ARKANSAS ARCHAEOLOGY

ARKANSAS ARCHAEOLOGY

Essays in Honor of Dan and Phyllis Morse

Edited by

ROBERT C. MAINFORT JR.
AND MARVIN D. JETER

THE UNIVERSITY OF ARKANSAS PRESS • FAYETTEVILLE, 1999

Manufactured in the United States of America

03 02 01 00 99 5 4 3 2 1

Designed by Ellen Beeler

♾ The paper used in this publication meets the minimum requirements of the American National Standard for Permanence of Paper for Printed Library Materials Z39.48-1984.

This project is supported in part by a grant from the Arkansas Humanities Council and the National Endowment for the Humanities.

Library of Congress Cataloging-in-Publication Data

Arkansas archaeology : essays in honor of Dan and Phyllis Morse / edited by Robert C. Mainfort, Jr. and Marvin D. Jeter.
p. cm.
Includes bibliographical references (p.) and index.
ISBN 1-55728-571-3 (pbk. : alk. paper)
1. Indians of North America—Arkansas—Antiquities. 2. Excavations (Archaeology)—Arkansas. 3. Arkansas—Antiquities. 4. Morse, Dan F. 5. Morse, Phyllis A. 6. Archaeologists—Arkansas—Biography. I. Mainfort, Robert C., 1948– . II. Jeter, Marvin D. III. Morse, Dan F. IV. Morse, Phyllis A.
E78.A8A715 1999
976.7'01—dc21 99-30696
CIP

Contents

Figures

Tables

Preface

For thirty years, Dan Franklin Morse and Phyllis Anderson Morse have represented the Arkansas Archeological Survey, in the forefront of research in and near the Mississippi Valley, on and beyond the trails blazed by their University of Michigan mentors James B. Griffin and Albert C. Spaulding. Dan was hired as one of the fledgling Survey's first station archaeologists in 1967 and became the first station archaeologist to retire, at the end of 1997. From time to time during those three decades, Phyllis also worked for the Survey, and she has always collaborated with Dan in their research and other projects.

There was always plenty of work to go around. Dan's northeast Arkansas domain was by far the largest of the Survey's research station territories, and due to interactions of various past environmental and cultural factors, major portions of this territory had been heavily occupied during a number of different culture periods. Moreover, the Morses's tenure coincided with an unprecedented onslaught of archaeological site destruction due to agricultural land leveling, pot hunting, and various construction projects.

Indeed, as recounted in their co-authored classic volume (Morse and Morse 1983:217ff), two months after the Survey station opened in Jonesboro, the Morses plunged into research at the Zebree site. They immediately produced numerous insights into early Mississippian culture, and subsequently (in 1975–76) into methods of conducting multidisciplinary "salvage" excavations before Zebree was destroyed.

Meanwhile, and later, the Morses were riding off in other directions and bringing back important new data and ideas. Particularly noteworthy were their findings around the early and recent ends of the culture-historical sequence: Dan's work at late Paleoindian Dalton sites, Phyllis's with the Late Mississippian/Protohistoric Parkin phase, Dan's with the coeval Nodena phase, and their teamwork with Charles Hudson and others on the route of Hernando de Soto through Arkansas.

Retirement festivities for the Morses began at the 1997 Mid-South Archaeological Conference—organized and hosted by them in Jonesboro, appropriately enough, since they had done the same for the first Mid-South conference during the Zebree project. In addition to a series of papers on the history of Mid-South archaeology (one is included in this volume; the Survey is publishing the others), the 1997 meeting included two ceremonial highlights. The Morses were honored by the Quapaw tribe, represented by Carrie Wilson, who presented them with colorful tribal blankets. Later, the meeting concluded with a memorable feast and live jazz in the Morses's house and backyard.

After the Morses's impending retirement was announced in 1996, a group of their colleagues within and outside of the Survey hatched a plot to honor them with a Festschrift, based on papers to be presented in a symposium at the 1997 Southeastern Archaeological Conference (SEAC). As editors, we decided to give this project a sharper focus than most similar volumes by emphasizing Arkansas archaeology.

The introductory chapter by Kwas summarizes the professional careers of Dan and Phyllis Morse and provides a retrospective on the early days of the Arkansas Archeological Survey.

Chapter 2 provides an environmental and geomorphological context for the subsequent chapters on prehistoric archaeology. The authors, Paul and Hazel Delcourt and Roger Saucier, have worked closely with the Morses on collaborative research. This account will serve as a standard reference for many years.

A major strength of the Arkansas Archeological Survey is its system of nine research stations, each with a resident archaeologist, distributed across the state. The exhaustive review of the Saline River drainage by Marvin Jeter and Ann Early in chapter 3 demonstrates the value of long-term accumulation of intermittently acquired data and regional expertise. Although the approach here is very different from Anderson's intensive survey in the L'Anguille Basin in the following chapter, both suggest that at times a sort of "bifocal" occupation characterized these drainages, with population concentrations around their northern and southern extremes.

In chapter 4 David Anderson, a key participant in the Morses's 1970s Zebree project, reevaluates archaeological survey data from a poorly known portion of eastern Arkansas. His lengthy, detailed report on the L'Anguille River drainage had only limited distribution, and this valuable information has not heretofore been available to a wider audience.

Under the supervision of Dan Morse, Chris Gillam wrote an innovative master's thesis on a Geographic Information Systems approach to Paleoindian sites and lithic resources in northeast Arkansas. Gillam's contribution to this volume is the product of much additional analysis of his data set and benefits from the chapter by Delcourt, Delcourt, and Saucier.

For more than two decades, a major focus of Martha Rolingson's research has been the impressive Toltec Mounds site near Little Rock, Arkansas. Here, Rolingson compiles and discusses a number of early documents pertaining to the site and demonstrates the value of these in present-day interpretations.

Archaeologists traditionally have grouped sites of the same approximate age within a given region into "phases." Using large collections of ceramics, Mainfort in chapter 7 presents a multivariate statistical examination of late Mississippian sites in the Central Mississippi Valley and concludes that traditional methods for grouping sites are insufficient.

In recent years, Frank Schambach has been arguing forcefully for a new interpretation of the spectacular Spiro site in eastern Oklahoma, just across the state line from Arkansas. His arguments and data are presented at length in chapter 8.

Leslie Stewart-Abernathy addresses an often overlooked interest of the Morses, namely historical archaeology. Taking as his focus the entire Mid-South area, Stewart-Abernathy reviews in chapter 9 the history, problems, and prospects of historical archaeology while compiling a valuable bibliographic database for the region.

The volume closes with Michael Hoffman's look at early newspaper accounts of Arkansas archaeology and the insights that can be gleaned from them. His findings are certain to inspire other researchers to seek out and compile comparable early source material.

Short, draft versions of the papers included in this volume (except the chapter by Kwas) were presented on November 6, 1997, at the annual SEAC meeting in a symposium entitled "On Beyond Zebree: Papers in Honor of Dan and Phyllis Morse." At the SEAC business meeting the next afternoon, the Morses's regional colleagues unanimously approved, with a standing ovation, a resolution honoring Dan and Phyllis on the occasion of their retirement.

In addition to the individual authors, all of whom took time from their busy schedules to prepare contributions, a number of others contributed to the successful completion of this volume. Thanks must first go to Tom Green, director of the Arkansas Archeological Survey, for his encouragement and support since the inception of this project. Lindi Holmes, also of the Survey, expertly prepared the draft and final manuscript versions of the book and painstakingly compiled the conflated bibliography; without Lindi's pleasant and able assistance, this volume probably would not exist. Mary Lynn Kennedy and Jane Kellett, who produce the Survey's fine publication series, provided much appreciated assistance with the graphics. Finally, we wish to thank Kevin Brock, acquisitions editor for the University of Arkansas Press, for seeing the volume through to production in the face of numerous difficulties.

CHAPTER ONE

A RETROSPECTIVE ON THE CAREERS OF ARCHAEOLOGISTS DAN FRANKLIN MORSE AND PHYLLIS ANDERSON MORSE

MARY L. KWAS
(WITH CONTRIBUTIONS BY RONALD J. AND CAROL I. MASON,
LARRY CONRAD, ROBERT C. MAINFORT JR., AND HESTER A. DAVIS)

It was, undoubtedly, hot and muggy that day in late August 1967 when Dan and Phyllis Morse, with their three young sons in tow (one just a babe in arms), arrived in Jonesboro, Arkansas, to begin a long and fruitful association with Arkansas archaeology. What began on that sultry summer day now spans 30 years and two wonderful careers. Although this brief essay cannot hope to address all of their contributions to the field of archaeology, the highlights noted will reflect some of Dan and Phyllis's myriad interests and talents.

When the fledgling Arkansas Archeological Survey began its existence on July 1, 1967, the agency received initial funding to establish three research stations beyond the University of Arkansas base at Fayetteville. The colleges chosen for these stations were Henderson State University, Arkadelphia; Arkansas AM&N, Pine Bluff (later University of Arkansas at Pine Bluff); and Arkansas State University, Jonesboro. Even before funding was secure, organizers Bob McGimsey and Hester Davis began contacting archaeologists with experience in the Mississippi Valley to see who might be interested in the soon-to-be station positions. Dan Morse, then employed as highway salvage archaeologist in Idaho, was one of the first to be contacted. When he accepted the position at Jonesboro later that year, Dan was one of three hired in the first batch of new station archaeologists. But that hiring came with a bonus, for Arkansas archaeology got Phyllis too.

Before Dan and Phyllis arrived in Arkansas, however, they journeyed through several states and much archaeology, gaining knowledge and experience along the way. Both of them started that journey from the prairie state of Illinois.

Dan's interest in archaeology had been catalyzed while still a child living in Peoria, Illinois. His physician father's interest in archaeology, tempered by a strong adherence to the scientific method, led them in the 1940s to the Peoria Academy of Science and the Illinois Archaeological Society. Here Dan came to meet and understand a potpourri of collectors, from trophy hunters to intellectuals, while experiencing a rare glimpse of the nineteenth-century type of antiquarian scientist. He handled enormous quantities of artifacts and won special mentoring from Gregory Perino.

Even more fortuitous for a youngster, Dan's association with these organizations gave him the opportunity to interact with professional archaeologists. While still in high school, he settled on his life's work, thanks largely to the help and influence of Melvin "Mike" Fowler. Later Howard Winters and Stuart Struever pointed him in the direction of Beloit College, which he entered at age 17 and attended for two years. In 1954 he transferred to the University of Michigan, receiving a B.A. in anthropology in 1956.

Phyllis Anderson arrived at the University of Michigan from Crystal Lake, Illinois, and discovered archaeology while there. She completed her B.A. in anthropology, with distinction, the same year as Dan. Both then entered graduate school there and interacted in the same circle of students, which included, more or less intimately, Ron Mason, Carol Irwin (Mason), Patsy Gerstner, Mark Papworth, Art Jelinek, Pierre Gravel, Lewis Binford, and Charles and Phoebe McNutt. The graduate students studied under such luminaries as James B. Griffin, Albert C. Spaulding, Leslie A. White, Elman Service, and Marshall Sahlins.

From early on, Dan and Phyllis's careers—and lives—became intertwined. They both worked at Modoc Rock Shelter, both worked in various capacities at the University of Michigan Museum of Anthropology, and undoubtedly shared other field experiences and research interests during their student years. Phyllis's bright mind carried her along at a quick pace, and she finished her master's degree in 1958. Dan completed his master's the following year, by which time Phyllis had completed her course work and aced her preliminary exams for a Ph.D.

With his M.A. in hand in the spring of 1959, Dan was ready to set aside school for a while and begin work. He accepted a position as highway salvage archaeologist for the Georgia Historical Commission, but by then Dan and Phyllis were inseparable. Phyllis went with him to Georgia, intending to work on her dissertation there, and found work as a laboratory archaeologist for the same agency. Their first joint paper was published on the Williams Site, Gordon County, Georgia. Within a year, on March 26, 1960, they were married. Ten months later, their first son was born.

With the birth of Daniel Arthur, Phyllis put her dissertation and her career on hold. At that time, before the women's movement of the 1960s, there were few options open to women wanting to have a career. In school, women were discouraged from pursuing a career and rarely had female role models. Career-minded women tended to choose one of two paths: to pursue a career but remain single and childless, or to marry and become junior partners in their husband's research. Even the latter option was less of a choice than a response to the realities of the time. No university was likely to provide positions for two married Ph.D. archaeologists, and before the contract boom resulting from the passage of the 1974 Moss-Bennett Act, few jobs for archaeologists existed outside of universities or museums. Adding children to the equation of married archaeologists even further complicated matters. This was a time prior to daycare, when women still were expected to abandon paying jobs once offspring arrived. It was, undoubtedly, a daunting time for intelligent women. By the time the last of the Morse children entered grade school, however, the world of archaeology had changed—and Phyllis found a niche in it.

In 1961 Dan accepted a position as instructor with the University of Alabama, Huntsville Center, and in 1962 advanced to assistant professor at the University of Tennessee, Knoxville. While at UT, he conducted a brief but thorough testing program in the spring of 1963 at the later-to-be-renowned Middle Woodland site of Pinson Mounds. His work was the first extensive professional investigation conducted at the site. He also investigated the Archaic Robinson Shell Mound near Nashville, which he later used as the subject of his dissertation.

Meanwhile, Phyllis kept her hand in professionally, working as a lecturer in the UT Department of Anthropology and contributing her writing, editing, and intellectual skills on papers co-authored with Dan. In spring 1964 she gave birth to their second son, John Franklin. By this time, however, Dan was persuaded to return to the University of Michigan to complete his Ph.D., which he began in fall 1964 after a summer teaching stint at Indiana University.

While Dan immersed himself in graduate studies, Phyllis picked up work as a teaching fellow in the anthropology department. In 1966, with his doctoral work almost completed, Dan accepted a position as curator of archaeology and instructor at Idaho State University and as highway salvage archaeologist for Idaho. In March 1967, their third son, Robert James, was born. The same year, Dan received his Ph.D. and accepted the position of station archaeologist with the Arkansas Archeological

Survey. When they arrived in Jonesboro that day in late August, one wonders if they sensed a glimmer of the next thirty years.

When Dan accepted the job with the Arkansas Archeological Survey, he also accepted the inevitable growing pains of a new agency coming into its own. The goals set for the first year indicated his work would be cut out for him. Dan and the other new station archaeologists were charged with familiarizing themselves with the sites in their geographic areas, familiarizing the college and local community of the Survey's purpose, and writing a summary of what was then known about archaeology in their portion of Arkansas.

In subsequent years, Dan worked on becoming intimately familiar with the sites in his area, testing many to develop a better understanding of the chronology of northeast Arkansas. Because Philips, Ford, and Griffin had concentrated on Woodland and Mississippian sites, Dan initially tested older ones and began an inventory of Paleoindian points found in Arkansas. With his first graduate student, Al Goodyear, Dan excavated the Brand site, thus beginning his study and definition of the Dalton culture in northeast Arkansas; the resulting monograph is still much in demand.

Dan's background with collectors and amateur archaeologists in Illinois provided him with ready experience for interacting with the active members of the Arkansas Archeological Society, a group instrumental in the support of the Survey. Dan participated in the Society's two-week training program and submitted many articles to the Society's publications. He was always ready and willing to work with local amateurs and collectors.

In the middle 1970s, as the last of their children entered grade school, Phyllis returned to archaeology. She taught at Arkansas State University in Jonesboro, served as a consultant to museums in Memphis, and conducted research for the Arkansas Archeological Survey. She completed many individual contract projects, a sampling of which includes an Arkansas Civil War battlefield, investigations in Missouri, and work in the Arkansas counties of Poinsett, Mississippi, St. Francis, Cross, Crittenden, Fulton, Lawrence, Craighead, Greene, Randolph, Clay, and Independence. Through the 1970s and 1980s, her major research included work at the sites of Zebree and Parkin and co-authored articles with Dan. In 1981, Phyllis's monograph on Parkin and the Parkin phase was published by the Arkansas Archeological Survey in their research series. In addition to the above, the Morses's growing interest in and love for antiques led to the 1979 opening of Phyllis's still-active business, Possum Antiques, and her 1990 directorship of the Mid-West Tool Collectors Association.

During the same period, Dan divided his time among teaching at Arkansas State University, working with amateurs, participating in

Society activities, and conducting research in his area of Arkansas. He served as a consultant for a variety of museums and as a grant reviewer for national foundations. By the mid-1970s, his major research centered on the Zebree site, the Sloan Dalton cemetery, the Nodena phase, and work on the Cache River project. A major monograph on Nodena was published in the Survey's research series.

Dan's and Phyllis's research efforts became even more entwined after the mid-1970s, and they co-authored a number of books and articles on such diverse topics as the Zebree site, the Southeastern Ceremonial Complex, emergent Mississippian, and the Spanish exploration of Arkansas. Their important synthesis, *Archaeology of the Central Mississippi Valley,* was published in 1983 by Academic Press. During this time they also devoted considerable time to assisting colleagues in a variety of disciplines, with research ranging from geomorphology to the route of the de Soto expedition. Their work has continued into the 1990s, with Dan's most recent monograph on the Sloan site published in 1997 by the Smithsonian Institution Press.

Dan and Phyllis are regular contributors at myriad societies and conferences, a sampling of which includes the Society for American Archaeology, the Southeastern Archaeological Conference, the Plains Anthropological Conference, the Mid-South Archaeological Conference, the Society for Historical Archaeology, the Conference on French Colonial Archaeology, the Archaeological Institute of America, the Caddo Conference, the Southern Anthropological Society, and the Central Lowland Archeological Seminar and Symposium.

They have had research articles published in the following journals: *American Antiquity, Current Anthropology, Southeastern Archaeological Conference Bulletin, Eastern States Archaeological Federation Bulletin, Plains Anthropologist, Central States Archaeological Journal, Journal of the Illinois State Archaeological Society, Illinois Archeological Survey Bulletin, Florida Anthropologist, Journal of Alabama Archaeology, Tennessee Archaeologist, Wisconsin Archeologist, Arkansas Archeologist,* and *Papers of the Michigan Academy of Science, Arts, and Letters.*

They hold memberships, either individually or jointly, in the Society for American Archaeology, the Southeastern Archaeological Conference, the Plains Anthropological Society, the American Association for the Quaternary, the Society for Lithic Technology, the National Trust for Historic Preservation, the Early American Industries Association, the Mid-West Tool Collectors Association, the National Ornamental Metal Museum, and the Arkansas Antique Dealers Association, as well as many state archaeological societies.

With Dan's retirement from the Arkansas Archeological Survey in 1997, Dan and Phyllis moved from Arkansas, and their many friends and colleagues sadly miss them. But we all know that this retirement and move is not the end of Dan and Phyllis's association with archaeology. If anything, it will be the beginning of enough unencumbered time to let their research dreams take flight.

MEMOIRS OF THE MORSES

As far as I am concerned, Dan and Phyllis have done a fine job in northeast Arkansas, sometimes with great difficulty. I well remember their work in the University of Michigan Museum and Phyllis becoming interested in Dan's research actions. They will be missed.

—James B. Griffin

Dan has an excellent understanding of the views and wishes of amateur archeologists, for he was a dedicated amateur himself for many years. Later, when the Society for American Archaeology set up the Crabtree Award for amateurs, he was chosen to be the first to head the committee that administered it. His dedication has increased his ability to work with amateurs and has aided him in successfully reaching a number of different sorts of people.

—Leonard W. Blake

One of the most impressive and satisfying events we witnessed as graduate students centered on Phyllis. Carol had loaned Phyllis her notes from Marshall Sahlins's lectures on "primitive economics." When it came time for the dreaded prelims, Phyllis sailed through the economics section with aplomb, astonishing the faculty, who knew she had never taken the course.

—Ronald J. and Carol I. Mason

The environment of the Illinois Archaeological Society and Dickson Mounds provided the opportunity to handle, examine, and compare large numbers of artifacts, which has been invaluable to Dan in his later material culture studies. Though Dan spent time in an environment in which emphasis on material objects was considered old-fashioned and sterile, his work has reaffirmed that they are still the basis for most other observations on past cultures.

—Larry Conrad

It was, indeed, very hot that late August day in 1967. I remember Bob McGimsey and me driving into the agreed-upon gas station in Jonesboro, where the Morses were already sweltering in the heat. As we introduced ourselves, I watched Johnny (aged 3) squat down and try to let the air out of one of their tires! Unfazed, Dan and Phyllis went on to put northeast Arkansas on the archeological map with solid research on all 12,000 years.

—Hester Davis

In Jimmy Griffin's office were filing cabinets, many containing a wealth of photographs of archaeological specimens, sites, and archeologists—many taken long ago. Jimmy granted his graduate students free access to this archive, and these photographs were examined with appropriate gravity. With one exception, involving Dan and Phyllis and the two of us, a bit giddy after an extended day of serious academic work; we got it into our heads to search the files for a photograph of Jimmy Griffin with hair. We can still hear Phyllis's shriek of triumph when we found one.

—RONALD J. AND CAROL I. MASON

The Morses conducted a number of landmark survey and excavation programs including the Sloan site, the Brand site, Big Lake, Zebree, and Parkin. But their biggest contribution has been to establish a solid, dependable foundation for archeology in northeast Arkansas, one upon which Arkansas and the profession can continue to build in the years ahead.

—CHARLES R. MCGIMSEY III

Dan and Phyllis make up a team that is nearly unique. Both are archaeologists and are considered by many to be among the best in the field. Since coming to northeastern Arkansas, their achievements have been numerous, ranging from new information on the Dalton culture to studies which led to the linking of the Parkin site to accounts of the de Soto expedition.

—LEONARD W. BLAKE

Dan's contribution to my own career has been enormous. His fieldwork at Pinson Mounds and the resulting report, which included a number of specific research goals, provided the foundation for my own research at the site. When I later became more involved with Mississippian research, Dan gave me free access to the extensive collections at his station and always had time to discuss sites, artifacts, and interpretations with me.

—BOB MAINFORT

I first met those eminent archeologists, the Morses, when I was a rookie in Arkansas back in 1978, after having heard so much about them from my grad-school cohorts Al Goodyear and Mark Raab. I was most gratified (and greatly relieved) at the warm welcome Dan and Phyllis gave me to the Survey fold. Over the years since then, I have become even more grateful for the hospitality and knowledge they have shared on many occasions.

—MARVIN D. JETER

A SELECTED BIBLIOGRAPHY OF DAN F. AND PHYLLIS A. MORSE

Morse, Dan F.

1963 *The Steuben Village and Mounds: A Multi-Component Late Hopewell Site in Illinois.* Anthropological Papers No. 21. Museum of Anthropology, University of Michigan, Ann Arbor.

1965 The Hannah Site, Peoria County, Illinois. *Illinois Archeological Survey Bulletin* 5:129–46.

1967 The Robinson Site and Shell Mound Archaic Culture in the Middle South. Ph.D. diss., University of Michigan. University Microfilms, Ann Arbor.

1969 The Crable Site. In *Ancient Disease in the Midwest,* by Dan Morse, 63–68. Reports of Investigations No. 15. Illinois State Museum, Springfield.

1971a The Hawkins Cache: A Significant Dalton Find in Northeast Arkansas. *Arkansas Archeologist* 12:9–10.

1971b An Historic Indian Grave near Blytheville, Arkansas. *Arkansas Archeologist* 12:56–60.

1972 A Pot Full of Beads. *Arkansas Archeologist* 13:67–76.

1973a Dalton Culture in Northeast Arkansas. *Florida Anthropologist* 25:28–38.

1973b Natives and Anthropologists in Arkansas. In *Anthropology Beyond the University,* edited by Alden Redfield, 26–39. Southern Anthropological Society Proceedings No. 7.

1973c (ed.) *Nodena: An Account of 75 Years of Archeological Investigation in Southeast Mississippi County, Arkansas.* Research Series No. 4. Arkansas Archeological Survey, Fayetteville.

1975a Paleo-Indian in the Land of Opportunity: Preliminary Report on the Excavations at the Sloan Site (3GE94). In *The Cache River Archeological Project,* edited by Michael B. Schiffer and John H. House, 135–43. Research Series No. 8. Arkansas Archeological Survey, Fayetteville.

1975b *Report of Excavations at the Zebree Site 1969.* Research Report No. 4. Arkansas Archeological Survey, Fayetteville.

1975c Research Potential in Terms of Questions of Regional Prehistory. In *The Cache River Archeological Project,* edited by Michael B. Schiffer and John H. House, 187–98. Research Series No. 8. Arkansas Archeological Survey, Fayetteville.

1976 An Analysis of the Dalton Complex in the Central Mississippi Valley. In *Habitats Humains Anterieurs a L'Holocene en America,* edited by James B. Griffin, 136–66. Colloque 17, Union Internationale des Sciences Prehistoriques et Protohistoriques, Nice, France.

1977a Dalton Settlement System: Reply to Schiffer. *Plains Anthropologist* 22:149–58.

1977b The Penetration of Northeast Arkansas by Mississippian Culture. In *For the Director: Research Essays in Honor of James B. Griffin,* edited by Charles E. Cleland, 186–211. Anthropological Papers No. 61. Museum of Anthropology, University of Michigan, Ann Arbor.

1978 Comment on "Temporal Models in Prehistory: An Example from Eastern North America" by James B. Stoltman. *Current Anthropology* 19:735.

1982a A Paleo-Indian/Early Archaic Cemetery Possibility in Arkansas. In *Peopling of the New World,* edited by Jonathon E. Ericson, R. E. Taylor, and Rainer Berger, 147–62. Anthropological Papers No. 23. Ballena Press.

1982b Regional Overview of Northeast Arkansas. In *Arkansas Archeology in Review,* edited by Neal L. Trubowitz and Marvin D. Jeter, 20–36. Research Series No. 15. Arkansas Archeological Survey, Fayetteville.

1986a McCarty (3-Po-467): A Tchula Period Site Near Marked Tree, Arkansas. In *The Tchula Period in the Mid-South and Lower Mississippi Valley,* edited by David H. Dye and Ronald C. Brister, 70–92. Archaeological Report No. 17. Mississippi Department of Archives and History, Jackson.

1986b Preliminary Investigation of the Pinson Mounds Site: 1963 Field Season. In *Pinson Mounds: A Middle Woodland Ceremonial Center,* by Robert C. Mainfort Jr., 96–119. Research Series No. 7. Tennessee Department of Conservation, Division of Archaeology, Nashville.

1986c Protohistoric Hunting Sites in Northeast Arkansas. In *The Protohistoric Period in the Mid-South: 1500–1700,* edited by David H. Dye and Ronald C. Brister, 89–94. Archaeological Report No. 18. Mississippi Department of Archives and History, Jackson.

1986d The Second Mid-South Archaeological Conference—1971. In *The Tchula Period in the Mid-South and Lower Mississippi Valley,* edited by David H. Dye and Ronald C. Brister, 9–10. Archaeological Report No. 17. Mississippi Department of Archives and History, Jackson.

1988 The Kellar Site: Its Implications for Interpreting the Late Marksville Period Occupation in Northeast Arkansas. In *Middle Woodland Settlement and Ceremonialism in the Mid-South and Lower Mississippi Valley,* edited by Robert C. Mainfort Jr., 68–75. Archaeological Report No. 22. Mississippi Department of Archives and History, Jackson.

1989 *Nodena: An Account of 90 Years of Archeological Investigation in*

Southeast Mississippi County, Arkansas. Research Series 30. Arkansas Archeological Survey, Fayetteville.

1990a The Nodena Phase. In *Towns and Temples Along the Mississippi,* edited by David H. Dye and Cheryl Anne Cox, 69–97. University of Alabama Press, Tuscaloosa.

1990b Scientific Instruments and Early Explorers in the United States. *Florida Anthropologist* 43(1):45–47.

1991a On the Possible Origin of the Quapaw in Northeast Arkansas. In *Arkansas Before the Americans,* edited by Hester A. Davis, 40–54. Research Series No. 40. Arkansas Archeological Survey, Fayetteville.

1991b Perforated Atlatl Weights in Northeast Arkansas. In *The Archaic Period in the Mid-South,* edited by Charles H. McNutt, 59–65. Mississippi Department of Archives and History, Archaeological Report 24, and Memphis State University, Anthropological Research Center, Occasional Papers No. 16.

1992 The Seventeenth Century Michigamea Village Location in Arkansas. In *Calumet and Fleur-de-Lys,* edited by John Walthall and Thomas Emerson, 55–74. Smithsonian Institution Press, Washington, D.C.

1993 Archeology and the Population of Arkansas in 1541–1543. In *The Expedition of Hernando de Soto West of the Mississippi, 1541–1543,* edited by Gloria A. Young and Michael P. Hoffman, 29–35. University of Arkansas Press, Fayetteville.

1994 Digging in Jersey County, Illinois, in 1951. In "Highways to the Past: Essays on Illinois Archaeology in Honor of Charles J. Bareis." *Journal of the Illinois Archaeological Survey* 5(1–2):247–55.

1997 *The Sloan Site: A Paleoindian Period Dalton Cemetery in Northeast Arkansas.* Smithsonian Institution Press, Washington, D.C.

Morse, Phyllis A.

1981 *Parkin: The 1978–1979 Archeological Investigation of a Cross County, Arkansas Site.* Research Series No. 13. Arkansas Archeological Survey, Fayetteville.

1990 The Parkin Site and the Parkin Phase. In *Towns and Temples Along the Mississippi,* edited by David H. Dye and Cheryl Cox, 118–34. University of Alabama Press, Tuscaloosa.

1993 The Parkin Archeological Site and Its Role in Determining the Route of the de Soto Expedition. In *The Expedition of Hernando de Soto West of the Mississippi, 1541–1543,* edited by Gloria A. Young and Michael P. Hoffman, 58–67. University of Arkansas Press, Fayetteville.

Morse, Dan F., and Phyllis A. Morse

1960 A Preliminary Report on 9-GO-507: The Williams Site, Gordon County, Georgia. *Florida Anthropologist* 13:81–99.

1964a Archaeological Survey of the J. Percy Priest Reservoir, Tennessee. *Journal of Alabama Archaeology* 10:1–12.

1964b The Brake Site: A Possible Early 19th Century Log Cabin in Stewart County, Tennessee. *Florida Anthropologist* 17:165–76.

1964c 1962 Excavations at the Morse Site: A Red Ocher Cemetery in the Illinois Valley. *Wisconsin Archeologist 45:79–98.*

1976 (eds.) *Zebree 1975: A Preliminary Report of the Zebree Project, New Approaches in Contract Archeology in Arkansas.* Research Report No. 8. Arkansas Archeological Survey, Fayetteville.

1980 *Zebree Archeological Project: Excavations, Data Interpretation, and Report on the Zebree Homestead Site, Mississippi County, Arkansas.* Final report submitted to the Memphis District, U.S. Army Corps of Engineers, by the Arkansas Archeological Survey.

1983 *Archaeology of the Central Mississippi Valley.* Academic Press, New York.

1986 Late Prehistoric Control of Critical Upland Resources in the Central Mississippi Valley USA. In *The Social and Economic Contexts of Technological Change,* edited by Sander van der Leeuw and Robin Torrence, 1–13. The World Archaeological Congress, London.

1989 The Rise of the Southeastern Ceremonial Complex in the Central Mississippi Valley. In *The Southeastern Ceremonial Complex: Artifacts and Analysis,* edited by Patricia Galloway, 41–44. University of Nebraska Press, Lincoln.

1990a Emergent Mississippian in the Central Mississippi Valley. In *The Mississippian Emergence,* edited by Bruce D. Smith, 153–73. Smithsonian Institution Press, Washington, D.C.

1990b The Spanish Exploration of Arkansas. In *Columbian Consequences,* edited by David Hurst Thomas, 197–210. Archaeological and Historical Perspectives on the Spanish Borderlands East, vol. 2. Smithsonian Institution Press, Washington, D.C.

1996a Changes in Interpretation in the Archaeology of the Central Mississippi Valley Since 1983. *North American Archaeologist* 17(1):1–35.

1996b Northeast Arkansas. In *Prehistory of the Central Mississippi Valley,* edited by Charles H. McNutt, 119–35. University of Alabama Press, Tuscaloosa.

Morse, Phyllis A., and Dan F. Morse

1990 The Zebree Site: An Emerged Early Mississippian Expression in Northeast Arkansas. In *The Mississippian Emergence,* edited by Bruce D. Smith, 51–66. Smithsonian Institution Press, Washington, D.C.

Griffin, James B., and Dan F. Morse

1961 The Short-Nosed God from the Emmons Site, Illinois. *American Antiquity* 26:560–63.

Morse, Dan F., Phyllis A. Morse, and John Waggoner Jr.

1964 Fluted Points from Smith County, Tennessee. *Tennessee Archaeologist* 20:16–33.

Morse, Dan F., and Albert C. Goodyear III

1973 The Significance of the Dalton Adze in Northeast Arkansas. *Plains Anthropologist* 18:316–22.

Morse, Dan F., and Samuel D. Smith

1973 The Hazel Site: Archeological Salvage During the Construction of Route 308. *Arkansas Archeologist* 14:36–77.

Morse, Dan F., G. Daniel Morse, and Daniel A. Morse

1974 A Biconcave Pottery Discoidal from Northwest Florida. *Florida Anthropologist* 27:59–61.

Morse, Dan F., and Louis D. Tesar

1974 A Microlithic Tool Assemblage from a Northwest Florida Site. *Florida Anthropologist* 27:89–106.

Morse, Dan F. (with contributions by Neal Trubowitz, Phyllis Morse, Timothy Klinger, and Ross Dinwiddie)

1982 Northeast Arkansas. In *A State Plan for the Conservation of Archeological Resources in Arkansas,* edited by Hester A. Davis, NE1–NE26. Research Series No. 21. Arkansas Archeological Survey, Fayetteville.

Morse, Dan F., and David G. Anderson

1983 Zebree: An Example of Problem-Oriented Contract Research in Northeast Arkansas. *Southeastern Archaeological Conference Bulletin* 20–21:136–40.

Delcourt, P. A., Hazel R. Delcourt, Dan F. Morse, and Phyllis A. Morse

1993 History, Evolution, and Organization of Vegetation and Human Culture. In *Biodiversity of the Southeastern United States: Lowland Terrestrial Communities,* edited by William H. Martin, Stephen G. Boyce, and Arthur C. Echternacht, 47–79. John Wiley and Sons, New York.

Morse, Dan F., David G. Anderson, and Albert C. Goodyear

1996 The Pleistocene-Holocene Transition in the Eastern United States. In *Humans at the End of the Ice Age: The Archaeology of the Pleistocene-Holocene Transition,* edited by Lawrence Guy Straus, Berit Valentin Eriksen, Jon M. Erlandson, and David R. Yesner, 319–38. Plenum Press, New York.

CHAPTER TWO

LATE QUATERNARY VEGETATION DYNAMICS IN THE CENTRAL MISSISSIPPI VALLEY

PAUL A. DELCOURT, HAZEL R. DELCOURT, AND ROGER T. SAUCIER

Introduction

Since the late Pleistocene, human cultures have developed in southeastern North America within an environmental context that has been characterized by dynamic changes in climate, geomorphology, hydrology, and vegetation (Delcourt et al. 1993). In this chapter, we characterize the major changes in geomorphology and vegetation since the Late Wisconsinan full-glacial interval in the Central Mississippi Valley (hereafter referred to as the CMV). Following the definition of Morse and Morse (1983), this geographic area (fig. 2.1) extends along the lowlands of the Mississippi Alluvial Valley between the Ohio River and the Arkansas River. To depict late Pleistocene and Holocene changes in geomorphology and vegetation, we prepared paleoenvironmental maps for (1) the Late Wisconsinan full-glacial interval (18,000 radiocarbon years before present [B.P.]) (fig. 2.2a); (2) the late-glacial interval (14,000 B.P.) (fig. 2.2b); (3) the Paleoindian cultural period (12,000 B.P., at the late Pleistocene/Holocene transition) (fig. 2.2c); (4) the Dalton cultural period (10,000 B.P., in the early Holocene interval) (fig. 2.2d); (5) the Early Archaic cultural period (8000 B.P., in the early Holocene interval) (fig. 2.2e); (6) the Middle Archaic cultural period (6000 B.P., in the middle Holocene interval) (fig. 2.2f); (7) the Late Archaic cultural period (4000 B.P., in the middle Holocene interval) (fig. 2.2g); (8) the Woodland cultural period (2000 B.P., in the late Holocene interval) (fig. 2.2h); and (9) the Mississippian cultural period (ca. 1000 B.P. [A.D. 700–1500], in the late Holocene interval) (fig. 2.2i). The series of paleoenvironmental maps represents a synthesis of data gathered over the past several decades of interdisciplinary research into the vegetational and geomorphic history of the CMV.

Methods

Geomorphic Setting

Saucier (1994) produced a mapped synthesis for the 2.5 million-year history of the Lower Mississippi Alluvial Valley, a region extending from Cairo, Illinois, at the confluence of the Mississippi and Ohio Rivers, to the mouth of the Mississippi River, where it enters the Gulf of Mexico. For the late Quaternary time interval, this atlas (Saucier 1994) contains paleogeographic maps for 30,000 B.P. and for two-thousand-year intervals from 12,000 B.P. to the present. Paleogeographic reconstructions within the CMV (fig. 2.1) depict the locations of uplands and dynamic Pleistocene depositional environments, including both active and inactive valley trains that represented braided streams formerly carrying glacial outwash. Holocene Mississippi River environments include active meander belts, inactive meander belts, and backswamp environments. Saucier (1994) distinguished as a distinct map unit the floodplains and active meander belts of smaller streams such as the Black and Cache Rivers.

The paleoenvironmental maps presented in this chapter depict a series of prominent paleogeographic features, such as Crowley's Ridge, a north-south oriented upland ridge of late Tertiary and early Quaternary gravels (Guccione et al. 1990). Crowley's Ridge divides the Western Lowlands, which are bounded farther to the west by the escarpment of the Ozark Plateaus, from the Eastern Lowlands, which are bounded along the eastern Mississippi Valley by the uplands of the northern Blufflands (Delcourt et al. 1980). The paleoenvironmental maps are based on several key premises. On the map for 18,000 B.P. (fig. 2.2a), the Western Lowlands are the route through which glacial meltwaters and coarse sands and gravels were transported in braided streams of the full-glacial Mississippi River (level Pve 2; Saucier 1994). The corresponding valley train of the meltwater-fed Ohio River is mapped along the eastern half of the Eastern Lowlands. Flanking Crowley's Ridge, abandoned braided-stream terraces record the locations of older Quaternary valley trains (levels Pve 4 and Pve 3; fig. 2.1; also shown on the Middle Wisconsinan paleogeographic map for 30,000 B.P. in Saucier [1994]).

The paleoenvironmental map for 14,000 B.P. (fig. 2.2b) depicts the initial diversion of Mississippi River meltwater through the Bell City-Oran Gap breach in northernmost Crowley's Ridge. Powers Fort Swale, located in the Western Lowlands, records the substantial reduction of

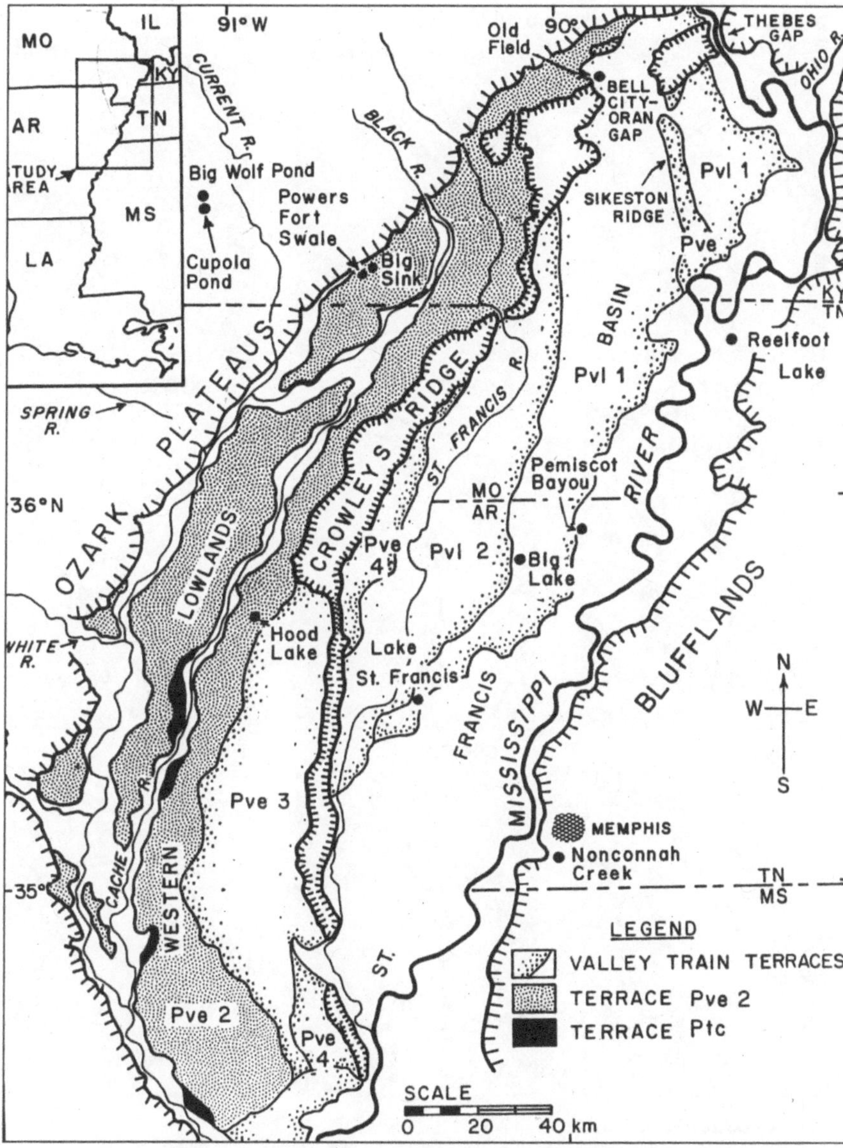

FIGURE 2.1. Late-Quaternary geomorphic environments and paleoecological sites from the Central Mississippi Valley, the Ozark Plateaus, and the Bluffiands (modified from Royall et al. 1991 and Saucier 1994). Alluvial surfaces Pve (Sikeston Ridge) and Pve 4 to Pve 1 represent Pleistocene valley train levels of Early Wisconsinan age (Saucier 1994). Valley train level 2 (Pve 2) was abandoned after 11,500 B.P. Late-glacial terraces along the Cache River (Ptc) formed with fluvial incision between approximately 14,500 and 11,500 B.P. Late Wisconsinan valley trains, levels Pvl 2 and Pvl 1, formed in the late glacial and early Holocene intervals.

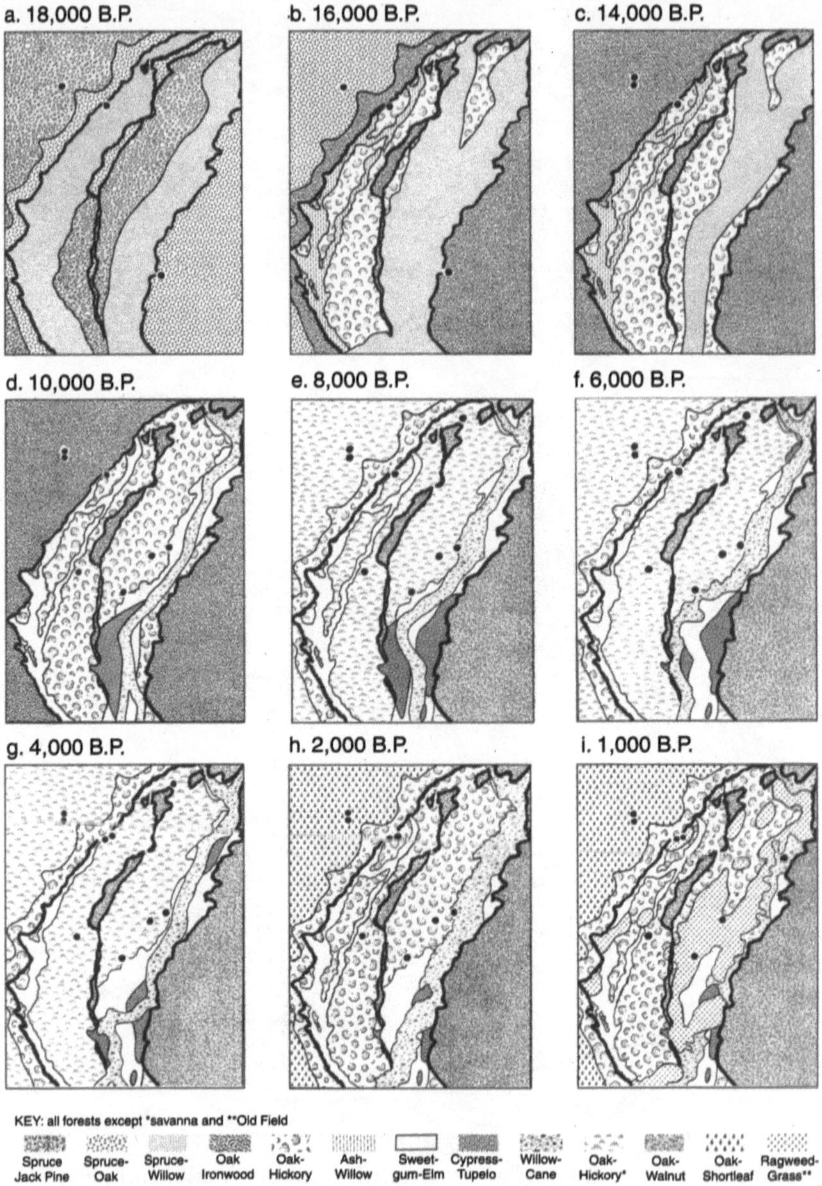

FIGURE 2.2. Paleoenvironmental maps for late-Pleistocene and Holocene paleovegetation types in temporal sequence from their first (oldest) occurrence.

meltwater flow by the Mississippi, starting about 16,300 B.P., and its cessation by 14,500 B.P. (Royall et al. 1991). By 14,000 B.P., with the increasing flow of braided streams east of Crowley's Ridge, a prominent Mississippi River valley train (level Pvl 2 of Saucier [1994]) formed across the Eastern Lowlands (F. L. Smith and Saucier 1971) and merged with the Ohio River valley train.

The 12,000 B.P. paleoenvironmental map (fig. 2.2c; Saucier 1994) shows an eastward shift of Mississippi River flow through the central portion of the Eastern Lowlands. Reduction of meltwater discharge by this time resulted in valley incision and abandonment of newly inactive valley trains along the margins of the Eastern Lowlands. The topographically lowest and youngest valley train (the Pvl 1 surface designated by Saucier [1994]), situated between Crowley's Ridge and Sikeston Ridge, remained active until at least 10,890 ± 130 B.P., based upon a radiocarbon assay associated with paleo-llama remains buried within channel-fill deposits and exposed along the Buffalo Ditch (D. F. and P. A. Morse, personal communication 1997). Within the Western Lowlands, between 14,500 and 11,500 B.P., the former braided-stream channels of the Cache and Black Rivers became ephemeral sluiceways (e.g., level Ptc; fig. 2.1) and increasingly captured water flow from the southeastern Ozark Plateaus.

The paleogeographic setting at 10,000 B.P. (fig. 2.2d) is based on Saucier's (1994) reconstruction for 10,000 to 9000 B.P. and depicts Stage 6 (the oldest Holocene) meandering Mississippi River. Between 11,000 and 10,500 B.P., the last pulse of Mississippi River outwash flow (Teller 1990) carved a diversion route through Thebes Gap (fig. 2.1), and braided streams built up the Charleston alluvial fan east of Sikeston Ridge (Porter and Guccione 1994). By approximately 10,000 B.P., both the Mississippi and Ohio Rivers changed from braided to meandering regimes and incised at least 7 m, forming an active floodplain restricted along the eastern border of the CMV (fig. 2.2d; Guccione et al. 1988).

The 8000 B.P. paleoenvironmental map (fig. 2.2e) is based on the reconstruction from 9000 to 8000 B.P. (Saucier 1994), showing the Stage 5 meander belt of the Mississippi River. Between 10,000 and 8000 B.P., buildup of alluvial fans along the Ozark Border deflected flow from the St. Francis River eastward within the Western Lowlands and through a breach in Crowley's Ridge, forming the extensive drainage occupying abandoned braided-stream channels of the westernmost Eastern Lowlands (fig. 2.1).

The combination of major earthquake events at 8100 B.P., 4000 B.P., and 200 B.P. (New Madrid earthquake) caused tectonic deformation and episodic ponding within what is recognized today as the St. Francis Sunk Lands (Guccione and Van Arsdale 1995; Saucier 1970).

The 6000 B.P. map (fig. 2.2f) is derived from the 6000 to 4500 B.P. reconstruction, including meander belt Stage 3 of the Mississippi River (Saucier 1994). During this time, a crevasse diversion of the Mississippi River shifted its location against the southeastern portion of Crowley's Ridge. Within the Eastern Lowlands, the sizes and shapes of abandoned meander channels indicate that middle Holocene flow of the Mississippi River was substantially less than that of the early Holocene. Reduced discharge of the Mississippi River suggested by Saucier (1994) may have been a result of Hypsithermal warmth and aridity, as prevailing westerly winds dominated across the Midwest region (Bartlein et al. 1984; King and Allen 1977). With reduced surface-water flow from the Ozark Plateaus, the only permanently flowing rivers in the Western Lowlands were the Black and White Rivers flanking the Ozark Border. Farther east within the Western Lowlands, a middle Holocene drop in the groundwater table within the braided-stream terraces caused the Cache River and Bayou DeView to decline significantly in base-flow discharge (Delcourt et al. 1997).

The 4000 B.P. paleoenvironmental map (fig. 2.2g) is based on the Stage 2 position of the Mississippi River 4500 to 3000 B.P. (Saucier 1994). In the late Holocene, increased discharge of the Mississippi River coincided with a shift in the meander belt to a position along the eastern Blufflands near Memphis, Tennessee (fig. 2.1).

Paleoenvironmental maps for 2000 B.P. and 1000 B.P. (fig. 2.2h–i) are both based on the paleogeographic reconstruction for 2000 to 1000 B.P., meander belt Stage 1 for the Mississippi River (Saucier 1994). After 3000 B.P., increased discharge of the Mississippi River produced very broad meander belts in the Eastern Lowlands. Late Holocene increases in precipitation brought recharge in the Ozark Plateaus and resulted in increased flow within the Cache, White, and Black Rivers.

Vegetation Mapping

We used the regional survey of modern pollen rain from surface samples collected across the Lower Mississippi Valley (Delcourt et al. 1983) to characterize the diagnostic "signatures" produced by contemporary vegetation (Braun 1950). The subcontinental-scale atlas of modern pollen rain for eastern North America (Delcourt et al. 1984) documents pollen assemblages from mixed conifer–northern hardwood forests and from boreal forests, providing present-day analogues for late Pleistocene vegetation types (Delcourt and Delcourt 1987; E. Smith 1984).

We compiled fossil pollen data available from 11 paleoecological sites within or on uplands bordering the CMV (table 2.1). Delcourt and Delcourt (1996) previously summarized vegetation histories inferred from fossil evidence for seven of these published records.

TABLE 2.1. LATE QUATERNARY PALEOECOLOGICAL SITES IN THE CENTRAL MISSISSIPPI VALLEY

Geomorphic Setting	Time Span yr B.P.	No. ^{14}C Dates	Oldest Valid ^{14}C Date yr B.P.	Publication
OZARK PLATEAUS				
Cupola Pond, Ripley Co., MO	17,100 to 0	10	17,110 ± 340	Smith 1984; Delcourt and Delcourt 1994
Big Wolf Pond, Shannon Co., MO	12,500 to 0	6	11,760 ± 150	Delcourt and Delcourt 1994
WESTERN LOWLANDS				
Powers Fort Swale, Butler Co., MO	18,300 to 0	10	17,370 ± 170	Royall et al. 1991
Big Sink Pond, Butler Co., MO	4300 to 0	10	4300 ± 90	J. P. Gardner, unpublished ms.
Hood Lake, Poinsett Co., AR	11,250 to 0	11	10,620 ± 320	Delcourt et al. 1997
EASTERN LOWLANDS				
Lake St. Francis, Poinsett Co., AR	10,000 to 0	4	8130 ± 60	Cummings 1987; Dixon 1987; Guccione and Van Arsdale 1995
Big Lake, Mississippi Co., AR	10,000 to 0	3	9050 ± 150	King 1978; Scott and Aasen 1987
Pemiscot Bayou, Mississippi Co., AR	10,000 to 2000	2	8530 ± 30	Guccione et al. 1988; Scott and Aasen 1987
Old Field, Stoddard Co., MO	9200 to 3500	4	8810 ± 90	King and Allen 1977
Reelfoot Lake, Lake Co., TN	1000 to 0	2	240 ± 80	Mirecki 1996
NORTHERN BLUFFLAND UPLANDS				
Nonconnah Creek, Shelby Co., TN	>33,000 to 13,000	5	>33,000	Delcourt et al. 1980; Delcourt and Delcourt 1996

For each of the late Quaternary paleoenvironmental maps, we defined broad vegetation types based upon four criteria: (1) from the fossil-pollen diagrams, we determined the suite of taxa represented and the timing of immigration or of local extinction at each site; (2) for each landscape setting represented by paleoecological data, we selected the dominant pollen type and a second, subdominant, or "indicator," pollen type, based on ecological requirements for temperature, soil fertility and moisture, and tolerance to disturbances such as wildfire and flooding (Burns and Honkala 1990); (3) for each paleoecological site, we designated a spectrum of vegetation types potentially occupying nearby hydric wetlands, mesic terraces or uplands, and more xeric upland settings; and (4) we extrapolated the mapping of the vegetation units across the corresponding habitat as portrayed on the paleogeographic reconstructions of geomorphic environments.

Results

For the time series of paleoenvironmental maps, we recognized thirteen vegetation types as spanning part or all of the past 18,000 years (fig. 2.2). During the late Pleistocene, from 18,000 to 12,000 B.P., we distinguished six paleovegetation types; we mapped nine vegetation types for the Holocene time interval from 10,000 to 1000 B.P. On the map legend (fig. 2.2), paleovegetation types are shown in temporal sequence, based on the time at which they first appeared in the time series of maps.

On the uplands of the southeastern Ozark Plateaus and the fertile, mesic loessial soils mantling Crowley's Ridge and the northern Blufflands, late Pleistocene plant communities included Spruce-Jack Pine Forest, Spruce-Oak Forest, and Oak-Ironwood Forest. Holocene vegetation of these upland areas included Oak-Ironwood Forest, Oak-Hickory Forest, Oak-Hickory Savanna, Oak-Walnut Forest, and Oak-Shortleaf Pine Forest.

Within the CMV, intermediate-level braided-steam terraces, characterized by gently rolling sand plains with droughty, acidic, nutrient-poor soils, supported late Pleistocene forests of Spruce-Jack Pine and Oak-Hickory. In the Holocene, these environments were occupied by Oak-Hickory Savanna and Oak-Hickory Forest.

Bottomland habitats within the CMV changed over at about 10,000 B.P. from a glacial-age, braided-stream regime to an interglacial-age, meandering-stream regime. During the late Pleistocene, active valley trains and sand dune fields maintained relatively open Spruce-Willow Forest. This forest type was replaced by Ash-Willow Forest after 14,500 B.P. in the Western Lowlands, after the diversion of glacial meltwater southeastward through the Bell City–Oran Gap. Holocene bottomland vegetation was linked with major geomorphic environments associated with floodplains of meandering streams. Willow-Cane Forest occupied active river channels, young point bars, well-drained levees, and newly abandoned channel cutoffs. At the map scale used in this chapter, however, the width of the Willow-Cane communities is exaggerated to include the width of the active meander belts of the Mississippi River. Thus the area mapped as Willow-Cane Forest also includes a patchwork of successional hardwood forests on former floodplain remnants abandoned up to 1000 years prior to the interval depicted on the maps (Saucier 1994). Areas of inactive Holocene meander belts, resulting from lateral shifts in river meanders and characterized by mesic to poorly drained, sandy and silty soils on sites flooded during the winter and spring, are mapped as Sweetgum-Elm Forest. Cypress-Tupelo Forest is mapped in backswamps situated between levee crests of active and former meander belts and in rimswamps located between levee crests and adjacent terrace or upland escarpments. These poorly drained depressions are characterized by relatively long periods of standing water and chemically reducing environments.

Several of the paleovegetation types are designated for only one or a few mapped times. For example, Spruce-Jack Pine Forest occurred only at 18,000 B.P. Ash-Willow and Oak-Ironwood forest types appeared only during the late-glacial interval, from 14,000 to 12,000 B.P. and from 14,000 to 10,000 B.P., respectively. Ragweed-Grass Old Field, shown only on the map for 1000 B.P., developed in the late Holocene as an anthropogenic product of forest clearance, cultivation, and abandonment of old fields by Native Americans.

Paleoenvironmental Map for 18,000 B.P. (Fig. 2.2a)

During the Late Wisconsinan full-glacial interval, the entire mapped region was occupied by boreal forest communities dominated by spruce (*Picea* spp.), but with a variety of codominants that varied across the environmental gradient from uplands to lowlands. Peak glacial-age forests of the southeastern Ozark Plateaus were primarily composed of evergreen conifers, including spruce and boreal jack and/or red pines *(Pinus banksiana/resinosa)*, with minor amounts of fir *(Abies)*, oak *(Quercus)*, ironwood *(Ostrya/Carpinus)*, black ash *(Fraxinus nigra)*, and birch *(Betula)* also present (Delcourt and Delcourt 1996; E. Smith 1984). Oak probably was codominant with spruce along the mesic, dissected uplands of the Ozark Border region. The active valley train with meltwater-fed braided streams within the Western Lowlands was occupied by spruce, fir, and tamarack *(Larix laricina)*, as well as willow *(Salix)*, indicating a disturbance regime marked by frequent flooding within a shifting network of midchannel bars (Royall et al.

1991). We speculatively map Spruce-Willow Forest in the Eastern Lowlands in the valley train fed by Ohio River glacial meltwater. We infer that the mesic, loess-mantled Crowley's Ridge was occupied by Spruce-Oak Forest, and that the intermediate terraces of inactive valley trains bordering Crowley's Ridge provided a drier sand-plain habitat for Spruce-Jack Pine Forest. The mesic, loess-mantled Blufflands bordering the Eastern Lowlands supported a mixed forest of spruce, oak, and cool-temperate hardwoods, including sugar maple *(Acer saccharum)*, beech (*Fagus grandifolia*), tulip tree *(Liriodendron tulipifera)*, black walnut *(Juglans nigra)*, hickory (*Carya* spp.), ironwood, and ash (Delcourt et al. 1980).

Paleoenvironmental Map for 14,000 B.P. (Fig. 2.2b)

After 15,350 B.P., jack pine populations collapsed across the southeastern Ozark Plateaus in response to climate warming; cold-hardy species of spruce, oak, and ash all increased in importance within a late-glacial Spruce-Oak Forest (Delcourt and Delcourt 1991a; E. Smith 1984). Within the Ozark Border and Western Lowlands, spruce declined in importance as the Mississippi River–fed valley train was diverted southeastward through the Bell City–Oran Gap in Crowley's Ridge. By 14,500 B.P., cool-temperate deciduous hardwoods such as oak, ironwood, hickory, beech, and maple predominated within the Ozark Border in the Oak-Ironwood Forest community (Delcourt and Delcourt 1994; Royall et al. 1991). In the bottomlands, a species-poor Ash-Willow Forest established in ephemeral sluiceways (Royall et al. 1991). Oak-Hickory Forest replaced Spruce-Willow Forest on the intermediate-level braided-stream terraces of the Western and Eastern Lowlands. We speculatively map Spruce-Willow Forest along the active valley trains fed by Mississippi and Ohio River meltwater east of Crowley's Ridge. Spruce-Oak Forest was replaced by Oak-Ironwood Forest on Crowley's Ridge and in the Blufflands (Delcourt and Delcourt 1994; Delcourt et al. 1980).

Paleoenvironmental Map for 12,000 B.P. (Fig. 2.2c)

By 12,000 B.P., Oak-Ironwood forest was the predominant vegetation cover throughout the southeastern Ozark Plateaus, including the Ozark Border. Ash-Willow Forest still occupied ephemeral sluiceways in the Western Lowlands. Oak-Hickory Forest expanded to occupy abandoned braided-stream terraces both west and east of Crowley's Ridge. Spruce-Willow Forest became more restricted as the active channel of Ohio River–fed meltwater shifted to the east. Oak-Ironwood Forest persisted in the Blufflands. Both the Ash-Willow Forest (mapped at 14,000 and 12,000 B.P.) and the Oak-Ironwood Forest (14,000 to 10,000 B.P.) were plant communities with only poor modern analogues (Royall et al. 1991; E. Smith 1984). These ephemeral plant communities developed during the late-glacial interval in response to rapidly changing climatic and hydrologic conditions within the CMV (Delcourt and Delcourt 1996).

Paleoenvironmental Map for 10,000 B.P. (Fig. 2.2d)

At 10,000 B.P., uplands bordering the CMV to the west in the Ozark Plateaus, on centrally located Crowley's Ridge, and to the east in the Blufflands were occupied by poor-analogue, mixed deciduous forests. Throughout the lowlands of the CMV, the vegetation had become temperate to warm temperate in character, reflecting the northward recession of the climatic Polar Frontal Zone and increased frequency of storms in the warm and highly seasonal climates of the early Holocene interval (Delcourt and Delcourt 1994), as well as the modernization of the Mississippi River as a meandering stream (Saucier 1994). The first continuous representation of sweetgum pollen *(Liquidambar styraciflua)* at about 10,000 B.P. in the Western Lowlands at both Powers Fort Swale (Royall et al. 1991) and Hood Lake (Delcourt and Delcourt 1996; Delcourt et al. 1997), as well as in the Eastern Lowland sites of Big Lake and Pemiscot Bayou (Scott and Aasen 1987), records the replacement of Ash-Willow Forest by Sweetgum-Elm Forest in sluiceways throughout the lowlands. Oak-Hickory Forest continued to expand on midlevel abandoned braided-stream terraces both west and east of Crowley's Ridge. Willow-Cane Forest vegetation developed on levee systems within the active meander belt of the Mississippi River. Cypress-Tupelo Forest occupied backswamps of the Mississippi River. At Hood Lake, the oldest fossil pollen occurrences of bald cypress *(Taxodium distichum)* and tupelo gum *(Nyssa)* are dated at 11,250 and 9500 B.P., respectively, documenting their immigration in the early Holocene interval (Delcourt and Delcourt 1996; Delcourt et al. 1997).

Paleoenvironmental Map for 8000 B.P. (Fig. 2.2e)

With Hypsithermal climatic warming and drying that characterized the middle Holocene interval through the mid-continent region, vegetation throughout the mapped area became composed largely of drought-tolerant species in response to both diminished precipitation and lowered groundwater tables. Along the southeastern flank of the Prairie Peninsula, on the southeastern Ozark Plateaus, Oak-Hickory Savanna developed. This vegetation was characterized by sparse woodland with an understory of grass *(Poaceae)* and herbs (E. Smith 1984). Along the fire-protected escarpment of the Ozark Border, cool-temperate, mesic trees including beech, ironwood, sugar maple, basswood *(Tilia)*, and butternut *(Juglans cinerea)* were eliminated as the vegetation changed to

Oak-Hickory Forest (Royall et al. 1991). Sweetgum-Elm Forest, including sycamore *(Platanus occidentalis)*, planer tree *(Planera aquatica)*, hackberry (*Celtis/Maclura* type), box elder *(Acer negundo)*, water locust *(Gleditsia aquatica)*, and river birch *(Betula nigra)*, continued to occupy abandoned valley trains and ephemeral sluiceways in the Western and Eastern Lowlands as the water table continued to drop (Delcourt and Delcourt 1996; Delcourt et al. 1997; Guccione and Van Arsdale 1995; Royall et al. 1991; Scott and Aasen 1987). Oak-Hickory Forest thinned to become open savanna on midlevel, abandoned braided-stream terraces. For example, at Old Field on the Pvl 1 terrace surface, between 8700 and 4800 B.P. the fossil-pollen assemblages were dominated by herbs including grass (65 percent Poaceae) and ragweed (5 percent *Ambrosia*) in addition to trees such as oak (15 percent) and hickory (4 percent) (King and Allen 1977). Willow-Cane Forest continued on levees of the active Mississippi River meander belt, and Cypress-Tupelo Forest expanded in backswamps of the Mississippi River (Guccione et al. 1988; Guccione and Van Arsdale 1995).

By 8000 B.P., middle Holocene reduction in seasonal extremes produced a more equable range in temperatures than in the early Holocene, favoring warm-temperate hardwood trees over cool-temperate ironwood and ash (Delcourt and Delcourt 1994). We speculate that the former Oak-Ironwood Forest changed to mesic Oak-Walnut Forest both on Crowley's Ridge and in the northern Blufflands. The Oak-Walnut Forest could have maintained a diverse mixture of temperate hardwood species through the droughty middle Holocene interval because of the ameliorating effect of the fertile, mesic silt-loam soils developed in thick loess deposits.

Paleoenvironmental Map for 6000 B.P. (Fig. 2.2f)

The middle Holocene or Hypsithermal trend toward more arid conditions continued between 8000 and 6000 B.P., evidenced in the loss of many flowing streams and the areal restriction of riparian marsh and lowland swamp environments throughout much of the Western Lowlands (Delcourt et al. 1997; Royall et al. 1991). Oak-Hickory Savanna expanded there at the expense of Sweetgum-Elm Forest. Closed, deciduous forests dominated by oak continued to occupy Crowley's Ridge and the northern Blufflands. Extensive areas of Willow-Cane Forest and Cypress-Tupelo Forest were confined to the easternmost portion of the Eastern Lowlands along a relatively narrow meander belt of the active valley train of the Mississippi River. Within the central portion of the Eastern Lowlands, the Mississippi River probably provided lateral recharge through the sandy deposits of the adjacent braided-stream terraces, locally supplementing the dropping water tables and otherwise ameliorating the severity of Hypsithermal aridity. Mesic lowland forests expanded at the expense of permanently inundated backswamps of Cypress-Tupelo Forest.

Paleoenvironmental Map for 4000 B.P. (Fig. 2.2g)

Paleovegetation remained xeric, with wetlands restricted to a narrow meander belt of the Mississippi River, until after 4000 B.P. In addition to the southeastern Ozark Plateaus, much of the Western and Eastern Lowlands were occupied by dry Oak-Hickory Savanna, with more hydric Sweetgum-Elm Forest occupying intermittent drainage ways close to the Ozark Border and the Blufflands escarpment. Willow-Cane and Cypress-Tupelo vegetation continued to track the shifting meanders of the Mississippi along the easternmost portion of the Eastern Lowlands.

Paleoenvironmental Map for 2000 B.P. (Fig. 2.2h)

Late Holocene increases in precipitation resulted in both rising groundwater levels and increased overbank flooding of rivers traversing the CMV. This change in hydrology is evident after 3000 B.P. in the broadening Mississippi River meander belt (Saucier 1994). The shift from warm, dry middle Holocene climate to warm, wet late Holocene climate is variously recorded at 4500 B.P. in Powers Fort Swale, 3500 B.P. in Hood Lake, about 4700 B.P. at Pemiscot Bayou, and 3800 B.P. at Big Lake (Delcourt and Delcourt 1996). This spread in radiocarbon ages reflects local site differences in fluvial and groundwater responses to climate change.

Between 4000 and 3000 B.P., warm-temperate tree taxa, such as shortleaf pine *(Pinus echinata)*, immigrated northward onto the southeastern Ozark Plateaus, resulting in development of a late Holocene Oak-Shortleaf Pine Forest. By 2000 B.P., Oak-Hickory Forest probably reestablished along the Ozark Border, and Sweetgum-Elm Forest reexpanded along drainage systems throughout the Western Lowlands (Delcourt et al. 1997; Royall et al. 1991), as well as in the southern part of the Eastern Lowlands (Guccione et al. 1988). Willow-Cane vegetation occupied a broadened and shifting Mississippi River meander belt in the easternmost Eastern Lowlands. Oak-Walnut Forest continued to occupy both Crowley's Ridge and the Blufflands.

Paleoenvironmental Map for 1000 B.P. (Fig. 2.2i)

The patterns of natural vegetation portrayed on the paleoenvironmental map for 1000 B.P. are similar to those at 2000 B.P., with minor changes in location of Willow-Cane, Sweetgum-Elm, and Cypress-Tupelo Forests according to the shifting position of the active Mississippi River meander belt. This map differs substantially from the previous ones, however, in that it includes the area of prehistoric human impact for the CMV, based upon archeological maps of the extent of human occupation and agriculture from A.D. 700 to 1650 (figs. 10.1, 11.1, and 12.1 in Morse and Morse [1983]). We designate a Ragweed-Grass Old Field vegetation type to characterize a cumulative mosaic of secondary succession on anthropogenically disturbed landscapes. These areas would have included agricultural fields where maize *(Zea mays)* was cultivated by Native Americans, adjacent areas of human settlement, and early successional grasslands and thickets invading abandoned old fields that would have resulted from extensive human occupation and utilization of the Western Lowlands and (especially after about A.D. 1350) the Eastern Lowlands during the Mississippian cultural period.

The paleoecological "signature" of cultural impact is characterized by occurrence of pollen grains of cereals such as maize; weedy herbs including ragweed, chenopods, and grasses; and spores of old-field ferns, such as bracken *(Pteridium aquilinum)*. For example, the plant-fossil assemblage for 600 B.P. at Powers Fort Swale contains trace occurrences of *Zea mays,* 20 percent *Ambrosia* type, 5 percent Poaceae, and pollen grains of *Iva*, *Chenopodium* type, and *Plantago*. Palynological spectra from nearby archeological sites (Price 1978a) contained this suite of indicator pollen types, as well as spores of *Pteridium aquilinum,* reflecting prehistoric anthropogenic disturbance in the form of forest clearance and cultivation (J. P. Gardner, unpublished manuscript; Royall et al. 1991).

Discussion

Pleistocene full-glacial climatic, geomorphic, and vegetational environments in the CMV were all profoundly different from those of the Holocene. Colder regional climate, combined with major meltwater flow funneled down the Mississippi Alluvial Valley, provided a paleoenvironmental context in which boreal species of plants thrived and from which temperate plant species were generally excluded, except along the fertile soils of the Blufflands bordering the CMV. The changeover of the Mississippi River from a braided to a meandering regime in the late-glacial interval (Royall et al. 1991; Saucier 1974, 1994) was a geomorphic event that coincided with global and regional climatic amelioration. Paleoclimatic and geomorphic changes in the CMV during the late-glacial interval resulted in a fundamental change in the biota, with vegetation shifting from boreal coniferous forests to temperate deciduous forests (Delcourt and Delcourt 1987). As braided-stream environments became abandoned terraces, the vegetation changed in unpredictable ways as new and ephemeral combinations of plant communities assembled and then disassembled along changing topographic and hydrologic gradients (Delcourt and Delcourt 1994, 1996; Royall et al. 1991). The CMV world entered by Paleoindians was thus inherently unstable, with populations both of boreal plants and of certain mammals undergoing local extinctions related to major environmental change, and with populations of temperate species immigrating into the region to fill newly available niches. Plants that were to become valuable resources—for example, bald cypress (used for canoes as early as Dalton times)—established their populations in the CMV at the late Pleistocene/Holocene transition. These changes in environment may have been forcing functions for cultural change as Dalton people adapted to new and different conditions than those experienced by their Paleoindian predecessors; for example, shifting from hunting of Pleistocene megafauna such as mastodons to smaller game including white-tailed deer.

Alluvial forests along the meandering Mississippi River continued to change in distribution and composition throughout the Holocene (Delcourt and Delcourt 1996; Guccione et al. 1988) in response to a changing interglacial climatic regime. Because of astronomical changes in the Earth's eccentricity of orbit, tilt of its axis of rotation, and wobble about its axis of rotation, between 12,000 and 6000 B.P. northern hemisphere climates experienced greater extremes of temperature in both winter and summer compared with either full-glacial or modern climates (Kutzbach and Webb 1993). In the CMV, the early and middle Holocene intervals thus were times of accentuated seasonal extremes, along with decreased precipitation that may have resulted in changes in adaptive strategies for Archaic people. For example, as previously navigable streams dried up into ephemeral sluiceways, populations of hunters and gatherers may have responded by moving from unproductive bottomlands to adjacent uplands, where game and mast yield would have increased because of increased forest edge in open savannas. With a shift in the late Holocene to mesic, warm-temperate conditions, bottomland environments once again became favorable for human occupation, with Woodland and Mississippian people adapting to fertile bottomlands and increasing their populations as they developed agricultural fields on levees along active meander trains.

Widespread deforestation and conversion of bottomlands to agriculture began around A.D. 700 in the Mississippian cultural period and culminated in historic times (Morse and Morse 1983). From the paleoenvironmental map for 1000 B.P., it is evident that by the height of the Mississippian cultural period, prehistoric Native Americans had a substantial effect upon the composition and distribution of bottomland forests, both on active floodplains and on midlevel, abandoned braided-stream terraces. Prior to EuroAmerican contact, therefore, humans became active agents of ecological change in the CMV by fragmenting the once-contiguous bottomland forest cover into a patchwork of forests and fields.

Acknowledgments

We gratefully thank Dan F. Morse and Phyllis A. Morse, James E. Price, Cynthia Price, Marvin Jeter, and David Anderson for many productive discussions concerning the natural and cultural history of the Central Mississippi Alluvial Valley. Peggy Guccione graciously made available critical new discoveries for the late Quaternary geomorphic and paleo-ecological development of the Eastern Lowlands. This is Contribution No. 65 in Quaternary Ecology, University of Tennessee, Knoxville.

CHAPTER THREE

PREHISTORY OF THE SALINE RIVER DRAINAGE BASIN, CENTRAL TO SOUTHEAST ARKANSAS

MARVIN D. JETER AND ANN M. EARLY

The thrill of discovery is not necessarily that of finding a fine artifact but that of... translating a hodgepodge of information into a coherent model.

—DAN AND PHYLLIS MORSE,
Archaeology of the Central Mississippi Valley

Drainage basins are basic units for hydrological research, but they have had a variable history with regard to cultural situations. Archaeologically, it often has proved useful to subdivide them, especially in large-scale studies (Morse and Morse 1983; Phillips 1970). On a smaller scale, there have been some archaeological attempts to consider entire drainage basins. Not long ago, a controversy about such models involved Dan Morse, who proposed a "central interpretation... that each watershed represents a single [Dalton culture] band's territory" (1983:81–82; cf. Morse and Morse 1996:6). In any event, there is something to be said for holistic attempts to study human activities in entire drainage basins, if only to determine whether previously established subdivisions were really warranted. Certainly, it is most practical for small to moderate-sized drainages (e.g., Anderson, this volume). Here we consider one such situation, where nothing of the sort has been attempted before.

The Saline River drainage basin (fig. 3.1) covers nearly 8,500 km^2 (approximately 3,250 mi^2) in central to southeast Arkansas, or 6.1 percent of the state's area. It includes significant natural resources in two major physiographic provinces and some remarkable sites in marginal regions of two major archaeological areas. Yet, there have been no major professional excavations in the Saline Basin, and there are relatively few reports on individual sites. Modern land use is a major factor. Much of the basin is covered by dense vegetation (commercial pine forests, portions of the Felsenthal National Wildlife Refuge and the Ouachita National Forest, undeveloped woods, and pastures), so ground visibility is minimal. Also, the few cultural resource management projects have only involved early stages, not "mitigation" excavations.

Beyond the site level, the northern and southern portions of the Saline Basin generally have been discussed separately, as marginal parts of regions or areas centered elsewhere. One accidental factor has been involved: over the past three decades, during which modern archaeology has developed, the Saline Basin has been divided among three of the Arkansas Archeological Survey's research station territories. The southern portions, in Ashley, Bradley, Drew, Cleveland, and Lincoln Counties, are in the domain of the UAM station (occupied by Jeter for most of the time since 1978). Most of the northern portions, in Dallas, Grant, Saline, Garland, and Hot Spring Counties, are in the HSU station territory (where Early has worked since 1972). A small portion of the northeast margin, in Jefferson County, is in the UAPB station territory (where our colleague John House holds forth).

This has had a distracting or marginalizing effect on work in the Saline Basin. The major research attention in each station territory has been directed elsewhere. The UAM station has emphasized the "delta" lands of southeasternmost Arkansas, along the Mississippi River and (especially) former Arkansas River courses, plus the lowermost modern Arkansas River and the bottomlands of the Felsenthal Refuge, along the Ouachita River below the Saline's mouth. The HSU station has emphasized the middle and upper reaches of the Ouachita Valley, into the Ouachita Mountains. The UAPB station's major foci have been along the Mississippi and Arkansas, secondary but important rivers such as the lowermost White and St. Francis, and various bayous in between. Nevertheless, our databases for the Saline drainage have gradually increased on a more or less opportunistic basis.

The territorial research situation also has had a fragmenting effect with regard to consideration of the "big picture" of the Saline drainage basin. Here we begin to remedy this problem. After a consideration of the basic environmental factors, we present a chronological review of the major culture periods, emulating (on a much more limited scale) the example of our distinguished colleagues the Morses (1983).

Geoscientific Background and Environment

The Saline's Course and Tributaries

The stream under consideration here is sometimes called "the Saline River of the east" to distinguish it from a smaller, western Saline River

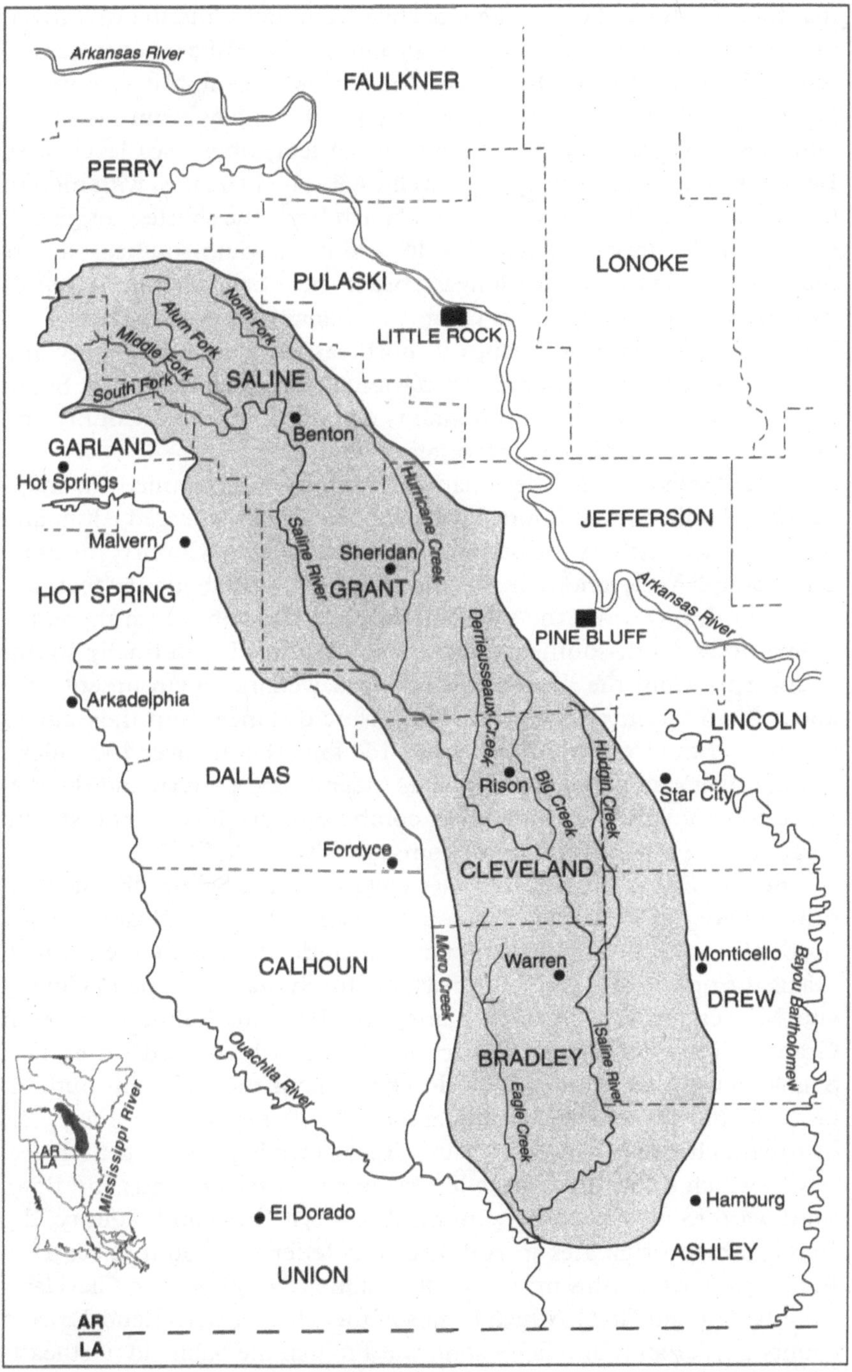

FIGURE 3.1. The Saline River drainage basin, central to southeast Arkansas.

that flows southward out of the Ouachita Mountains into the Red River. Our Saline River's headwaters are also in the Ouachitas, but in central Arkansas, west of Little Rock. Its major tributaries in this vicinity are known as "the Four Forks" (Dunnahoo 1993). They begin flowing at altitudes of more than 300 m (over 1,000 feet) above sea level (asl). Before they join, they are all fairly well-established streams, with modest floodplains along their lower reaches. North Fork, the shortest, originates near Saline County's northern border and flows south-southeast across that county. Alum Fork, the longest, begins near Saline County's northwestern borders with Garland County and flows southeast. Middle Fork heads up north of Hot Springs in northeastern Garland County and flows southeast to join Alum Fork in southwestern Saline County. South Fork has its sources in the mountains of eastern Garland County and flows east-southeast into southwestern Saline County.

The "Saline River" designation usually is first applied on maps below the point where South Fork joins the already-merged Alum and Middle forks, just west of Benton in southern Saline County; the adjacent floodplain elevations are on the order of 75 m (about 250 feet) asl. North Fork flows into the river northwest of Benton. From there, the Saline flows south-southeastward, then southward, and finally southwestward to join the Ouachita River in a wetland environment only about 20 m (about 65 feet) asl. The airline distance from the Saline's nominal origin to its mouth is about 160 km (slightly over 100 miles), but the river's arcuate course plus its meandering pattern and the distance to its northernmost sources combine to produce a total stream length on the order of 325 km (about 200 "river miles").

Below Benton, several tributary creeks join the Saline; archaeologically, all are poorly known, but some are already of significance. From north to south, the major tributaries include Francois Creek, which drains the uplands east and northeast of Hot Springs in Garland County and Malvern in Hot Spring County and joins the Saline in western Grant County; the lengthy Hurricane Creek, which heads in eastern Saline County just west of Little Rock and joins the Saline in southern Grant County in an extensive wetland locality featuring a confusing snarl of stream channels; Derrieusseaux Creek (locally pronounced "Deer-saw"), which drains the Grant-Jefferson county borderlands and flows southward to meet the Saline in northwestern Cleveland County; Big Creek, which originates in southwestern Jefferson County near Pine Bluff and flows southward to join the Saline in southeastern Cleveland County; Hudgin Creek, which begins in the Jefferson-Cleveland-Lincoln county borderlands and flows southward to join the Saline in northeasternmost Bradley County; and Eagle (L'Aigle) Creek, which drains central Bradley County, flowing south to meet the Saline in southernmost

Bradley County just above the Saline-Ouachita junction. There are also several small creeks below Hudgin Creek, flowing westward into the Saline in Drew and Ashley Counties.

The Saline's overall course is of comparable length, and similar shape, to that of Bayou Bartholomew, a short distance to the east and southeast. The cultural sequences along these streams, which are in different physiographic (and cultural) situations, offer interesting opportunities for comparisons and contrasts (cf. Jeter 1982; Jeter et al. 1989).

Physiographic Provinces and Resources

The Saline's headwaters are in the southeastern portion of the Ouachita Mountains physiographic province (Fenneman 1938:663ff), between, but not including, the immediate vicinities of Hot Springs and Little Rock. From the Benton vicinity, the Saline flows through various subdivisions of the West Gulf Coastal Plain province (Fenneman 1938:100ff).

Ouachita Mountains

The Ouachitas are true mountains in the structural-geological sense, with often steep, ridge-and-valley topography, trending east-west. Elevations in the Saline-drained portions sometimes exceed 300 m (about 1,000 feet) asl, and local relief of 30 to 50 m (100 feet or more) is common. This landscape was formed by erosion of strongly folded and locally faulted Paleozoic sedimentary rocks, locally interspersed with significant metamorphic rock formations. These ancient formations were intruded by Cretaceous volcanic action near and in the upper Saline Basin.

Natural overhangs, or rock shelters, are present in the Ouachitas, but are much less common, and apparently were not occupied as intensively, as the famous "bluff shelters" of the Ozarks. There are a few shelters in the Saline Basin, and one allegedly had pictographs (Dunnahoo 1993:6), but none have been professionally excavated or even tested. Some may be due to historic quarrying rather than natural processes.

The major resource of relevance here is the famous Arkansas Novaculite Formation, involving a varicolored, weakly metamorphosed cherty stone, and probably the greatest set of aboriginal lithic quarries in North America (Early 1988:6–7; Jeter and Jackson 1994:159–60). Most of the quarries are on ridgetops in the Ouachita River's drainage basin, including some near and along the Saline drainage divide; some are within the Saline drainage.

The abundant lithic resources of this zone also include Bigfork chert, quartz crystals, shales and slates (Early 1988:8; Jeter and Jackson 1994:173–78), sandstones and quartzites (Early 1993a:17), and igneous rocks (Rolingson and Howard 1997). Lamprophyres, apparently the most commonly used igneous materials, were available from dikes in the eastern Ouachitas, some of them in the upper Saline drainage.

Magnetite, a remarkable iron-oxide mineral, has known outcrops only in the Magnet Cove locality in northeastern Hot Spring County (Jeter and Jackson 1994:167). This is in the Ouachita drainage, but very near the Saline drainage divide. Hematite is much more widely distributed and variable in texture; no rigorous studies have been made in these regions, but nodules are available in the Magnet Cove locality.

West Gulf Coastal Plain

The boundary between the Ouachita Mountains and West Gulf Coastal Plain provinces is a geological unconformity or discontinuity between the much older, consolidated Paleozoic rocks of the mountains and the late Mesozoic to Cenozoic, generally unconsolidated deposits of the Coastal Plain.

The late Cretaceous period saw several igneous intrusions beyond the southeastern margin of the Ouachita Mountain front. The "Saline County Intrusive" is one of these, now surrounded by younger Cenozoic deposits, as is Fourche (Granite) Mountain overlooking the Arkansas Valley, near Little Rock (Divine 1972:75–76). Granite like syenites and chemically similar trachytes are best known from the Fourche Mountain locality, but the Magnet Cove and Saline County formations also were used as sources. Syenite artifacts found as far west as east Texas have been identified by a "distinctive . . . crystalline structure" characteristic of the Saline County source (Rolingson and Howard 1997:45).

Bauxite, an aluminum-rich mineral produced by intense Cenozoic weathering of the Cretaceous syenites, has been commercially exploited in southeast Saline County (Divine 1972:75–76). Archaeologists have long speculated that "Arkansas bauxite" was the raw material for some late prehistoric figurines, effigy pipes, etc., but this has not yet been borne out by physical-chemical testing. In the early 1980s, Jeter and others, including the Morses, provided artifactual and raw material samples to the Smithsonian Institution for testing; in that sample, the bauxite specimens did not resemble the artifacts, which instead were provisionally identified as a "fire clay" from southeast Missouri (Bruce D. Smith to Jeter 1982).

The Cenozoic region of the Coastal Plain (Divine 1972:171ff) surrounds the Saline River from the Benton vicinity to its mouth. Southward, the river valley traverses progressively younger formations: first, a narrow band of the Paleocene Midway Group, followed by more extensive Eocene members of the Wilcox, Claiborne, and Jackson groups.

Along the river and surrounding its southern reaches, there is another unconformity, blanketed by Quaternary terraces and floodplains. Local relief varies from moderately hilly to rolling to virtually flat. Elevations of more than 150 m (over 500 feet) asl occur in the hilly country surrounding the Saline near Benton. Near the river's mouth, the nearby hills are still often above 60 m (approximately 200 feet) asl. On a smaller scale, thousands of prairie mounds are present on nearly flat landforms more than 5,000 years old. They are of undetermined natural origin (Saucier 1994:162–65), but are often thought to be "Indian mounds" by the general public, and were occasionally occupied prehistorically, most frequently in the case of those near streams.

Saucier (1987; Saucier and Smith 1986) recently has mapped and discussed the Quaternary deposits and landforms (especially terraces) along the Saline, from below Benton to the juncture with the Ouachita. He has called for increasing integration of archaeological project planning and interpretation with geomorphic data (Saucier 1987:63–64). Saucier also has suggested that there is a relatively low probability of finding buried sites in the Saline floodplain setting; instead, "the terraces adjacent to the floodplain should contain the best and most complete record of human habitation" (Saucier 1987:68). This has not been fairly tested as yet.

Although there are no bedrock outcrops in the Coastal Plain formations, the uplands and terraces do include abundant deposits of gravel. Pebble cherts (and other materials) from these sources, and from gravel bars along streams dissecting these formations, were used extensively in prehistoric times. Although novaculite gravels also are present and were used prehistorically in the upper Saline drainage, they do not appear to have been used much in the lower portion. Instead, larger pieces of novaculite obtained from the sources in the Ouachita Mountains seem to have been preferred, especially in the Archaic period, when large points were made (Hemmings 1982:219ff, 242).

These gravel deposits have long been used in road construction and maintenance (Dunnahoo 1993:7). In recent decades, sandpit and/or gravel-pit and fill-dirt operations have greatly intensified. The upland and terrace portions of regional topographic quadrangle maps appear moon cratered by these pits (or ponds, where they have filled with water). Many archaeological sites, some quite important, have been damaged or destroyed by such activities.

Another interesting lithic component of the Coastal Plain deposits is petrified wood, mostly from the Redfield Formation of the Jackson Group, which is present over much of the surface of Jefferson, Lincoln, and eastern Grant Counties (Divine 1972:190–91, figs. 19, 20). It is of generally poor quality, not comparable to petrified woods that were flaked prehistorically in areas such as Arizona. Nevertheless, small unworked pieces of this material occur in archaeological sites in the lower Saline Valley, as if prehistoric "rockhounds" had collected them; rarely, some were minimally flaked and/or used.

Also among the resources of archaeological significance are abundant and varied clays. Efforts are now under way to correlate chemical trace-element signatures of clays and prehistoric ceramics from these regions, with promising results (Jeter et al. n.d.).

The resource that earned the Saline River its name is, of course, salt. There do not, however, appear to be any significant salt deposits in the entire basin. Instead, early explorers' descriptions of the lower Saline, and passing remarks in geological reports, seem to indicate patchy and generally minor concentrations of ancient marine salt in some of the Coastal Plain formations, in the form of seeps and licks used by animals (Dickinson 1989:154). We know of no prehistoric Native American saltworks in this drainage, although such sites are well documented in the nearby Ouachita Valley around Arkadelphia (Early 1993a).

The Lowermost Saline River

Near the Saline's juncture with the Ouachita, land below 30 m (about 100 feet) asl is fairly common, and some is even below 20 m (approximately 65 feet) asl. Along the Ouachita, between the Saline's mouth and the Louisiana state line, is the lowest land (and water) in the state of Arkansas: the Ouachita leaves Arkansas at low-water elevations around 18 m (less than 60 feet) asl. The Ouachita does not have well-developed natural levees in this vicinity (King 1990:87; Schambach 1981:105); extensive long-term flooding, involving the lowermost Saline Valley, was common under natural conditions (Hemmings 1982:13ff, fig. 70). Not even modern mechanized agribusiness practices had been able to establish significant farming in or near these lowlands before the Felsenthal Refuge was established in the 1970s. Recent dam construction created Lake Jack Lee, with a maximum water elevation of about 19.8 m (65 feet) asl, covering about 4,000 hectares (approximately 10,000 acres) for much of the year.

Archaeological Areas and Regions

Arkansas archaeologists, using the taxonomic systematics of large archaeological areas subdivided into regions, have included portions of the Saline Basin within two major areas and three regions. The upper reaches are within the Trans-Mississippi South (TMS) area, and the lower portions are part of the Lower Mississippi Valley (LMV) area.

The TMS was defined by Schambach (1970, 1971, 1982a:133ff) as an area of Southeastern-like cultural ecology west of the Mississippi Valley and east of the Plains. He suggested that the TMS designation would be more appropriate than the culturally laden term *Caddoan area*, which is still sometimes used for a major portion of the same territory.

Within the TMS, the uppermost Saline Basin is in the very large Ouachita Mountains region, which extends into Oklahoma and is coextensive with the Ouachita Mountains physiographic province. Some recent research has been done by the HSU station in portions of the Ouachitas drained by the Ouachita River and its other tributaries (e.g., Early 1988), but there are no modern publications dealing with the Saline-drained portions.

The middle portions of the Saline drainage are called the Middle Saline region (Early 1982a:13). It has seen little in the way of formal archaeological study and is the most problematical of the three regions under consideration here (cf. Early 1982a:65). It is split among the Survey's HSU, UAM, and UAPB stations and has never been formally defined as belonging to the LMV or TMS archaeological areas, although it is generally considered as part of the latter. Quite probably, any prehistoric cultural "boundaries" here were generally permeable and shifted through time (as occurred in the Felsenthal region, below).

The lower reaches and tributaries of the Saline, entirely within the UAM station territory, are included in the Felsenthal region of the LMV. This large region was defined by Schambach (1979, 1981) as "basically a zone of Lower Mississippi Valley environment, extending up the Ouachita [drainage basin] from Louisiana into Arkansas, that seems to have supported [LMV] cultures for most of [prehistory]" (Schambach 1979:21). It should be noted that a later major survey suggested that the LMV-TMS cultural boundary had shifted significantly several times, both up and (especially) down the Ouachita Valley from the present Camden, during the course of prehistory (Weinstein and Kelley 1984:515).

Schambach (1979, 1981) did not discuss the extent of the LMV area and Felsenthal region up tributaries of the Ouachita, such as the Saline, but did provide a large-scale map (Schambach 1981:fig. 22) that depicted the region's boundary with the Middle Saline region as an uncertain dashed line. That situation continued in a more recent rendering (Schambach 1990:fig. 1). Our discussions will note some evidence for fluctuation of a cultural boundary zone, especially during the later prehistoric to protohistoric periods.

Archaeological Sequence

The largest gap in data is the Saline River drainage . . . It was not, however, a no-man's land.

—Martha Ann Rolingson, *Toltec Mounds and Plum Bayou Culture*

Here we will summarize the Saline Basin's culture history in chronological order. For present purposes, approximate dates will be given in B.C. and A.D. terms. It must be emphasized, though, that these are only a convenient shorthand. For more accuracy, radiocarbon and other absolute dates, and appropriate conversion tables, should be used.

Our basic data are derived from recent larger scale overviews (Early 1982a; Jeter 1982; Jeter et al. 1989; Schambach 1982b), supplemented significantly by our knowledge of subsequent published and unpublished research in these regions. We also have used the Survey's computerized AMASDA database for some basic information (e.g., as of January 1997, AMASDA contained data on more than 30,000 sites in Arkansas, but only 765 [2.5 percent] of these were in the Saline Basin). Beyond the most basic levels, however, AMASDA must be used with caution, as noted some time ago (Jeter et al. 1989:77–78). The data are no better than the site forms on which they are based, and many older forms include inaccurate assessments, based on outmoded or mistaken interpretations.

Early Paleoindian (Clovis, Fluted Point) Period, 9500–8500 B.C.

A few fluted points have been found in the Ouachita Mountains region, but so far none have come from the upper Saline drainage. Other fluted points have been found on old river terraces in the Middle Ouachita region, but none are yet known from the Middle Saline (Early 1982a: 34–35) or Felsenthal regions.

Late Paleoindian Period, Dalton Culture, 8500–8000 B.C.

Research on the Dalton phenomenon is best exemplified by Dan Morse's efforts in and near northeast Arkansas, where a major concentration of Dalton sites has been found (Morse 1997a; Morse and Morse 1983:71ff). Early (1982a:43) noted that there had probably been "a major Dalton presence in southwest Arkansas" since Dalton diagnostics had been found in "a variety of locations" in all of our regions. Rumors persist of remarkable deeply buried finds by relic collectors, but the surface has barely been scratched scientifically. Only one minor Dalton site in the Saline drainage has been professionally tested. In 1981 Jeter tested site 3DR146, overlooking an intermittent stream in northwestern Drew County, but found no evidence of undisturbed subsurface deposits.

San Patrice Complex, 8000–7500 B.C.

The San Patrice complex may be related to Dalton and may at least partly overlap it in time. Its elements are found into northern Arkansas (Morse and Morse 1983:104), but it is best known in and near northwest Louisiana (Jeter et al. 1989:81–84). On the basis of data from the western part of the region, Schambach (1982b:45) stated that San Patrice culture was probably "strongly represented" in the Felsenthal region, but only one San Patrice site (3AS40) is recorded in the entire Saline drainage basin. This multicomponent site has been extensively surface collected, but has not been scientifically tested.

Early Archaic Period, 7500–6000 B.C.

Early (1982a:46–47) and Schambach (1982b:47–48) reserved this designation for any remains other than Dalton or San Patrice for this general period in southwest Arkansas. They mentioned finds of stemmed, corner-notched, and early variants of side-notched points (cf. Morse and Morse 1983:104–6), which might belong to this period, but noted the lack of type definitions and good contexts.

Scottsbluff Intrusion, 7000–6000 B.C.

Scottsbluff points are generally believed to represent an intrusion from the Great Plains into western Arkansas and northwestern Louisiana (Jeter et al. 1989:87–89). There has been some difference of opinion on the dating of the Scottsbluff complex, with some regarding it as a late Paleoindian phenomenon, possibly even preceding Dalton (Early 1982a:43). Data from the Plains, however, suggest a date range as given above (Jeter et al. 1989:89). Morse and Morse (1983:106–8) have compared/contrasted Scottsbluff points to Hardin points of the Central Mississippi Valley and suggested that they are coeval, around 7000–6000 B.C., citing an apparent eastward expansion of prairie environments and Plains cultural influence related to the onset of the hot and dry Hypsithermal climatic interval.

Early (1982a:40) noted that a few Scottsbluff points, including one from western Garland County in the Ouachita drainage, have been found in the Ouachita Mountains region, but none were yet known from the portions draining into the Saline Basin. However, "occasional" specimens had been reportedly found in northwestern Grant County "on high promontories overlooking the Saline alluvial valley in the Middle

Saline region" (Early 1982a:40). A Scottsbluff find was made at a site in the Derriesseaux Creek drainage in southwestern Jefferson County; still farther east and barely outside the Saline drainage, a Scottsbluff point recently was found on the southwestern outskirts of Pine Bluff (House 1991a:fig. 1).

Middle Archaic Period, 6000–3000 B.C.

In and near the Saline Basin there appears to be little evidence of basally notched or "lobed" point styles such as those found in portions of north Arkansas and adjacent regions and dating roughly 6000–4000 B.C. (Morse and Morse 1983:108–10). Perhaps only "a very minimum of human activity" around the Hypsithermal peak, as in the northeast Arkansas lowlands (Morse and Morse 1983:108, 110), was also the case in the Saline Basin.

In the Arkansas *State Plan* (Early 1982a:48–55; Schambach 1982b: 50–54, 57–59), four Middle Archaic "study units" were discussed as occurring in and near southwest Arkansas: the Tom's Brook culture (including its Spoon Bend phase), the Crystal Mountain phase, the White Oak phase (discussed below, in the Late Archaic section), and the Big Creek culture (including the Dorcheat phase).

Tom's Brook Culture

The Tom's Brook culture is relatively well defined for the period circa 5000–4000 B.C. in much of central and western Arkansas, especially the Ouachita Valley (Jeter et al. 1989:91–93, fig. 8; Schambach 1970:384–85). The principal diagnostic artifact is the distinctive Johnson point/knife, which has a very broad stem and a concave to straight base. This culture, or at least its major Hypsithermal riverine adaptation, also is characterized by notched pebbles that may have been netsinkers. It is well represented in the Felsenthal region along the Ouachita, where the Spoon Bend phase was defined (Schambach 1982b:50). There is scarcely any evidence from the eastern part of the region, though. It seems likely that the Saline Basin was near the southeast margin of the Tom's Brook cultural interaction zone (Jeter et al. 1989:fig. 8), but this may be due to inadequate investigation.

Crystal Mountain Phase

Schambach (1970:385–87) defined the Crystal Mountain phase for the Middle Ouachita region based on the co-occurrence of Big Sandy (or similar late side-notched) points and notched pebbles (apparently a continuation of the Tom's Brook adaptation). Its representation appears "weak" in the Felsenthal region, though (Schambach 1990:fig. 78). Such points are quite common to the north and east, dating circa 4000–3000 B.C. (Morse and Morse 1983:110–11), but are poorly represented to the south in Louisiana (Jeter et al. 1989:93). However, Joe Saunders (personal communication to Jeter 1997) has found a variant side-notched point form at the Hedgepeth site in extreme north-central Louisiana associated with a radiocarbon age of roughly 3000 B.C. Side-notched points occasionally are seen in private collections from these regions; Survey station collections should be examined for them, and site forms should be systematically searched for mentions of them. For example, site 3CV11 in eastern Cleveland County near Hudgin Creek was recorded in 1966 as having produced 12 "dart points, side notched near stem."

Big Creek Culture

The concept of the Big Creek culture has gradually evolved to significant proportions over nearly three decades of research by professionals, expanding on some remarkable collections and notes begun by amateurs and WPA excavators in Arkansas and Louisiana at least as early as the 1930s (Jeter et al. 1989:36, 98). The basis of the concept is the widespread distribution of the distinctive "double-notched" or "blade-notched" Evans points/knives.

On the basis of the literature and interviews with archaeologists, in the Arkansas-Louisiana overview the primary Big Creek culture (Evans point distribution) area was shown as a huge oval, elongated north-south, from the Little Rock vicinity to central Louisiana and about the width of the two states (Jeter et al. 1989:fig. 9). This is one of the most glaring culture-historical differences between the sequences for the Saline Basin (and adjacent regions) and for northeast Arkansas, where the Evans point type is essentially unknown (Morse and Morse 1983: 99–122; Dan Morse personal communication to Jeter 1995).

Schambach (1970:175ff, 389ff) defined the Dorcheat phase on the basis of Evans points and other artifacts, probably including (at least in the western Evans range) straight-stemmed Bulverde points/knives at the Cooper site in the Middle Ouachita region. Later, he expanded this phase into the newly designated Felsenthal region (Schambach 1979:27) and showed some inclination to consider it as a "culture" designation (Schambach 1979:fig. 3.1). He had already noted, however, the finds of numerous Evans points at the Big Creek site (3CV18) in Cleveland County (Schambach 1970:178–80, 392), and did so again (Schambach 1979:27). In a more detailed review of Felsenthal regional archaeology (Schambach and Rolingson 1981:179, table 19), the "Big Creek culture" designation was unveiled. In the *State Plan*, the Dorcheat phase concept was expanded to include at least parts of the Felsenthal, Middle Saline, and Ouachita Mountains regions (Early 1982a:58–59; Schambach 1982b:57).

The culture-sequential and chronological placements of Evans points and associated phases and cultures have varied considerably (Schambach 1970:389ff, table 27, 1979:fig. 3.1; Schambach and Rolingson 1981:179). In the *State Plan* (Schambach 1982b:57), the Dorcheat phase and Big Creek culture were subsumed within the Middle Archaic period, with a chronological placement "between approximately 4000 and 2000 B.C." (this now appears to have been the most accurate, if not precise, of these early estimates; see below).

Jeter and Jackson (1994:144–47) conjectured that Big Creek culture may have been an important early Late Archaic precursor of the Poverty Point culture, but the concept of Evans points and Big Creek culture as Late Archaic now appears questionable. Recent work at several northeast Louisiana sites (Saunders et al. 1994; Saunders to Jeter 1997) has produced a calibrated radiocarbon date of about 3300 B.C. associated with an Evans point and unusual "clay block" fragments, and a virtually contemporary date for the "blocks" (which may come to be called "Watson Brake objects" [Saunders et al. 1998]) without associated points. Evans points and "blocks" appear to be associated at several of these sites with mound and other earthwork construction and Bulverde points. Saunders's data seem to indicate a late Middle Archaic placement (or beginning date), before 3000 B.C., for the Evans/blocks/mounds complex.

Within the Saline drainage, the Big Creek site itself, near the northern margin of the Felsenthal region, was the scene of intensive occupation(s) by the makers of Evans points. The Chowning collection (Rolingson 1993) includes more than 600 specimens from this site alone. Several minor Evans point components are known nearby; sites 3CV105 and 3CV110 are examples. The former was on a "prairie mound" only a few km upvalley from the Big Creek site itself. The latter, in a deep-woods location less than 1 km (approximately 0.5 miles) from the Big Creek site, produced two Evans points and a scraper. Sites 3CV11, 3CV12, and 3CV14, to the southeast on the margins of Hudgin Creek's valley, have all reportedly yielded Evans points, as did 3BR97 on a tributary stream just north of Warren.

Survey collections from a number of other sites in these regions, and the hoards of regional collectors, contain many Evans points. Clearly, some inventories are in order, but beyond that, it will take major excavations of undisturbed and isolated components at a variety of site types to begin compiling adequate definitions of Big Creek as a coherent culture. As it is, we really have only the Evans points, plus vague categories like fire-cracked rock and mostly local chert debitage. Relationships with more specific artifact classes, such as the Bulverde points (more common to the west), Williams points (see below), and the clay "blocks" (and mounds) of northeast Louisiana, remain problematical.

Late Archaic Period, 3000–600 B.C.

Williams Point Complex

The "early" dating for at least some Evans variants creates a new question about the placement of the corner-notched, convex-based Williams points/knives. Schambach's (1970:393–94, tables 24, 27) analyses found them to co-occur with Evans points in arbitrary levels at the Cooper site, possibly tending to precede the Evans complex slightly. Here we will consider the possibility that the two overlap, but that Williams points tend to be slightly later than the Evans complex, and that the Williams points date mainly if not completely after 3000 B.C. This is reinforced by the Morses's (1983:116–18, fig. 6.2a–b) placement of a Williams variant called the Big Creek point type (not to be confused with the Big Creek culture) between 3000 and 2000 B.C.

In the *State Plan*, the "Middle Archaic" White Oak phase was called a "minimally defined . . . amorphous entity" based on Williams points but poorly represented outside the Middle Ouachita and (perhaps) Ouachita Mountains regions, possibly primarily an adaptation to the relatively unstudied uplands (Early 1982a:56; Schambach 1982b:53). Williams points do occur in lowland sites to the southeast, though. Collections from the Saline Basin have not been systematically studied, but in 1985–87 H. Edwin Jackson examined UAM collections from 52 sites in the Delta lowlands. The Williams type, with 13 specimens from six sites, was the sixth most common of 20 identified types (Jackson and Jeter 1991:42–44, table 2).

Gary and Other Late Archaic Stemmed Point/Knife Types

Numerous other Late Archaic stemmed point/knife types have been assigned to generalized Late Archaic placements in these and nearby regions. They are not well dated, however, nor associated with well-defined assemblages of other artifacts (see Jeter et al. 1989:98–99 for a summary). The almost ubiquitous contracting-stemmed Gary point/knife type, or at least its larger varieties, is easily the most common type of this period. It definitely is associated with sites of the Poverty Point culture, but is also found on sites outside the Poverty Point orbit. Gary points are quite common in collections from sites in the Saline Basin, but there have been no excavations to document associated materials and features. There was an obvious significant increase in the use of novaculite during this period (Jackson and Jeter 1991:43–45; Jeter and Jackson 1994: 159–66), coinciding with the use of relatively large points/knives and other stone tools.

Poverty Point, or "Terminal Archaic" Subperiod, 1700–600 B.C.

The remarkable Poverty Point site in northeast Louisiana was the hub of a far-flung network of interactions, with some emphasis on lithic raw material extraction and/or exchange and long-distance transport. A significant amount of this interaction involved Arkansas lithics (e.g., novaculite, magnetite, hematite, slate, quartz crystals) from the Ouachita Mountains (Jeter and Jackson 1994). Probably many contemporary people in and near the LMV did not participate significantly in the Poverty Point network; they are usually regarded as culturally "late Late" or "Terminal" Archaic rather than Poverty Point peoples. An initial assessment of this situation for the Bartholomew-Macon region documented a large number of point types, especially the larger varieties of Gary points, for this general time span (Jackson and Jeter 1991:42–44, table 2).

During this period, the Saline River would have been a secondary tributary, via the Ouachita River, of the Arkansas River system. The Arkansas then flowed in the present Bartholomew meander belt and was joined by the Ouachita near present-day Monroe. The Poverty Point site, on Macon Ridge, then commanded the divide between the major Arkansas and Mississippi valleys (Jeter et al. 1989:103; Jeter and Jackson 1994:139–40; Saucier 1994:273–74, fig. 50). The lithic sources in and near the Ouachita Mountains would have been accessible to Poverty Point peoples via the Saline River's headward tributaries, as well as the Ouachita Valley itself and the Arkansas Valley (Jeter and Jackson 1994:135–42).

The Calion site and others along the Ouachita upstream from the Saline's mouth have long been regarded as closely affiliated with Poverty Point (Webb 1982:7, figs. 1, 4). Schambach (1979:fig. 3.1) designated the Calion phase as a strong presence of Poverty Point culture in the Felsenthal region. He has reaffirmed that "Poverty Point culture, rather than just isolated traits" (Schambach 1982b:62) existed along the Ouachita, but he has not discussed the Saline Valley. Hemmings (1982:126, 128) noted two Calion phase components among the 40 sites he found along the lowermost Saline River. He also found a major Poverty Point/Calion component at the Marie Saline site (3AS329) on the Ouachita River, a short distance downstream from the Saline's present mouth, and suggested that the nearby Marais Saline Lake might represent a former mouth of the Saline (Hemmings 1982:159ff).

No definite Poverty Point culture assemblages (*sensu* Webb 1982: 68–69, table 18) have been found in the Saline-drainage portion of the Ouachita Mountains region nor in the Middle Saline region (Early 1982a:63–64). The novaculite (and other lithic) outcrops are in the former region, but it is unknown whether Poverty Point peoples themselves, or intermediaries from outside these regions, extracted materials from the outcrops directly or obtained lithic materials via exchange with local/regional residents. In the Middle Saline region, along the river in southern Saline and adjacent Grant Counties, there are several deep, multicomponent midden sites containing many thousands of pieces of novaculite debitage. Many, if not all, of these sites have been "sluiced" by commercial relic collectors seeking points (Early 1982a:53), and none have been professionally excavated, but it appears that during the Late Archaic period (and others?) people were taking blanks from the novaculite outcrops to workshop (and base camp?) sites like these (Jeter and Jackson 1994:150). A possibly similar situation may involve Poverty Point–related magnetite workshops in the Felsenthal region, away from the source, as postulated by Schambach (1982b:63).

Jeter and Jackson (1994:157–58; Jackson and Jeter 1991:39) have suggested that at least some of these sites may have been occupied by peoples coming seasonally from the Bartholomew-Macon lowlands to the east (if not from Poverty Point itself), as seasonal (summer?) base camps from which to hunt, fish, gather, and visit the lithic quarries (or their "proprietors" or local traders) to bring back blanks for knapping (and later down-the-line exchange of preforms or finished artifacts toward Poverty Point). The Morses (1983:130–32) have suggested a similar model, minus the Poverty Point connection, for Late Archaic peoples using the lowlands and uplands of northeast Arkansas. Early, however, suggests that the regions containing the quarries and these "workshop" sites probably were already inhabited and not readily available for expeditions from other regions.

Undifferentiated Woodland and Fourche Maline Periods, 600 B.C.–A.D. 1000

A number of sites in the Saline drainage are represented only by small collections of undecorated or undiagnostic grog- or bone- (or grog/bone) tempered potsherds (cf. Hemmings 1982:254–55). Archaeologists tend to label such sites by the general Eastern U.S. term *Woodland* when unable to apply LMV terms such as Tchula, Marksville, Baytown, or Coles Creek. In the TMS, Schambach (1982a) has refined the definition of Fourche Maline culture to include remains covering a long span of time before about A.D. 900, during which the ceramics were predominantly plain and tempered with bone, grit, or grog. He also has called attention to the potentially crucial significance of the Middle Saline region for defining TMS-LMV cultural relationships (Schambach 1982a: 160). More and better data are needed before these sites can be culturally and chronologically differentiated.

Early Woodland (Tchula) or Early Fourche Maline Period and Tchefuncte Culture, 600–100 B.C.

Schambach (1982a:165, 1982b:87–88) has recognized the presence of "*bona fide* Tchefuncte ceramic assemblages" and "a real intrusion of Tchefuncte culture" in the Felsenthal region, where he has defined the Coon Island phase. It is recognizable by the "distinctive laminated paste" of the pottery and by diagnostic decorated types and vessel shape modes (e.g., podal basal supports). The poorly made (essentially untempered and scarcely kneaded) ceramic paste found here resembles that found in the classic Tchefuncte regions to the south in the LMV, in contrast to the relatively well-made pottery found in coeval Early Woodland sites to the north (Morse and Morse 1983:137–38, 142).

Hemmings (1982:252–54) found a small cluster of Tchula period sites in the vicinity of the Saline-Ouachita junction. These sites produced specimens of the pottery types Tchefuncte Plain, Tchefuncte Incised, Tchefuncte Stamped, and Lake Borgne Incised (Hemmings 1982:252, 254, fig. 65). To the north, a Tchefuncte Stamped rim sherd was found at site 3JE68, near Derriesseaux Creek in southwestern Jefferson County (House 1984:3, fig. 1a). This brings the Middle Saline region (or at least its eastern margin) into the Tchula period picture but may represent only trade by local Early Woodland/Fourche Maline people with Tchefuncte culture people. Schambach (1982a:table 7-1) has designated a "Fourche Maline 2" period as a TMS equivalent to the LMV Tchula period, but no sites of this affiliation have been identified for the Ouachita Mountains or Middle Saline regions.

Middle Woodland (Marksville-related) or Middle Fourche Maline Period, 100 B.C.–A.D. 400

For the Felsenthal region, the identification of LMV Marksville culture is problematical at best (Schambach 1982b:90). Weinstein and Kelley (1984:498) suggested that the TMS-LMV cultural boundary may have shifted southeastward and virtually out of the Felsenthal region during the Marksville and Baytown periods. Schambach (1982a:164–66, 189–90,

1982b:88–89) found no convincing evidence for the presence of true Marksville cultural assemblages, as opposed to occasional Marksville traits (usually ceramic types), for the TMS in general. Jeter et al. (1989: 127ff, figs. 12, 13) agreed; they designated an earlier "Hopewellian" subperiod (cf. Morse and Morse 1983:161ff), circa 100 B.C.–A.D. 100, and a later "Plainware" subperiod, circa A.D. 100–400. Whatever the cultural affiliation(s), no phases have yet been designated in the Felsenthal region (Schambach 1990:fig. 78) or in the other regions of concern here.

The Goulett Island site (3BR8), in the Felsenthal Refuge, and the nearby Godfrey Landing site (3BR2) were briefly visited by C. B. Moore (1913:81–83). He found no obvious Marksville artifacts, but recent visits by Survey personnel have found a few items suggestive of occupation during this period. Jeter's 1995 excavation into the small Mound D at the Eagle Lake site (3BR4) in the Refuge recovered two Marksville Incised sherds and one of Marksville Stamped, resembling late varieties of those types, from mound fill contexts (the mound itself was built much later; Jeter n.d.a).

In the Middle Saline region, three sites with Marksville pottery were found near Derriesseaux Creek (House 1984:3, figs. 1b, 1c, personal communication 1997). A site near Sheridan produced two Marksville Incised sherds. Here too, we are reluctant to use the Marksville culture name; "Middle Woodland" or "Middle Fourche Maline" will have to suffice.

Schambach (1982a:table 7-1) designated the Fourche Maline 3 and 4 periods as TMS equivalents to early and late Marksville. Although he listed no phases or sites of these periods in the Middle Saline region or the Saline-drainage portion of the Ouachita Mountains region, he did define the Oak Grove phase for the nearby Middle Ouachita region as coeval with the late Marksville period (Schambach 1982a:141, table 7-1). Early (1982a:84) noted that ceramics resembling those of the Oak Grove phase had been found in the eastern Ouachita Mountains and Middle Saline regions, but samples are insufficient for phase identification.

Late Woodland or Late Fourche Maline Period, A.D. 400–700

We are again departing from the use of LMV terminology. It is quite likely that LMV Baytown culture did not exist in any of the regions under consideration here (Schambach 1982b:91; Weinstein and Kelley 1984:498). The (admittedly often rare) LMV decorated pottery types of this period, particularly Mulberry Creek Cord Marked, have not been found in these regions (Jeter et al. 1989:145; Schambach 1982b:95). This is a matter of even larger cultural-geographical significance. During the Late Woodland period, cord-marked pottery was common over a huge area: north-south from the Midwest to the East Gulf Coastal Plain, and east-west from western Alabama to the "delta" of northeastern Louisiana and eastern Arkansas (cf. Morse and Morse 1983:183–95).

Schambach (1982b:91) has suggested that in the Felsenthal region, given large samples of potsherds of this period, there may be a chance of differentiating Fourche Maline assemblages dominated by the Williams Plain type from Baytown assemblages dominated by the similar Baytown Plain type, based on an apparent "predominance of flat-bottomed vessels in the former type, and round-bottomed bowls in the latter." However, Baytown (or Troyville) assemblages from the eastern delta part of the UAM station territory very commonly include flat-bottomed jars. Quantitative comparative studies are needed.

Schambach (1982a:141, table 7-1) has defined the Dutchman's Garden phase of late Fourche Maline culture for the Middle Ouachita region, involving the latter part of the period under consideration here. Similar remains are found in the eastern Ouachita Mountains region and may occur in the Middle Saline region. We should not leave this time period without noting that the Plum Bayou culture probably began around A.D. 600 in the Arkansas Valley, not far from the northeastern Saline drainage (Rolingson 1982a; see below).

Coles Creek Period, Coles Creek and/or Plum Bayou Cultures, Fourche Maline-Caddoan Transition, circa A.D. 700–1200

Coles Creek Culture

In contrast to the Middle and Late Woodland situations, there does appear to be evidence of more or less genuine LMV Coles Creek culture (or at least pottery) in the Felsenthal region, or portions of it. Although highly critical of claims of Coles Creek culture in the TMS Caddoan heartland, Schambach (1979:29–30, fig. 3.1, 1982a:166–72, 190, 1982b: 92–96) has all along been open to the possibility of a Felsenthal manifestation of Coles Creek culture. Most recently, he has stated that "ceramically, at least, . . . a regional variant of Coles Creek culture" was present in the Ouachita Valley, as far northwest as the Bangs Slough site (Schambach 1990:115).

The Saline-drainage portion of the Felsenthal region has at least produced some evidence of Coles Creek period traits, whatever culture(s) may be represented. It does appear highly probable that mound building began in the Felsenthal region before A.D. 1000, at several sites overlooking and surrounding the seasonally flooded lowlands (Schambach 1990:115; Schambach and Rolingson 1981:182, 189, 200–201). At the Eagle Lake Mounds (3BR4), recent investigations directed by Jeter (n.d.a) produced small rim sherds probably representing varieties of Coles Creek Incised and related types and probably coeval Homan arrow points from two separate nonmound midden zones. A few similar items have been found in mound fill at the two mounds tested so far. At least some of this material may belong instead to the post–A.D. 1200 Gran Marais phase of Plaquemine culture (see below).

The Gordon site (3AS152) in northwestern Ashley County was intensively excavated during the 1970s and produced evidence of both middle and late Coles Creek period occupations (White 1987:9, table 1, figs. 5–7). The Fraser site (3BR40), just east of Warren, was salvaged by Society members in the late 1970s. No report has been published, but data on file at the UAM station indicate that a few dozen Coles Creek Incised sherds, representing varieties from early to late subperiods, were recovered.

Plum Bayou Culture

This is also the period during which the Plum Bayou culture of central to eastern Arkansas flourished, especially at the Toltec Mounds site (Rolingson 1982a). Toltec had long been infamous among LMV archaeologists for the "overwhelming predominance of Baytown Plain" and the "extremely rare" occurrence of any kind of decorations, which (when present at all) tended to be minimal and on the uppermost portions of otherwise plain vessels (Phillips 1970:916).

Although the Saline River's middle to upper reaches and northerly tributaries, in the Middle Saline and Ouachita Mountains regions, are adjacent to the Arkansas River's drainage basin near the Toltec site itself, the relationships of these portions of the Saline drainage to Toltec and Plum Bayou culture are uncertain (Rolingson 1998). Whether or not Plum Bayou culture extended even farther southward into the Felsenthal region is doubtful (Schambach 1982b:93–94), but there is slight evidence for Plum Bayou ceramic traits at some sites in the Saline-drainage portion of this region.

An amateur's collection from site 3BR119, overlooking the Saline north of Warren, includes three Coles Creek Incised sherds, identified by Rolingson (to Jeter 1995) as *vars. Keo* (one specimen) and *Plum Bayou* (two). It would be of great interest to compare the Coles Creek period sherds from these sites (and others nearby) directly to materials from Coles Creek sites farther down the Ouachita Valley and in the LMV proper, and from Toltec and other Plum Bayou sites.

The Middle Saline region is a virtual unknown for this period. It was not even mentioned in the *State Plan* sections on Coles Creek culture (Schambach 1982b:92–96) and was only briefly noted as having no known cultural resources in the coeval Caddoan section (Early 1982a: 102). Plum Bayou and/or transitional Fourche Maline to Caddoan components are at least logical possibilities.

FOURCHE MALINE–EARLY CADDOAN CULTURAL TRANSITION IN THE TMS

The end of the Fourche Maline tradition and the archaeologically recognizable beginnings of the Caddoan tradition occurred during this period (Schambach 1982a:191–92, table 7-1). As Early (1982a:102) has noted, however, the Saline Valley appears to have been "the easternmost frontier of the Caddo area" for most of that tradition's existence. In particular, the earliest significant developments seem to have occurred to the west and southwest (Early 1982a:99).

The Caddo I period dates from about A.D. 900 to 1200 (Early 1982a:99). There are no clearly identifiable Caddo I components in the Middle Saline or Ouachita Mountains regions, but there is slight evidence in the nearby Middle Ouachita region (Early 1982a:102–3).

Undifferentiated Caddoan, A.D. 900–1600

A number of undifferentiated Caddoan sites are known in the northerly portions of the Saline drainage basin, especially in Saline County, and as far south as northern Cleveland County. They are only vaguely identifiable on the basis of inadequate samples, including a few engraved sherds and/or incised or punctated sherds from utilitarian vessels.

Middle Mississippi Period, Plaquemine and Caddo II Cultures, A.D. 1200–1400

GRAN MARAIS PHASE, PLAQUEMINE CULTURE

The Gran Marais phase was defined by Schambach (1979:30, fig. 3.1) as a possible Plaquemine occupation, probably involving increasing population in the Felsenthal region. The phase definition was refined on the basis of finds at the Shallow Lake site (3UN9/52) in the Ouachita bottomlands (Rolingson and Schambach 1981). In that site report, the Gran Marais phase ceramics were the primary impetus for the first published exposition of the "collegiate" descriptive system of ceramic classification (Schambach 1981). Nevertheless, some Gran Marais phase sherds and partial vessels were identifiable by the Phillips (1970) type-variety system. Baytown Plain was most common, while the predominant decorated type appeared to be Kiam Incised. Also present were varieties of Avoyelles Punctated, Coles Creek Incised, Harrison Bayou Incised, Lapile Incised, and Pargoud Incised, plus Mazique Incised (Schambach and Rolingson 1981:190, 195). Fingernail-punctated body sherds were common; at least some were probably from vessels of the LMV type Evansville Punctated, but they could have come from the lower portions of Kiam Incised or Lapile Incised vessels (Schambach and Rolingson 1981:158, fig. 37a, 162, 166). Schambach (1979:30, 1981:105–6) first suggested that some form of agriculture had contributed to Gran Marais subsistence, but he later doubted this (see below).

Hemmings (1982:258) found "many small Gran Marais phase components" in the form of temporary camp sites in the Felsenthal bottomlands. Six were along the lowermost Saline River (Hemmings 1982:126, 128, fig. 26), and one, False Indigo (3AS285), produced a dense concentration of Gran Marais materials (Hemmings 1982:168–74, 258–63, figs. 40–43, 66, 68–69, tables 23–24). A Gran Marais midden was also tested at site 3BR76 (Hemmings 1982:185–87, fig. 50). Hemmings (1982:151, 153, fig. 34) noted a pattern of Gran Marais mound centers and base camps on terrace edges overlooking the bottomlands and proposed a "seasonal model for extractive activity" in the flood-prone lowlands (Hemmings 1982:275, 277, fig. 70).

Weinstein and Kelley (1984:505–6) stated that the LMV-TMS boundary appeared to have moved up the Ouachita Valley during this period, to "the vicinity of Camden," with Caddoan culture above that latitude. This is essentially the maximum northwestward boundary of the Felsenthal region (Schambach 1981:103ff, fig. 22).

With still more data in hand, Schambach in the Bangs Slough site report (1990:60–61, 121–22) confirmed that the Gran Marais phase "appears to be a northern regional variant of Plaquemine culture" with ceramic diagnostics as listed above, plus (in some components) Plaquemine Brushed (or the Caddoan trade wares Bossier Brushed or Pease Brushed-Incised). Bulbous-stemmed Ashley arrow points are also common, if not diagnostic. A number of these artifact types also occur in Bartholomew phase assemblages of northern Plaquemine culture in the Bartholomew-Macon region (Rolingson 1976:115–16).

A significant aspect of the Bangs Slough site report was its emphasis on subsistence. The report was explicitly entitled "Coles Creek and Mississippi Period *Foragers* in the Felsenthal Region" (emphasis added). Schambach (1990:120, 122) cited "steadily accumulating data suggesting that horticulture was absent or unimportant in the Felsenthal region *in all periods*" (emphasis added). Kidder (1991:80–81, 85), however, suggested that the sampling and recovery techniques used for plant remains at Bangs Slough were inadequate, as was the overall regional database. Since then, corn has been found at a Felsenthal upland site, possibly in a Gran Marais context (see below). In any event, Schambach has never addressed the issue of Gran Marais occupations in the northeastern part of the Felsenthal region—for example, the Saline Basin. It is therefore incumbent on us to do so.

At the Eagle Lake Mounds site, Jeter's controlled surface collections have produced Gran Marais materials from both the northeastern and western midden zones (Jeter n.d.a). Small samples of similar materials have also been found in two mound fills during brief tests. At Goulett Island, Moore (1913:83, fig. 35) recovered a Pease Brushed-Incised vessel closely resembling one from Shallow Lake (Schambach 1981:168, fig. 42c, mislabeled "e"). A revisit by Hemmings in 1979 confirmed a Gran Marais component.

The Gordon site produced abundant ceramic and lithic evidence of Gran Marais occupation(s) (White 1987:7ff, 20f). A fairly common class of pottery was called Gordon Brushed-Incised (White 1987:9, 18, fig. 11); it closely resembles Felsenthal regional varieties of Kiam Incised (White 1987:table 1; cf. Schambach 1981, above). The Evans Field site (3AS40), just north of Gordon, has long been surface-hunted and looted but has never been tested under controlled conditions; collections include several Gran Marais pottery types. Two nearby small sites, 3BR111 and 3BR113, have produced probable Gran Marais sherds.

White (1970, 1987:7) also found Gran Marais materials at Gee's Landing (3DR17) on the Saline in southwestern Drew County and the Fraser site near Warren. Both assemblages included pottery with the Gordon (Kiam) decoration (White 1987:18). A small site (3BR97) on the northern outskirts of Warren has also produced Gran Marais pottery.

At the Saline-Fifteen site (3BR119) on the upland edge overlooking the Saline above Warren, 1990 salvage investigations produced fairly abundant materials suggestive of at least a late Gran Marais phase occupation, possibly transitional to the Caney Bayou phase (Jeter n.d.b). Although the "collegiate" classification scheme has been emphasized, varieties of many classic LMV Plaquemine (and most Felsenthal Gran Marais) ceramic types may be present, plus presumably Caddoan intrusives. Potentially the most significant finding, though, is that maize was virtually "ubiquitous" in the flotation samples (Lopinot n.d.). Some may have been associated with the Gran Marais occupation, but more analyses (e.g., AMS dating of maize specimens) are needed to support this.

A short distance to the east is site 3DR40, surface collected and tested in 1981 by Jeter. Ceramics included variants of Mazique Incised and fingernail-punctated body sherds. In 1986 House found a multicomponent site (3CV110) farther north, in northeast Cleveland County, with sparse ceramics including two sherds possibly indicative of a Gran Marais component. This last location is actually within the Middle Saline region. As noted by Jeter et al. (1989:210), the northernmost probable component of the Bartholomew phase of Plaquemine culture is at about this same latitude, in central Lincoln County.

In any event, the evidence appears reasonably good for a significant dispersal of legitimate Gran Marais sites of various sizes (and probably functions) over the landscape of the Saline-drained northeastern portions of the Felsenthal region, and possibly a short distance beyond to the north. This supports the impressions of Schambach and Rolingson (1981:200–201) for the region as a whole, and resembles the findings of Weinstein and Kelley (1984:512) for the region's northwest part. The foci appear to have been the ceremonial centers surrounding the Felsenthal bottomlands, with mound building probably reaching its regional peak and with habitation at some mound sites. There was ample use of seasonal fishing-foraging camps in the flood-prone wetlands, with a concentration near the Saline River's mouth (Hemmings 1982). The new data from 3BR119 suggest that Schambach's original intuition about upland maize-farming sites may have been correct.

CADDO II CULTURE

Early (1982a:108–9) noted a definite Caddo II presence, including at least one ceremonial center, farther west in the Ouachita Mountains region. She found insufficient data for the Middle Saline region but enough general evidence to hypothesize that Caddoan culture had appeared in this region during this subperiod. Again, it would appear that these regions were peripheral to the earlier Caddoan developments.

Late Mississippi and Protohistoric Periods, Mississippian and Caddo III–IV Cultures, A.D. 1400–1700

CANEY BAYOU PHASE, LATE MISSISSIPPIAN (PROTOHISTORIC TUNICAN?) CULTURE

The Caney Bayou phase was defined on the basis of vessels from a cemetery at the Shallow Lake site as representing an "unknown" culture with "a late Mississippi period time placement . . . of A.D. 1500 to 1700" (Schambach and Rolingson 1981:193, table 19). It was viewed as possibly indicating "small groups of people, perhaps refugees . . . a recent mixing of diverse cultural groups" after population reduction due to European diseases (Schambach and Rolingson 1981:201). Jeter (n.d.b and this chapter) proposes as an alternative hypothesis that this is basically a Protohistoric LMV Mississippian (probably Tunican) assemblage, augmented by Caddoan trade ceramics. Kidder (1988:29) has also suggested that "the complex as a whole appears to be locally inspired" and that it may relate to the (probably Tunican) Ķoroa. All Tunicans appear to have moved southward out of Arkansas by 1700 (Jeter 1986).

Caney Bayou ceramics at Shallow Lake (Schambach and Rolingson

1981:193, 195; cf. Schambach 1982b:97) included the LMV shell-tempered types Parkin Punctated and Winterville Incised, plus late varieties of the LMV grog-tempered types Baytown Plain and Coleman Incised. Also present were types often regarded as "Caddoan," such as Cowhide Stamped and possibly Hodges and/or Natchitoches Engraved and Keno Trailed. More recently, Kidder (1986:328ff) redefined much of the material formerly called Cowhide Stamped as a western LMV type, Mound Tract Incised and Brushed. At least two specimens called Cowhide in the Shallow Lake report (Schambach and Rolingson 1981: 156, figs. 29j, 36b) appear to have the body treatment characteristic of the Mound Tract type. Another two Shallow Lake "Cowhide" vessels have "divergent" unzoned body decorations (Schambach and Rolingson 1981:156, figs. 36c–d); they probably should be called Grace Brushed, a late type common in northeast Louisiana (Kidder 1986:306ff) which has recently been identified in the Saline Valley (Jeter n.d.b and below). Finally, another Shallow Lake "Cowhide" vessel (Schambach and Rolingson 1981:156, fig. 36a) could also be called a variant of Winterville Incised (cf. Phillips 1970:173).

The LMV type name Mississippi Plain was not used in the Shallow Lake report, but plain shell-tempered ceramics definitely were present. In fact, one whole vessel classed as Parkin Punctated but noted as aberrant (Schambach and Rolingson 1981:167–68, fig. 41c) is plain except for "a double row of tool punctations around the rim." This decorative accent closely resembles the so-called "Tunica mode," which cross-cuts types at the Trudeau site in Louisiana (Brain 1979:224, 234–39), including one Mississippi Plain vessel (Brain 1979:229). Jackson (1992:51–52, 89–90) defined a similar "Tillar mode" at the Ables Creek site in the Bartholomew-Macon region, noting it on two varieties of Mississippi Plain (Jackson 1992:56, 60, figs. 51x, 52c, 53p–q).

A number of the Caney Bayou mortuary vessels at Shallow Lake bore a black "carbon" encrustation (Schambach and Rolingson 1981: 195). Similar deposits are common on protohistoric burial vessels at other sites in the Felsenthal and Bartholomew-Macon regions (Jeter 1986:55; White 1970:7, 10) and are obviously present on many of the illustrated vessels from the putatively historic Tunican Trudeau site (Brain 1979:225–39).

Hemmings (1982:128, 130, 263) found a number of shell-tempered sherd scatters attributable to this phase, estimated to date A.D. 1400–1600. He took some pains to differentiate these from an even later "Quapaw phase" Mississippian occupation, estimated to date about A.D. 1600–1700 and found at two sites on the lowermost Saline River. But in his most recent published statement, Schambach (1990:122) moved his beginning estimate for the Caney Bayou phase to circa A.D. 1550, noting that he still considered it "a post-contact phase representing a mixed or 'Seminolized' group of Koroans, Tunicans, and Caddoans who took refuge in the Felsenthal region under the stress of European contact."

Schambach never has explicitly addressed the issue of the relationship(s), if any, between the Gran Marais and Caney Bayou phases. There is some evidence suggestive of continuity between them, however, despite the impressions that might be fostered by a strict normative typological separation between their ceramic complexes. Hemmings (1982:263, fig. 26, table 25) called attention to an apparent transition from mostly grog-tempered to mostly shell-tempered pottery at four sites along the lowermost Saline River. Such a transition may also be reflected by trends found at site 3BR119 (Jeter n.d.b).

Schambach's Caney Bayou discussions make no mention of the lower Saline drainage basin. So again we will attempt to round out the regional perspective with summaries and evaluations of very late sites in our territories.

The cemetery at Gee's Landing, excavated in the late 1960s, produced 34 burials (which were not preserved), mostly extended-supine with heads to the southeast (White 1970:fig. 2) and associated with 32 whole or nearly complete shell-tempered vessels. The vessels were illustrated and briefly discussed; several were compared to types then in the literature (White 1970:12–13). Jeter has reanalyzed these vessels, concluding that most are related to standard LMV Mississippian assemblages regarded by several archaeologists (Brain 1979, 1988; Jackson 1992; Jeter 1986; Kidder 1986, 1988, 1992) as probably Tunican. Following Jeter, the assemblage includes 10 Mississippi Plain vessels, five Winterville Incised, and one each of Barton Incised, Grace Brushed, Parkin Punctated, and Pouncey Ridge-Pinched, plus eight examples comparable to the "Tillar" or "Tunica(n)" modes. Probable or possible Caddoan types include three examples of Hudson Engraved and one each of Cowhide Stamped, Karnack Incised, and Keno-like trailed or incised.

A similar situation was found nearby at the Gordon site, where 16 burials were excavated (most extended-supine with heads to the southeast or south) (White 1987:33, fig. 2); 18 whole or partial shell-tempered vessels were recovered (White 1987:37ff, figs. 26–30). Most vessels are Mississippian (Tunican?). The 11 typable examples (White 1987:table 4) include four specimens of Winterville Incised, three of Mississippi Plain, and one of Mound Tract Incised and Brushed. The "Tillar/Tunica mode" is present on five vessels. Probable Caddoan vessels included one each of Belcher Engraved, Hudson Engraved, and Karnack Incised.

Importantly, the Gordon site human skeletal materials have been analyzed by bioanthropologist Jerome C. Rose and his students at the

University of Arkansas in Fayetteville. These represent the only professionally studied human burials from any period within the entire Saline Basin. Although a complete report has not been published, some important findings have been summarized by Burnett (1990a:155): "[T]he dental features indicate a relatively soft diet, few abrasive particles, and the consumption of hickory nuts. This microwear pattern is substantially different from all other Lower Mississippi Valley molars and suggests the presence of a distinctive diet . . . the high rate of porotic hyperostosis . . . and high caries rates . . . suggest that maize consumption was high." These findings, plus the actual presence of maize in another probable Caney Bayou component, greatly strengthen the case against the presence of nonagricultural Mississippian "foragers" in the Felsenthal region.

Moore (1913:91–92) found "a place of burial to a considerable extent" near Wire Fence Landing (3BR115), a short distance south-southeast of Warren. He dug extensively there, and found 11 ceramic vessels. One, "more interesting than the rest" (Moore 1913:fig. 40), is a small jar with patches of a sooty encrustation; it appears to be shell-tempered and classifiable as Pouncey Ridge Pinched. This type is best known from regions north of the Arkansas River (Phillips 1970:154–55), but has been found at Winterville, Lake George, elsewhere in the Lower Yazoo Basin (Williams and Brain 1983:200). A few specimens also are known from the Tillar phase and as far south as northeast Louisiana (Jackson 1992:68), and one was found at Gee's Landing (White 1970:fig. 6d), near Wire Fence Landing.

During a 1978 salvage effort at the Fraser site near Warren, Jeter excavated a bulldozed burial with two badly broken but reconstructible shell-tempered vessels. One is a small, rounded-base conoidal open bowl bearing a Winterville Incised festoon design; the vessel form and decorative motif resembles vessels that have been called "Wallace Incised" (Ford 1961:161, fig. 11f). The other is a small Mississippi Plain jar. Both are encrusted with black (carbonized) deposits.

So far, our discussions of Caney Bayou-like components in the Saline drainage have dealt only with burial sites and apparently ephemeral or seasonal campsites. There is some evidence for longer occupations, though. Schambach (1990:123) noted that one such situation appeared to have been found by Weinstein and Kelley (1984:382ff) in the northwest part of the region. A similar situation probably existed at the Saline Fifteen site (3BR119), above Warren. The 1990 salvage excavations there (Jeter n.d.b) found an undisturbed midden remnant with 70 percent or more shell-tempered pottery in its upper portions. Both floral and faunal remains were recovered, and samples of these have been analyzed. It appears that the site was occupied (or seasonally reoccupied) multi-seasonally, if not year-round, over a fairly extended period, perhaps as long as 200 years, bridging a Gran Marais-Caney Bayou transition (or mixing separate occupations by peoples of these phases).

As might be expected from nonmortuary, midden contexts, the shell-tempered pottery sample was dominated by Mississippi Plain sherds, but a number of LMV decorated types also were recovered. Grace Brushed was the most common of these: an unusual variant accented by tiny punctations on thin ware is being designated as *var. Bradley.* Also present is Winterville Incised, plus individual sherds of Owens Punctated and Parkin Punctated and possible single examples of the Tillar/Tunica(n) mode and the type Leland Incised. Other regions are represented by a probable Foster Trailed-Incised rim fragment, and late types including Belcher Ridged and Bossier Brushed (Jeter n.d.b).

As mentioned earlier, flotation samples from this site produced specimens of maize from most of the analyzed pit fills (Lopinot n.d.). At least some of these may relate to the Gran Marais component, but given the predominance of shell-tempered pottery, and perhaps an inherent long tradition of resistance to agriculture in this region (Schambach 1990), it seems more likely that most, if not all, of the maize derives from Caney Bayou occupation(s).

Felsenthal "Terminal Mississippian" Sites: the "Quapaw Phase" Question

Hemmings (1982:128) separated two late sites from the Caney Bayou phase category. At One Cypress Point (3AS286), systematic surface collections and fairly extensive testing produced a "distinctive" assemblage, "previously unknown in the Felsenthal region and likely to be intrusive" (Hemmings 1982:178). The site produced 15 Nodena arrow points, a Madison-like triangular arrow point, a barbed arrow point fragment, two fragmentary "thumbnail" endscrapers, and debitage (Hemmings 1982: 178ff, figs. 48, 58a–c, table 20). Much of this is comparable to materials from the Nodena phase of northeast Arkansas and the then-extant Quapaw phase of the lower Arkansas Valley. Hemmings (1982:182) regarded the site as an outlier occupation "by Quapaw phase people, regardless of their linguistic identity and point of origin." His second site (3AS310) was located nearby and was represented by only one Nodena point.

The "Quapaw phase" question has been a vexing one for some time (Phillips 1970:943–44; Morse and Morse 1983:320). During the 1980s, a growing realization of discordance between various aspects of the phase on the one hand, and the ethnohistorically described Quapaw tribe on the other, led to the label "the Quapaw paradox" (Hoffman 1986:30ff). In reviewing the problem, Jeter (1990a:148–49; Jeter et al. 1990) noted that many, if not most, Arkansas archaeologists had ceased using the Quapaw phase terminology, instead using the ethnically neutral "Menard complex," and argued that much, if not all, of this complex might be the remains of very late Tunican groups. At least one former "Quapaw phase" adherent has agreed with the "probably Tunican" hypothesis (Hoffman 1992), but the question remains open; perhaps it could be resolved by extensive DNA testing.

Culturally Indeterminate Sites in Cleveland County

The status of 3BR119 as having a good Caney Bayou component seems reasonably secure (Jeter n.d.b), but in Cleveland County, the protohistoric cultural situation is not clear. Only a few sites are known, all in the northern portion of the county in the vague borderland between the Felsenthal and Middle Saline regions, and the meager information is ambiguous and insufficient. Adding to the problem is the recurring presence of apparently panregional (if not pancultural or multicultural) very late shell-tempered ceramic types such as Cowhide Stamped, Foster Trailed-Incised, and Keno Trailed, and the unavailability of most of the materials for examination in the light of modern comparative typology. Sites include 3CV4, west of Rison; 3CV18, the Big Creek site itself, where two Foster Trailed-Incised jars were found with a burial; 3CV24, destroyed by gravel-pitting (Reaves and McClurkan 1970); and 3CV109, where House recorded finds of two Keno Trailed bottles.

Caddo III–IV Sites

Caddo III is "a hazy intermediate or transitional period" estimated to date between A.D. 1400 and 1500 (Early 1982a:111). Although some "fundamental changes" occurred in ceremonial and mortuary behavior, and in material culture, in some of the TMS regions (Early 1982a:112), there is little evidence of this in the Saline Basin.

In the northern Middle Saline region near Benton, there is one known multiple mound site, Hughes (3SA11), that may have been a ceremonial center during Caddo III times. A number of small sites, possibly related, include small house mounds, nonmound habitation sites, and perhaps small mortuary sites (Early 1982a:112). The extent (if any) of related occupations up into the Ouachita Mountains and down the valley is unknown.

The Caddo IV period, circa A.D. 1500–1700 (Early 1982a:115), is the temporal equivalent of the LMV Protohistoric period. If the de Soto *entrada* of the 1540s and/or the French refugees led by Joutel in 1687 (Jeter 1986; Joutel 1714) contacted any Native Americans in the Saline drainage basin, they may well have been those whose remains are called

Caddo IV. Also, not far from here on the Arkansas River, trade goods may have started trickling in without direct European contacts (Jeter et al. 1990). Similarly, European-derived diseases may have been involved in Native American deaths (Burnett 1990a).

Early (1982a:116) noted that Caddo IV remains, though probably present, were unidentified in the Ouachita Mountains region and that there was no good evidence for the Middle Saline region. It now appears, though, that use of the Hughes mound center and neighboring small sites (possibly farmsteads) continued into this period. House (personal communication to Jeter 1997) suggests that some Caddoan sites in the upper Saline Basin may well relate to a protohistoric Caddoan presence in the Arkansas Valley. At the Kuykendall Brake site, almost due east of Benton and overlooking the Arkansas Valley, he has found structural remains associated with a number of Foster Trailed-Incised vessels. These regions apparently were abandoned by Caddoans before 1700 (Early 1982a:122–23).

Summary

Our perceptions of patterning in the archaeological record of the Saline drainage basin undoubtedly are distorted by grossly insufficient and biased samples, but at least a few tentative findings can be stated. One is that this relatively minor river valley does indeed appear to have been culturally peripheral throughout most if not all of prehistory. Additionally, there is a fair amount of evidence that cultural boundaries involving LMV cultures fluctuated significantly through time (see discussions of Baytown and Plaquemine). And even though there is a late prehistoric to protohistoric Mississippian presence in the southerly portions, nowhere in the entire Saline Basin do we find evidence for nucleated settlements such as the Morses (1983:237ff) have dealt with. One of us (Jeter) would argue that this Felsenthal Mississippian (Caney Bayou phase) variant shows some evidence of continuities with the preceding Plaquemine (Gran Marais phase) cultural variant, with contemporary Mississippian cultures to the east and north, probably representing Tunican peoples.

Within the Saline drainage basin itself we can at least hypothesize a sort of geographically based "bifocal model" for settlement and regional cultural activities during some, if not all, of prehistoric time. The first focal zone is the ecotonal locality around the Saline's lower reaches, as it approaches the wetlands at the heart of the Felsenthal region. This is best seen via the remains of what was apparently that region's prehistoric cultural and population climax, the Gran Marais phase, featuring ceremonial mound centers such as Eagle Lake, dispersed hamlets and possibly maize-based farmsteads, and seasonal extractive camps. The Gran Marais picture may be biased by findings of intensive work within the Felsenthal Refuge, but these seem to be supported by a fair amount of data from sites to the north, in the Saline Valley itself and along its tributaries into the uplands.

A second focal zone can be suggested for the locality around Benton. Unlike the Felsenthal focal situation, this is near the hypothetical boundary of two archaeological regions: barely within the very large Ouachita Mountains region, most of which is to the west, and just north of the poorly known Middle Saline region. This also constitutes an ecotone, and here the "four forks" come together, with modest floodplains of their own, to form the Saline. Their valleys and tributaries offered relatively easy access to the lithic and other resources of the Ouachita Mountains. Here the prehistoric cultural and population climax may have occurred slightly later, during the Caddo III–IV periods, with a single ceremonial center (Hughes) surrounded by dispersed hamlets or farmsteads and extractive camps.

With regard to an issue mentioned at the outset, we can see no definite evidence that the Saline drainage basin was the scene of a more or less culturally isolated and self-sufficient entity at any time. Instead, it appears to have been swallowed up within larger early cultural areas (e.g., Dalton) or was peripheral to other large entities centered elsewhere (the Poverty Point interaction sphere); and sometimes it appears clearly divided between two (or more?) larger entities centered elsewhere (e.g., Plaquemine vs. Caddoan; Mississippian vs. Caddoan). Possibly influencing this situation are the facts that the Saline is tributary to the Ouachita, and its drainage divides with the Ouachita and Arkansas valleys are not formidable.

Perhaps the closest approach to self-centered self-sufficiency came with the Big Creek culture, with a possible cultural focus at the Big Creek site, near the center of the Saline drainage basin. The overall distribution of Evans points covers a much larger area, from central Arkansas to southern Louisiana, but there are some hints of differentiated traditions within that area. The predominance of local or regional lithic materials for Evans points and apparently associated artifacts argues for a good measure of self-sufficiency, but excavations at a number of sites, including Big Creek, are needed to test such notions.

Indeed, many more modern, intensive excavations and specialized analyses are needed before we have a real grasp of any period and region within the Saline drainage basin. We have only barely scratched below the surface.

Postscript and Acknowledgments

This chapter was condensed toward "Morse telegraphic style" from a much longer unpublished manuscript (on file at the UAM station), which includes more detailed sections on the Saline drainage basin's geology, environments, and cultural sequences, plus sections on its early history and the history of archaeological investigations. Jeter wrote most of the introductory sections and the portions dealing with the Felsenthal region. He also outlined the portions dealing with the Middle Saline and Ouachita Mountains regions, largely based on previous publications by Early, after which she provided more up-to-date information.

We would like to thank, first of all, Dan and Phyllis Morse for welcoming us aboard the Survey back in the 1970s and for the inspiring examples they have set for us all. Our Survey colleagues John House, Martha Rolingson, Frank Schambach, and Bob Mainfort, plus Joe Saunders from his Louisiana perspectives, Charlotte Copeland from her perspectives as UAM research librarian, and Jeter's wife and manuscript reader are thanked for providing information, comments, and corrections. We also thank Jami Lockhart and Lela Donat of the Survey's Fayetteville staff; the former for GIS graphics and both for information about AMASDA. Mary Lynn Kennedy prepared figure 3.1. We, of course, are ultimately responsible for the portions related to our own research and our Survey station territories.

CHAPTER FOUR

ARCHAEOLOGY IN THE L'ANGUILLE RIVER BASIN, NORTHEAST ARKANSAS: LARGE-SCALE SURVEY IN THE SOUTHEAST

DAVID G. ANDERSON

Introduction

If anything characterizes modern archaeological research in the Southeast, it is intensive survey work. This is in marked contrast to earlier times, when excavation comprised much of the fieldwork undertaken and certainly the vast majority of what was reported. The Bureau of Ethnology's Mound Exploration program during the 1880s, for example, included extensive excavations at many of the 2,000 mounds examined (B. D. Smith 1985), while dozens of large sites were largely or completely excavated during the New Deal era (Lyon 1996). In many of the so-called "survey" projects undertaken during these eras, in fact, the amount of excavation that occurred often vastly exceeded what is opened in many of today's "data recovery" projects (e.g., DePratter 1991; Wauchope 1966).

The kind of large-scale survey work in the Southeast that comes close to resembling modern activity—the examination of landscapes, localities, or regions to locate sites followed by the systematic surface or limited subsurface collection of artifacts from them—did not get started until the late 1920s and early 1930s. James A. Ford's (1936) classic analysis of primarily surface materials from 103 sites in Louisiana and Mississippi collected over the preceding decade—a study that went a long way toward establishing the basic cultural chronology for the Lower Mississippi Valley—was one of the earliest and, to this day, still one of the best examples of the research potential of survey data. The most outstanding contributions to our understanding of southeastern archaeology based on survey level data are the monumental overviews produced by the Lower Mississippi Survey (LMS) under the direction of Philip Phillips, James A. Ford, and James B. Griffin (1951; Phillips 1970). These overviews, based on materials from hundreds of sites from across several regions—with each site carefully located, recorded, and then collected according to the best standards of the time—documented the distribution in time and space of many of the prehistoric cultures of the Lower Mississippi Valley. In a very real sense, much of the survey work done in this area since has been directed to filling in the details of a record whose broad outlines were revealed by these investigations.

The LMS work was exceptional in another way, in that the fieldwork and analyses were thoroughly written up and published and, as a result, had a profound impact on our understanding of southeastern prehistory. Survey work was not typically reported until the 1970s, although site data began to be compiled in many southern states during the 1930s. Thus, while a number of large-scale reservoir projects were conducted from the late 1940s through early 1960s across the Southeast, the survey work associated with many of them usually was cursorily written up, at best. Fortunately, modern researchers are beginning to analyze and synthesize this information (e.g., Elliott 1995; Ledbetter et al. 1987).

With the passage of the National Historic Preservation Act of 1966 (NHPA) and the rise of the modern cultural resource management (CRM) era, archaeological research has undergone a dramatic change in the Southeast. Survey, rather than excavation, has come to be viewed as primary, the essential first step in responsible research and resource management. This emphasis is driven by Sections 106 and 110 of the NHPA, which call for the location, evaluation, and treatment (i.e., preservation or mitigation) of historic properties—archaeological and historic sites—on all federal lands, and on private lands if projects conducted on these lands require federal approval or make use of federal funding. While excavations still occur, these are viewed as a last resort by responsible professionals. That is, sites determined to be significant under the current process are to be preserved and protected wherever possible and only excavated on a large scale if there is no other alternative.

As a result of this change in emphasis and legal mandate, a vast number of archaeological survey projects encompassing a wide range of geographic scales have occurred in the Southeast in recent years. This has lead to a massive increase in information. The number of known archaeological sites in the Southeast has increased from roughly 10,000 in 1970 to close to 200,000 at the present, with about 10,000 new sites added per year (Anderson and Horak 1995:3). The total area examined is growing at a comparable rate. Project survey tracts range in size from under an acre to thousands or even tens of thousands of acres, and cumulatively millions of acres have been intensively surveyed during the past three decades. Locational data on the occurrence of archaeological sites exists from contiguous tracts that may be up to hundreds of thousands of acres in extent. Some military reservations, for example, have been completely or nearly completely examined in recent years (e.g., Anderson et al. 1997; Poplin and Roberts 1992; Thomas and Campbell 1993).

Research designs have been set in place for the comprehensive survey of all of the National Parks in the Southeast (Keel et al. 1996), and most other federal agencies have management plans detailing how the lands under their control are to be examined. The U.S. Forest Service, for example, maintains active archaeological survey programs on every national forest. In many parts of the Southeast, large data sets are thus available that can be used to address research questions about population distribution and growth, settlement systems, and even regional political organization (e.g., Anderson 1994:165–70, 1996; Kowalewski and Hatch 1991; Milner et al. n.d.; Sassaman and Anderson 1995).

Modern survey research has resulted in an information explosion since, unlike previous eras, completion of technically adequate reports is a requirement of the historic preservation process. Attention also has been directed to properties not typically considered during earlier eras, such as historic sites, smaller sites of all kinds, landscapes, sacred sites, and traditional cultural properties. Unfortunately, while the survey work that has been conducted is important, it has not had as profound an impact as it could, in part because there are thousands of projects and because the reports, while often excellent, typically are printed in low numbers, in many cases no more than 10 to 20 copies. The volume of information being generated has challenged archaeologists' ability to deal with it, to the point where for many localities and regions it is difficult to find lists of reports and projects that have been conducted, much less find the primary documents themselves.

Some of the largest and best-known archaeological survey projects of the CRM era have occurred in northeast Arkansas and southeast Missouri, work that is continuing to this day. The Cache River Basin survey, conducted in the early 1970s, for example, helped set high standards for survey work not only in the Southeast, but across the country and beyond (Schiffer and House 1975). Other major survey projects that have made solid contributions to knowledge encompassed the Village Creek watershed (Klinger 1986), portions of the White River Basin (Spears et al. 1975), portions of the St. Francis River drainage (Klinger and Mathis 1978), the Little Black and Fourches Creek watersheds (J. Price and C. Price 1975, 1981), and the Tyronza River watershed (Lafferty et al. 1984; Lafferty, Spears, et al. 1985); as well as a great many ditching projects (e.g., Cande et al. 1990; Lafferty et al. 1987). One of the earliest intensive survey projects, a transect between the Little River and the St. Francis River, was conducted by Dan and Phyllis Morse. A total of 80 prehistoric sites were recorded in an effort to interpret the Late Woodland and Emergent Mississippian assemblages at the Zebree site (Morse and Morse 1980, 1983:183).

In the pages that follow, one of the many large-scale survey projects that have been undertaken in northeast Arkansas in recent years is briefly summarized. In June and July 1987 an intensive archaeological survey and paleoenvironmental research program was conducted along the margins of the L'Anguille River, locating 222 sites. The survey was directed to a zone within 300 feet (about 100 m) of either side of the main channel for 90 miles north from its confluence with the St. Francis River, in portions of Lee, St. Francis, Cross, and Poinsett Counties (fig. 4.1). The work was conducted by archaeologists from Garrow and Associates, Inc., a private company based in Atlanta, Georgia, under the direction of the author (Anderson et al. 1989). The project was performed under a contract from the Memphis District, U.S. Army Corps of Engineers (hereafter, Memphis District). A program of limited vegetation and channel clearing was being considered along the river, and the equipment maneuvering and earth removal associated with the project had the potential to seriously damage archaeological resources along the channel margin.

It is unknown beyond a small circle of scholars that the L'Anguille project, while extensive in scope, occurred at all. Only a limited number (25) of final reports were printed; the results were not summarized in journal articles; and subsequent mitigation projects did not redirect attention to the locality (the proposed channelization never happened). Accordingly, the summary that follows illustrates the kinds of information that lie buried in the nation's CRM reports, field notes, and artifact collections.

Environmental Conditions

Northeast Arkansas is characterized by three major physiographic zones. The Eastern and Western Lowlands, areas of relict late Quaternary braided-stream terraces, are separated by Crowley's Ridge, a remnant landform that survived the extensive erosion associated with the Pleistocene movement of the Ohio/Mississippi River systems (Saucier 1982:25–31, 1994:25). The St. Francis and the White Rivers and their major tributaries constitute the major drainage systems of northeast Arkansas (Morse and Morse 1983:3). These channels are oriented roughly parallel to one another and trend from north to south. The White River and its tributaries drain much of the Western Lowlands, while the St. Francis and its tributaries drain the Eastern Lowlands. The L'Anguille River is the only major stream originating in the Western Lowlands flowing into the St. Francis River Basin.

The L'Anguille River Basin generally trends from north to south and is bounded on the west by the low divides of Bayou DeView and Big

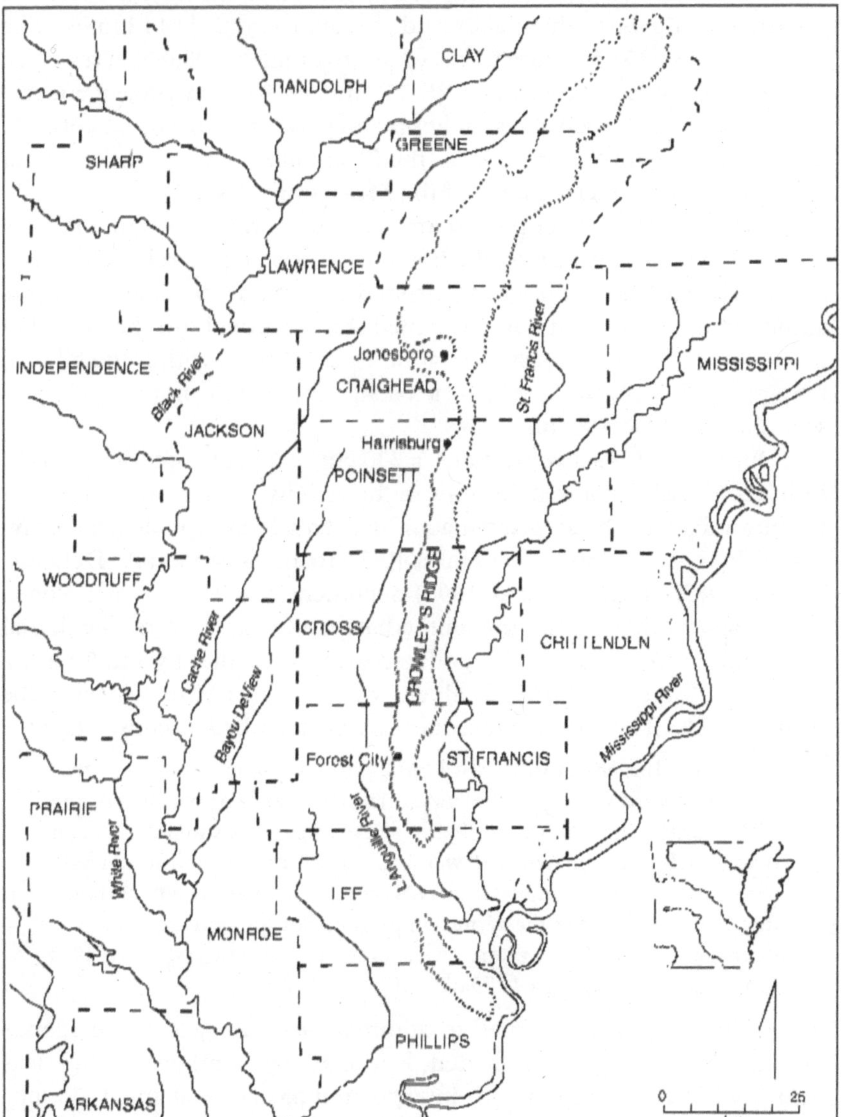

FIGURE 4.1. The L'Anguille River survey area.

Creek, tributaries of the White River, and on the east by Crowley's Ridge. Crowley's Ridge separates the L'Anguille Basin from the St. Francis Basin, except in the vicinity of the confluence of the two streams, where the L'Anguille veers to the east and flows through the Marianna Gap into the St. Francis. The river originates in the Crowley's Ridge escarpment in Craighead County, Arkansas, near the modern town of Jonesboro. The main channel extends for approximately 112 miles. The basin occupies 937.5 square miles, or approximately 608,000 acres (U.S. Army Corps of Engineers 1985:EIS-45); the 1987 survey project encompassed just under 7,000 acres, or approximately 1 percent of the total. At its confluence with the St. Francis, the L'Anguille comes to within about 20 miles of the modern course of the Mississippi River.

The L'Anguille River project area is characterized by comparatively recent alluvial deposits along the floodplains and considerably older, late Pleistocene surficial deposits away from the channel. The upland terraces adjoining the floodplain have remained stable throughout the period of human occupation, at least in relation to conditions within the alluvial floodplain. Evidence for prehistoric occupation is thus more readily preserved on these landforms.

During the 1987 investigations, a 330 cm sediment core was obtained from Hood Lake, Poinsett County, in the vicinity of the northern part of the basin. Palynological, plant-macrofossil, and geomorphological analyses of the core's contents by Hazel R. Delcourt and Paul A. Delcourt (1989a, 1989b; Delcourt et al. 1997) document vegetational, hydrologic, and climatic changes in the immediate study area from the initial Holocene to the present. The pollen core showed that by 11,250 B.P. a deciduous forest was present, albeit with traces of boreal species like spruce and fir. The vegetation sequence was described as consisting of

> bottomland swamp forests with bald cypress, planer tree, and other temperate hardwoods. . . . Upland xeric forests were primarily oak and hickory, and, in addition, on mesic slopes, the forests included sugar maple, beech, hornbeam, and walnut . . . maximum expansion of oak-hickory forest occurred between 7750 yr B.P. and 3500 yr B.P., and during that time interval the representation of bottomland trees such as river birch, sycamore, planer tree, elm, willow, and ash increased (Delcourt and Delcourt 1989a:29–30).

After 3500 B.P., oak continued to dominate assemblages, and evidence for extensive swamps is indicated. Interestingly, sunflower pollen was recovered in two samples with interpolated ages of 980 and 1350 B.P., perhaps reflecting cultivation by local Woodland and Mississippian populations (Delcourt and Delcourt 1989a:27, 31).

Today the L'Anguille River Basin consists of about 504,000 acres in bottomlands and 104,000 acres in uplands. The predominant habitat types include cultivated farmland, bottomland hardwoods, and upland hardwoods. Most of the basin (approximately 438,000 acres) is in farmland, although much of the land immediately along the channel (i.e., within 10 to 30 m of the water) itself remains wooded, particularly in lower, undrained areas that are difficult to cultivate. The basin is characterized by extensive permanently to seasonally inundated backwater areas, producing a diversity of aquatic habitats conducive to a wide range of fauna.

Twentieth-century drainage projects have markedly altered the pre-European contact landscape, which was characterized by extensive hardwood swamps throughout much of the later Holocene. Modern aquatic habitats range from narrow channelized stream courses (primarily in the upper portion of the drainage) to wide swamplands in the lower part of the basin. Oxbows and other cutoff channels, which formerly characterized much of the drainage prior to modern channelization, act as a nursery and growth area for many fish species; these populations replenish the main stream during periods of flooding, making oxbows and cutoff channels excellent fishing grounds for prehistoric populations (U.S. Army Corps of Engineers 1985:EIS-48, 49; see also Smith 1975:52–64). Crappie, bluegill, and largemouth bass are the dominant game fish, while nongame fish include gizzard shad, river carpsucker, and buffalo. Catfish are common in the drainage and are grown commercially along its length.

Large-scale agriculture has significantly altered natural conditions in the L'Anguille Basin. Extensive land leveling to facilitate rice cultivation and other forms of agriculture has occurred and has dramatically altered the physical appearance of the locality as well as vegetation and wildlife patterns (Medford 1972). This has stripped most of the hardwood vegetation from the basin and has severely impacted local archaeological resources. Many previously recorded sites, and no doubt hundreds that were unrecorded, have been land leveled.

In addition to land modification caused by modern agricultural practices, twentieth-century flood control projects have altered natural drainage systems and changed local topography, particularly in stream floodplains. There are approximately 193 channel miles of rivers and streams within the L'Anguille Basin comprising 2,100 flooded surface acres, almost all of which is "contiguous to the L'Anguille River and its major tributaries" (U.S. Army Corps of Engineers 1985:6). The main channel of the L'Anguille River is the principal water body in the basin. Its upper reaches (from Mile 85.5 to 113) were channelized prior to 1945 and are characterized by relatively long, straight stretches having moderate to fast currents; most of this area was outside the project survey zone. Downstream from the Cross-Poinsett County line, the L'Anguille

River remains a natural meandering channel with slow to moderate current (U.S. Army Corps of Engineers 1985:EIS-46). The low incidence of archaeological sites discovered during the 1987 survey in some portions of the drainage was directly related to the presence of large expanses of open water and wetlands adjacent to the main channel. At the time of the survey, well over half the terrain within 100 m of the main channel, particularly large portions of northern Lee County through St. Francis County and into southern Cross County, was flooded and hence inaccessible.

Previous Archaeological Research in the L'Anguille River Basin

There is a long history of archaeological fieldwork in the Eastern and Western Lowlands of northeast Arkansas, both by professional and amateur archaeologists (Klinger, Imhoff, and Cochran 1983:36–50; Lafferty and Watkins 1987:42–45; McNutt 1996; Morse and Morse 1983:17–49). Prior to the 1987 survey, however, the L'Anguille River had seen only a comparatively modest amount of previous research (J. Stewart-Abernathy 1982).

In the 1880s, archaeologists from the Mound Exploration Division of the Bureau of Ethnology (hereafter Mound Division) visited a number of sites in northeast Arkansas (Thomas 1894), producing descriptions that are invaluable in light of the subsequent destruction that has occurred. During the explorations of the Mound Division, Dr. Edward Palmer briefly visited the towns of Marianna and Harrisburg in the L'Anguille Basin, the former in snowy/sleety weather in mid-January 1882 and the latter in late 1882 (Jeter 1990b:120–22, 148–49, 158, 160–62, 173–74, 176–78). Palmer was not at all impressed with the area's living conditions, complaining about "wretched beds," "food badly cooked & served," and "drinking water with insects in it" (Jeter 1990b:173). In early November 1882 Palmer spent a day visiting the Cherry Valley Mounds in Cross County and produced a sketch map of the site, while noting that at least one of the mounds had been dug into in the recent past (Jeter 1990b:178–80, 187–88, 379). Thomas (1894:231) briefly described what the lower L'Anguille may have looked like in the 1880s from an archaeological perspective: "A careful examination was made of the bluffs and valleys both of the L'Anguille and St. Francis rivers above their confluence for a distance of fully 20 miles, from which it was found that scarcely a terrace or hillock was without evidences of ancient occupancy, such as brick-red fire-beds, charcoal, ashes, etc., indicating camps or dwellings." The 1987 survey demonstrated that a century of intensive agriculture and collecting had removed much of this evidence.

The only site located and described in detail in the L'Anguille Basin as a result of the exploits of the Mound Division was Greer's Mound (3LE24), for which the following description was recorded:

> This is a very rectangular, oblong truncated or flat-topped mound, situated upon the point of a second or upper terrace of the L'Anguille river 2 miles above its confluence with the St. Francis. It is rectangular, measuring on the top 87 feet in length and 51 feet in width and is 30 feet high; the slope of the sides is very steep, being about 45 degrees.
>
> A shaft sunk in it near one end some years ago revealed, as it is stated by the parties who made the exploration, the stump of a small tree and a stake 4 or 5 feet long near the bottom, the former growing in the natural soil. Layers of swamp mud and fire beds were found at irregular distances through the whole depth (Thomas 1894:231).

Permission to make further exploration could not be obtained by Mound Division personnel. No professional archaeological investigations were reported over the next half century in the L'Anguille Basin.

During the Lower Mississippi Valley survey, Greer's Mound was again visited, this time by James A. Ford and James B. Griffin on March 19, 1940. The site was described as having "thin village site indication"; that is, a low artifact density around the mound. Ford and Griffin made a collection of sixty sherds from the vicinity of the main mound and from a knoll to the northwest (Phillips et al. 1951:49, fig. 20). Most of the pottery was Baytown Plain, with minor amounts of other wares, and occupation fairly early in the local Mississippian sequence was indicated by the ceramic seriation. The Greer's Mound was revisited by the 1987 L'Anguille project team, which spent four person-hours in a 100 percent general surface collection of the area around the mound. Only 71 artifacts were found, however, of which 30 were sherds. Again, minimal evidence for an associated village was found, suggesting the site may have been a vacant ceremonial center or a chiefly compound (Williams 1995).

Prior to the 1987 survey, the most intensive program of archaeological survey in the L'Anguille Basin was the Ford-Redfield Dalton Project, which occurred in 1961 and 1962. This project, conducted by James A. Ford and Alden Redfield, focused on the discovery of preceramic sites in portions of the Lower Mississippi Alluvial Valley in Louisiana, Arkansas, and Missouri. The survey method employed was essentially opportunistic, as described by Redfield (1971:20):

> When Ford began this project, he described his method of surveying as resembling the selling of Bibles from door to door. We basically followed each road and stopped at each occupied house, asking about past discoveries of Indian relics. Answers ranged from the most helpful to such blunt statements as "We don't want to subscribe to another newspaper!" In many cases, of course, sites must have been

> missed if the land was not being farmed or if no residents could be found. In some cases other surveys reported farmers bragging about how they mislead or misdirected us (Morse, personal communication). Other farmers may not have accurately known what was in the area. . . . Despite lack of informants, unhelpful informants, and mis-informed informants, about 400 sites were visited. A few, like Poverty Point, were easily found; some had been reported earlier and were on the Lower Mississippi Valley Survey maps already (Phillips et al. 1951). The majority of our sites, however, were shown to Ford and Redfield by local collectors.

A vast amount of data was collected, and a preliminary report on the project's findings was released by Redfield (1971).

Ford and Redfield's survey incorporated most of the 1987 project area in the L'Anguille Basin. A concentration of Dalton sites was found in the central portion of the basin and along adjoining portions of Bayou DeView, between Forrest City and Harrisburg; a second, lesser concentration was reported near Helena. These have since been interpreted as the nuclei, or central foraging areas, of Dalton social groups (D. F. Morse 1975a, 1975b, 1997a; P. A. Morse 1977a; see also Gillam 1996a, this volume).

In 1987 minor concentrations of Dalton points were found in Lee and Cross Counties in the southern and central portions of the basin, in the vicinity of the concentrations observed during the 1961–62 survey. Eleven Ford-Redfield sites were in the project right-of-way and were revisited. Some had been land leveled and most yielded far fewer artifacts than were found during the original survey, indicating that appreciable surface collection and site destruction has occurred in the intervening years.

Four prehistoric sites in the L'Anguille Basin saw some level of excavation from the late 1950s to the late 1980s, including the Cherry Valley Mounds (Perino 1967), Lace Place (Redfield and Moselage 1970), Brand (Goodyear 1974), and Sloan (Morse 1975a, 1997a). The Cherry Valley Mound Group, located in Cross County, just to the west of Crowley's Ridge, was examined in 1958 by Gregory Perino (1967). Although the mounds had been extensively disturbed by vandals, three were excavated, and the site has since been recognized as the type locality for an initial Middle Mississippian phase dating to circa A.D. 1050–1150 (Morse and Morse 1983:243). Submound structures were found under two of the three mounds examined. A charnel house/mortuary complex was documented, characterized by numerous bundle burials, with lesser quantities of extended burials and remains from cremations. The site apparently served as a center where local Mississippian populations came to dispose of their dead. Although other Cherry Valley phase mound centers have been reported, all have been destroyed (Jeter 1990b:179; Morse and Morse 1983:246).

Lace Place (3PO17) was a large, multicomponent site in Poinsett County, examined in 1961 during the Ford-Redfield Dalton project (Morse and Morse 1983:83; Redfield and Moselage 1970). Perino (1967:12) first drew attention to the site and made collections from it during the late 1950s and after. Literally hundreds of Dalton points, adzes, and other tools have been collected from the site, which Dan Morse (1977a) has interpreted as a probable base camp for Dalton populations living in the central L'Anguille Basin. Three test pits were opened in the central portion of the site, documenting the presence of an artifact-rich Dalton midden with pronounced organic staining. Unfortunately Lace Place was land leveled and hence presumably completely destroyed in 1980 (Morse and Morse 1983:83). The vicinity was visited during the 1987 survey and 194 artifacts (mostly debitage) were collected from the surface.

Brand (3PO139), a Dalton site in Poinsett County, was excavated in 1970 (Goodyear 1974). This site was located on a small natural hillock several kilometers west of the L'Anguille River. About half the site area was excavated and several hundred tools were recovered. Several concentrations of tools were interpreted as discrete short-term occupations by male hunting/butchering task groups (Goodyear 1974:16). The large sample of points and associated tools were used to develop the concept of the Dalton toolkit.

Sloan (3GE94), located on the summit of a sand dune along the edge of the Cache River floodplain, was a Dalton cemetery completely excavated in 1974 by Dan Morse (Morse 1975a, 1997a). Several hundred chipped stone tools and over 100 identifiable human bone fragments were found in an approximately 11 by 12 m area (Morse 1975a:137–38). Most of the artifacts were clustered into a number of groups that have been interpreted as discrete burials (Morse 1975a:138, 1997a).

Only a few small survey projects were conducted in the L'Anguille Basin between the Ford-Redfield survey and the 1987 project. In 1966, James A. Scholtz (1968) surveyed archaeological sites in northeast and southeast Arkansas to study the effects of modern agricultural practices. In northeast Arkansas, he examined sites in Cross County, visiting 83 of the 88 sites that had been recorded as of that time, many by the Ford-Redfield Dalton survey. Approximately one-quarter of the sites had been destroyed by land leveling, an extremely high attrition rate given that most of them had been recorded within the previous decade.

In 1970 Larry Medford (1972) conducted a more detailed examination of archaeological site destruction in northeast Arkansas, using a sample of 1,293 sites in 11 counties. In all, 545 sites were found to have undergone destructive agricultural practices, indicating an alarming rate of site destruction. The L'Anguille Basin north of Lee County was included in Medford's study and was noted as ideal for rice cultivation. Because rice requires level, flooded field conditions, extensive land-leveling, ditching, and dike construction is associated with its cultivation. Medford (1972:77) argued that much of the archaeological record in the region would be destroyed if these agricultural practices continued unabated.

Finally, in 1981 an intensive survey was performed along approximately 50 miles of proposed drainage ditches in the Larkin Creek Watershed in Lee and Francis Counties (Bennett et al. 1982). The survey recorded 39 sites, including 21 historic and 29 prehistoric components. Most of the historic components were recently leveled tenant houses, while most of the identifiable prehistoric components were found to date to the Late Archaic and Late Woodland periods (Bennett et al. 1982). One site discovered during the 1981 survey, 3LE101, was revisited in 1987, and a well-executed Dalton point was found.

As shown by this review, little formal archaeological research had been conducted and reported in the vicinity of the L'Anguille channel prior to 1987. If not for the Ford-Redfield Dalton Project, in fact, the project area would be considered virtually unexplored. As the first systematic examination encompassing virtually the entire main channel, the sites documented in 1987 provide a wealth of new information about past life in the basin, particularly in the immediate channel and floodplain environments.

Survey and Analysis Procedures

The 1987 field investigations along the L'Anguille consisted of an intensive survey of the entire impact area, coupled with limited testing at sites along miles 0 to 16. A total of 222 sites were found, 137 in the right-of-way and 85 immediately adjacent to it, but still within about 200 m of the main channel (fig. 4.1). These latter sites were thoroughly documented to determine whether they extended into the impact zone. Because the vast majority of the project terrain was in plowed fields offering excellent visibility, surface collection formed the primary method of data collection. General surface collections were made at 172 sites (fig. 4.1), controlled surface collections were made at 45 sites, and shovel testing was conducted at 9 sites. In addition, 1 m test units were opened at 47 sites, encompassing all of the sites located in the right-of-way within the first 16 channel miles, as per the scope of work, since that was where project construction activity was to be initiated. Detailed site forms, including locations plotted on 1:5000 project aerials, USGS quads, and county soils maps were submitted with the final report. Additional investigations at these sites, and at the sites along channel miles 17 through 90, as well as a detailed geomorphological examination for buried sites were, at the request of the Memphis District, deferred to later stages of the project; because the construction plans were shelved, this work remains unaccomplished.

Prior to fieldwork, a records check was conducted with the Arkansas Archeological Survey (AAS) registrar's office. Original site forms and locational data were obtained for all previously recorded sites within 1,000 m of the main channel of the L'Anguille in the project area. A total of 103 sites had been recorded, 19 of which lay in the direct impact zone. These site locations were marked on project maps, and all sites within or at the margins of the right-of-way were revisited during the fieldwork to determine their extent and condition.

Compared with other areas of northeast Arkansas, the incidence of previously recorded sites was quite low, for a number of reasons. First, the L'Anguille channel margin had seen little formal survey by either amateurs or professionals in the past. Second, the area within 100 m of the main channel along much of the drainage is low and seasonally to permanently flooded. Third, the scarcity of large Mississippian or other prominent archaeological sites in close proximity to the channel has limited interest in this area. Fourth, the L'Anguille Basin does not appear to have attracted amateur collectors, at least those who record sites. Finally, the county with the fewest previously recorded sites in the project area, Lee County, is the farthest from the nearest AAS stations, at Pine Bluff and Jonesboro.

To delimit relationships between archaeological site locations, landforms, and past vegetation, a program of preliminary geomorphological investigation was conducted during the 1987 survey. A major goal was to identify specific areas likely to contain significant archaeological remains and areas unlikely to contain such deposits. During the fieldwork Drs. Paul A. Delcourt, Hazel R. Delcourt, and John E. Foss visited the project area and offered advice on the possibility of finding buried sites. Soil columns were taken and analyzed from a dozen project sites by Foss (1989), documenting local depositional conditions, and project terrain and maps were examined by P. Delcourt and J. Foss to identify locations conducive to buried site preservation. A number of settings were recommended for deep testing using a backhoe and sample screening should construction ever occur.

In conjunction with the geomorphological investigations, palynological and paleoenvironmental analyses were conducted under the overall direction of Hazel and Paul Delcourt. As noted, a major success was the recovery of the approximately 11,250-year pollen/plant-macrofossil record from Hood Lake in the northern part of the project area. This work was described in detail in the final survey report and has since been included as a chapter in Dan Morse's (1997a) Sloan site report (H. and P. Delcourt 1989a; Delcourt et al. 1997).

Field Procedures

Archaeological fieldwork during the L'Anguille River survey project consisted of a site discovery phase followed by a data collection phase. The site discovery phase entailed two major tasks, each with specific methods: (1) site discovery in wooded or overgrown areas; and (2) site discovery in open agricultural lands. Throughout the project, a site was defined as any grouping of five or more nonmodern (i.e., greater than 50 years old) historic or prehistoric artifacts from surface context within an area 20 by 20 m in maximum extent in open areas, or any positive shovel test in wooded or overgrown areas. Five or fewer artifacts from within larger areas were considered *isolated finds*. The project total of 222 sites includes 209 sites and 13 isolated finds assigned site numbers.

Shovel testing on a 30 m grid was employed in areas with greater than 50 percent ground cover. That is, in overgrown areas, a 30 by 30 cm shovel test was excavated to at least 50 cm every 30 m along transects spaced 30 m apart, with all fill screened through 0.25 inch mesh. The 30 m shovel test interval was paced; when sites were discovered, the interval was reduced to 10 m and all distances were taped. Transect and shovel test locations were marked on project aerials. Nine sites were discovered using the intensive shovel testing procedure, a very low number. This was due to the intensity of cultivation, however. Few areas of high ground in the basin have been left in an overgrown or wooded state. Fields extend right to the river channel, or else the terrain is low and flooded and hence overgrown in swamp hardwoods.

The principal site discovery technique in areas with greater than 50 percent surface visibility, typically in plowed fields, was pedestrian surface survey. This was accomplished by having crew members walk transects spaced 30 m apart oriented parallel to the L'Anguille River. In practice, given the use of two- to four-person survey teams, and the fact that each area was covered twice (radiating out from a vehicle and then back), the transect intervals were more typically 10 to 15 m. When sites were located, the extent of the scatter was carefully determined, and a decision on data collection procedures was made, specifically whether a controlled random sample or 100 percent timed general collection strategy was warranted.

In areas of uneven visibility, characterized by differential ground cover or erosional conditions, or where artifact density was extremely low (i.e., typically under 1 artifact per 10 by 10 m area), and on sites located outside of the project right-of-way, a 100 percent general collection strategy was followed. Each scatter was inspected using transects roughly 2 m apart, with all observed artifacts collected. Collection time was recorded in person hours or fractions thereof, permitting some degree of intersite comparability. Boundaries were paced or taped and drawn on project aerials and USGS quadrangle sheets.

A probabilistic sampling collection procedure was used on surface scatters in the right-of-way characterized by uniform visibility and a moderate to heavy artifact density. The sampling procedure entailed the collection of artifacts from equal-sized units dispersed over the site area using a stratified systematic unaligned sampling frame (Haggett 1966: 196–98; Redman and Watson 1970). The artifact scatter was arbitrarily divided into grid blocks 10 m on a side, and one 3.38 m radius circle (approximately 6.75 m in diameter) was collected from each block, providing a 36 percent sample from each grid. The use of a stratified systematic sampling scheme ensured even coverage, while the use of the unaligned unit dispersion procedure ensured that the actual collection points were not placed at regular intervals. The procedure thus provided for even coverage while avoiding possible periodicity in the data. This technique provided a representative, standardized artifactual (and areal) sample from the site surface—useful not only for the delimitation of intrasite patterning and specific assemblage parameter estimation, but also of value in intersite comparative analyses.

The controlled surface collection procedure was quick and easy to use. Collection points were predetermined in the lab and implemented in the field. The angle and distance to each sample point was calculated from a centrally fixed referent and placed on a standardized collection form that included space to record the elevation at each point (fig. 4.2). Once in the field, a transit was set up on a point equated with this referent and sample points were laid out and elevation values recorded using a stadia rod and tape. All that is necessary is to place the instrument in a location to ensure coverage of the entire scatter. This temporary reference point can then be tied in to a permanent datum placed in a secure location. At sites where the scatter extended over the 100 by 100 m size of the predetermined collection grid, secondary datum points were located at 100 m intervals from the primary datum, along cardinal directions, and a second series of points were collected. As each sample point was located, a stake or surveyor wire flag was planted and numbered. This number corresponded to that listed with the appropriate angle and distance on the record sheet (fig. 4.2). If more than one datum was required, sample location numbers were increased by 100 for the second datum, 200 for the third datum, and so on (i.e., 101, 102, 103, 201, 202, 203, etc.).

A two-person team conducted the mapping and collection-point dispersal activity, with one person on the transit and one person holding the stadia, tape, wire flags, and marking pen. Once a few points were dispersed, the remaining crew members began their collection. Since a stadia rod was used, elevations were recorded for each point, providing the basis for a site contour map. Using a dog-leash method, a 3.38 m radius circle was scribed about each sample point with chaining pins and string, and all artifacts were collected from within this circle. Artifacts were bagged and labeled in reference to each collection point. To further ensure standardized collection samples, each circle was collected for a minimum of five minutes (collection proceeded until all visible artifacts were picked up). This minimum collection time prevented cursory examination and ensured that areas with low artifact density were not quickly written off. Once the controlled surface collection had been

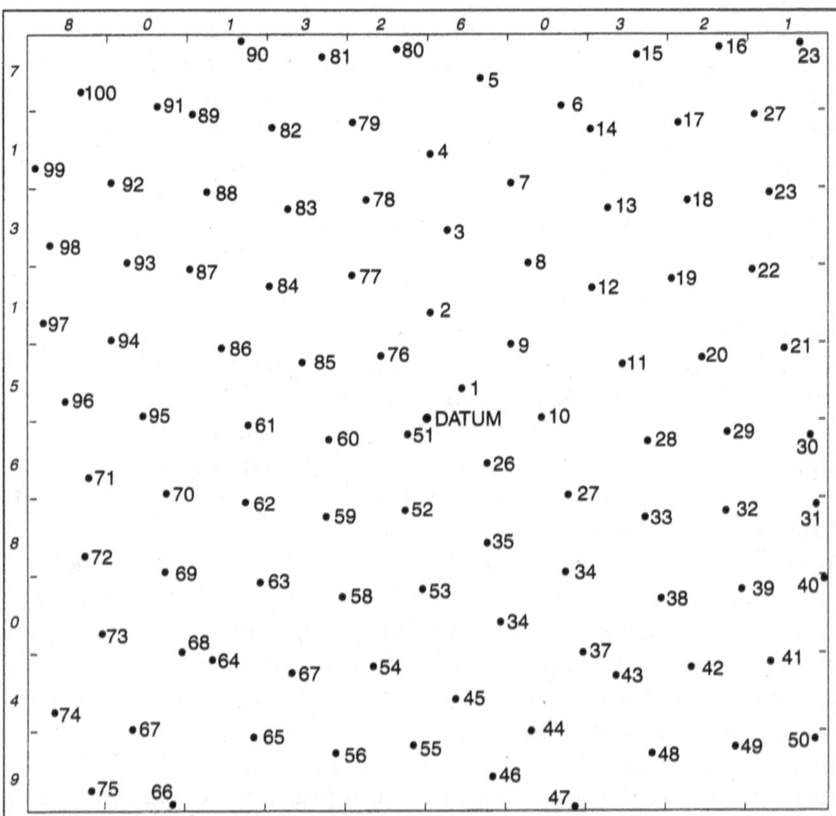

FIGURE 4.2. L'Anguille River project sampling frame, summer 1987 field program.

completed within the sample circle, a general or "grab sample" collection was made of the surrounding area, to roughly half the distance to adjacent sample flags. In this manner, tight spatial control was maintained over every surface artifact collected whose locations are thus known to within approximately 10 m in the overall scatter.

An example of a large site collected using this procedure was 3SF270, which required three separate temporary datum points (fig. 4.3). The entire 3SF270 scatter, some 20,000 square m in extent, and stretching over 300 m along the river margin, was mapped and surface collected in two days by a crew of eight. The 3,019 artifacts recovered, including 59 diagnostic projectile points, are located to within about 10 m, indicating the high degree of spatial resolution that can be obtained from use of this procedure at a comparatively low cost. Traditional general surface collection procedures, in contrast, combine all artifact provenience data into one gross sample and hence eliminate any possibility that these materials can be used to resolve intrasite patterning. Fine-grained provenience data using the stratified systematic unaligned sampling procedure described here was obtained from 45 project sites. Most average-sized sites of approximately 0.5 hectares in extent and requiring about 50 sample points were mapped and collected in about four hours with an eight-person crew.

A stratified systematic unaligned sampling procedure was adopted by Dan and Phyllis Morse at Zebree during the 1975 field season to disperse test pits over the site midden. This sample was used to produce artifact distribution maps and to provide estimates of overall assemblage content (Anderson 1975; Morse and Morse 1980). Based on its success at Zebree, the author has used this procedure on a range of site types and data categories, including during the 1987 L'Anguille survey (Anderson 1979; Anderson and Schuldenrein 1985).

Finally, a 1 m test unit was excavated at each site in the project right-of-way along miles 0.0 to 16.0. All test units were excavated using arbitrary 10 cm levels, or by natural strata where these were present, and all fill was dry screened through 0.25 inch mesh. Excavations were taken to at least 20 cm below artifact bearing soils, and a 30 by 30 cm test was excavated in a corner of each unit to at least 40 cm below this depth. Test units, like all other controlled collection units, were tied into a permanent site datum with a transit and tape. Representative profiles were drawn and color slides and black and white photographs were taken of each unit.

Laboratory Analysis Procedures

All artifacts were sorted and cataloged using descriptive and techno-functional categories. This was done in consultation with the AAS registrar's office, and the Arkansas State University and University of Arkansas-Pine

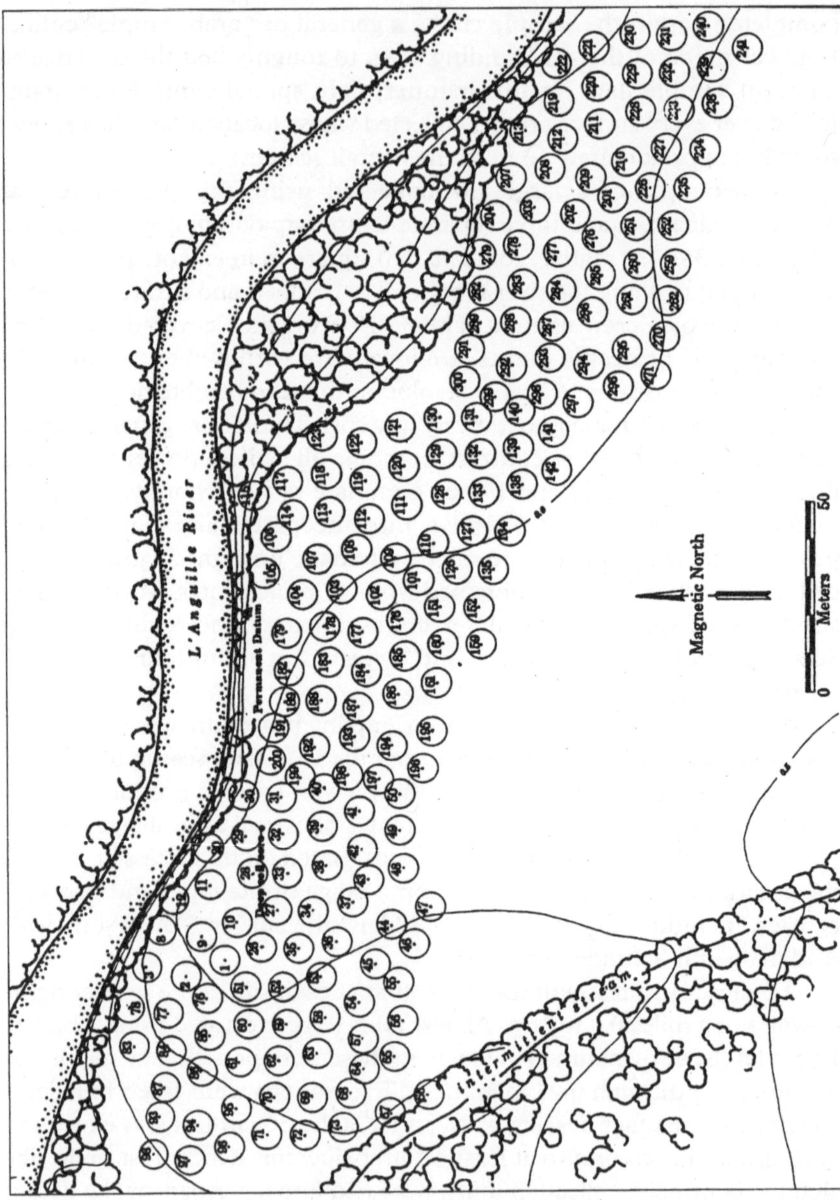

FIGURE 4.3. Site 3SF270 proveniences and controlled surface collection circles.

Bluff station archaeologists, where the collections were to be curated. Analysis included the description of all recovered prehistoric and historic artifacts. For the prehistoric assemblage, count or weight data were recorded by artifact category and raw material. For ceramic artifacts, temper type and surface finish were initially recorded, and a typological analysis of the collections was then conducted. Stone tools were cataloged using the functional typology developed by John House (1975a) during the Cache River project.

Count data were recorded for stone tools, including intentionally retouched and wear-retouched flakes, thick and thin bifaces, dart and arrow points and point fragments, hafted scrapers, spokeshaves and notches, adzes and axes, denticulates, and a range of cobble forms. An "other" category was established to accommodate unusual tools. Count and weight data was recorded for all core, quarry waste, and debitage categories, as defined by White (1963:5) and House (1975a). Raw material was recorded for all debitage and tool forms, with primary categories including thermally altered and unaltered Crowley's Ridge chert, Pitkin chert, chert breccia, white (Boone?) chert, quartzite/orthoquartzite, and banded chert. Again, an "other" category was used to handle unusual materials. Raw material identification followed descriptions advanced by House (1975b) and Mathis (1986) and the advice of Dan Morse. Firecracked rock was recorded by count and weight. Count data were recorded for all historic artifacts.

The results of the cataloging and analysis were combined into a comprehensive *Final Data Appendix and Catalog* prepared as a separate, limited distribution set of volumes curated with the AAS and at the Memphis District (Anderson 1988). This catalog, which was produced in both hard copy and electronic form, contains the analysis data by provenience for all 222 sites. All artifacts, photographs, original analysis sheets, and field notes from the 1987 archaeological survey, as well as copies of the technical report and the data appendix volume, have been curated with the AAS.

Technical Observations about Past Human Occupation of the L'Anguille Basin

The 222 sites found in 1987 were distributed along much of the length of the basin, offering an excellent opportunity to initiate descriptive and comparative analyses about past use of the L'Anguille channel margin. The number of sites discovered varied considerably from county to county, figures directly related to the nature of terrain along the channel (fig. 4.1). In Lee County, for example, the main channel of the L'Anguille flows through the Marianna Gap in Crowley's Ridge. As a result, the river is fairly deeply incised through much of the county, particularly in the southern reaches, and a considerable expanse of elevated, comparatively well-drained terrain conducive to past settlement is present close to the channel. To the north, particularly in St. Francis County, where few sites were found, the river is less deeply entrenched and broad swamplands parallel the main channel in many areas. In the narrow upper reaches of the basin, in Cross and Poinsett Counties, where extensive clearing and drainage have occurred, site density increased, reflecting both greater survey accessibility and the proximity of older land surfaces to the main channel.

Evidence for Prehistoric Occupations in the L'Anguille Basin

A total of 39,791 prehistoric artifacts was collected from 219 sites during the 1987 survey, including 3,400 sherds, 4,486 stone tools, and 25,723 pieces of debitage, as well as several thousand pieces of fire-cracked rock, cracked rock, and fired clay. Summary data on the distribution of stone tool forms by county are presented in table 4.1. Percentage figures are presented by type within a county and between counties in an effort to indicate, and control for, the differing sample sizes (i.e., numbers of sites and artifacts) from the four counties. Assemblage differences are readily apparent from county to county over the various tool categories. At least some of this variation appears to reflect intensity of prior visitation. Collection of virtually every open field along the L'Anguille drainage by relic hunters must be assumed, given previous research into collector behavior in the general region (see House and Schiffer 1975:50–52; Morse and Morse 1983:30–33), and information provided by informants during the survey itself.

Dart points, adzes, and intentionally retouched flake tools were more commonly recovered in the southern part of the basin, and a clear decline in the total number of tools was observed proceeding from south to north. These figures do not appear closely linked to the number of sites examined per county, as large numbers of artifacts were found in St. Francis County, which had the lowest site total. What the overall assemblage figures suggest is that avocational collection intensity seems to vary within the basin, with greater collection in the northern counties (Poinsett and Cross) and somewhat less in the southern counties (Lee and St. Francis). This is likely due, in part, to the proximity of a large population center, Jonesboro.

The most common tool forms recovered throughout the project area were wear-retouched and intentionally retouched flake tools, artifact categories least likely to have been picked up by relic hunters. Given their relatively expedient nature, however, these artifact categories

TABLE 4.1. PREHISTORIC STONE TOOL CATEGORIES RECOVERED DURING THE 1987 L'ANGUILLE RIVER SURVEY: TOTALS BY COUNTY

County	# of Sites	Wear Ret. Flakes	Int. Ret. Flakes	Thick Bifaces	Thin Bifaces	Dart Points	Unid. Points	Arrow Points	Adze/ Ax	Hammer Stones	Pitted Abrader	Unmod. Cobble	Cobble	Grinding Basin	Grand Totals
LEE	107 Sites	664	192	86	188	183	71	7	26	66	9	20	27	5	1544
	100%	43.01%	12.44%	5.57%	12.18%	11.85%	4.60%	0.45%	1.68%	4.27%	0.58%	1.30%	1.75%	0.32%	100%
	48.20%	28.39%	38.71%	47.78%	39.33%	44.74%	37.97%	38.89%	54.17%	39.76%	34.62%	39.22%	35.06%	45.45%	34.42%
ST. FRANCIS	20 Sites	790	162	37	117	111	42	1	12	26	3	10	15	1	1327
	100%	59.53%	12.21%	2.79%	8.82%	8.36%	3.17%	0.08%	0.90%	1.96%	0.23%	0.75%	1.13%	0.08%	100%
	9.01%	33.78%	32.66%	20.56%	24.48%	27.14%	22.46%	5.56%	25%	15.66%	11.54%	19.61%	19.48%	9.09%	29.58%
CROSS	67 Sites	594	91	23	104	75	51	8	6	37	9	13	16	5	1032
	100%	57.56%	8.82%	2.23%	10.08%	7.27%	4.94%	0.78%	0.58%	3.59%	0.87%	1.26%	1.55%	0.48%	100%
	30.18%	25.40%	18.35%	12.78%	21.76%	18.34%	27.27%	44.44%	12.50%	22.29%	34.62%	25.49%	20.78%	45.45%	23%
POINSETT	28 Sites	291	51	34	69	40	23	2	4	37	5	8	19	0	583
	100%	49.91%	8.75%	5.83%	11.84%	6.86%	3.95%	0.34%	0.69%	6.35%	0.86%	1.37%	3.26%	0%	100%
	12.61%	12.44%	10.28%	18.89%	14.44%	9.78%	12.30%	11.11%	8.33%	22.29%	19.23%	15.69%	24.68%	0%	13%
Grand Totals	222 Sites	2339	496	180	478	409	187	18	48	166	26	51	77	11	4486
	100%	52.14%	11.06%	4.01%	10.66%	9.12%	4.17%	0.40%	1.07%	3.70%	0.58%	1.14%	1.72%	0.25%	100%
	100%	100%	100%	100%	100%	100%	100%	100%	100%	100%	100%	100%	100%	100%	100%

ret.=retouched; int.=intentional

probably were also the most common tool forms produced by prehistoric populations.

A total of 409 dart points and 18 arrow points were recovered, of which 288 could be assigned to specific cultural-historical types (table 4.2). Fairly appreciable occupation of the basin during the Archaic and Woodland periods was suggested by the large numbers of dart points recovered. The comparatively low number of arrow points, in contrast, indicates settlement may have been sparse during the Mississippian period. Few Mississippian period shell-tempered sherds were recovered, supporting this inference.

Among the diagnostic projectile points were a single Clovis base and 20 Dalton points, indicating fairly appreciable Paleoindian, and particularly late Paleoindian Dalton culture, occupation within the basin. The early Paleoindian Clovis point, found at 3SF270 (table 4.3), was made of exceptionally fine-grained chert of unknown origin; no other artifacts of this material were found within the scatter. Use of such high-quality stone at this time level is thought to be linked to an extensive mobility strategy and a concomitant need to maximize raw material usage (see Goodyear 1979). The largest incidence of Dalton points was in Cross County, near the center of the Dalton site concentration documented in this area during the Ford-Redfield survey and where Dan Morse (1975b, 1977a) posited a Dalton band was residing. A second concentration of Dalton points in the southern part of the basin, in Lee County, may be related to the Ford-Redfield concentration noted west of Helena and may document the northern extent of a second Dalton territory.

A moderate number of Early and Middle Archaic projectile points was found in about equal numbers over each period (table 4.3). During the Early Archaic period, Hardin Barbed forms are the most common, while Hickory Ridge and Eva-like forms tend to characterize Middle Archaic assemblages. While a partial depopulation of the Western Lowlands has been posited following Dalton locally, particularly in the Middle Archaic period during the Hypsithermal warm interval (Morse and Morse 1983:103), roughly equivalent numbers of diagnostics were found along the channel margin during the late Paleoindian, Early Archaic, and Middle Archaic periods. Given this, initial Holocene population reduction may not have been as extreme as has been thought. If a population decline did occur during the immediate post-Dalton period, this may have been the result of changes in technological organization rather than, or in addition to, changes in climate (e.g., Jeter and Williams 1989:78–79; Morse and Morse 1996:6).

Across the Southeast, the Early Archaic period is one in which great technological changes occurred. A gradual replacement of logistical systems by more residentially mobile adaptations took place in many areas

TABLE 4.2. PREHISTORIC PROJECTILE POINTS RECOVERED DURING THE 1987 L'ANGUILLE RIVER SURVEY: TOTALS BY TYPE AND COUNTY

Point Type	Lee 107 Sites	St. Francis 20 Sites	Cross 67 Sites	Poinsett 28 Sites	Totals	Period
Clovis	0	1	0	0	1	Early Paleoindian
Dalton	8	3	7	2	20	Late Paleoindian
San Patrice	1	2	0	0	3	Early Archaic
Hardin	9	4	3	1	17	Early Archaic
Searcy	0	0	1	0	1	Early Archaic
Hickory Ridge	4	3	2	1	10	Middle Archaic
Rice Lobed	0	0	1	0	1	Middle Archaic
Cache River	0	1	0	1	2	Middle Archaic
Eva-like	5	2	1	0	8	Middle Archaic
Big Creek	12	8	1	3	24	Late Archaic
Burkett	12	10	1	3	26	Late Archaic
Gary	20	17	9	7	53	LA/Woodland
Weems	44	21	6	6	77	LA/Woodland
Motley	1	0	0	0	1	LA/Woodland
Harrison Turkey-Tail	0	1	0	0	1	LA/Woodland
Marksville	2	0	4	0	6	Woodland
Woodland Stemmed	5	0	0	0	5	Woodland
Baytown Stemmed	4	1	1	0	6	Woodland
Dickson	2	0	0	0	2	Woodland
Steuben	4	2	2	1	9	Woodland
Scallorn	1	0	5	1	7	Mississippian
Schugtown	1	0	1	1	3	Mississippian
Sequoyah	1	0	0	0	1	Mississippian
Madison	2	0	1	0	3	Mississippian
Nodena	1	0	0	0	1	Mississippian
Totals	**139**	**76**	**46**	**27**	**288**	

TABLE 4.3. PREHISTORIC PROJECTILE POINTS RECOVERED DURING THE 1987 L'ANGUILLE RIVER SURVEY: TOTALS BY MAJOR PERIOD AND COUNTY

County	# of Sites	Early Paleo-indian	Late Paleo-indian	Early Archaic	Middle Archaic	Late Archaic	Late Archaic/ W'land	Woodland	Mississippian	Grand Totals
Lee	107 Sites	0	8	10	9	24	65	17	6	139
	100%	0%	5.76%	7.19%	6.47%	17.27%	46.76%	12.23%	4.32%	100%
	48.20%	0%	40%	47.62%	42.86%	48%	50%	60.71%	40%	48.26%
St. Francis	20 Sites	1	3	6	6	18	39	3	0	76
	100%	1.32%	3.95%	7.89%	7.89%	23.68%	51.32%	3.95%	0%	100%
	9.01%	100%	15%	28.57%	28.57%	36%	29.10%	10.71%	0%	26.39%
Cross	67 Sites	0	7	4	4	2	15	7	7	46
	100%	0%	15.22%	8.70%	8.70%	4.35%	32.61%	15.22%	15.22%	100%
	30.18%	0%	35%	19.05%	19.05%	4%	11.19%	25%	46.67%	15.97%
Poinsett	28 Sites	0	2	1	2	6	13	1	2	27
	100%	0%	7.41%	3.70%	7.41%	22.22%	48.15%	3.70%	7.41%	100%
	12.61%	0%	10%	4.76%	9.52%	12%	9.70%	3.57%	13.33%	9.38%
Grand	222 Sites	1	20	21	21	50	132	28	15	288
Totals	100%	0.35%	6.94%	7.29%	7.29%	17.36%	45.83%	9.72%	5.21%	100%
	100%	100%	100%	100%	100%	100%	100%	100%	100%	100%

as part of a broad regional adaptation by human populations to post-glacial-era conditions (Anderson and Hanson 1988; Cable 1996; Morse et al. 1996). The same patterning likely occurred in northeast Arkansas. That is, the Dalton adaptation, with its highly curated toolkit and logistically organized technological system characterized by central base camps, hunting camps, and cemeteries, and its apparent large attendant local populations, became an increasingly untenable means of dealing with postglacial Holocene environmental conditions, population levels, and resource structure. Thus the so-called "Dalton collapse" may not be so much a population *decline* as a population and organizational *rearrangement.* That is, populations that formerly exploited territories from central core areas were now much more residentially mobile, ranging over greater areas, and leaving a less concentrated, and hence less pronounced, archaeological record of their activities. This pattern apparently continued locally through the Middle Archaic.

A major population increase within the L'Anguille Basin is indicated during the Late Archaic period and may be tied to the rise in local water tables and the expansion of swamplands that occurred at this time. Big Creek, Burkett, Gary, and particularly Weems points are common, although it must be cautioned that some of these forms, particularly the latter two types, continue in use into the Woodland era. For this reason, Big Creek and Burkett points were assigned to a preceramic Late Archaic category (see tables 4.2 and 4.3), while Gary and Weems points were placed in a transitional Late Archaic/Woodland category, together with the isolated examples of Motley and Harrison Turkey Tail points that were found.

Most Late Archaic and Late Archaic/Woodland points, as over all periods, came from the southern part of the basin, something that has been linked to prior collection intensity (tables 4.2 and 4.3). When the figures are standardized by county using percentages, however, two concentrations of Late Archaic and Late Archaic/Woodland projectile points are evident within the basin in the northern and southern areas. Comparatively few diagnostics dating to these periods occur in Cross County, at least when compared with the areas to the north and south. The pattern is most pronounced during the Late Archaic (4.35 percent in Cross County versus a range of from 17.27 to 23.68 percent in the other three counties), and trends toward a somewhat more even distribution during the Late Archaic/Woodland period (32.61 percent in Cross County versus a range of from 46.76 to 51.32 percent in the other three counties). The emergence of discrete Late Archaic/Early Woodland groups occupying the northern and southern parts of the basin, with a vacant zone between them in Cross County, may be indicated by these distributions.

Fewer diagnostic point forms attributable solely to the Woodland period were found, and on first appraisal a population decline might be indicated within the basin (table 4.3). Given the moderate occurrence of grog-tempered pottery (table 4.4), and the fact that the point types placed in the Late Archaic/Woodland category also were used during the Woodland era, an actual population decline is unlikely. Two discrete concentrations of points are again indicated in the northern and southern parts of the basin. Again the southern concentration is centered in Lee County. The northern concentration, however, is centered on Cross County, while St. Francis County to the south and Poinsett County to the north are relatively underrepresented. A shift in population concentrations in the northern part of the basin, from the northern to the north-central area, may be indicated from the Late Archaic to the Woodland periods. The projectile point distribution is paralleled by that of grog-tempered pottery (table 4.4), indicating that this patterning is probably a fairly accurate appraisal of Woodland population concentrations in the basin.

TABLE 4.4. PREHISTORIC CERAMICS RECOVERED DURING THE 1987 L'ANGUILLE RIVER SURVEY: TOTALS BY MAJOR TEMPER GROUP AND COUNTY

County	# of Sites	Grog	TEMPER Shell	Sand	Grand Totals
Lee	107 Sites	1110	87	12	1209
	100%	91.80%	7.20%	1%	100%
	48.20%	32.65%	2.56%	0.35%	35.56%
St. Francis	20 Sites	50	3	0	53
	100%	94.30%	5.70%	0%	100%
	9.01%	1.47%	0.09%	0%	1.56%
Cross	67 Sites	1941	21	9	1971
	100%	98.50%	1.10%	0.40%	100%
	30.18%	57.09%	0.62%	0.26%	57.97%
Poinsett	28 Sites	133	23	11	167
	100%	79.60%	13.80%	6.60%	100%
	12.61%	3.91%	0.68%	0.32%	4.91%
Grand Totals	222 Sites	3234	134	32	3400
	100%	95.10%	3.90%	1%	100%
	100%	100%	100%	100%	100%

What is represented by these apparent Late Archaic and Woodland population concentrations and realignments remains unknown. It is tempting to speculate that what we are seeing is territorial realignment and circumscription brought about by population increase over the Late Archaic and Woodland eras. In this scenario, the Late Archaic assemblage distributions reflect the presence of two social entities within the basin. The Woodland pattern may reflect the movement of the northern group southward or, alternatively, the emergence of yet another social entity in the northern part of the basin, in northern Poinsett County or beyond, that led to the southward movement of the peoples formerly living in this area. In this view, three or more Woodland groups may have been present within or near the basin. These social entities need not have been culturally distinct or antagonistic. They may have been part of a larger cultural entity, such as separate lineage-based communities within D. Morse's (1977b) hypothesized Baytown segmentary tribal configuration; these may have kept separate for a number of reasons, such as the need to maintain viable hunting territories, firewood supplies, or other resources. So few sand-tempered sherds were found within the basin that it was not possible to examine Morse's (1977b) idea that the distribution of Barnes versus Baytown ceramics in the general region represents the location and movement of discrete and possibly antagonistic Woodland cultural systems (see also Jeter and Williams 1989:143–45).

Comparatively few Mississippian period diagnostics were found (tables 4.2 to 4.4). Arrow points accounted for just over 5 percent of the diagnostic projectile points recovered in the basin (table 4.3), while just under 4 percent of the prehistoric ceramics are shell tempered (table 4.4). A population decline may be indicated, at least in comparison with the Woodland period. At the time of the de Soto *entrada,* the L'Anguille vicinity was described as a vast unoccupied swampland (Hudson 1985). The basin may have been largely depopulated, serving as a buffer or hunting territory for the complex Mississippian chiefdoms occupying the Eastern Lowlands (see also Morse and Morse 1983:271–301).

There are minor concentrations of Mississippian artifacts in two areas. Shell-tempered pottery tends to occur in Lee and St. Francis Counties in the southern part of the basin and in Poinsett County to the north, while arrow points are concentrated in Lee County in the southern part of the basin and Cross and Poinsett Counties in the northern reaches. These assemblages did not come from large or extensive Mississippian period sites, so whatever is represented by these "concentrations," dense settlement is not indicated. The Mississippian sites in the southern part of the basin are tentatively interpreted as outlying Kent phase hamlets and hunting stations. The main centers and population concentrations from this and earlier ancestral phases are for the most

TABLE 4.5. PREHISTORIC DEBITAGE RECOVERED DURING THE 1987 L'ANGUILLE RIVER SURVEY: TOTALS BY REDUCTION STAGE AND COUNTY

County	# of Sites	Quarry Waste	Cores	Primary Flakes	Secondary Flakes	Interior Flakes	Shatter	Grand Totals
Lee	107 Sites	105	339	414	2659	2802	1121	7440
	100%	1.41%	4.56%	5.56%	35.74%	37.66%	15.07%	100%
	48.20%	35%	30.62%	28.85%	29.18%	32.50%	21.78%	28.92%
St. Francis	20 Sites	46	238	385	2261	3037	1153	7120
	100%	0.65%	3.34%	5.41%	31.76%	42.65%	16.19%	100%
	9.01%	15.33%	21.50%	26.83%	24.82%	35.22%	22.40%	27.68%
Cross	67 Sites	90	318	377	2406	1513	1679	6383
	100%	1.41%	4.98%	5.91%	37.69%	23.70%	26.30%	100%
	30.18%	30%	28.73%	26.27%	26.41%	17.55%	32.61%	24.81%
Poinsett	28 Sites	59	212	259	1785	1270	1195	4780
	100%	1.23%	4.44%	5.42%	37.34%	26.57%	25%	100%
	12.61%	19.67%	19.15%	18.05%	19.59%	14.73%	23.21%	18.58%
Grand	222 Sites	300	1107	1435	9111	8622	5148	25723
Totals	100%	1.17%	4.30%	5.58%	35.42%	33.52%	20.01%	100%
	100%	100%	100%	100%	100%	100%	100%	100%

part located to the south and east, along the St. Francis (House 1987, 1993). Only Greer's Mound lies within the L'Anguille Basin, and it has yielded little evidence for Mississippian occupation (29 of the 30 sherds collected in 1987 were grog tempered, with only one shell tempered). Mississippian sites in the northern part of the basin may be outlying sites from the late prehistoric Parkin and Nodena/Armorel phase chiefdoms to the east across Crowley's Ridge. Alternatively, some of these northern sites may represent earlier, Cherry Valley phase occupations.

Evidence for variability in prehistoric lithic raw material utilization and reduction practices also is evident (table 4.5). Considerable localized reduction is implied by the presence of appreciable primary and secondary decortication flakes and by large numbers of cores. Procurement of lithic raw materials in cobble form is indicated, at least during some periods. Given the comparatively small number of quarry waste pieces (tested cobbles with no subsequent reduction), local populations were adept at selecting high-quality chert cobbles from within the nearby Crowley's Ridge gravel deposits, where much of this material is assumed to have originated.

Some difference in overall reduction behavior is evident between the north and south ends of the basin. Interior flakes comprise a higher proportion of assemblages in the southern part of the basin, in Lee and St. Francis Counties, than they do in the two northernmost counties examined (table 4.5). The opposite pattern is evident with the shatter category, which is comparatively infrequent in the southern counties and more common in the northern part of the basin. The significance of this is unclear. It may be related to the quality of lithic raw material sources, with poorer quality stone more likely to shatter occurring more commonly in the northern part of the basin. Alternatively, and perhaps more probable, this pattern may be linked to the distance local populations had to travel to obtain raw materials. Sites in the southern part of the basin, particularly in Lee County in the vicinity of the Marianna Gap, are somewhat farther from Crowley's Ridge, and hence raw material sources, than sites in the northern part of the basin. This greater distance may have prompted greater care in cobble selection during procurement forays and in reduction. Occupants of the northern part of the basin, in contrast, having to expend less effort to obtain stone, may have been comparatively profligate in its use. This is also suggested by firecracked rock, which shows a clear pattern of increase from south to north, presumably indicating greater ease of procurement (table 4.6).

The distributions of lithic raw materials within the basin support some of the inferences noted (see table 4.7). Crowley's Ridge chert accounts for the vast majority (87.11 percent) of all lithic raw material and occurs in roughly equivalent proportions in each of the four counties.

TABLE 4.6. PREHISTORIC FIRECRACKED ROCK RECOVERED DURING THE 1987 L'ANGUILLE RIVER SURVEY: TOTALS BY COUNTY

County	Number of Sites	Incidence of Firecracked Rock
Lee	107 sites	526
	48.20%	9.10%
St. Francis	20 sites	1049
	9.01%	18.14%
Cross	67 sites	1783
	30.18%	30.84%
Poinsett	28 sites	2424
	12.61%	41.92%
Grand Totals	222 sites	5782
	100%	100%

The sum of intentionally thermally altered and unaltered Crowley's Ridge chert, in fact, ranges from a low of 83.32 percent in Cross County to a high of 89.55 percent in St. Francis County. Thermal alteration is more evident in the northern part of the basin, however, where it accounts for approximately one-third of the total raw material assemblage, as opposed to about one-fifth in the southern part of the basin. This may be linked to the greater incidence of firecracked rock in these same counties. That is, some of the firecracked rock observed in these counties may be thermal alteration production failures. Some of the intentionally thermally altered chert debitage and shatter may also be misidentified and may have been firecracked rock fragments.

Materials other than Crowley's Ridge chert make up only a minor part of the basin assemblages, although again some variation in the occurrence of these materials was noted. Chert breccia decreased in incidence from south to north in the basin. Mathis (1986:297) noted that a similar material was common in the central Village Creek Basin to the north. The L'Anguille breccia, a well-cemented conglomeritic-like material, thus probably derives from a different source than the Village Creek materials. White chert, presumably from the Ozark escarpment, is infrequent throughout the basin, with a low in St. Francis County, where black Pitkin chert, also probably from the Ozarks, was the most common. The distribution of gray chert, which is a very high-quality material, is similar to that of the white chert, suggesting that the two materials came from the same localities or were utilized in the same fashion.

TABLE 4.7. PREHISTORIC LITHIC RAW MATERIAL UTILIZATION IN THE L'ANGUILLE BASIN: TOTALS BY RAW MATERIAL CATEGORY AND COUNTY

County	Number of Sites	Crowley's Ridge Chert	ITA Crowley's Ridge	Pitkin Chert	Chert Breccia	White Chert	Quartzite	Banded Chert	Other Unknown	Gray Chert	Novaculite	Grand Totals
LEE	107 Sites	5877	1908	161	62	107	216	373	72	61	28	8865
	100%	66.29%	21.52%	1.82%	0.70%	1.21%	2.44%	4.21%	0.81%	0.69%	0.31%	100%
	48.20%	32.42%	23.06%	25.64%	52.10%	39.78%	16.95%	29.94%	46.75%	34.86%	63.64%	29.24%
ST. FRANCIS	20 Sites	5949	1941	269	34	22	220	322	35	11	8	8811
	100%	67.52%	22.03%	3.05%	0.39%	0.25%	2.50%	3.65%	0.40%	0.12%	0.09%	100%
	9.01%	32.81%	23.46%	42.83%	28.57%	8.18%	17.27%	25.84%	22.73%	6.29%	18.18%	29.07%
CROSS	67 Sites	3627	2489	133	16	84	484	392	35	72	8	7340
	100%	49.41%	33.91%	1.81%	0.22%	1.14%	6.59%	5.34%	0.48%	0.98%	0.11%	100%
	30.18%	20.01%	30.08%	21.18%	13.45%	31.23%	37.99%	31.46%	22.73%	41.14%	18.18%	24.22%
POINSETT	28 Sites	2677	1936	65	7	56	354	159	12	31	0	5297
	100%	50.54%	36.55%	1.22%	0.13%	1.06%	6.68%	3%	0.23%	0.59%	0%	100%
	12.61%	14.77%	23.40%	10.35%	5.88%	20.82%	27.79%	12.76%	7.79%	17.71%	0%	17.47%
GRAND	222 Sites	18130	8274	628	119	269	1274	1246	154	175	44	30313
TOTALS	100%	59.81%	27.30%	2.07%	0.39%	0.89%	4.20%	4.11%	0.51%	0.58%	0.15%	100%
	100%	100%	100%	100%	100%	100%	100%	100%	100%	100%	100%	100%

ITA=intentionally thermally altered

Banded chert, a high-quality jasper-like material that may derive from Crowley's Ridge gravels (given the frequent presence of pebble cortex) was found in about even incidence throughout the basin. Quartzites, another material originating on Crowley's Ridge (House 1975b), are comparatively more common in the northern part of the basin as opposed to within the southern counties. Finally, novaculite, while extremely uncommon within the basin, occurred most frequently in Lee County. This area presumably was the closest to the sources for this material in central and southwest Arkansas and also to the transportation routes by which it likely was transported into northeast Arkansas, along the Arkansas and White rivers. A south-to-north decrease in the incidence of novaculite was also observed by Jeter (1988:26–27) in an analysis of collections from a gas pipeline corridor running from near Little Rock to the Missouri border just west of Crowley's Ridge.

Evidence for Historic Occupations in the L'Anguille Basin

Historic artifacts were found at 101 of the 222 sites examined during the 1987 survey along the L'Anguille channel margin. Most were light scatters of material, typically isolated pieces of glass or pottery, but dense debris scatters were found at 26 sites that appear to be the remains of farm or tenant houses. Some were, in fact, identified by informants as the locations of former tenant houses. Architectural debris from some of these structures was found on the riverbank below the scatters, where it had been pushed by heavy equipment. Twenty house sites date to the early to mid-twentieth century, while the remaining six reflect earlier, mid-to-late nineteenth-century farmsteads. Most historic sites were found in Lee County, something that appears linked to drainage conditions in the basin. Only in Lee County were appreciable areas of elevated, well-drained terrain found close to the channel margin. Three somewhat unusual historic assemblages were found. One site yielded an eighteenth- or early-nineteenth-century French gunflint amid an otherwise (inferred) prehistoric assemblage, and two early-to-mid twentieth-century trash dumps were found near the town of Marianna.

Conclusions

The 1987 L'Anguille River survey is typical of the kind of CRM projects that have been undertaken in large numbers across the Southeast in recent years. As the preceding discussions have indicated, these projects are resulting in the compilation of vast quantities of high-quality data that can be used by future generations of scholars to address a wide range of questions. As the archaeological record in the region continues to deteriorate, such collections will prove increasingly important. As such, the study highlights the importance of federal support for archaeology and historic preservation.

Acknowledgments

Funding for the 1987 L'Anguille Basin project was provided under terms of a contract (DACW66-87-C-0046) between Garrow and Associates, Inc., and the Memphis District office of the U.S. Army Corps of Engineers. Site records and collections are curated with the AAS, at the Survey registrar's office in Fayetteville and at Arkansas State University and the University of Arkansas-Pine Bluff. Dan and Phyllis Morse provided advice and assistance throughout the course of the L'Anguille project and have done much to shape my career and attitudes about archaeology in general. Finally, Bob Mainfort and Marvin Jeter have my thanks for their advice and patience in the preparation of this chapter.

CHAPTER FIVE

PALEOINDIAN SETTLEMENT IN NORTHEASTERN ARKANSAS

J. CHRISTOPHER GILLAM

Introduction

The Paleoindians occupying the Western and Eastern Lowlands of the Mississippi Valley of Arkansas witnessed dynamic changes in their environment during the terminal Pleistocene (Delcourt et al., this volume). Perhaps there was a time when the elder generation had hunted Pleistocene megafauna, whereas the younger generation had not. During this time, the potential for cultural change would have been at its greatest had large game been the primary focus of hunting activity. Cultural change during this period was not, however, necessarily related solely to changes in fauna. Many factors, including changes in regional vegetation communities, increased knowledge of local resources, decreased range of group movement, and population increase could have resulted in significant cultural change.

Given the nature of the Paleoindian archaeological record, it is very difficult to determine if such change occurred. Populations remained relatively low during this period, and tool kits changed gradually over time. This gives the impression that few changes occurred in the lifestyle of the Paleoindians following the demise of the megafauna. Sites such as Kimmswick indicate that a generalized foraging adaptation, including big-game hunting, was prevalent in the region (Graham et al. 1981; Graham and Kay 1988). Increasing dependence on deer and other modern game species may have been transparent over time, not evoking significant cultural change.

The consistency of regional adaptations may be evaluated by examining the spatial characteristics of site distribution over time. Clearly, if cultural change occurred in the region during the Paleoindian period, that change would be reflected in the spatial distribution of archaeological sites. This chapter demonstrates the temporal variability of Paleoindian settlement in northeastern Arkansas during the terminal Pleistocene. This is accomplished by comparing the distribution of sites containing fluted points (an "early" data set) to those containing Dalton cultural materials (a "late" data set) with a Geographic Information System (GIS). This early versus late approach was chosen due to the limited number of fluted-point bearing sites (*n*=68) compared to those of the Dalton Period (*n*=767). Past research by the author has demonstrated the significant association between early and late Paleoindian site location and the lithic resources of the Crowley's Ridge landform (Gillam 1995, 1996a, 1996b). This chapter presents new information on site distribution bias, examines the relationship of sites to lithic resources available in the Ozark Plateau, evidences the occurrence of seasonal variation in early Paleoindian settlement, presents a model of early Paleoindian settlement, and provides support for Morse's model of Dalton settlement in the region.

Changes in site distribution are demonstrated to reflect cultural change in late Paleoindian Dalton culture. This is seen in the riverine focus of site location, growth in population size, and the general increase of Oak-Hickory Forests in the Lowlands region. Crowley's Ridge remained a significant landscape feature throughout the period. Seasonal variation in site location occurred primarily during the early Paleoindian occupation. Such a pattern of site distribution supports the hypothesis that the Paleoindians practiced a generalized foraging adaptation (Morse 1997b). Megafauna probably were not exclusively hunted by these early populations. The Oak-Hickory Forests occupied by the Paleoindians were better environments for modern game than their Pleistocene-adapted counterparts. Greater utilization of the landscape occurred during the Dalton period although *significant* landscape associations indicate a riverine focus by this late Paleoindian culture.

Regional Setting

The geomorphology and vegetation dynamics of the region have been presented in detail elsewhere (Delcourt et al., this volume). I will therefore concentrate on the significance of these characteristics to Paleoindian settlement. Lithic resources of the region will be discussed in greater detail.

Most archaeological materials from the Paleoindian period have come from zones dominated by Oak-Hickory Forests throughout the terminal Pleistocene and early Holocene (Delcourt et al., this volume). Spruce communities no longer were widespread, potentially indicating a substantial decline in megafauna populations before 12,000 rcbp. This is significant when considering the potential for a generalized foraging adaptation by human populations in such a setting. There probably were many more deer in this environment than Pleistocene megafauna. It is therefore likely that deer were a primary focus of hunting activity, even at a very early date (e.g., 11,200 rcbp).

There are four major landscape features in the vicinity of the Lowlands. These include Crowley's Ridge, the valley train terraces, dune sand deposits, and the Holocene meander belts (Saucier 1997). The Pleistocene terraces, dune sand deposits, and Crowley's Ridge are the only landforms ancient enough to have relevance to Paleoindian settlement. Indeed, it will be demonstrated that the terraces and dune sand fields were the primary areas of habitation during this period. Crowley's Ridge provided lithic resources suitable for expedient tools and will be described further below.

Neighboring environments, such as the Ozark Plateau, have not yielded the vast quantity of Paleoindian sites and cultural materials present in the Mississippi Valley. This may be an issue of preservation or discovery, but it is more likely related to population size. The poorly drained environment of the Lowlands would have provided abundant game and floral resources—likely unmatched in neighboring environments—and allowed for greater population sizes to develop over time. This is not to say that the Ozarks were unoccupied. There probably were permanent residents of the Ozarks throughout the Paleoindian period. Contact may have been maintained through trade of high-quality lithic materials, a resource nearly absent in the Lowlands.

The lithic resources of the study region are primarily restricted to the Crowley's Ridge landform and the Ozark Plateau. Crowley's Ridge contains Tertiary strata covered by Quaternary sediments (Autin et al. 1991:550). These strata contain an abundance of chert cobbles, which were used throughout prehistory as a raw material source (House 1975b; Morse 1969).

The origins of the gravels remains a matter of debate. In northeastern Arkansas, their distribution is restricted to the Crowley's Ridge landform and sediments bordering the Ozark Plateau (Ray 1995). What is certain is that the gravels of Crowley's Ridge (hereafter, Crowley's Ridge chert) and those of the Plateau-Valley margin are from multiple sources. The source areas most probably are located in the Ohio and Mississippi drainage systems. The following discussion draws heavily from the published descriptions of chert resources in the region (House 1975b; Manger 1986; Mathis 1986; Morse 1969; Ray 1995).

Crowley's Ridge cherts are highly variable due to their secondary context; they were deposited by braided-stream activity and are blanketed by Pleistocene loess deposits. The cherts are most easily exploited from gravel beds formed by streams flowing from Crowley's Ridge.

Composition is highly variable, with chert colors including shades of brown, gray, and yellow; white and red cherts also occur, although with less frequency.

The Ozark Plateau is a dome of sedimentary bedrock that has witnessed considerable uplift and erosion. Cherts from the Ozark Plateau generally originate from the Everton, Penters, Boone, and Pitkin geologic strata. Those from the Middle Ordovician Everton formation are quartz-bearing, sometimes oolitic, white, brown, red, and gray cherts of uniform composition. The Middle Devonian Penters formation contains mottled chert that is very pale brown in color and lacks fossiliferous inclusions. Boone chert is highly variable in color and composition, frequently sharing characteristics with other cherts from the region. Pitkin chert is a distinctive, very dark gray chert that originates in the Upper Mississippian Pitkin limestone formation.

Although the diversity of chert-bearing strata suggests the potential for an abundance of readily available cherts in the Ozark Plateau, these strata make up only 13 percent of the study area's land cover. Of this, only a small fraction consists of chert-bearing deposits. The chert quarried from this region may have been extracted from the gravel beds of streams cutting through these formations, a pattern of exploitation shared with Crowley's Ridge.

The diversity of resources make it clear that the Lowlands were a great environment for hunter-gatherer occupation during the terminal Pleistocene. Unfortunately, many Paleoindian sites are currently being destroyed by the radical agricultural practices in the region. In 1994, Dan Morse and I visited several sites that had been leveled for increased agricultural productivity, including the Lace (3PO17) and Brand (3PO139) sites—two very significant Dalton sites in the region. Once rich in cultural materials, it was difficult to even locate debitage in the former site areas. Corporate farming, concerned with precision agriculture, is destroying sites in the Mississippi Valley at an unprecedented rate. The existing archaeological record for this region will become more and more important in the next century, as fieldwork becomes less productive due to site destruction.

The fact that the regional landscape was largely formed during the Pleistocene is remarkable when one considers the potential for studying the distribution of Paleoindian sites across the study area. Unfortunately, depositional sequences have been modest at best during the past 15,000 years, so we have a Paleoindian record that is dominated by surface finds lacking the stratigraphy necessary for chronological control. Therefore the chronology adopted here relies upon evidence from surrounding regions.

The primary diagnostic artifacts of the Paleoindian period include variants of Clovis, Folsom-like Sedgwick, basally-thinned/fluted Pelican, and traditional Dalton point types. Due to the limited number of fluted points with site provenience, sites yielding these distinctive artifacts were combined to form an "early" data set for comparison with the later Dalton site distributions. It is assumed here that local fluted-point technology represents the period from 11,200 to 10,700 rcbp, followed by the Dalton cultural expression from 10,700 to 10,200 rcbp (Goodyear 1982; Haynes 1992; Morse 1997b).

Extant Models of Paleoindian Settlement

Early attempts to characterize the prehistory of the lower Mississippi Valley failed to identify the richness of the Paleoindian record there (Griffin 1952; Jennings 1952; Phillips et al. 1951). This was primarily due to the nature of archaeological survey in the first half of the century. Although Woodland and Mississippian mounds were easily identified, buried and forested Paleoindian and Archaic sites had very limited archaeological visibility.

The Ford-Redfield Dalton Survey was the first to target the earliest cultures of the region (Redfield 1970, 1971; Redfield and Moselage 1970). This project revealed the potential of the region for understanding the development of Dalton culture. Paleoindian fluted points, Dalton points, and San Patrice points were identified and their distributions delineated within the project area. The occurrence of fluted points remained poorly understood, but general patterns in distribution of Dalton and San Patrice materials were recognized. Dalton artifacts were most common in the northern portion of the survey area, from southeastern Missouri to east-central Arkansas, while San Patrice artifacts were found to occur most commonly in the southern portion, from east-central Arkansas to northeastern Louisiana.

After the Ford-Redfield survey, interest in the Paleoindian record of the region continued to grow (e.g., Perino 1965; Williams 1965). Dan Morse and his colleagues have given meaning to the Dalton culture over the past 30 years. In addition to identifying the diversity of the Dalton tool kit, Morse developed a complex model of Dalton settlement in the Lowlands of northeastern Arkansas. Morse's model inspired a long-standing controversy, and there remain two contrasting Dalton settlement models for the region: D. Morse's (1970, 1971a, 1973, 1975a, 1975b, 1977a, 1977b, 1997b; Morse and Morse 1983) single drainage model, and Schiffer's (1975a, 1975b) mobile cross-drainage settlement model. Morse maintains that Dalton settlement centered around single drainage systems and that band-level territories of at least 7 bands may be delineated in the region (fig. 5.1). Site types proposed by Morse include long-term base camps, hunting and gathering loci, quarries, and cemeteries. Support for the Morse model has come primarily from his own fieldwork, including the recently published report on the Sloan site, a Dalton cemetery in the Cache River Basin (Morse 1975b, 1997a, 1997b). The diversity of Dalton site types in the region and ethnographic analogy formed the basis for Morse's model. Unfortunately, only limited excavations were ever conducted at a hypothesized base camp, namely the Lace site (Redfield and Moselage 1970). The lack of controlled excavation at a proposed base camp is the "missing link" needed to verify Morse's model.

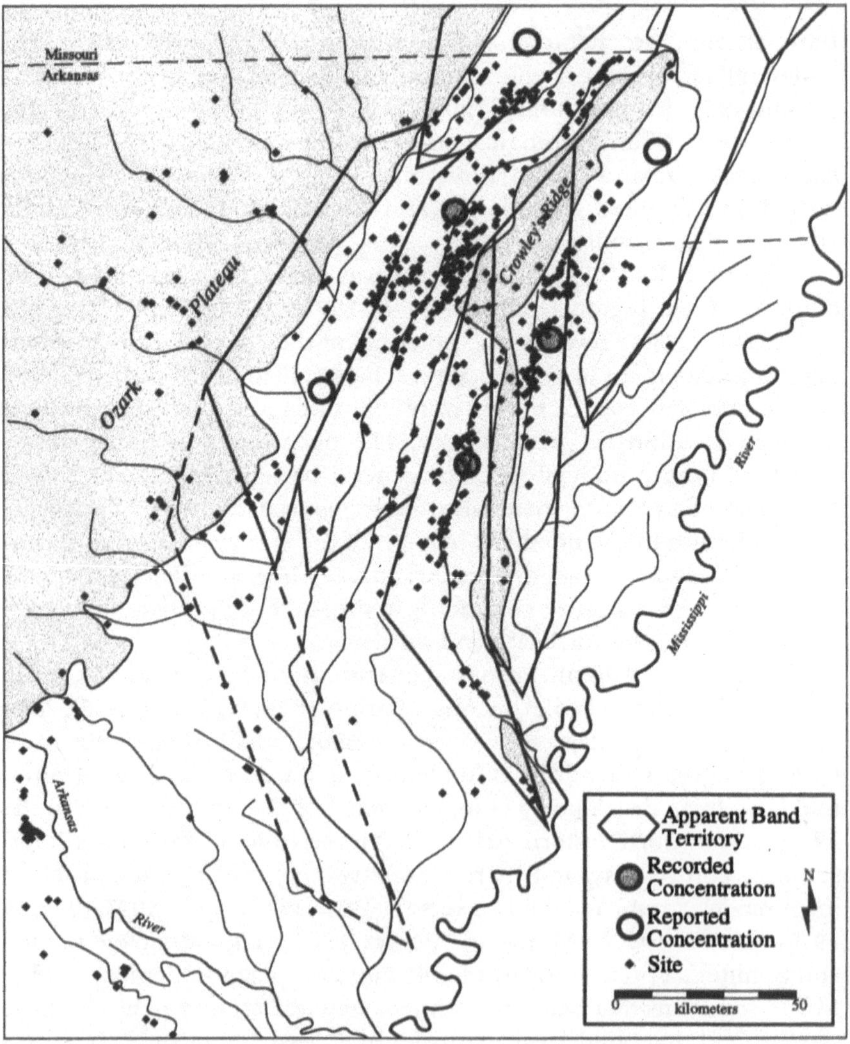

FIGURE 5.1. Morse's model of Dalton settlement compared to the actual distribution of sites. Note the close correspondence of sites to the hypothesized territories (after Gillam 1996b).

Schiffer (1975a, 1975b) considered Dalton settlement to be more generalized than Morse proposed, suggesting that band-level territories crosscut drainages to exploit contrasting environmental zones, and that these territories are best represented by regularly spaced hexagons (fig. 5.2). Sites that Morse interpreted as long-term base camps are simply sites that were frequently reoccupied under Schiffer's model. Schiffer also believed that sites such as hunting loci would be archaeologically

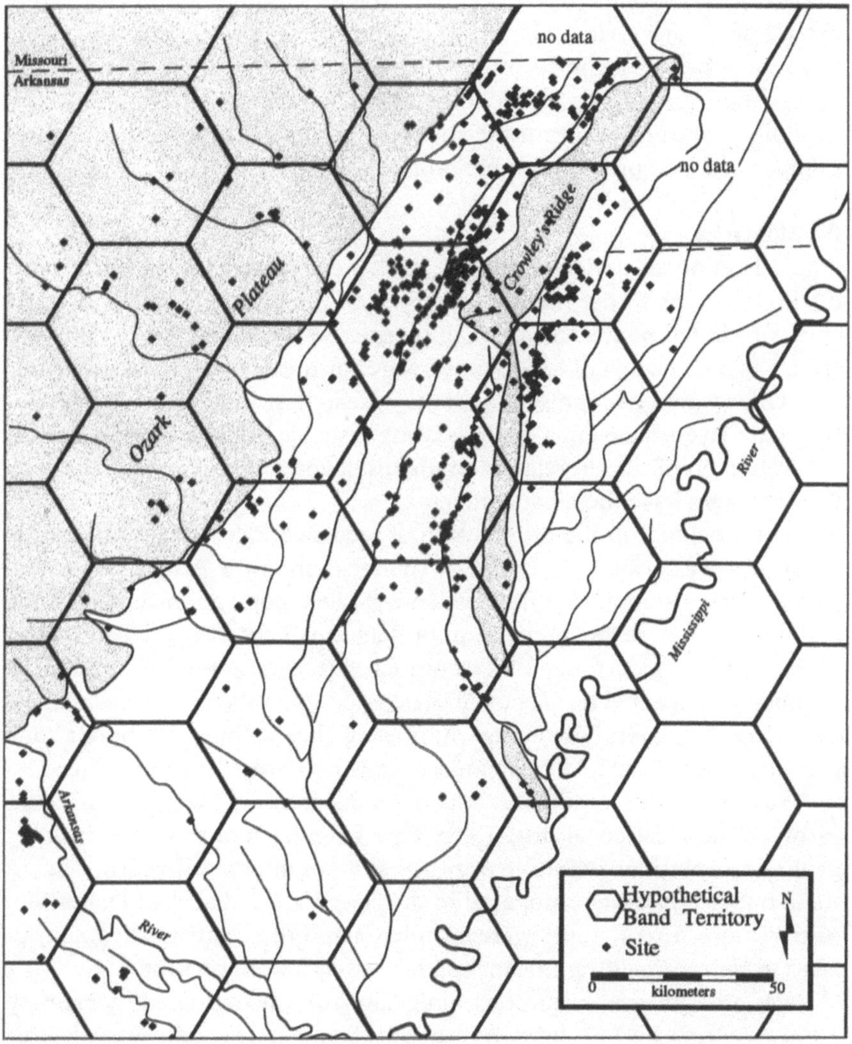

FIGURE 5.2. Schiffer's model of Dalton settlement compared to the actual distribution of sites. Note that the hexagonal territories do not match the clustered distribution of sites. (after Gillam 1996b).

"invisible." Partial support for Schiffer's hypothesis was presented in the Cache River survey report (House et al. 1975) and by Price and Krakker (1975) for the Ozark border in southeastern Missouri.

As a graduate student at the University of Arkansas, my thesis research examined the distribution of early Paleoindian and Dalton sites in the study area (Gillam 1995, 1996a, 1996b). That research demonstrated the significance of the Crowley's Ridge landform to Paleoindian settlement in the Lowlands. Distributional analysis revealed that Paleoindian settlement centered on the Crowley's Ridge landform, rarely extending greater than 30 km from its lithic resources, despite the occurrence and use of lithic resources in neighboring regions. It was concluded that the combined richness of the Lowlands environment and local lithic resources permitted the development and spread of Dalton populations into previously unexploited areas.

Methods

Central to an understanding of settlement patterns is the correlation of site locations to the natural resources of the region. Sixty-eight early sites with fluted points and 767 Dalton sites were evaluated in the analysis (figs. 5.3, 5.4) using GRASS GIS software for the various spatial analyses. The GIS operations represented in this research include reclassification of base data layers, proximity analysis using distance buffers, and the statistical evaluation of sites in relation to the distance buffers. Most raster-based GIS packages have these capabilities.

Potential bias in the distribution of recorded Paleoindian sites in the study area was evaluated relative to the location of the Arkansas Archeological Survey station in Jonesboro and modern population centers in the region. From these locations, 1 km buffers were calculated, radiating outward, and site occurrences were compared to each zone. From the total number, an expected frequency of sites based upon the area of each buffer zone was calculated. The actual number of sites within each buffer zone was then used to calculate chi-square statistics to test for significance.

Similarly, examining the spatial relationship of sites to lithic resources involved the creation of distance buffers from each of the chert-bearing geologic formations radiating outward at 5 km intervals. In turn, each of these buffer layers was compared to the early Paleoindian and Dalton site distributions. Frequencies were calculated and then statistically manipulated to determine if significant spatial patterns were present.

Variation in site location within drainages was evaluated by creating 1 km distance buffers from rivers. Site frequencies again were determined and statistically evaluated for significance. This part of the analysis was designed to reveal patterns of seasonal variation in site location by providing evidence of bottomland versus upland land use.

Results

Evaluation of Site Distribution Bias

Sample bias is always a concern in archaeological research. The archaeological "visibility" of sites may not be assumed to represent the actual distribution under most circumstances. Therefore, methods for evaluating the bias of site distribution across the region were developed using

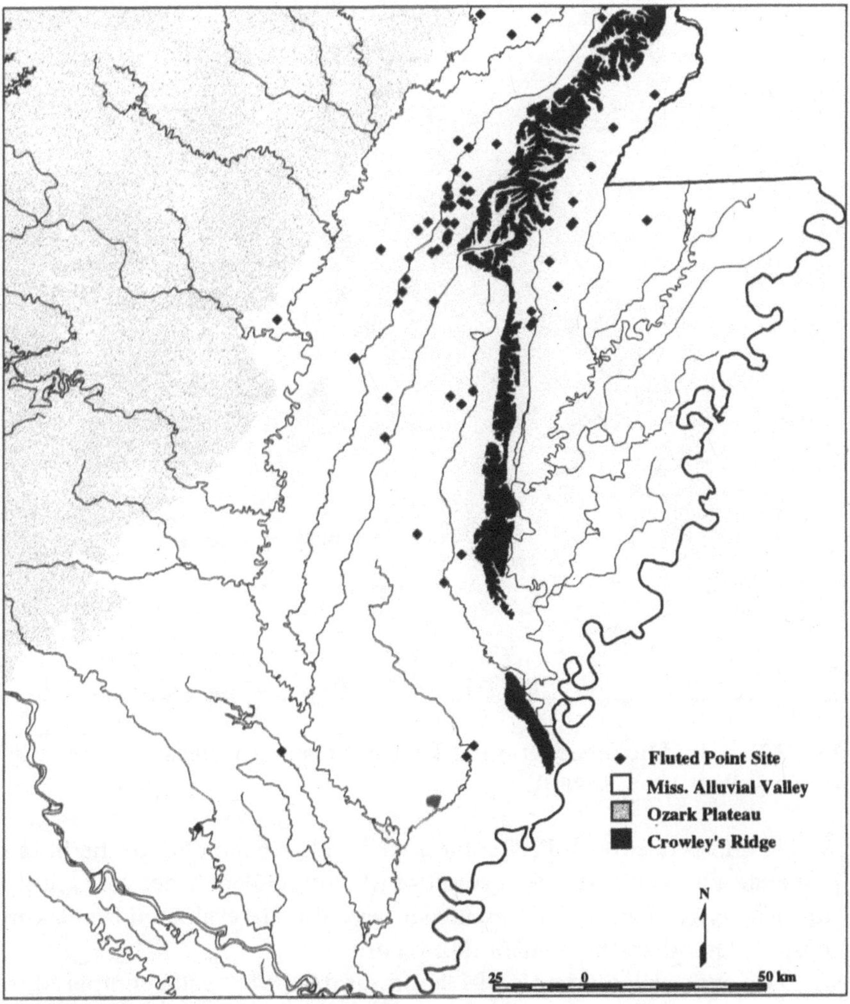

FIGURE 5.3. The distribution of early Paleoindian sites containing fluted points in northeastern Arkansas (after Gillam 1995, 1996a, 1996b).

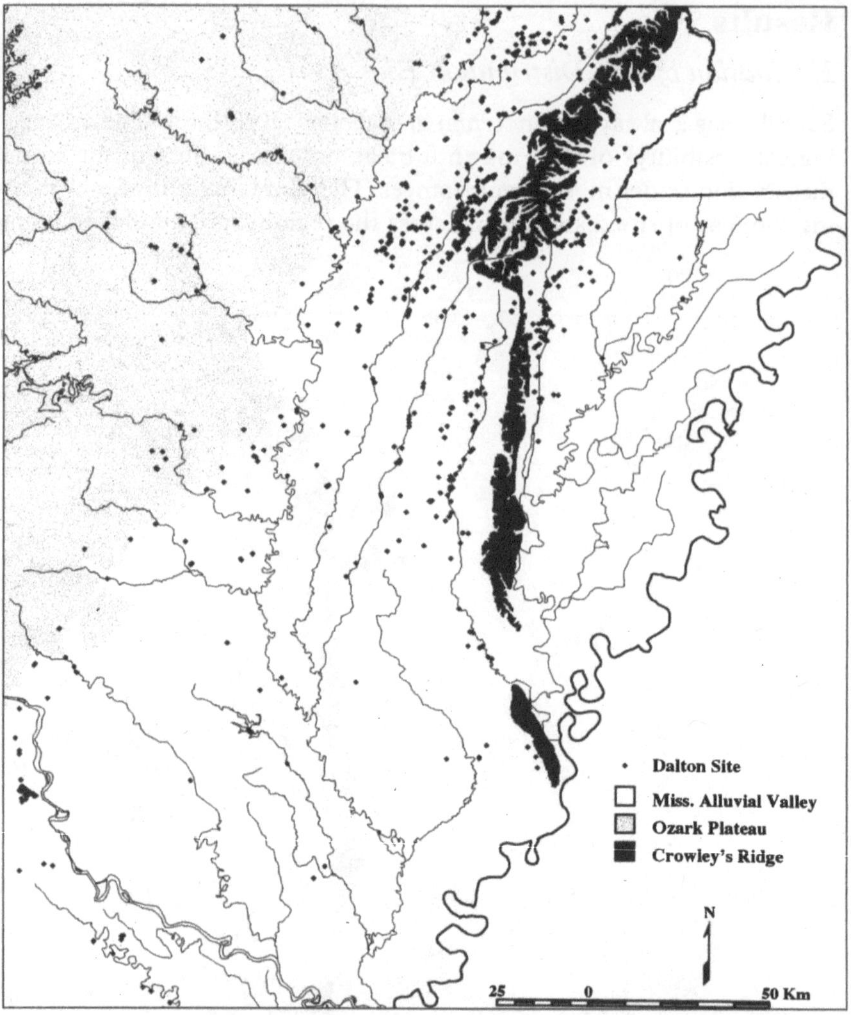

FIGURE 5.4. The distribution of Dalton sites in northeastern Arkansas (after Gillam 1995, 1996b).

simple GIS procedures. Particular attention has been paid to the fluted point sample, as it is largely a result of Morse's collector network within northeastern Arkansas. Systematic surveys also are evaluated in relation to the Paleoindian site distribution record.

The early Paleoindian and Dalton samples were each compared to the location of the Arkansas Archeological Survey (AAS) station at Arkansas State University, Jonesboro. A data layer of distance buffers from this location was produced, and results were evaluated using chi-square tests. The patterns revealed were not unexpected considering the relative density of sites near Jonesboro. Locations of early Paleoindian and Dalton sites are not significantly clustered within 10 km of the AAS station (fig. 5.5). However, early sites were found to significantly occur between 11 to 30 km, and Dalton sites occurred in significant numbers from 11 to 50 km from the AAS station. This illustrates that significant numbers of Paleoindian sites have been identified in the surrounding region.

The significant occurrence of sites in neighboring localities is not solely due to sample bias. Rather, the concentrations of sites near Jonesboro probably reflect population preference during the Pleistocene, as this location is centrally placed along Crowley's Ridge and major stream systems. The fact that both early fluted point sites and later Dalton sites cluster at different distance ranges also suggests that the pattern is related to factors other than bias from Morse's collector network. Significantly fewer sites than expected by chance alone do not occur until distances greater than 100 km away for early sites and 80 km for Dalton sites.

The distribution of these sites in relation to modern population centers also indicates minimal bias. If the location data were biased, sites should cluster close to densely populated areas; but, again, sites are not concentrated within 10 km of population centers (fig. 5.6). Although significant numbers of both early Paleoindian and Dalton sites do occur within 11 to 20 km of modern cities, this zone represents 43 percent of the regional coverage. Moreover, these modern population centers tend to be located on landscape features, such as Crowley's Ridge and stable

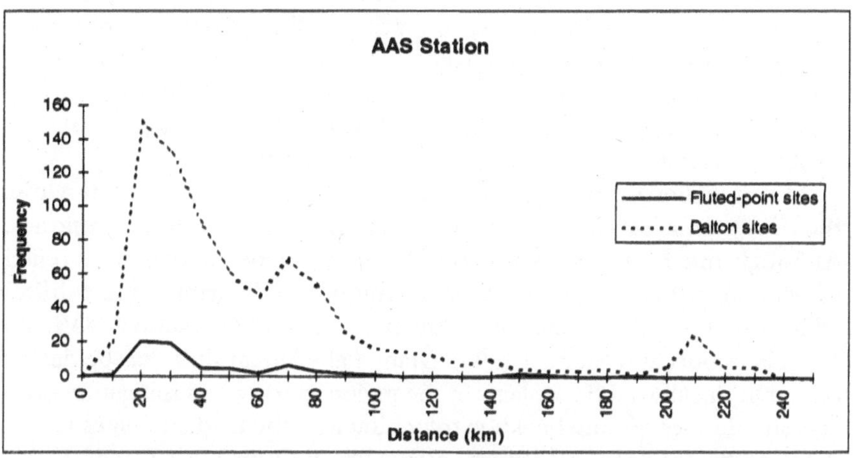

FIGURE 5.5. Distance decay graph for early Paleo-Indian and Dalton sites in relation to the AAS station in Jonesboro, Arkansas.

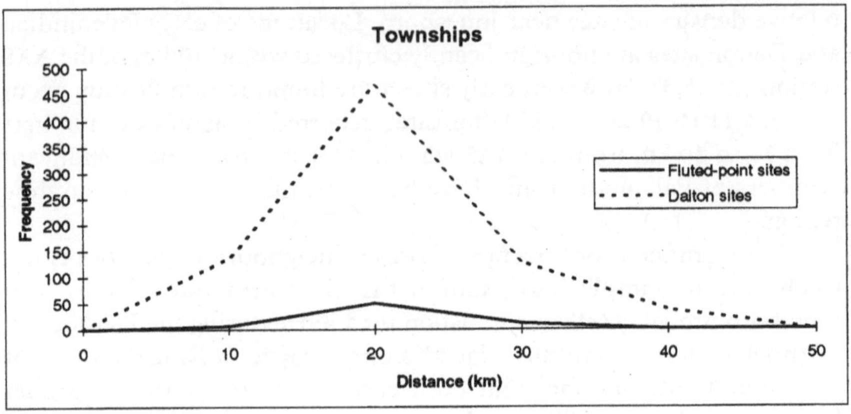

FIGURE 5.6. Distance decay graph for early Paleo-Indian and Dalton sites in relation to the towns of northeastern Arkansas

drainage systems that were important to prehistoric settlement in the region. Significantly fewer early sites than expected occur at distances greater than 30 km, and for Dalton sites, at distances greater than 20 km.

Although numerous systematic surveys have been conducted in the study area, rarely have Paleoindian sites been encountered. The most frequent Paleoindian occurrences recorded during systematic surveys have been Dalton components. During the L'Anguille River survey, only one fluted point was recovered despite the fact that this drainage lies in close proximity to Crowley's Ridge (Anderson, this volume; Anderson et al. 1989). This probably relates to the location of systematic surveys in relation to Paleoindian remains. Examination of the spatial distribution of Paleoindian sites relative to archaeological projects reveals several interesting patterns. Only four recorded fluted point sites fall within the boundaries of a systematically surveyed region. In marked contrast, 115 Dalton sites have been recorded during such surveys.

Examination of the field methods used in some survey projects across the study area reveal several problems in data recovery techniques. Although much of this area is in cultivation, many surveys have relied heavily on surface reconnaissance techniques to determine the cultural affiliation of prehistoric sites (e.g., Anderson et al. 1989; Fehon and Viscito 1974; Harcourt and Stewart 1993). Many Paleoindian sites may be deeply buried in the alluvial floodplains of the region. Survey and mitigation projects should incorporate backhoe trenching into the field strategies to test the potential for deep site deposits across the study area (see Cande 1979). Additionally, when sites are encountered during survey, they should be shovel-tested to evaluate subplow zone deposits (see Cande 1978).

Given the limited influence of sample bias in the data, the distributional analyses that follow will lead to robust interpretation. It is likely that the patterns recognized in relation to the AAS station and modern population centers reflect prehistoric settlement preferences that correspond, in part, to modern ones. The distribution of modern population centers along Crowley's Ridge and along stream systems that have remained relatively stable over the past 12,000 years creates an artificial pattern of site bias within the data set. It is likely, however, that some bias results from Morse's local collector network near Jonesboro, Arkansas. This is most severe in the early Paleoindian data set, which consists of only 68 sites.

Site Distribution and Lithic Resources

Few recorded Paleoindian sites are located near the Pitkin formation. Early Paleoindian sites do not occur in significant numbers until a distance greater than 60 km from this chert source locality (fig. 5.7). Likewise, significant numbers of Dalton sites do not occur until a distance of greater than 40 km away, and significantly fewer Dalton sites than expected by chance occur within 30 km of the Pitkin source locality.

Recorded Paleoindian sites also do not occur near the Penters exposure. Early Paleoindian sites do not occur in significant numbers until a distance of greater than 25 km (fig. 5.8), and Dalton sites only occur in significant numbers beyond 20 km in distance. Significantly fewer Dalton sites than expected by chance are located within 15 km of the Penters formation.

Paleoindian site location relative to the Everton formation demonstrates a similar relationship. The early Paleoindian sites cluster significantly at distances exceeding 20 km from the locality (fig. 5.9), while Dalton sites occur in significant numbers at distances farther than 15 km from the formation. Significantly fewer Dalton sites than expected occur within 10 km of the Everton formation.

This lack of association also holds true for Boone chert. Early Paleoindian sites only occur in significant numbers beyond 40 km from the deposits (fig. 5.10), and Dalton sites are only present in significant numbers at distances greater than 40 km from the locality. Significantly fewer Dalton sites than expected by chance occur within 30 km of the Boone formation.

Clearly, recorded Paleoindian sites are not significantly associated with the lithic sources of the Ozark Plateau. Conversely, the association of Paleoindian sites with the Crowley's Ridge landform is very robust. Early Paleoindian sites significantly occur within 15 km of the ridge, and Dalton sites cluster significantly within 25 km of the landform (fig.

5.11). Reinforcing this close association with Crowley's Ridge, significantly fewer Dalton sites occur at distances greater than 30 km from the landform.

Site Distribution in Relation to Streams

Comparison of site location to distance from major streams suggests seasonal variation in settlement by early Paleoindians. There is a bimodal distribution of sites corresponding to alternating episodes of exploitation

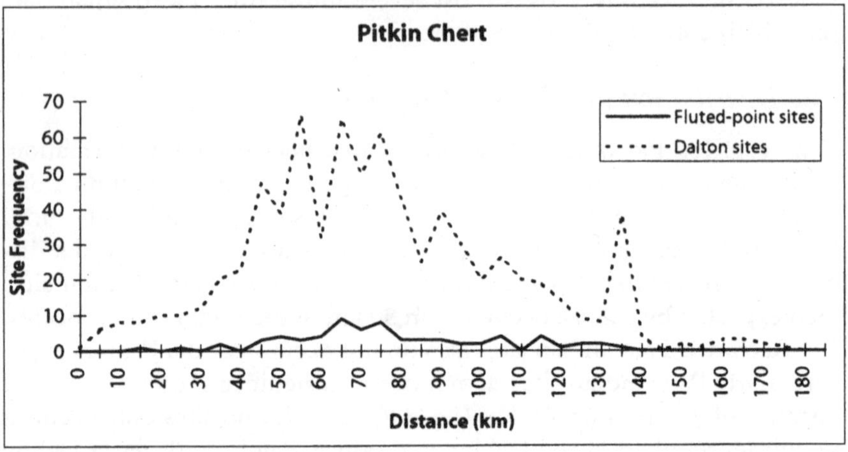

FIGURE 5.7. Distance decay graph for early Paleo-Indian and Dalton sites in relation to Pitkin chert.

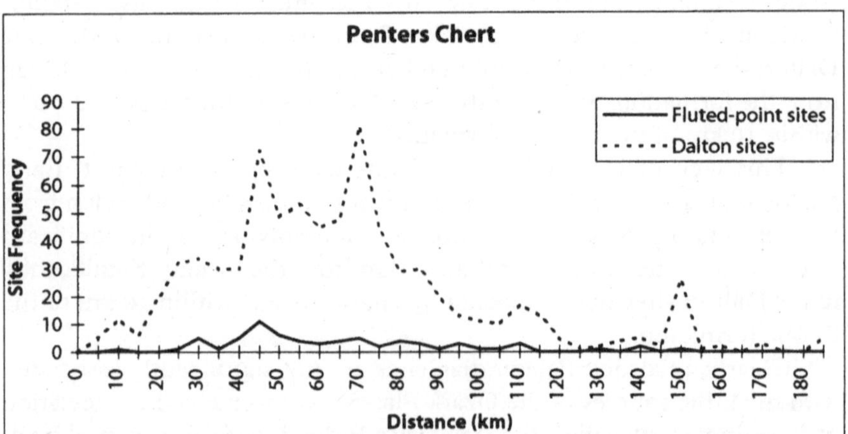

FIGURE 5.8. Distance decay graph for early Paleo-Indian and Dalton sites in relation to Penters chert.

of bottomland and upland environments (fig. 5.12). This is an interesting and unexpected finding. Very little is known about seasonal variation in Paleoindian settlement, and such variation is unexpected due to the amelioration of seasonality of the time period. Cooler and wetter than today, seasonal shifts in temperature and rainfall were less extreme in the terminal Pleistocene.

Nonetheless, a pattern suggestive of seasonal variation is present. Sites with fluted points significantly occur within 1 km of streams and

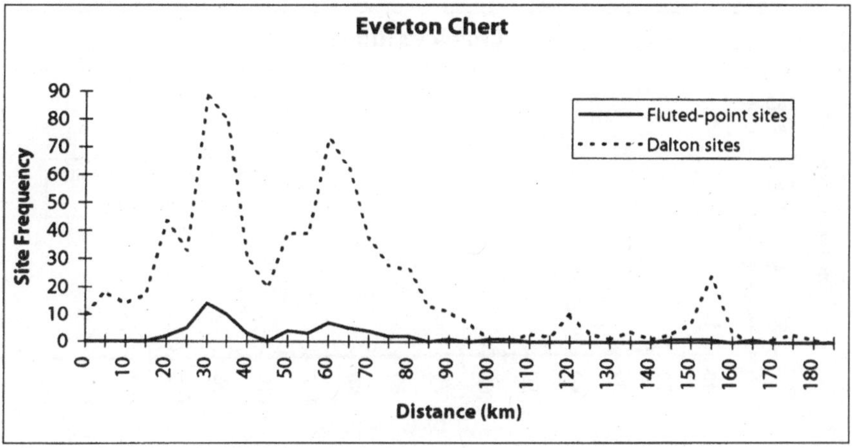

FIGURE 5.9. Distance decay graph for early Paleo-Indian and Dalton sites in relation to Everton chert.

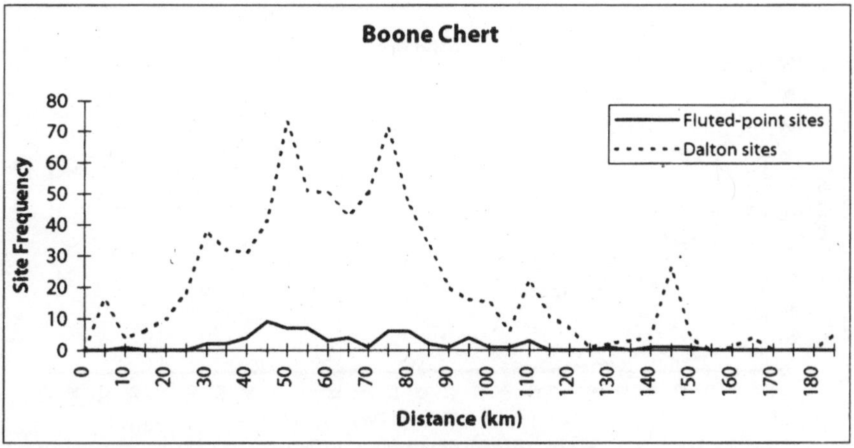

FIGURE 5.10. Distance decay graph for early Paleo-Indian and Dalton sites in relation to Boone chert.

within a zone between 3 to 4 km. This pattern is particularly strong for distributions in the Cache River Basin, where the site data are best. The concentration of sites within 1 km of streams corresponds to river terraces immediately within and adjacent to modern floodplains. These level 1 terraces contain abandoned braided-stream channels that add to the diversity of the local environment (Saucier 1997).

The zone between 3 to 4 km corresponds to the early valley train terraces and dune sand formations. These second-level terraces repre-

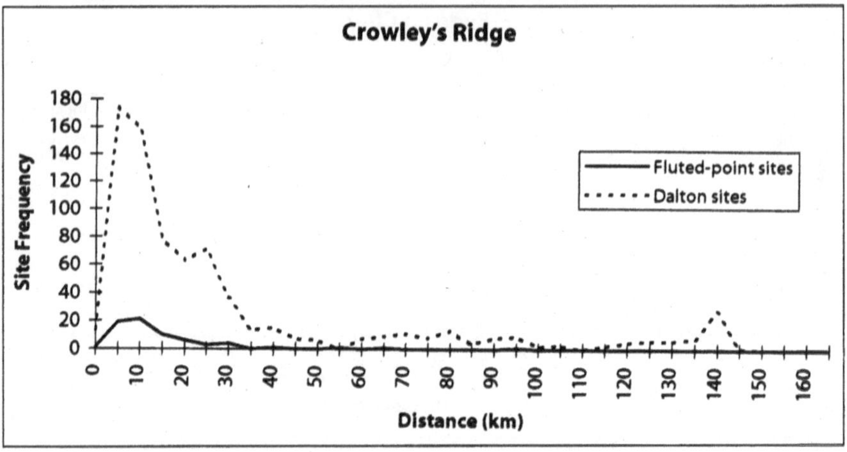

FIGURE 5.11. Distance decay graph for early Paleo-Indian and Dalton sites in relation to Crowley's Ridge chert.

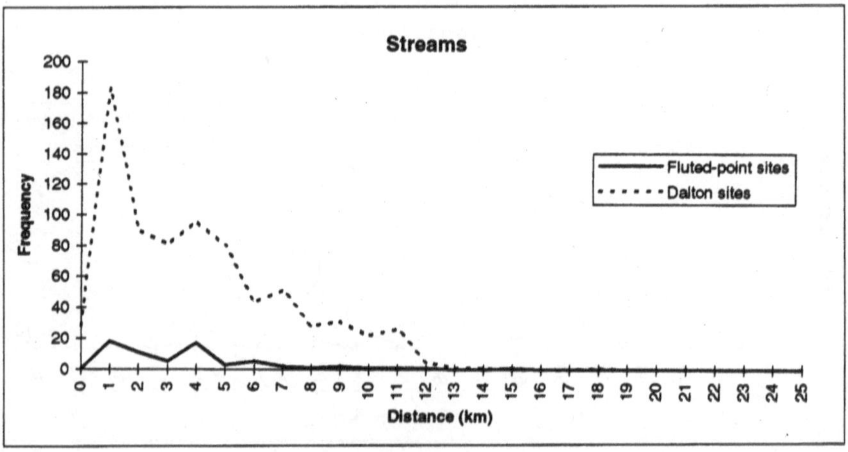

FIGURE 5.12. Distance decay graph for early Paleo-Indian and Dalton sites in relation to major streams in northeastern Arkansas.

sent an upland environment with different resources than the bottomland locations. The alternating exploitation of bottomland and upland resources further suggests that early Paleoindian populations were generalized forager-hunters.

In contrast to the early Paleoindian distribution, the Dalton data point to a riverine focus by later populations. The primary concentration of sites falls within 1 km of rivers throughout the region (fig. 5.12). Although sites are also common within 11 km of rivers, they only occur in significant numbers immediately adjacent to the water courses.

Additionally, distances greater than 11 km from streams exhibit significantly fewer Dalton sites than expected by chance. For most river basins in the study area, the zone within 11 km of the rivers encompasses the active floodplain, multiple terraces of varying age, dune sand fields, and major upland features (e.g., Crowley's Ridge and the Ozark escarpment). These localities likely consisted of different vegetation and animal communities and the neighboring landforms—Crowley's Ridge and the Ozark escarpment—additionally offered lithic resources.

Discussion

The geographic analyses revealed several interesting patterns in the distribution of Paleoindian sites across the region. Bias is present in the archaeological record, but this is not linked to the distribution of modern townships and the central location of the AAS station in Jonesboro. Major towns lie on or adjacent to major physiographic features, such as rivers and Crowley's Ridge, and are evenly distributed throughout the region. The AAS station is located on Crowley's Ridge, near the geographic centroid of this prominent landscape feature.

Comparisons of early Paleoindian and Dalton sites relative to lithic resources of the Ozark Plateau verify that these resources were of secondary importance compared to those of Crowley's Ridge. Only Crowley's Ridge, with its cherty gravel deposits, has significant frequencies of sites in surrounding localities. Thus, early Paleoindian and Dalton populations shared a pattern of lithic exploitation centered upon the Crowley's Ridge landform. The significance of Crowley's Ridge is such that settlement focused on the major river systems in the immediate neighborhood of the landform.

A pattern of seasonal variation was revealed in the early Paleoindian record of the region; this was unexpected due to the mild character of seasonal variation during the terminal Pleistocene. Apparently summers were cooler and wetter and winters were cooler and dryer than that of today. Thus, the bimodal distribution of sites corresponding to an alternating pattern of exploitation of bottomland and upland resources is surprising.

Early Paleoindian data are strongest in the Cache River Basin, where 50 percent of the sites (n=34) are recorded. The model presented below focuses on the Cache River Basin but may be generally applicable to most drainages in the region. I suggest that early Paleoindians alternated their base camp locations on a seasonal basis (fig. 5.13). During the spring and summer months, these early peoples occupied the bottomlands and lower-terrace, remnant braided-stream environment. The bottomlands would have provided access to aquatic resources, as well as terrestrial species of plants and animals. Short-term extraction sites would be plentiful throughout this environment, but these probably produced minimal artifact residues. In the fall and winter, the bands moved to more upland environments, particularly the second-level terraces and dune sand fields of the study area, where nut mast and terrestrial fauna would have been plentiful. Close proximity to Crowley's Ridge would have facilitated the replenishment of stone tools. Hunting and gathering activities likely occurred on Crowley's Ridge as well, although few early Paleoindian sites have been recorded there. Short-term extraction sites involving hunting, gathering, and tool kit renewal likely occurred throughout the uplands.

The riverine focus of Dalton sites provides support for Morse's model of Dalton settlement in the region. Under the Loschian model of Schiffer, it is expected that sites would be evenly distributed across environmental zones in the region (fig. 5.2), but Dalton sites only occur in significant numbers within 1 km of the major river systems. This pattern

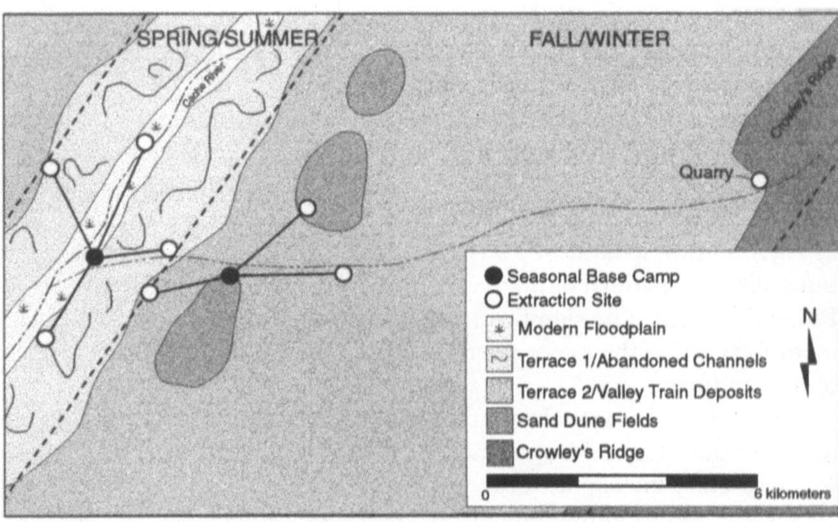

FIGURE 5.13. A model of early Paleo-Indian settlement on a hypothetical landscape in the Cache River Basin.

fits Morse's single drainage, base camp hypothesis rather well (fig. 5.1). Short-term, extractive activities are inferred from the numerous, yet insignificant, occurrences of sites in adjacent environments. Many more extraction sites likely are present, but remain unidentified due to the limited archaeological visibility of the deposits. Lithic artifacts testify to exploitation of lithic resources in the neighboring Ozark Plateau by Dalton people. Yet, significant numbers of Dalton sites do not occur adjacent to these lithic resources. This further supports the notion that short-term extractive activities were a regular part of Dalton lifeways, and that long-term settlement was primarily focused on rivers in the Lowlands region near the Crowley's Ridge landform.

Conclusion

This chapter has demonstrated the degree of integrity of the northeast Arkansas Paleoindian site data, examined the interrelatedness of Paleoindian settlement and Crowley's Ridge, revealed the seasonal character of site distributions resulting in a model of early Paleoindian settlement, and provided support for Morse's model of Dalton settlement by verifying the riverine focus of Dalton site location. The methods of analysis involved simple GIS analytical routines that can be replicated by most commercial GIS software. The analyses incorporated basic environmental data with the archaeological data gathered by Morse and others conducting research in northeastern Arkansas over the past 30 years.

The Dalton data are clearly the most robust, having some 767 sites represented. The early Paleoindian data are limited to 68 sites but are complete enough for the development of a general model of settlement within the region. Early Paleoindian and Dalton populations maintained close proximity to the Crowley's Ridge landform. The cherty gravels of this ridge provided an expedient source of stone for the replenishment of tool kits.

Early Paleoindians, exhibiting fluted-point technology, alternated their site locations on a seasonal basis. In the spring and summer, bottomland and lower-level terrace environments were primarily exploited. During the fall and winter, upland locations, including second-level terraces, dune sand fields, and Crowley's Ridge, were occupied. This pattern of seasonal exploitation of regional resources is an exciting discovery and warrants further research.

Dalton settlement centered on the river systems adjacent to Crowley's Ridge. Most sites are immediately adjacent to the river floodplains with fewer sites occurring throughout the surrounding region. This pattern supports Morse's Dalton settlement model for the region by verifying the riverine focus of the period.

By way of future directions, a survey of the primary chert outcrops in the Ozark Plateau is desperately needed. The actual occurrences of chert in the geologic strata used to measure distances in this study are much more restricted than the geographical extent of these formations, and this may introduce considerable error in evaluating the quarry behavior of prehistoric populations with a spatial methodology. Once identified, the quarry locations could be easily mapped using a GPS receiver. The primary outcrops are particularly important because secondary gravel beds along streams, such as those mapped by Mathis (1986), may or may not correspond to prehistoric source areas. Locations also should be recorded for quarry areas along the Crowley's Ridge landform.

Likewise, a comparative study of the chert gravels from Crowley's Ridge and those from the Ozark escarpment of Arkansas and Missouri may appreciably increase our ability to assign an appropriate source to artifacts recovered in the Lowlands and adjacent regions. Ray (1995) is currently working toward this goal. Unless distinctive characteristics can be identified, I propose that the source for artifacts made of extralocal cherts be assigned based on the minimum distance criteria. If evidence exists that these cherts were acquired through trade or some other cultural mechanism, not direct acquisition, the source assignment could then be modified.

The seasonal variation of early Paleoindian settlement needs further scrutiny. Effort must be maintained to record the location of fluted-point artifact finds in the study area. Without better distribution data, this model will be difficult to verify. Sites containing early materials need to be identified and excavated so that a comparison of the full range of associated cultural material can be made. The seasonal variation of site location should also correspond to variation in site-specific artifact components.

Acknowledgment

This research would not have been possible if not for the career-long commitment of Dan and Phyllis Morse to maintain the Paleoindian record of northeast Arkansas. The support and encouragement of Mark J. Brooks and Bruce Rippeteau at the South Carolina Institute of Archeology and Anthropology is gratefully acknowledged. Most data used in this study were derived from the Arkansas Archeological Survey's AMASDA database. My appreciation is extended to Malcolm Williamson and the Center for Advanced Spatial Technologies, University of Arkansas, for supplying a compiled version of the GRASS GIS software for this research. I thank Robert Mainfort, Marvin Jeter, and David Anderson for providing comments on drafts of this paper.

CHAPTER SIX

THE TOLTEC (KNAPP) MOUNDS GROUP IN THE NINETEENTH CENTURY

MARTHA ANN ROLINGSON

Research on large archaeological sites with mounds and other architectural features is often enhanced by examining information and descriptions in early reports. These early descriptions provide views of the features that can no longer be observed because the earthworks have been altered and damaged during the past 200 years. In the eastern United States the large mounds and monuments fascinated travelers, traders, explorers, and historians. Interest during the eighteenth and nineteenth centuries was directed toward the question of who had built the mounds, since most of the Indian tribes were not, at that time, doing so. As a result of this interest, sites with mounds were described in various reports (Willey and Sabloff 1974:21–41). By the 1840s, expeditions were undertaken to investigate and describe architecture and monuments in a systematic manner. These reports, the most notable of which is *Ancient Monuments of the Mississippi Valley* by E. G. Squier and E. H. Davis (1848), provided maps based on measurements and detailed descriptions (Willey and Sabloff 1974:42–50). Other reports are in obscure publications or are unpublished notes in museum archives, and their discovery may be serendipitous to other research.

The importance of these earlier works to modern research is evident in the fact that the nineteenth-century reports continue to be cited and are being reissued. Data from early descriptions of the Cahokia site in Illinois beginning in the early nineteenth century have been integral to the modern research (Fowler 1989). Phyllis Morse (1981:20–21), in her report on the Parkin site in Arkansas, made use of the descriptive reports of Edwin Curtiss for the Peabody Museum, Harvard University, and publications by Clarence B. Moore of the Academy of Natural Sciences of Philadelphia. In a preface to the reissue of Moore's reports on his two expeditions to the Moundville site in Alabama, Knight (1996:vii–viii) pointed out the continuing importance of the Moore volumes to site research. The analysis of the community pattern at the Macon Plateau site in Georgia made use of late-nineteenth-century descriptions (Hally and Williams 1994).

Late-nineteenth-century descriptions of the Toltec Mounds site (3LN42) in central Arkansas have been incorporated into the modern research (Rolingson 1982b, 1998). This site has been considered a well-known local landmark since the early nineteenth century and, as a result, was described by several archaeologists and other visitors. The best known and most readily available of the early descriptions of Toltec (then known as the Knapp Mounds) is that of Cyrus Thomas, published in 1894, in his *Report on the Mound Explorations of the Bureau of Ethnology.* Thomas began his description with the opinion that "These works form, without doubt, the most interesting group in the state, and, in fact, one of the most important in the United States" (Thomas 1894:243). Since that time the site has been damaged and altered by farming operations, so much so that when the Toltec Mounds research project began in 1976 the site did not closely resemble Thomas's description. As a result, his description of the mounds and plat of the site (Thomas 1894:plate X) have been significant to the development of the concept of what the site may have looked like in the late nineteenth century.

Information from descriptions by travelers, the landowner, archaeologists, and local historians have accumulated slowly in the research files, providing significant information. The descriptions varied in quality and amount of detail, and they must be considered in the context of the time in which they were made and compared against other descriptions to gain useful information from them. Some of these descriptions have been discussed previously (Jeter 1990b; Rolingson 1982b), but others have not. In this chapter, all of the known descriptions from the nineteenth century are discussed and the site is placed in historical context beginning with the 1790s and ending in 1908.

The Toltec Mounds site is located on the bank of an oxbow lake of an ancestral channel of the Arkansas River (Rolingson 1982b, 1990). Today this location is 3 miles from the left bank of the river and 16 miles from Little Rock on the opposite side of the river from the city. The site (fig. 6.1) encompasses about 100 acres (40 hectares) and is delineated by an earthen embankment and exterior ditch forming an oval boundary on three sides, with the oxbow lake on the fourth side. Portions of the embankment and ditch are still present, but are not prominent features. Only three mounds are prominent today, with heights of 49 feet (15 m), 39 feet (11.5 m), and 12 feet (4.2 m). Most of the other mounds have been plowed down and smoothed over or have been leveled and used as sources of fill both on and off the site. Recent research has established the probable location of 18 mounds arranged in a rectangular pattern. Excavations have been conducted on six of the mounds, all of which still have layers of fill preserved.

The earliest known descriptions of the site are from travelers in the region in 1812 and in 1819. Arkansas Post had been established in 1686 by the French on the lower Arkansas River (fig. 6.2) near the Quapaw village of Osotouy for the purpose of trade with the Indians and to establish the French presence in this part of Louisiana (Arnold 1991). The post was under the administration of the French colonial government in New Orleans. Louisiana was ceded to Spain in 1762 but was returned to France in 1800. France then sold Louisiana in late 1803 to the U.S. government, which took control in 1804. Arkansas Post had a small population of soldiers and settlers. The population increased slightly in the late eighteenth century, with the greatest increase after 1790. By 1798 there were 120 households enumerated in the census, most of them French

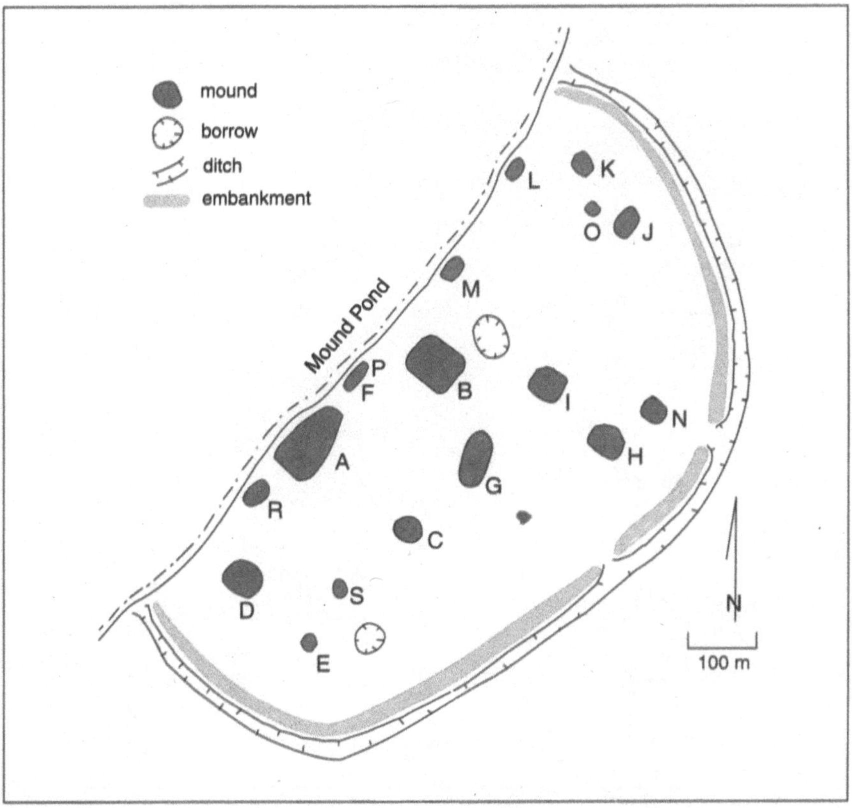

FIGURE 6.1. Map of the Toltec Mounds site, with mound locations established by research between 1977 to 1996.

(Arnold 1985:98–99). Residents were primarily families of hunters, some of whom did a little farming. These hunters undoubtedly explored much of the country around the lower Arkansas River, even though such exploration and knowledge cannot be documented.

Louis Bringier was a Frenchman who traveled widely in Upper Louisiana from 1810 to 1812, apparently as a result of gambling losses in New Orleans (Williams 1989:108–12). Born in 1773 in France, Louis was the eldest son of Emanuel Marius Pons Bringier, a prominent and wealthy citizen of Louisiana. Documents in the official records from Arkansas Post establish his presence in Arkansas as early as November 29, 1810, and as late as August 18, 1812 (Williams 1989:110–11). He was interested in minerals, the potential for production, and the native peoples. He was in the New Madrid, Missouri, area on January 6, 1812, during the famous earthquakes (Bringier 1821:20), and he explored the Hot Springs area, among other places. He wrote a description of what he had seen in the form of a letter that was published in 1821 in the *American Journal of*

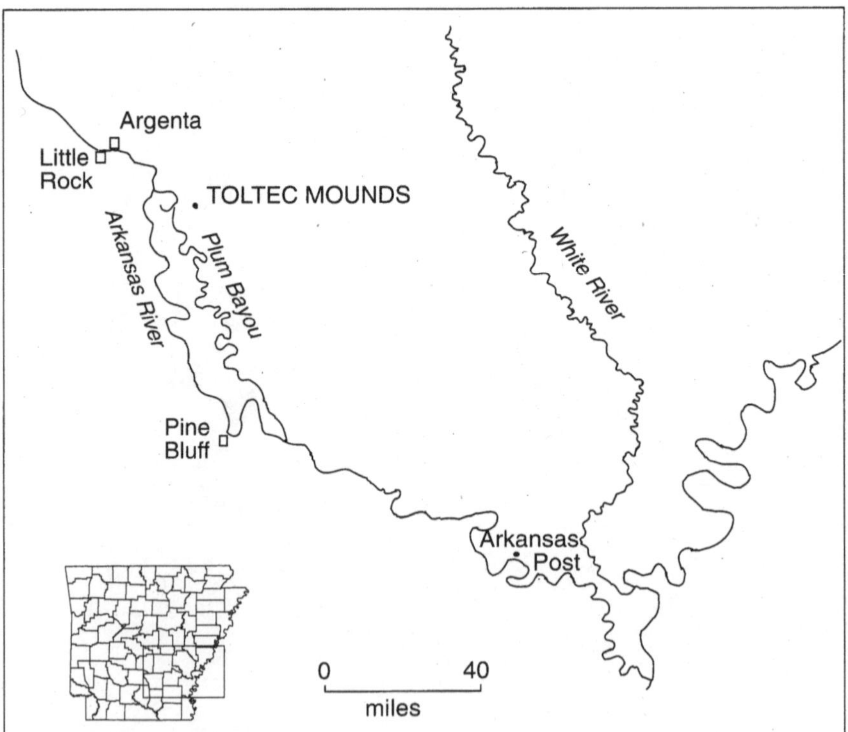

FIGURE 6.2. Lower Arkansas and White Rivers, with locations of nineteenth-century settlements.

Science and Arts, edited by Benjamin Silliman of Yale University. The correspondence was dated March 20, 1818, and was not a travel narrative but a series of topics entitled "Notices of the Geology, Mineralogy, Topography, Productions, and Aboriginal inhabitants of the regions around the Mississippi and its confluent waters" (Bringier 1821).

Bringier's description identified the site as an "ancient fortification . . . within two miles from the banks of the Arkansas" (Bringier 1821: 37–38; Williams 1989:132–33) and said:

> This fortification is tolerably regular, covering an area of about twenty-five acres; the trenches remain about eight feet high, and the ditches which are nearly filled up, seem to have been very deep, and about twenty-five feet wide. There are two gateways, in the inside of which there is a large well, which probably was a covered way; and in the centre there are two mounds about eighty feet in height, whose bases are about three hundred feet in diameter, with a truncated summit offering a surface of about ninety feet across. Both are artificial, and perhaps were formed from the dirt of the ditches. The country around is perfectly level.

His figure for the acreage within the embankment was low—just 25 acres, while it is now considered 95 acres. The heights of the two large mounds, at 80 feet, were considerably more than the 49 feet and 39 feet measured today and may represent slope lengths rather than actual heights. It is now difficult to know what he meant by a "large well" and "a covered way," although the two openings in the embankment or "gateways" were still deep enough to hold water most of the year into the 1970s, and thus they may have been thought of as a well. This description of the site likely resulted from a personal visit by Bringier, as he seems to have been familiar with the region.

An interesting sidelight about Bringier is that he returned to Arkansas in 1816 with a group of men on a mission organized by the pirate Jean Lafitte (Williams 1989:112). The official objective of this expedition was mining, and Bringier bought a preemption claim on land west of Crystal Hill near the mouth of Palarm Creek, upstream from present-day North Little Rock. Bringier built a sawmill, the remnants of which were a local landmark for travelers on the river. The location of his presumed silver mine has not been identified (Williams 1989:113–14).

The second early-nineteenth-century description was made by Thomas Nuttall, a botanist (Lottinville 1980). Originally from England, Nuttall (1786–1859) came to America, to Philadelphia, in 1808. He was interested mainly in plants and secondarily in the manners and customs of Indians. By 1810 he began a long career in scientific expeditions to discover and describe plants. Nuttall published a number of books on plant taxonomy and became a lecturer and curator of the Cambridge

Botanical Garden of Harvard University (Lottinville 1980:ix–xxiv). One of his expeditions was up the Arkansas River in 1819, the account of which was published in 1821 as *A Journal of Travels into the Arkansas Territory during the Year 1819, with Occasional Observations on the Manners of the Aborigines* (Lottinville 1980).

Near the mouth of Plum Bayou was the residence of Lewismore Vaugine, the son of a French gentleman who had held a position under the Spanish government (Lottinville 1980:108–9). At that time Plum Bayou entered the Arkansas River some 10 miles (more or less) downstream from a cluster of houses at the location of present-day Pine Bluff. At Vaugine's place, Nuttall recorded:

> Fifteen miles above this place, Monsieur Vaugin informed me of the remains of an aboriginal station of considerable extent, resembling a triangular fort, which the Quapaws on their first arrival in this country say, was inhabited by a people who were white, and partly civilized, but whom, at length, they conquered by strategem. The hunters possess an opinion, by no means singular, that this embankment is of antediluvial origin (Lottinville 1980:109).

This description of the site is minimal, but the embankment is unique to Toltec Mounds and there is no other site nearby that could be confused with this one. This description also indicated the Quapaws were familiar with the site. The direction "above" in this case, probably meant north or up Plum Bayou rather than the Arkansas River. The distance of 15 miles was not a correct distance across land, which was about 25 miles; the distance by water, however, was much greater. The land bordering Plum Bayou is relatively high in elevation, interspersed with swamps, and would have been relatively dry and accessible part of the year. In 1892, local residents at the village of Toltec reported that the land around the site and village remained several feet above the higher than average overflow that spring, nor had it been covered by the great flood of 1844 (*Arkansas Gazette,* June 19, 1892, 3).

Labeling the site a "fortification" in the descriptions of Bringier and Nuttall was probably based on the similarity in appearance of the exterior ditch and inner earthen embankment to military fortifications and battlefield entrenchments of the eighteenth century. Neither description provides much useful information in terms of archaeological details. Nevertheless, it is noteworthy that the site apparently was commonly known at this time, although there is no evidence that anyone lived on it. The General Land Office (GLO) survey of Township 1 South and Range 10 West, Pulaski County (Chastain 1827), in which the site is located, was made in 1827, just eight years after Nuttall's trip. On the survey map, the oxbow lake adjacent to the site was labeled "lake mound pond," indicating general knowledge of the site at that time. In fact, the section line crosses one of the big mounds, but the mound was not indicated on the plat. No mention of the mounds was made in the GLO notes, but notation of cultural features was not included in the instructions to surveyors at that time.

Nuttall's journal provided information about the settlement of the lower Arkansas River in his identification of the locations of homes for a number of families, many of whom he named. The position of the river has changed during the past 175 years, both in the normal course of events for a meandering river and by the efforts of the U.S. Army Corps of Engineers to control the channel for navigation. The GLO township plats show the location of the river in the 1820s and 1830s when the township and section lines were surveyed, although some townships were resurveyed in the 1850s. The segment of river of most interest here is between the location where Plum Bayou joined the Arkansas River, downstream from Pine Bluff, and the cluster of houses at present-day Little Rock. In 1819, Nuttall noted 18 families, both French and English, along this segment. Some of the same names were recorded in the GLO surveys. Unfortunately, many of these locations have been destroyed by the shifting river.

The dates of filing for patents on land in Township 1 South Range 10 West began in 1830, and most patents in this township were filed during the 1830s (Bureau of Land Management 1993). There is, of course, no assumption here that the locations of land patents in the 1830s are the same as where people were living in 1819; nevertheless, they are useful as an indication of land settlement patterns. Peter E. LeFave (LeFevre) filed on land in 1837 on the left bank of the Arkansas River in Sections 18 and 19 T1S R10W, 3 miles west of the Toltec Mounds site. Peter LeFave's property was adjacent to a bend of the river where Reeds Landing was located in the 1880s (fig. 6.3). This is approximately the location where Nuttall (Lottinville 1980:114) reported the "Jean Le Feve" (LeFevre) family and a second LeFeve family. In the 1830s, five LeFeve/LeFevre brothers (John B., Acan, Ambrose, Egnace [Ignace], and Francis G.), in addition to Peter, filed on lands between Toltec and Argenta (North Little Rock) on the left bank of the river (Allen and McLane 1991a). Four censuses taken at Arkansas Post during the 1790s record Pierre LeFevre and his family in residence (Arnold and Core 1986:43–91). Pierre was the father of the men who settled in the 1830s.

While specific locations of residences may have been easily changed, a number of French families had considerable stability in the region. Through the 1700s, settlers kept close to Arkansas Post. The Osage were hostile to the French hunters, killing or depriving them of their deer

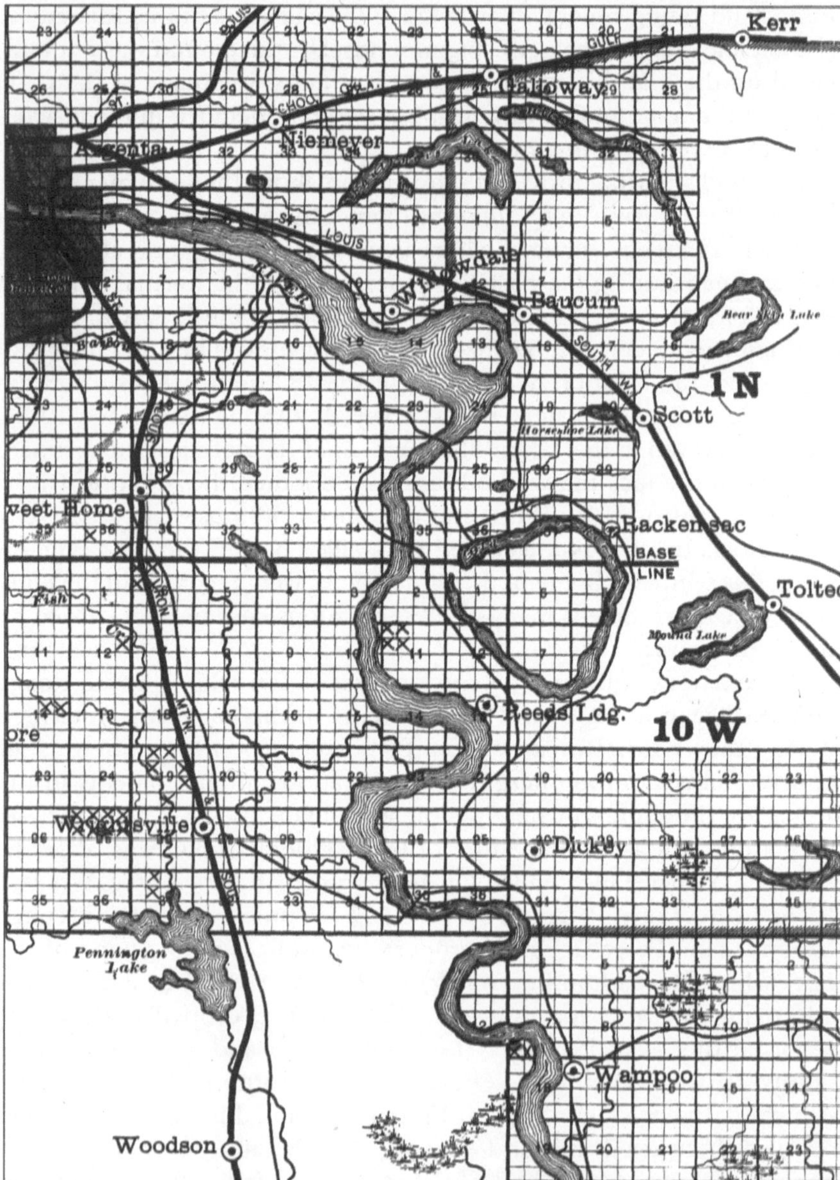

FIGURE 6.3. Map of southeastern Pulaski County showing the Arkansas River, adjacent lands, late-nineteenth-century communities, roads, and railroads (from map of Pulaski County, Arkansas, showing the land grant of the St. Louis, Iron Mountain and Southern and Little Rock and Fort Smith R'ys. Land Commissioner, Little Rock, 1900. Courtesy of Arkansas History Commission).

hides and possessions (Arnold 1985:72–77). Isolated families attempting to live up the Arkansas River from the post would have had a hard time surviving, but hunters would have been familiar with the land. In the early 1800s they were living up the river. The U.S. government took control of Louisiana in 1804. A treaty with the Big and Little Osage tribes in 1808 effectively removed them from lands in Arkansas and stopped the raiding of the dissident Arkansas Osage along the lower Arkansas River (Din and Nasatir 1983:375–82). In treaties of 1818 and 1824, the Quapaw tribe ceded all their lands in Arkansas and by 1834 were removed to Indian Territory (Baird 1980:57–78, 101).

The community of Plum Bayou, located on the Arkansas River in northeastern Jefferson County, upstream from Pine Bluff and 12 miles south of Toltec Mounds, established a post office in 1843 (Baker 1988). A post office for Reeds' Landing (fig. 6.3) on the river was applied for in 1870, one of the first in this region. Towns were developed late in the century in the region east of the river in southeastern Pulaski and southern Lonoke Counties. A few towns developed in the 1880s, but most of them followed the railroad in 1888.

William Peay Officer (1810–1851) filed patents for 160 acres of the land on which the Toltec Mounds site is located in 1849 (Allen and McLane 1991b; First State Abstract and Insurance Corp. 1975). He married Mary Eliza Feild (1825–1905) in early 1846 and the land remained in the family, through Mary Eliza, until it was sold to settle her estate in 1907. Mary Eliza purchased additional adjacent land after William's death. William and Mary Eliza Officer had one child who lived to adulthood, Eustis Feild Officer (1849–1900). Six years after William Officer's death, Mary Eliza Officer married Gilbert Knapp (1827–1900), and he purchased additional land adjacent to her property. The land on which the site was located actually was owned by Mary Eliza or her son, Eustis Feild Officer, but was part of a larger farm managed by Gilbert Knapp. The property was known as the Lake Mound Plantation. The Knapps lived in Little Rock and had a house at the plantation. Gilbert Knapp was at Lake Mound when he died.

Mary Eliza Knapp maintained an active interest in archaeology and history. She was acquainted with Dr. William H. Barry, a physician practicing in Hot Springs. Barry had been editor of several newspapers in Arkansas and mixed in local politics (Allsopp 1922:17). Barry was interested in Indian customs and artifacts and corresponded with Joseph Henry, secretary of the Smithsonian Institution. Mrs. Knapp wrote a letter with a description of the site to Dr. Barry, who forwarded her letter to Henry (Knapp 1876a). At Barry's request she also wrote directly to Henry (Knapp 1876b) and sent a sample of artifacts (Rolingson 1982b:71). An abstract from her letter to Barry was published in the

Annual Report of the Board of Regents of the Smithsonian Institution for 1877 (Knapp 1878:251). The sections of her letters quoted here provide additional pertinent information.

> Little Rock Ark
> April 8th, 1876
> Dr Barry
> Dear Sir
>
> . . . We were attracted to the place by the immense artificial Mounds and a wall similar to our Levees about six to ten feet hight enclosing 90 acres or rather coming around a half circle to the Lake bank which in those days might have been the Ark. River. In the wall are two openings Both deep pools of water. they were evidently *water gates* or *baths.*
>
> Skilled engineers pronounce it a perfect fortification. Possibly a walled city. The Quawpaw Indians who had it in possession had no tradition relating to the builders. Within the area between the Lake (which is three miles long) and the wall are numerous mounds but only two of Great Size. The hights are variously estimated one which was called one hundred feet high we have cultivated for 20 years. I presume it makes more than a Bale of cotton so you may imagine the size. As the years go by it washes and these rude relics of a prehistoric possibly an Indian race are picked up. It was certainly a place of sepulcher for human bones rest tier up tier but mingled with those of deer and other animals. They are of great age and crumble on coming to the air.
>
> One of the tall mounds is still covered with trees some-times gives a sonorous ringing Sound as if it were hollow when wagons are driven 'round it. These two large Mounds are exactly similar to the mounds of the *Sun* and *Moon* at the city of Mexico. They you know had burial chambers in them.
>
> During the war I lost the only perfect piece of pottery *a cup* that I had. I found it in a mass of adobe brick which seemed to have been made with straw on the outside after the fashion of the Egyptians. I put some of the pieces in the box, one mound is covered with it.
>
> I picked up these specimens this winter. My attention was called to them by noticing the *engravings* in Sir John Lubbock and Sir Charles Lyells books on the antiquity of man that these Stone Hatchets are precisely similar to those found in Europe called by the Archaeologist *'Celts'* and some of the pottery bears the ornamental Greek border. It is exceedingly rude, colored Red, Brown & Black some with shells beaten in. You must bear in mind the situation of the place 16 miles South east of Little Rock in the Alluvial Valley of the Arkansas where the black deposit is ten feet deep & no stone or pebble was ever seen. But the by-gone race who made it their home brought Crystals from Hot Springs Flints Jasper granite sandstone all kinds of stone evidently are picked up here.

> . . . I know I have wearied your patience Dr. but I am so glad after all these years to interest someone in opening these mounds. We hope you will succeed in having it done. We will do all in our power to facilitate it.
>
> Very respectfully
> Mrs Gilbert Knapp [signed]

Mrs. Knapp's second letter, to Professor Henry, provided less information than the one to Barry. It accompanied a box of artifacts that are still present in the collections (catalog numbers 22088–22095) at the National Museum of Natural History, Smithsonian Institution (Rolingson 1982b:85).

> Little Rock Ark
> April 11th 1876
> Professor Henry
> Dear Sir
>
> Dr. Barry requests me to Send you the Indian hatchets, pottery and Arrow heads which I do with pleasure. . . .
>
> . . . I wished to call your attention to these *Mound*s. Sixteen miles South-East of Little Rock located in a walled enclosure pronounced by Engineers a perfect fortification, & one of the greatest wonders of the *Lowlands* this Side of the City of Mexico, for the large Mounds are Similar in Shape to those of that City.
>
> The smaller mounds of which there a great number in the enclosure have tier upon tier of human & animal bones—some long mounds were evidently covered with buildings of Adobe brick. I enclose Some of the pieces in the box. The Stone weapons are exactly like the engravings of those discovered in Europe.
>
> . . . We have never opened one of our mounds yet—But at *anytime* they are at *your service* if you *wish* to *investigate*.
>
> Being an old resident and knowing many places in the State of Archaeological interest should you ever send an expedition in our direction will take pleasure in giving what information we can.
>
> Very respectfully
> Mrs. Gilbert Knapp [signed]

Several things are noteworthy in these letters. In the line of the embankment the two openings were deep enough to make pools of water and these openings were aboriginal, not cut through recently. The top of the second highest mound was cultivated, and both human and animal bones were exposed by plowing. The smaller mounds also had both human and animal bones plowed out, and one or more of these mounds had a building made with daub ("adobe brick") walls. Mrs. Knapp even noted the presence of shell temper in some of the pottery. She wanted to have the mounds explored and was pleased that Professor Henry expressed an interest in them. Recent excavations have not exposed human bone or evidence of buildings with mud daubed walls; these may have been destroyed by plowing and reduction of the heights of the mounds.

The response was rather prompt, following closely on the publication of Mrs. Knapp's (1878:251) description in the *Annual Report . . . for 1877.* Edwin Curtiss, working for the Peabody Museum of Harvard University, arrived to investigate the mounds in the fall of 1879, and Edward Palmer of the Bureau of Ethnology, Smithsonian Institution, arrived at the end of 1882. Both investigated the Knapps's mounds.

Edwin Curtiss (1830–1880) had worked with Frederick Ward Putnam of the Peabody Museum in the Nashville, Tennessee, area in 1877. Curtiss investigated sites in northeastern Arkansas during the winter of 1879–80 and is considered to have conducted the "first well-documented excavations" (Morse and Morse 1983:19) along the St. Francis River (Jeter 1990b:377; Putnam 1880:717). Curtiss visited the Knapps's mounds in the fall of 1879 but noted in a letter to Putnam (Curtiss 1879a):

> I was not permited to explore whare I wanted and I left in disgust I supose I could have done so if I had given old Knapp 10 or 15 dollars which I did not choose to do it is a remarkable place but there are hundreds of places in the state that are equaly as good so I would not waist time and money with him old Knapp now the quarentine is broke and one can travl with out getting a health Surtificate I will go up crowlys ridge along the St. Francis river whare there has never been any of the Kind of work done and by what I hear I will be able to get some good things.

Curtiss did, in fact, do some digging before Knapp's instructions were delivered to the farm. "Old" Gilbert Knapp would have been 51 years of age that fall, while Curtiss was 48. The quarantine against yellow fever was lifted by the Little Rock Board of Health on October 31, 1879, following similar action by the State Board of Health (*Arkansas Gazette*, November 1, 1879, 8).

Curtiss made a "rough sketch" of the site and surrounding country (fig. 6.4) on the back of his letter (Curtiss 1879a), which was written on lined paper. This sketch showed his route from Little Rock, across the Arkansas River by ferry, with an approach to the site from the north. A portion of Curtiss's route is shown on the 1900 map (fig. 6.3). The perspective of the site in relation to the country was distorted as he showed them, with the site much too big in relation to the adjacent oxbow lake. A number of mounds and the embankment were marked, but the southwest end was badly distorted and compressed. The line for the southern end of the embankment appears to have been changed on the map, from a slightly curved line to a straighter and shorter line. A small circled area was labeled "where dug—Best place in the bottom" and could be Mound D. Features are difficult to place on the south end of the site because of the distortion in the sketch. It is possible that the sketch was done from memory after Curtiss left the site and when he wrote the letter.

Curtiss (1879b) made notes describing the site's appearance, his digging, and the artifacts, as well as his relations with the people. He recorded that he left Little Rock and went to Mrs. Knapp's farm, so he talked to the Knapps first. His description is quoted here, with periods added for clarity, but capitalization is his own.

> I left Little rock and went on mrs. Knapps farm 16 miles below Little rock 4½ miles from the ark river on what is called mound lake farm[.] here I found an entrenchment enclosing 90 acres of bottom land commensing at the waters edge and ending in the waters edge the two ends being about one half mile a part[.] this earth work encloses Some remarkable Mounds there is two that are between 40 and fifty ft high[.] one Sets on the banks of the lake and the other Sets 175 ft from the waters edge just north of the first one mentioned[.] There are twenty or more mounds in the enclosure that are ritch in archological treasures[.] I explored with few hands on saturday and found human remains and broken pottery and I Should have remained and finished the mound although there is cotton growing on the mound[.] Mr Knapp Sent a letter down to his agent for me not to dig in any of the mounds whare the land was tilled or ploughed and that I might dig in a

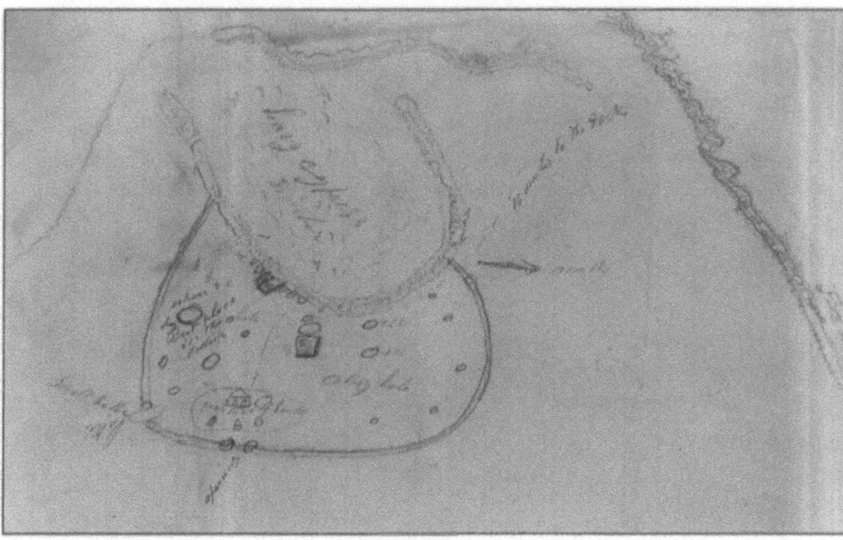

FIGURE 6.4. "Rough sketch or drawing of earthworks in mound bottom, Lonoke Co., Ark." by E. Curtiss. Courtesy of Peabody Museum, Harvard University. Photograph by Hillel Burger.

> mound near the quarters if I would levell it off after getting through digging which I do in all cases whare the land is in cultivation or likely to be but this mound was one that I did not want to explore[.] it is one of those Sacrifical mounds and I would not waste time and funds exploring in Such as I have worked in Such and found nothing and I think this is one of there devotional ones[.] the man who owns the cotton on the mound I first explored was anxious for me to explore the mound and Said I Should pull up the cotton Stalks and Set them aside and that he would pick the cotton out when it opened which it would do and he would be none the looser So he could not take that for an excuse in refusing me a place to dig I think he though I would pay him for the chance to dig and I think I have trouble anough with out paying for a chance to get fooled or sold[.] so I mooved back to the rock but I got quite a lot of worked Stones crystals and celts Some diferant from those that are found in other Localities[.] the mound I Started to open was one that had been Tilled for many years and was some what worn down by constant ploughing and had yealded many things[.] there was a vesel of pottery and a earthen pipe found there last spring[.] I found in one grave 5 boddies and two broken Jars[.] the bones were in a good state of preservation but the plough had disturbed & broken them So badly that I did not try to save any of them[.] I Sent on some burned pieces of clay or brick like material and a few things that I found in the grave[.] charcoal ashes and burned earth were found in the graves and all the mounds I saw but the total absence of shells I noticed other wise they were like all other Mounds I have ever Seen[.] Some of the mounds have been ploughed level with the Surounding bottom while others Show vary plainly whare once Stood there burrial mounds[.] this is truly a wonderful place one whare many once lived as there works plainly Show and whare they could live at there ease plenty of fish game etc and the ritch alluvial bottoms would produce there corn & other things that they cultivated with an hundred fold[.] So I left this place and passed through the Rock with out stopping and left for little red river White Co Ark.

The annual report of the Peabody Museum (Putnam 1880:739) listed "arrowheads and javelin points, and knives of stone from Old River near Little Rock, Ark., collected and presented by Mrs. Knapp" and "burnt clay, iron ore, earthen disk and fragments of small human figure in terra cotta, hammerstones with and without finger pits, rubbing stones, borers, arrowheads, knives and other implements of flint from mound on Pond Bottom, sixteen miles south of Little Rock, Ark." collected by Curtiss.

A number of comments are significant in these notes. The sketch map will be discussed further in relation to the plats of Thomas and Palmer, below. The two large mounds he reported as 40 to 50 feet in height, closer to what was apparently the correct height than was indicated by most other visitors. He also reported 20 or more mounds, more than anyone else reported. That he could see so many mounds may be an indication that most of the site was in cultivation, as is also his comment that some mounds were plowed level with the ground. The mound where he dug had been lowered by plowing, having been cultivated for many years. The plat is so compressed at this end of the site that the mound where he dug could have been D, E, or S. The closeness of the place where he dug to the embankment may be an indication this was Mound S or E; also the fact that he thought he could have finished it in one day of digging. Mound S was probably no more than 2 feet high, Mound E was probably 4 feet high. Mound D, at least 5 feet high and the fourth largest on the site, would seem to have been much too big to have "finished" in a day. Nevertheless, it could have been Mound D, because the things Curtiss reported— charcoal, ashes, burned earth, and graves with pots—were the same as Palmer reported from his digging on Mound D in 1883.

Curtiss was soon followed by Edward Palmer to the mounds on the Knapps's place. Palmer (1830?–1911) came as an agent of the Division of Mound Exploration of the Bureau of Ethnology. His work in Arkansas from 1881 to 1884 has been extensively researched (Jeter 1990b) and will not be elaborated on here. The Division of Mound Exploration was formed in 1881, and Cyrus Thomas was made director of the Division early in 1882 (Jeter 1990b:7–37; B. D. Smith 1985). The objective of the Division was to investigate the prehistoric mounds in the eastern United States and the "Mound Builders," the most important question being "were the mounds built by the Indians?" (Thomas 1894:21). Thomas produced the final report and, from detailed documentation of the sites investigated, concluded that the mounds had been built by the Indians and their ancestors.

Palmer made three visits to the Knapp place (Jeter 1990b:251–69, 351–55; Rolingson 1982b), approaching the south end of the site from the west, where he had gotten off the river steamer at Reed's Landing 3.5 miles away (fig. 6.3). The first visit was on Christmas Day in 1882 and the second was for three or four days in mid-January 1883. The third, on July 1, 1884, was solely to remeasure the two big mounds, as his previous measurements were unacceptable to Thomas. On the initial visit he was assisted by Henry J. Lewis, an African American artist from Pine Bluff. Lewis made four sketches, or views, and a plat showing the arrangement of mounds, embankment, and lake (fig. 6.5). They collected artifacts from the surface but did no digging. Leaving the Knapps's place, Palmer went to Pine Bluff (December 29), visited several sites down river from that town, and continued on to Arkansas City by January 10 (Jeter 1990b:158; Rolingson 1982b:72). In Arkansas City, Palmer received a letter from Thomas instructing him to release Lewis and to return to the Knapp group and excavate in the mounds. Palmer was on the site from January 16 to 18, 1883. He hired local men to do the work, excavating in eight of the mounds.

Four sources of information for Palmer's work became available to the research in the following order. Thomas (1894:243–45) provided a summary description, a view of the site, and a plat (fig. 6.6). Palmer's notes were published by the Arkansas Historical Association in 1917, six years after Palmer died. Unfortunately, the editors made corrections, deleted passages, and introduced errors (Jeter 1990b:106–7). The artifacts are in the National Museum of Natural History, Smithsonian Institution (Rolingson 1982b:83–86). The National Anthropological Archives has Palmer's letters to Thomas describing his activities and several illustrations of the site, including three of the four sketches and the plat drawn by Lewis. Palmer's personal notes and copies made by scribes are in the Arkansas History Commission archives (Jeter 1990b:99–119). The descriptions of the site and excavations in these sources have been extremely useful to the modern research (Rolingson 1982b, 1992:3, 1998).

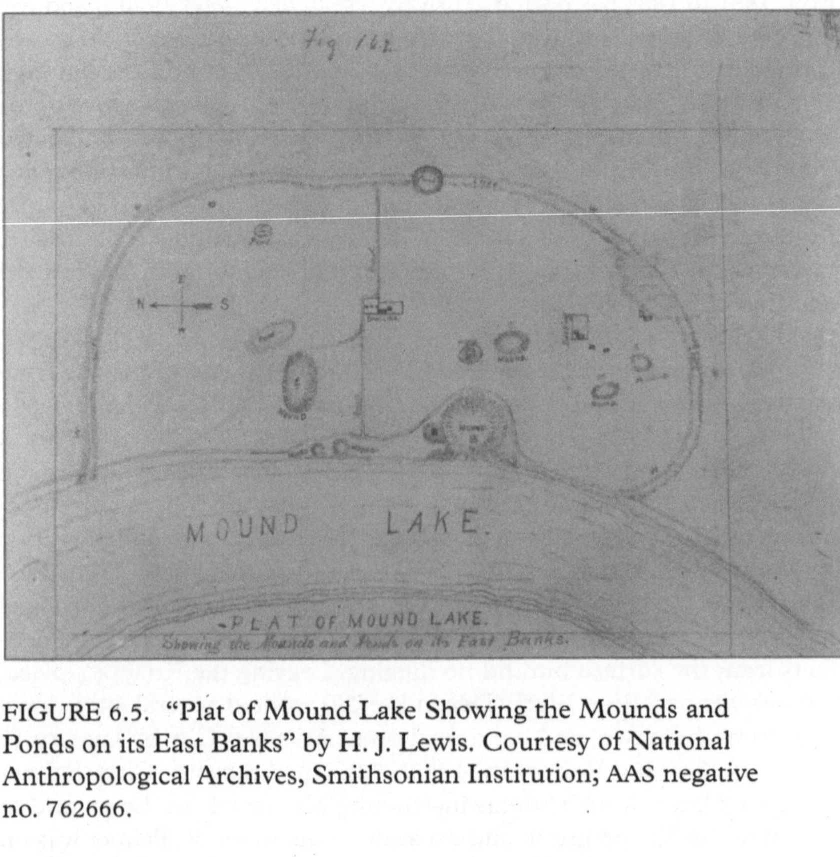

FIGURE 6.5. "Plat of Mound Lake Showing the Mounds and Ponds on its East Banks" by H. J. Lewis. Courtesy of National Anthropological Archives, Smithsonian Institution; AAS negative no. 762666.

Palmer's work was also reported in the newspapers (*Arkansas Gazette,* January 27, 1883, 4). *Frank Leslie's Illustrated Newspaper,* in New York, brought national attention to Palmer's discoveries (Anonymous 1883). The illustrations of Knapp Mounds, adapted from Lewis's sketches, were inaccurate (Jeter 1990b:267–69, 361–62; Rolingson 1982b:74), and the articles are not useful sources of information.

Both Thomas (1894:243–45) and Palmer (1917:423–26; Jeter 1990b:251–69) described the features of the site and Palmer's excavations in the four largest mounds (A, B, C, and D). Both reported that the largest mound had trees and brush growing on it, while the top of the second largest mound was in cultivation for a garden or cotton. Palmer's excavations were most productive in Mound D, where he uncovered places "which have burnt clay . . . [and] with ashes & human bones only" (Jeter 1990b:260). The burials he encountered included portions of three shell-tempered pottery vessels that dated to the late Mississippi or Protohistoric periods and were probably intrusive into the mound (Rolingson 1982b:85).

Concerning the four small mounds he excavated, Palmer merely reported: "Holes 4 ft. deep were dug in them from the centre. Their composition was a light sandy soil with an admixture of vegetable mould with here & there pieces of pottery, animal bones, Mussel shells, and stone implements" (Jeter 1990b:260).

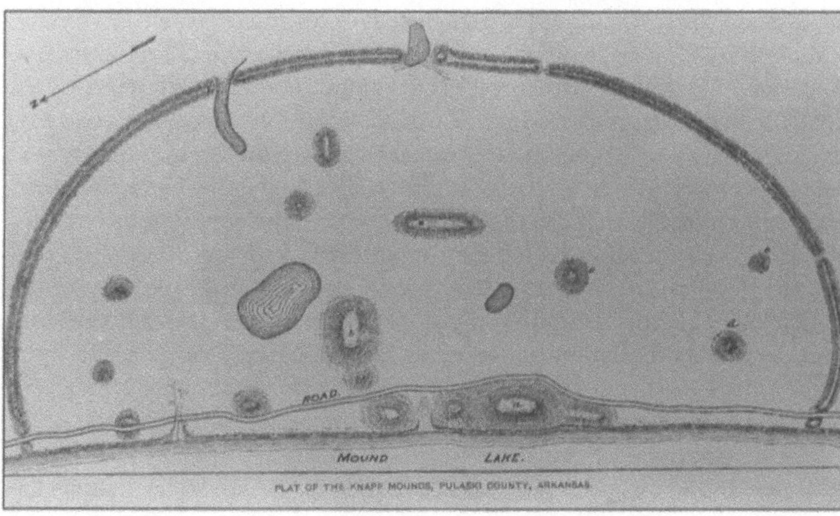

FIGURE 6.6. "Plat of the Knapp Mounds, Pulaski County, Arkansas" by W. H. Holmes. (From Thomas 1894:plate X, courtesy of Smithsonian Institution; AAS negative no. 762680.)

These four mounds, about 4 feet high, were not clearly identified. Lewis's plat showed eight mounds, the four small ones being E, F, P, and Q, and these may be the ones dug by Palmer, although Mound Q had a small log building on it. Another mound (R) on the lake bank is an alternative possibility. My current interpretation is that "Q" is part of the basal platform of Mound A and not an independent mound. Local treasure hunters say burials have been dug from this portion of the mound. Sometime in the last 100 years the soil of "Q" has been borrowed away and only an outer rim is now present. Mounds F and P are now in a similar, nearly destroyed condition.

Interestingly, neither Thomas's nor Palmer's descriptions recorded the ditch on the outside of the embankment, which they termed a wall (Thomas) or a levee (Palmer). Thomas attributed a defensive function to the "earthen wall," which "reaches 5 or 6 feet in height where preserved, but where most reduced by cultivation is about obliterated" (Thomas 1894:243). Palmer's brief description for the levee is "one mile long, five feet high, five feet across at top and eight feet at the base" (Palmer 1917:423). This is grossly different from the 60 foot wide base for the portion of the embankment still preserved among trees.

The discrepancies between the Thomas and Palmer descriptions have been disconcerting, especially the dimensions of the two large mounds and the layout of the site in the two plats (figs. 6.5 and 6.6). Some of these differences may have resulted from additional observations made by William H. Holmes in 1890, when he was in Arkansas to investigate the novaculite quarries near Hot Springs (Powell 1894:xxiv). Palmer's (1917:426) "height" measurements for the two tall mounds, 100 feet and 75 feet, were measured on the slope. The measurements of the two big mounds published by Thomas, 48 and 38 feet, were made by Holmes. The plat of the site in Thomas (1894:plate X) apparently was adapted by Holmes from the plat drawn by Lewis, with changes resulting from Holmes's visit (Jeter 1990b:263–67). The discrepancies between the two plats, the published version and the drawing, have been discussed in detail by Jeter and Rolingson (Jeter 1990b:263–67), with the conclusion that the version published by Thomas was drawn by Holmes and the sketched map in the National Anthropological Archives files was drawn by Lewis, correcting the previous hypothesis concerning the authorship of the maps as proposed by Rolingson (1982b:73–74).

A comparison of the three maps—Curtiss 1879, Lewis 1882, and Holmes 1890—produces some significant information. All show the embankment around the site, but none show the exterior ditch. Curtiss shows two openings, one of which is a "small lake"; Lewis had one opening labeled "pond"; and Holmes shows four openings, two containing water. On all maps the two big mounds were emphasized. On the

Curtiss map the mounds are shown as small ovals, with 13 or 14 of these, not the 20 indicated in his notes. The ovals were scattered around the site, perhaps schematic rather than accurate locations. The Lewis map shows only eight mounds (including Q), possibly including the ones excavated by Palmer on his return in 1883. The Holmes map shows 15 mounds, with greater similarity to the modern map than the others. There are several borrow pits on the site. Curtiss's map shows one northeast of Mound B and one between Mounds C and A. Lewis's map shows "ponds" northeast of Mound B, near Mound C, and one on the northeast side of the site. Holmes's map has one northeast of Mound B and one near Mound C. None of the maps shows the large borrow pit east of Mound E that is still present today.

These three maps also show dwellings present at the time each map was made. The Curtiss map shows one cluster of buildings labeled "quarters of hands" with a two-door dwelling and three smaller buildings. These are circled along with a mound oval and thus are probably adjacent to this mound, the location of which suggests it represents Mound G. Curtiss also drew in the road from the north and across the site to the house. The Lewis map shows two dwellings. One is a large dwelling, and there are three small buildings, all fenced, in the location of Mound G, but he did not show the mound. A second dwelling with a fence around it is located southeast of Mound C. Two smaller buildings are outside the fence, one of which is likely to have been on or adjacent to Mound S. Excavation of Mound S exposed a small pit filled with gray-white ash and square-cut nails (Rolingson 1992:3). The map shows a road the length of the site from south to north and a crossroad to the Mound G dwelling, continuing on to the embankment but not through it. A single building is also present on the lower platform of Mound A. The Holmes map has only the north-south road and one black square to indicate a dwelling on the end of Mound G.

The condition of Mound G is perhaps the most intriguing information that remains unresolved from these descriptions and maps. It was sufficiently prominent for Holmes to see it and place it on his map. Curtiss only commented in his notes that it was a "sacrificial" mound and he would not bother to dig here since he had dug in others like it and found "nothing." Lewis and Palmer ignored it completely. It is still a puzzle that with the mound apparently as large as it was, they did not place it on the map or in the sketches. Today the mound is estimated to have once been 300 feet long and 148 feet wide. During the 1960s, much of Mound G was used to fill in the large borrow adjacent to Mound B and the remaining rise of ground pushed east to level it with the adjacent ground. Excavation trenches, however, have exposed 1 foot of fill present at the north end and 2 feet at the south end; while beneath the mound fill, a rich, undisturbed deposit is preserved. It must have been 3 feet high, or more; although, if it was in cultivation for 25 years, it could have been considerably rounded off by 1879.

The name "Toltec" was first used in the late 1880s for a post office and a proposed town (fig. 6.3). Jeter (1990b:369) concluded that while Mrs. Knapp (1878) had compared the mounds to those near Mexico City, the identification with the Toltecs developed from Palmer's visit. Palmer, while working in the west, had concluded that there were two classes of Indians. The Toltecan class was superior and built mounds, while the inferior warlike people were classed as Aztec. He is likely to have introduced this idea to the Knapps (Jeter 1990b:61–63, 253–55). A branch line of the St. Louis, Arkansas and Texas Railroad was completed into Little Rock in early April 1888, and Gilbert Knapp and Eustis Officer platted a town site on a portion of their property, expecting to sell lots (*Arkansas Gazette,* March 28, 1888, 5). Knapp applied for a post office on March 26, 1889 (Post Office Department 1980), to be named Toltec, located in the center of the SW ¼ of Sec. 2, T1S R10W. The town did not develop, but there was a Toltec station (Hempstead 1978 [1890]:1170; Pope 1895:96) and village. The post office was finally closed in 1932 (Baker 1988). At present, the name survives in the Toltec Baptist Church and among the community of people.

The mounds were well known in Arkansas and were specifically mentioned and described in a number of local histories published around the turn of the century (Goodspeed 1889; Hempstead 1978 [1890]; Pope 1895; Reynolds 1906). The local authors seem to have acquired most of their information about the site from the Knapps and did not add much that was not in Mrs. Knapp's letters, quoted above. They made note of the two largest mounds and of the earthen wall and ditch, but they only remarked that there were a number of small mounds. The heights of the two large mounds varied in these reports. Goodspeed (1889:20) said the larger cone-shaped mound was "supposed to have been 100 feet high" and the smaller square mound was "about seventy-five feet" and that all of the small mounds were in cultivation. Hempstead (1978 [1890]:1170) reported "the two largest being respectively sixty and seventy feet high" and further stated that they "are the most extensive works of the mound-builders to be found in the southwestern portion of the United States." This was published before a similar statement by Thomas (1894:244), quoted at the beginning of this chapter.

Pope's book is his recollections of early days in Arkansas. He reported that Mrs. Knapp said both tall mounds were "about one hundred feet in height each in 1846" (Pope 1895:96–97) but had been lowered to 80 and 75 feet by 1895, while the levee was 10 feet high. Pope

FIGURE 6.7. "Lake Mound Earth Works By the Toltecs" (from W. F. Pope 1895:97; AAS negative no. 762679).

published a view of the site, but no artist was acknowledged (fig. 6.7). This is one of the more fanciful depictions of the site; nevertheless, it shows seven of the mounds with heights for each. The shape of the embankment is erroneous and further depicts the embankment along the lake bank, forming a complete enclosure.

Reynolds, in the first publication of the Arkansas Historical Association, said, "The largest mounds in Arkansas are those at Toltec in Lonoke County" (Reynolds 1906:275). He reported four large mounds at 65 feet high, 50 feet, 15 or 20 feet, and "not exceeding ten feet high" (Reynolds 1906:275), while the embankment was 3 to 4 feet high. Reynolds himself dug around for "about an hour . . . and found parts of two or three skeletons" (Reynolds 1906:275).

None of the people who actually dug at the Knapp Mounds was particularly impressed with the artifacts recovered. They all were impressed with the mounds, but artifacts that could be used in museum displays were not present. The site certainly did not impress Clarence B. Moore, the last archaeologist of the turn-of-the-century period to visit. For more than 20 years he systematically worked his way along the coast and up the rivers of the southeastern United States recording and excavating sites. He worked along the Arkansas River in 1908. He used the name "The Toltec Mounds" and after a brief visit said that "investigation was not deemed advisable, as there seemed to be no history of the discovery of artifacts in the vicinity" (Moore 1908:557).

The investigations of the nineteenth century ended with the visit by Moore, whose opinion of the site and artifacts probably dampened the interest of future potential investigators. The end of the century was also marked by the deaths of family members, Gilbert Knapp and Eustis Officer in 1900, and Mary Eliza Knapp in 1905, and the subsequent settlement of the estate and sale of the land to William R. McLaughlin.

Review of the Toltec Mounds site as described in the nineteenth century is important to current research in a number of ways. The historical context establishes a framework for discovery, early descriptions, and knowledge of the site. No descriptions are known from the colonial period, prior to 1800, but this is not to say that they do not exist, rather they have not yet been discovered. By the early 1800s the mounds were a landmark known to the Quapaws and to the French settlers. By 1850 the land was in agricultural production, and it is possible to begin to document occupancy and use of the land and consequent damage to the earthworks.

The nineteenth-century descriptions by Knapp, Curtiss, and Palmer/Thomas provide perceptions of site conditions that are different from what can be seen today. With only three prominent mounds and most of the embankment and ditch plowed away, only a fragment of the original monumental earthworks are now present. The Palmer/Thomas description and the Thomas/Holmes plat have strongly influenced modern perception of what the site looked like. The Knapp and Curtiss descriptions and Curtiss and Lewis plats provide comparative perceptions that increase our understanding of the site. An example of this is the number of mounds present: Curtiss reported 20 or more mounds, Knapp said there were numerous low mounds, the Palmer/Lewis plat showed eight; and the Thomas plat showed 15. With the count of mounds now up to 18, Curtiss appears to be the most accurate, even though the locations of the mounds on his sketch map are not realistic. Even with plowing done by mules, the low mounds were seriously damaged in the 25 or so years of cultivation between 1849 and 1879. Measurements of the earthworks varied greatly among the descriptions, so that the higher figures appear to have been exaggerated and cannot be used as an indication of erosion in this 30 year period.

Reports of burials and artifacts in the descriptions were generalized but are useful. Data from the 1966 and 1977 to 1990 excavations in six mounds indicate that they were mostly low platforms rather than burial mounds, with the exception of one. Knapp, Curtiss, Palmer, and Reynolds reported burials in the mounds, but these are now thought to have been intrusive. Mrs. Knapp noted the presence of shell temper in the pottery, and the pottery from Palmer's excavation on Mound D is shell tempered with decoration characteristic of the late Mississippi period. There may have been considerable use of the mounds after construction had stopped. People who later used the mounds for burials were not necessarily residents on the site. Masses of adobe brick or daub were indicated by Mrs. Knapp on the long mounds, one of which was probably Mound G. Such masses have not been encountered in the recent excavations and may have been a feature of the late period of construction or post-construction use of the platforms.

Historical data about a prehistoric site may be collected, or come to light, sporadically during a long-term research project. No matter how minor or extensive it appears to be, it is likely to contribute information that is significant to the research. As with the archaeology, the collection of historical data is an ongoing process that provides insight into the past as well as to the current research goals.

Acknowledgments

I am grateful to Mary Lynn Kennedy for her years of research on the nineteenth-century history of the Toltec Mounds site and adjacent lands. She generously provided me with documents about the land and the Knapp family members, as well as advice and comments on this chapter. Information on the artifacts in the collections of the Smithsonian Institution was made available to me by an inventory made by Michael P. Hoffman in 1975 and photographs of artifacts made by Stephen Loring in 1977. A conference in 1980 sponsored by the National Museum of Natural History, Smithsonian Institution, and the Lower Mississippi Survey, Peabody Museum of Archaeology and Ethnology, gave direct access to both notes and artifacts. I also want to thank Ian W. Brown for first drawing my attention to the sketch and notes by Edwin Curtiss and for providing initial copies of these documents in 1991. Figures 6.1 and 6.2 were drawn by Jane Kellett and Mary Lynn Kennedy, Arkansas Archeological Survey. Figure 6.3 is printed with permission of the Arkansas History Commission. Figure 6.4 was photographed by Hillel Burger of the Peabody Museum and permission to publish is given by the president and fellows of Harvard College. Permission to use the maps in figures 6.5 and 6.6 is given by National Anthropological Archives, Smithsonian Institution. Figure 6.7 is in the public domain.

CHAPTER SEVEN

LATE PERIOD PHASES IN THE CENTRAL MISSISSIPPI VALLEY: A MULTIVARIATE APPROACH

ROBERT C. MAINFORT JR.

In spite of adequate warnings about the unsatisfactory nature of the archaeological data . . . it is inevitable that his alignments will be accepted as defined archaeological units into which new data will be forced.

—JAMES B. GRIFFIN,
"Review of Archaeological Survey in the Lower Yazoo Basin, Mississippi, 1945–1955"

Introduction

The late period archaeological phases (ca. A.D. 1400–1600) of the Central Mississippi Valley (fig. 7.1) are of considerable interest because of their potential relationship to several polities mentioned in the chronicles of the de Soto *entrada* (e.g., Morse and Morse 1983:305). In particular, the Kent, Nodena, Parkin, and Walls phases figure prominently in recent attempts to reconstruct the route of the Spaniards (e.g., Hudson et al. 1990; D. Morse 1990; P. Morse 1990; Morse and Morse 1990). Serious questions have been raised, however, about the validity of existing phase definitions (e.g., Fox 1992; O'Brien 1994, 1995). Here I examine the current late period phases within the study area (Phillips 1970; Smith 1990) using multivariate statistical techniques. I will demonstrate that within the study area, groups of sites ("phases") generated by multivariate statistical methods are superior to current phase assignments of sites.

Phillips (1970:524) regarded an archaeological phase as "a geographically coherent group of site locations that one can . . . cautiously assume to have been occupied simultaneously or nearly so by local units of the same specific socio-political group." He defined a number of phases in the Lower Mississippi Valley based on similarities in artifact assemblages (primarily ceramics) and geographical proximity. Much to his credit, Phillips (1970:523–24) freely admitted the role of subjectivity in formulating his proposed phases and emphasized that his definitions were provisional.

Unfortunately, the decades that have elapsed since publication of the Yazoo Basin report have not given rise to the rigorous testing of phase

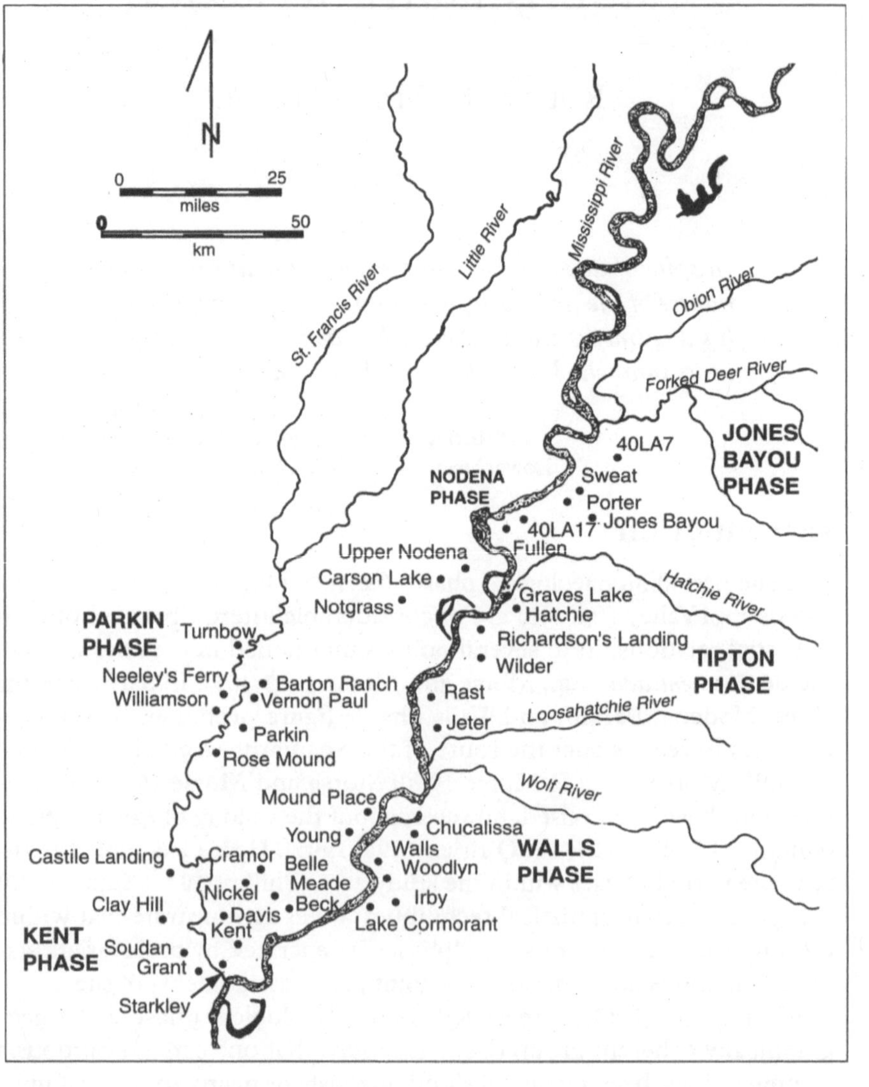

FIGURE 7.1. Late period sites and phases in the Central Mississippi Valley.

formulations envisioned by Phillips (1970:923–24). Even today most of our current knowledge about the sites included in this analysis (and, indeed, most sites in the Central Mississippi Valley) derives primarily from surface collections of potsherds, supplemented to varying degrees by assemblages of mortuary vessels excavated by relic hunters. Specific information on site structure, house styles, mortuary practices, and subsistence remains virtually nonexistent (see Fisher-Carroll 1997).

Lacking a robust radiocarbon chronology (see Mainfort 1996), researchers in the Central Mississippi Valley are not in a position to state that any of the late period phases encompass relatively short time spans, and, in fact, some are believed to have existed for more than 200 years (D. Morse 1990). This situation, bemoaned by Griffin (1978:xvii) two decades ago, has not improved significantly.

Although there has been a proliferation of additional phases within the study area, those considered here (and, in fact, the vast majority of phases defined throughout the entire Lower Mississippi Valley for all time periods) remain essentially intuitive constructs based on largely subjective impressions of artifact collections (Fox 1992; O'Brien 1995). Moreover, unlike Phillips, who called attention to the "inadequacy of [his] treatment of the quantitative problem" of assigning assemblages to phases, as well as the "inadequacy of the particular data [that is, sherds from surface collections]" (1970:973–74), more recent authors typically offer no caveats about newly created phases (see Fox 1992).

No one was more aware of the deficiencies of Phillips's phases than Phillips himself. Indeed, an outstanding feature of the Yazoo Basin report that is often overlooked by researchers is the frank discussion of uncertainties about such matters as ceramic groupings and the composition of archaeological phases, which as observed by Griffin (1973:375), "is perhaps too rare in anthropological studies or in pronouncements by one's colleagues." In offering a different perspective on certain late period phases here, I view my efforts as building on Phillips's (1970) excellent work and, like Phillips, I will note what I see as potential problems with my data set and methods.

Archaeological Background

Although some earlier studies included discussions of late period phases or foci in the Central Mississippi Valley (e.g., Griffin 1952; Phillips et al. 1951; Williams 1954), it is Phillips's (1970) broad areal synthesis that provides the baseline for late period phase definitions throughout the study area. Of the late period sites included in this study, Phillips assigned most to the Nodena, Parkin, Kent, and Walls phases, which are among the best-known and best-documented late period archaeological constructs in the Lower Mississippi Valley (House 1991b; D. Morse 1989, 1990; P. Morse 1981, 1990; see also O'Brien 1995). With the exception of the last, these phases encompass a significant portion of eastern Arkansas (fig. 7.1).

It seems virtually certain that some late period sites in eastern Arkansas were visited by the de Soto *entrada,* and there is a general consensus that the Parkin phase equates with the Spaniards' province of Casqui, while the Nodena phase represents Pacaha. Additionally, the Walls phase is a candidate for de Soto's province of Quizquiz, encompassing the point at which the *entrada* crossed the Mississippi River (Hudson 1985; Morse and Morse 1983, 1990; Young and Hoffman 1993). Pacaha evidently was the dominant polity in the region, as the Spaniards refer to Quizquiz and Aquixo as vassal polities of Pacaha; the latter perhaps includes sites variously assigned to the Kent and Walls phases (Phillips 1970), the Belle Meade phase (Morse and Morse 1990), and Horseshoe Lake phase (Smith 1990).

Thus the relationship of the late period sites and groups of sites (phases) in the Central Mississippi Valley to certain polities mentioned in the Spanish chronicles represents a problem of considerable anthropological and historical interest. The enormous historiographic and archaeological difficulties posed may be too great to overcome (Henige 1993), and I avoid positing strong linkages between the statistically derived groups of sites presented here and sociopolitical entities. Rather, I focus on deriving spatially limited groups of sites from ceramic sherd assemblages and explicitly documenting the variability within and between these groups. In doing so, I also examine the degree to which these groups correspond to existing, intuitively defined archaeological phases in the study area.

Virtually none of the western Tennessee sites considered here were included in Phillips's (1970) synthesis. Smith (1990) recently proposed several late period phases for the region, to which he assigned the majority of the relevant sites used in this study; Smith also proposed new and/or modified phase definitions for portions of eastern Arkansas and northwest Mississippi. The following discussion of current phases is based primarily on the work of Phillips (1970), with supplementary material taken from Smith (1990) and other researchers as appropriate.

The Nodena phase includes a group of sites located primarily within the Mississippi River counties of northeastern Arkansas. Phillips (1970: 933–36) states that "the outstanding feature" of this phase is "the low frequencies of Barton Incised and Parkin Punctated, which makes for a very different pattern from either the Parkin or Walls phases" (1970:935). Phillips (1970) included Carson Lake, Bell, Nettle Ridge, Notgrass, Upper Nodena, Shawnee Village, Bradley, Golightly, and several other sites in this phase, while D. Morse (1989, 1990) attributes more than 60 sites to the Nodena phase. Bradley, which actually includes at least three major late period sites (Morse and Morse 1983), has been interpreted as representing the capital of Pacaha, as recorded in the de Soto chronicles (Morse and Morse 1990). Only Upper Nodena, Notgrass, and Carson Lake have produced sufficiently large ceramic samples (cf. Phillips 1970) to be used in this study (fig. 7.1, table 7.1).

Situated along the St. Francis River drainage in northeastern Arkansas, the Parkin phase is characterized by very high frequencies of coarse shell-tempered Mississippi Plain (75–90 percent), relatively large amounts of Parkin Punctated, Barton Incised, Kent Incised, and a "fair but erratic showing of Old Town Red" (Phillips 1970:932). Major sites include Parkin, Barton Ranch, Rose Mound, Williamson, Vernon Paul, Neeley's Ferry, Cummings, Turnbow, Big Eddy, and Castile Landing (P. Morse 1981; Phillips 1970). The Parkin phase has been equated with de Soto's province of Casqui, with the Parkin site itself representing the capital (P. Morse 1981, 1990; Morse and Morse 1990). Ceramic samples from Parkin, Williamson, Barton Ranch, Rose Mound, Neeley's Ferry, Turnbow, and Castile Landing are used in this study (fig. 7.1, table 7.1). The relatively large sample from Vernon Paul was included in preliminary analyses; as discussed below, the site proved to be an extreme outlier and was subsequently dropped from analysis.

The Kent phase subsumes a group of late period sites that are located primarily within the lower St. Francis Basin of eastern Arkansas, although Phillips (1970) also includes two sites (Commerce and Hollywood) in northwestern Mississippi. More recently, House (1991b) has advocated limiting use of the Kent phase to sites of the lower St. Francis, a suggestion supported by the analyses that follow. Ceramically, this phase is said to be distinguished by "notably higher frequencies of the *Kent* variety of Barton Incised, Old Town Red, and painted types . . . than either Parkin or Walls. There is a great deal more Bell Plain than in Parkin but nowhere near so much as in Walls" (Phillips 1970:938); the percentages of Mississippi Plain and Bell Plain are roughly equal. In addition to the sites noted above, Phillips assigned Beck, Belle Meade, Kent, Clay Hill, Davis, and Starkley to the Kent phase. Smith (1990), like House, is more restrictive in his use of the Kent phase concept and assigned Belle Meade and Beck to his Horseshoe Lake phase (additional sites in this phase include Mound Place and Young). Sites with sufficiently large ceramic collections to be used in this study are Kent, Clay Hill, Starkley, and Davis of the Kent phase (in the more restrictive sense used by House), and Beck, Belle Meade, Mound Place, and Young of Smith's Horseshoe Lake phase (fig. 7.1 and table 7.1). Grant, another Kent phase site, proved to be a statistical outlier.

TABLE 7.1. CERAMIC SHERD COUNTS FROM SITES USED IN ANALYSIS

	Mississippi Plain	Bell Plain	Parkin Punctated	Barton Incised	Kent Incised	Ranch Incised	Old Town Red	Nodena Red/ White	Rhodes Incised	Walls Engraved	Vernon Paul Applique	Fortune Noded	Total*
Porter	1047	515	64	5	1	1	83	1	0	4	1	7	1780
40LA7	686	133	20	4	0	0	25	0	0	0	0	0	898
Hatchie	373	388	32	6	4	4	9	0	0	0	1	1	814
Richardson's Lg.	492	514	8	2	0	1	23	1	1	3	0	0	1067
Wilder	520	650	34	5	4	6	22	3	2	3	0	0	1266
Jones Bayou	1423	1140	87	2	1	2	99	6	0	2	2	0	2828
Fullen	504	477	33	5	0	0	70	2	0	2	0	0	1107
Jeter	363	448	35	2	4	1	10	2	1	4	0	1	874
Rast	617	927	61	2	0	2	12	2	3	6	0	2	1639
Lake Cormorant	361	781	83	16	8	18	37	2	3	17	0	0	1382
Upper Nodena	1299	1675	5	3	2	3	25	3	1	3	1	0	3034
Notgrass	2580	552	10	6	4	2	9	3	0	3	0	3	3172
Sweat	481	425	33	1	0	2	24	0	0	0	0	0	973
Irby	439	2134	162	2	21	37	21	1	18	50	0	0	3000
Castile Lg.	1567	68	268	36	8	3	70	0	4	0	1	3	2037
Hollywood	671	589	61	67	6	2	34	21	2	8	0	0	1513
Commerce	655	314	35	51	14	0	12	8	1	2	0	0	1108
Rose Mound	1123	35	154	62	1	1	22	0	0	0	1	1	1410
Cramor	814	56	91	27	9	1	7	0	0	0	0	3	1016

TABLE 7.1 CONTINUED

Neeley's Ferry	5992	2	760	463	4	9	14	3	0	0	0	5	7275
Turnbow	2913	10	20	87	0	1	12	0	0	0	0	7	3061
Williamson	4237	12	425	212	0	0	12	0	0	0	1	17	4923
Barton Ranch	4056	8	395	207	0	4	6	0	0	0	0	16	4712
Parkin	11203	135	1298	579	48	43	118	5	44	2	9	34	13671
Woodlyn	275	922	109	12	4	13	11	0	5	10	0	1	1433
Beck	486	693	231	122	44	6	80	19	8	9	1	0	1747
Nickel	592	81	114	37	4	4	20	2	2	0	1	2	886
Carson Lake	2753	577	39	51	4	9	22	13	0	0	0	0	3524
Mound Place	1593	2546	146	64	1	0	21	0	6	9	7	1	4425
Young	850	804	208	90	0	23	12	0	0	8	0	1	2020
Starkley	922	135	77	83	14	1	89	1	1	3	0	1	1355
Walls	993	3215	300	71	30	21	22	2	14	21	0	5	4862
Chucalissa	3190	2748	870	78	26	49	21	11	12	48	0	22	7129
Graves Lake	1514	995	51	19	11	30	46	4	3	1	3	1	2751
Kent	796	648	149	116	24	3	116	11	2	7	0	1	1920
Clay Hill	1638	92	190	124	1	0	166	0	2	4	0	0	2293
Soudan	1059	28	123	34	2	0	55	0	0	2	0	1	1311
Davis	536	137	87	28	2	0	57	4	0	0	0	0	861
Belle Meade	2957	1478	761	508	82	36	108	8	17	25	2	6	6087

*Row totals include miscellaneous shell-tempered sherds not used.

Phillips (1970:936) regarded the Walls phase as "perhaps the most satisfactory phase dealt with in this entire study." The "core" of the Walls phase is a group of sites in extreme northwestern Mississippi, including Irby, Lake Cormorant, Walls, and Woodlyn. Chucalissa, located to the north in Tennessee, often is referred to as a "secondary center" of the phase, and Smith (1990) considers Jeter (40SY28) to be the northernmost representative. Phillips also included at least four sites in eastern Arkansas (Rhodes, Mound Place, Pouncey, and Turner), but following Lumb and McNutt (1988) and G. Smith (1990), I limit the concept of the Walls phase to the east side of the Mississippi River. In reference to the associated ceramic assemblages, Phillips (1970:936) observes: "Outstanding is the plurality of Bell over Mississippi Plain," while Parkin Punctated, Barton Incised, and Old Town Red are "common." Ceramic collections from Walls, Lake Cormorant, Irby, Woodlyn, Chucalissa, and Jeter were used in this study (fig. 7.1 and table 7.1).

Moderately large ceramic collections are available from a number of other western Tennessee sites (fig. 7.1 and table 7.1). With only a few exceptions, this region was virtually ignored in Phillips's (1970) tome due to a paucity of reported sites at the time he was writing. Smith's (1990) recent paper represents the first attempt to describe the late period sites of this region. Smith's Tipton phase/district, which includes Rast, Hatchie, Richardson's Landing, and Wilder, is said to be distinguished by very low frequencies of decorated ceramics. In the comparative analyses that follow I also include Graves Lake (Mainfort 1996) because it falls within the geographic limits of Smith's Tipton district. To the north (primarily in the Lauderdale County, Tennessee, bottoms), the Jones Bayou phase/district also is said to be characterized by small quantities of decorated wares (Smith 1990); as will be seen below, several sites actually have relatively high frequencies of red painted pottery. Porter, Jones Bayou, Sweat, and several other sites are assigned to this phase; I have also included Fullen, which falls within the geographic limits of the Jones Bayou district but was discovered after the appearance of Smith's paper. Several sites considered by Smith (1990) to have late period components, notably 40LA3 and 40LA25, have produced no evidence whatsoever of late period occupations and are not used here (Mainfort 1991, 1996).

Methods

Cluster analysis is a technique for exploratory data analysis that encompasses a variety of methods that seek to objectively separate a set of objects (in this case, site assemblages) into consistent groups, such that the resulting subsets have high intracluster resemblance and low intercluster similarity. The literature of many disciplines abounds with discussions and applications of cluster analysis, and technical aspects will not be addressed here. Some major references include Anderberg (1973), Hartigan (1975), Jain and Dubes (1988), and Aldenderfer and Blashfield (1984). Problems in the applications of clustering methods to archaeological data also have been discussed (e.g., Baxter 1993 and Read 1989a, b). Potential pitfalls notwithstanding, cluster analysis has proven to be a useful and fairly robust means for recovering structure from data sets (e.g., Dubes 1993 and Milligan 1980; some archaeological examples include Glascock 1992; Gregg et al. 1991; Kintigh and Ammerman 1982; Mainfort 1979; O'Shea 1984; and Rigaud and Simek 1991). Here I use average linkage and K-means clustering, perhaps the two most reliable methods (see Baxter 1993 and Milligan 1980), largely as tools of discovery (see Dubes 1993; Dubes and Jain 1976).

The results of hierarchical clustering typically are displayed as dendrograms (see fig. 7.2) that provide graphical representations of statistically derived groups. K-means clustering has several advantages over hierarchical clustering, among these the ability of the user to specify the desired number of partitions (i.e., clusters). At each level of partitioning the statistically best group is separated, allowing the researcher to observe the progress of partitioning. Moreover, since assignment of members to clusters entails minimizing squared error on attributes (in this case, ceramic type percentages), not only can the attributes of greatest statistical significance be identified, but also the characteristics of each cluster —that is, the range of individual attributes within clusters—may be generated. This is of considerable value in documenting variation in late period ceramic assemblages because contrasts between phases typically are expressed in terms of variation in the relative frequencies of specific ceramic types (e.g., Phillips 1970). All cluster analyses utilized normalized Euclidean distances as input statistics and were performed using *SYSTAT* (Wilkinson 1989).

While the objective of cluster analysis is basically to find groups within a data set, discriminant analysis assumes that two or more groups are known to exist within the data and that individual objects within the data set belong to one of the groups. Among a number of potential applications, discriminant analysis can be employed to confirm the validity of the presumed groups and to identify objects that do not fit within the established groups (Baxter 1993). As discussed below, I use discriminant analysis to provide a degree of validation for the results of cluster analysis and, more importantly, to demonstrate that the groups obtained using cluster analysis are superior to the traditional phase assignments.

Data Set

As noted above, current late period phase definitions in the study area are based primarily on the contrasting relative frequencies of various pottery sherd types in collections (usually, but not exclusively, "grab samples" from the surface). The analyses presented here also rely heavily on surface-collected ceramic samples, but relationships between site assemblages are investigated using multivariate statistical methods.

It could be argued that such data are unsuitable for creating meaningful groups of sites or for assessing the validity of the phases under scrutiny, and some pertinent comments seem warranted. First, my use of surface-collected ceramic sherds in this study does not constitute advocacy of a research strategy that relies solely on such data for the definition of archaeological phases. Nonetheless, surface collections can be robust data sets and, hence, valuable indicators of past behavior. Second, I am using data comparable, and in some cases identical, to those used by previous researchers in the formulation phases (e.g., Phillips 1970 and Smith 1990). Any criticisms of sample size or representativeness of the collections analyzed here (see, for example, Phillips 1970:936) apply even more strongly to the efforts of previous researchers.

Some of the sites discussed here also have earlier, middle period Mississippian components that could skew the ceramic samples. Again, the same problem was faced by earlier researchers (see Phillips 1970: 932–33) and, like these individuals, I chose to work with the available data. It should be added that in light of the appalling loss of archaeological sites to agricultural practices, in some instances the original Lower Mississippi Valley Survey collections (Phillips et al. 1951) represent virtually the only material that will *ever* be recovered from some major archaeological sites in the study area.

Sample size was of critical concern in selecting collections for inclusion in this study. In the case of ceramic collections from late period sites in the Central Mississippi Valley, the relationship between sample richness and diversity and sample size is unclear (see various papers in Jones et al. [1983] for a general discussion of this problem). One implication of the phases conceived by Phillips (1970) is that ceramic richness and diversity vary between regions. Phillips himself expressed concern about sample size throughout his Yazoo Basin report and felt that "50 rim and decorated sherds (equivalent to a total sample of 400–500) is minimal" (1970:246, passim). Moreover, "since many minority types regularly occur in frequencies of less than one percent" (Phillips 1970:4), infrequently occurring types may not be present in small samples. Some small samples of sherds from late period sites in the study area, however, exhibit both considerable richness and diversity (see O'Brien 1994), although it has not been demonstrated that the specific samples are truly representative.

For the analyses presented here, I include only sites from which there are relatively large collections. Sites from which fewer than 800 sherds were available were excluded, and all but a few of the sites included have ceramic assemblages that number in excess of 1,000 sherds (table 7.1). As an example of the limitations imposed by the criterion of sample size, only three sites assigned by Phillips (1970) to the Nodena phase were included in this study, namely Upper Nodena, Notgrass, and Carson Lake; these represent only one-third of the Nodena phase sites that Phillips (1970:935) considered to have "provided samples of sufficient size for safe identification" and less than one-twentieth of the sites assigned to the phase by D. Morse (1989, 1990).

Since a substantial amount of the data used here was taken from the original Lower Mississippi Valley survey sherd counts made during the 1940s, I employed the ceramic typology of Phillips et al. (1951) rather than more recent type-variety designations (e.g., Phillips 1970). In fact, Phillips himself employed the 1951 classification in preparing the cumulative frequency graphs he used to distinguish archaeological phases in the study area (1970:930–39). In the case of more recent collections that I analyzed according to type-variety nomenclature (see below), the resulting information loss was minimal (e.g., Ranch Incised is now designated Winterville Incised, *var. Ranch*). Moreover, most existing type-variety definitions are intuitively derived and were not created for addressing a specific problem; they are often subject to greater analytic difficulties than those posed by the original type definitions (see O'Brien 1994).

The specific ceramic types used in the analyses are familiar to all researchers in the area: Parkin Punctated, Barton Incised, Kent Incised, Ranch Incised, Old Town Red, Nodena Red and White, Rhodes Incised, Walls Engraved, Vernon Paul Appliqué, and Fortune Noded. Importantly, the frequencies of all these types were instrumental in the formulation of existing phase definitions (Phillips 1970; Smith 1990).

Although shell-tempered plainwares (Mississippi Plain and Bell Plain) figure prominently in existing late period phase definitions (Lumb and McNutt 1988; Phillips 1970; Smith 1990), undecorated ceramics were excluded from most of the statistical analyses presented below. Within the study area, late period plainwares are subsumed within two "super-types" that intergrade and are based on the subjective judgments of researchers about the "coarseness" or "fineness" of crushed shell particles in the paste. If the tempering particles are considered to be "coarse," a sherd is classified as a variety of Mississippi Plain, while "fine" shell-tempered plainwares are grouped within the type Bell Plain. But assessments of "coarse" and "fine" shell temper can vary considerably among competent researchers.

While common decorated types, such as Parkin Punctated, Barton Incised, and Old Town Red are easily and consistently sortable based on readily identifiable surface treatments, plainwares are far more difficult to consistently sort due to subjectivity inherent in type definitions. Since undecorated sherds constitute the overwhelming majority of late period ceramic assemblages (e.g., table 7.1), this problem undermines the utility of using relative frequencies of plainwares as the primary attributes of phases in anything but a general sense. Further, the difference between coarse and fine shell-tempered wares is one of technology and function, and thus the two major plainware types are not comparable to the decorated (stylistic) types (see Feathers 1989; O'Brien 1994, 1995; O'Brien et al. 1994 for additional discussion). Worth noting too is the comment by Phillips et al. (1951:109) that the type Neeley's Ferry Plain (now Mississippi Plain) was useful only in the most general sense for posting "very broad chronological and areal relationships. This point should be insisted on so that it is clear to the reader that, for example, the presence of say 85% Neeley's Ferry Plain on two widely separated sites does not necessarily indicate an intimate cultural relationship between them." Finally, because plainwares usually constitute at least 80 percent of late period ceramic assemblages in the region (see table 7.1), inclusion of plainwares in multivariate analyses can mask variation in the frequencies of decorated types.

None of this is meant to suggest that technological differences implied by variation in the relative frequencies of Mississippi Plain and Bell Plain have no cultural importance. For example, the marked differences in the frequencies of these types between the Parkin and Walls phases strongly implies that these two groups of sites were not part of the same cultural system (see House 1991b for some discussion). Rather than considering this to be irrelevant, I simply claim that such technological/functional variability should be examined *independently* of stylistic variability.

Nonetheless, since most previous researchers have attributed great importance to relative proportions of fine and coarse shell-tempered plain ceramics in defining late period archaeological phases, several analyses using plainwares were performed for comparative purposes, as reported below.

The raw data are ceramic sherd counts from each site (table 7.1). These were converted into percentage occurrences for input into *SYSTAT.* Since, as previously noted by Phillips (1970), the frequency of plainwares relative to decorated types may be of importance in isolating groups of sites, the percentages of each decorated type reflect frequencies within the entire ceramic assemblage for each site, not frequencies relative to the total number of decorated sherds (see Fox 1992 for an alternative approach).

Some comments about the collections that were employed are in order. For much of eastern Arkansas and northwestern Mississippi, the sherd counts from the original analysis sheets compiled by Phillips et al. (1951) were used, and in some instances, these represent the only available data. Additional data for the Kent phase area were obtained from John House's (1991b) dissertation. Most counts for western Tennessee sites are based on collections housed by the Tennessee Division of Archaeology. Reanalysis of collections housed at the C. H. Nash Museum-Chucalissa (cf. Smith 1990) provided data for Walls, Beck, Belle Meade, and several other sites. Sherd counts from Chucalissa were taken from Lumb and McNutt (1988); counts for Parkin include material excavated during the mid-1960s (Davis 1966; Klinger 1977).

The discussion that follows is based on a sample of 39 late period Central Mississippi Valley sites. Several sites with reasonably large collections were revealed to be extreme outliers during the initial analyses and were excluded from subsequent analyses. Outliers can affect the results of multivariate analyses by causing samples to appear more similar when compared to the outliers (Jain and Dubes 1988:51–52, 98–99). In the case of Vernon Paul, the exceptionally high frequency of decorated types (almost 30 percent, n=2,595) suggests that the collection may not be representative. The outlier status of Grant cannot be attributed to sampling error; the site appears to have a distinctive ceramic assemblage but was dropped from consideration here in order to highlight broader trends.

Analysis and Results

Initial investigation of the data set employed average linkage clustering to generate the dendrogram shown in figure 7.2. Two large macroclusters are represented. The uppermost includes, but is not limited to, virtually all sites located east of the Mississippi River. With the exception of Chucalissa, all sites in the lower macrocluster are located west of the Mississippi River.

Eight subclusters are suggested by the dendrogram. Starting at the top of figure 7.2, the "core" Walls phase sites (Walls, Irby, Lake Cormorant, and Woodlyn) comprise a fairly distinctive subcluster, which is interesting because of the importance of plainwares (which were not included in these analyses) in Phillips's (1970) definition of the phase. Below this subcluster in the dendrogram are two sites within Smith's (1990) Jones Bayou district. The Nodena phase sites (Upper Nodena, Notgrass, and

Carson Lake), along with a number of western Tennessee sites (Jeter, Hatchie, etc.), Turnbow (a Parkin phase site [Phillips 1970]), and Mound Place form a large subcluster. Smith's (1990) Tipton and Jones Bayou phases in western Tennessee are unsupported by the dendrogram, as is his assignment of Jeter and Chucalissa to the Walls phase. Also contradicted is Phillips's inclusion of Mound Place, an eastern Arkansas site, within the Walls phase. Hollywood and Commerce (two putative Kent phase sites in northwestern Mississippi) form a small subcluster within the "eastern" macrocluster (fig. 7.2).

Sites of the Kent phase (Clay Hill, Kent, Starkley, Davis, and Soudan), particularly in the more restrictive sense used by House (1991b), constitute another distinct subcluster. The subcluster including Chucalissa (traditionally considered a Walls phase site), Nickel, and Castile Landing does not equate with a traditional phase. As demonstrated below using K-means analysis, the Chucalissa ceramic assemblage does not closely resemble the assemblages of the Walls phase sites.

The traditional Parkin phase is easily recognized in another subcluster, albeit with the addition of Young and Cramor. This is of considerable interest because one distinctive feature of the Parkin phase is considered to be the extremely high ratio of Mississippi Plain to Bell Plain (P. Morse 1981; Morse and Morse 1983; Phillips 1970). Plainwares were excluded from this study, yet many sites attributed to the Parkin phase are grouped together here based on a fairly distinctive assemblage of decorated ceramics. Beck and Belle Meade, a pair of presumably sequent sites within arrowshot of each other, exhibit the expectedly close relationship and are the sole members of the eighth subcluster.

An eight-cluster K-means analysis (table 7.2) produced groups very similar to those obtained using average linkage clustering, as well as providing insights into the basis of cluster formation. Most of the western Tennessee sites, those of the Nodena phase, as well as Turnbow, form a single, large cluster (Cluster 1) that is distinguished by relatively low frequencies of virtually all decorated types. The "Parkin phase" subcluster of the dendrogram is replicated (Cluster 2), with the addition of Soudan; appropriately, this cluster is distinguished by relatively high percentages of the type Parkin Punctated (8.4 percent to 10.9 percent). Kent, Starkley, Clay Hill, and Davis again form a distinctive group (Cluster 3); in fact, this subset was initially generated during a three-cluster solution. The defining characteristics of the cluster are relatively high percentages of Parkin Punctated (5.7 percent to 10.1 percent), Barton Incised (3.3 percent to 6.1 percent), and Old Town Red (6.0 percent to 7.2 percent). Belle Meade and Beck (Cluster 4) again stand apart from virtually all other sites; both exhibit very high frequencies of Parkin Punctated (12.5 percent to 13.2 percent) and the largest percentages of Barton Incised

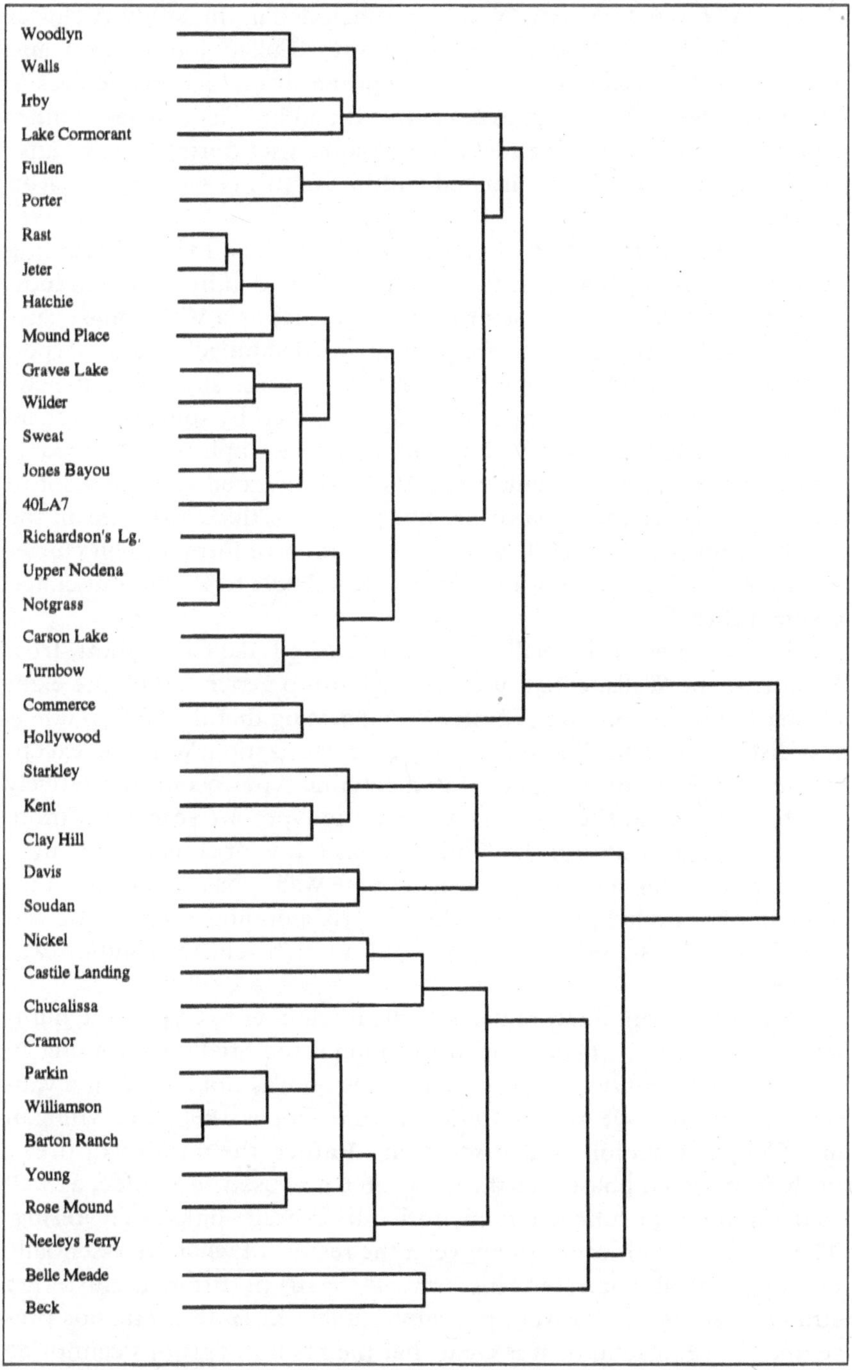

FIGURE 7.2. Dendrogram generated by average linkage clustering.

(7.0 percent to 8.4 percent) of any sites included in this study. A cluster of three Lauderdale County, Tennessee, sites (Fullen, Jones Bayou, and Porter; Cluster 5) was generated based primarily on high frequencies of Old Town Red (3.5 percent to 6.3 percent) and low frequencies of other types; two of these sites formed a minor subcluster during average linkage clustering and all are situated within Smith's (1990) Jones Bayou district.

The cluster consisting of Chucalissa, Nickel, and Castile Landing (Cluster 6) also appeared in the average linkage dendrogram and indicates that Chucalissa is not properly regarded as a Walls phase site, at least with respect to the frequencies of decorated ceramic types. Moreover, the high frequency of decorated types also suggests that viewing the site as a "secondary center," as suggested by some researchers (Lumb and McNutt 1988; Smith 1990) is at best simplistic and probably simply wrong. High percentages of Parkin Punctated (12.2 percent to 13.2 percent) are the most distinctive feature of this cluster. As in the dendrogram (fig. 7.2), Hollywood and Commerce form a small cluster (Cluster 7); a high ratio of Barton Incised relative to Parkin Punctated distinguishes the group.

Finally, sites of the Walls phase, including Lake Cormorant, Irby, Woodlyn, and Walls, constitute the final group generated by the eight cluster K-means solution (Cluster 8), suggesting that the Walls phase is less distinctive than Phillips's (1970) characterization. With the exception of Parkin Punctated, decorated ceramic types occur in relatively low frequencies at these sites, although the types are somewhat more common than in sites of the Nodena phase. It is of considerable note that although Phillips (1970) considered the Walls phase to be one of his strongest late period phases, the cluster corresponding to this phase was not isolated by K-means analysis until an eight-cluster solution was requested.

Since K-means analysis permits the researcher to choose the number of clusters generated, some justification is required for accepting an eight-cluster solution as "best." The decision was not based on a validation measure (see Dubes 1993, Jain and Dubes 1988, and Milligan and Cooper 1985 for some discussion). Rather, the number of previously formulated phases for the study area was used as a guide, as well as the number of subclusters identified by average-linkage clustering. The degree of isomorphism between the results of what are essentially methodologically opposed (hierarchical versus partitional) clustering strategies serves, in itself, to partially validate the interpretations presented above, insofar as it is clear that the resulting groups cannot be ascribed to serendipitous behavior by a single algorithm.

Following remarks made by Baxter (1993:206–9) regarding use of

TABLE 7.2. K-MEANS CLUSTERING: 8 CLUSTERS

Type	Between SS	DF	Within SS	DF	F-Ratio	Probability
Parkin Punctated	572.372	7	44.640	31	56.783	0.000
Barton Incised	181.406	7	30.200	31	26.601	0.000
Kent Incised	6.931	7	3.308	31	9.278	0.000
Ranch Incised	2.532	7	2.796	31	4.011	0.003
Old Town Red	127.688	7	38.532	31	14.676	0.000
Nodena R and W	2.314	7	1.135	31	9.031	0.000
Rhodes Incised	0.524	7	0.258	31	8.987	0.000
Walls Engraved	2.869	7	1.798	31	7.065	0.000
Vernon Paul Appl.	0.011	7	0.056	31	0.912	0.510
Fortune Noded	0.192	7	0.320	31	2.657	0.028

Cluster 1

Site	Distance	Type	Minimum	Mean	Maximum	S.D.
40LA007	0.50	Parkin Punctated	0.17	2.16	4.01	1.38
Hatchie	0.58	Barton Incised	0.10	0.69	2.84	0.77
Richardson's Lg.	0.56	Kent Incised	0.00	0.15	0.49	0.18
Wilder	0.27	Ranch Incised	0.00	0.23	1.09	0.29
Jeter	0.62	Old Town Red	0.28	1.26	2.78	0.79
Rast	0.56	Nodena R and W	0.00	0.11	0.37	0.11
Upper Nodena	0.68	Rhodes Incised	0.00	0.06	0.18	0.07
Notgrass	0.68	Walls Engraved	0.00	0.14	0.46	0.15
Sweat	0.58	Vernon Paul Appl.	0.00	0.03	0.16	0.05
Turnbow	0.88	Fortune Noded	0.00	0.06	0.23	0.07
Carson Lake	0.47					
Mound Place	0.51					
Graves Lake	0.33					

Cluster 2

Site	Distance	Type	Minimum	Mean	Maximum	S.D.
Rose Mound	0.47	Parkin Punctated	8.38	9.56	10.92	0.85
Cramor	0.58	Barton Incised	2.59	4.18	6.36	1.11
Neeley's Ferry	0.80	Kent Incised	0.00	0.19	0.89	0.29
Williamson	0.41	Ranch Incised	0.00	0.23	1.14	0.36
Barton Ranch	0.49	Old Town Red	0.13	1.06	4.20	1.26
Parkin	0.13	Nodena R and W	0.00	0.01	0.04	0.02
Young	0.43	Rhodes Incised	0.00	0.04	0.32	0.11
Soudan	1.12	Walls Engraved	0.00	0.07	0.40	0.13
		Vernon Paul Appl.	0.00	0.02	0.07	0.03
		Fortune Noded	0.05	0.19	0.34	0.12

TABLE 7.2. CONTINUED

Cluster 3

Site	Distance	Type	Minimum	Mean	Maximum	S.D.
Starkley	0.79	Parkin Punctated	5.68	7.96	10.10	1.58
Kent	0.40	Barton Incised	3.25	5.21	6.13	1.16
Clay Hill	0.31	Kent Incised	0.04	0.64	1.25	0.51
Davis	0.93	Ranch Incised	0.00	0.06	0.16	0.06
		Old Town Red	6.04	6.62	7.24	0.42
		Nodena R and W	0.00	0.28	0.57	0.25
		Rhodes Incised	0.00	0.07	0.10	0.04
		Walls Engraved	0.00	0.19	0.37	0.13
		Vernon Paul Appl.	0.00	0.00	0.00	0.00
		Fortune Noded	0.00	0.03	0.07	0.03

Cluster 4

Site	Distance	Type	Minimum	Mean	Maximum	S.D.
Beck	0.56	Parkin Punctated	12.50	12.86	13.22	0.36
Belle Meade	0.56	Barton Incised	6.98	7.66	8.35	0.68
		Kent Incised	1.35	1.93	2.52	0.59
		Ranch Incised	0.34	0.47	0.59	0.12
		Old Town Red	1.77	3.18	4.58	1.40
		Nodena R and W	0.13	0.61	1.09	0.48
		Rhodes Incised	0.28	0.37	0.46	0.09
		Walls Engraved	0.41	0.46	0.51	0.05
		Vernon Paul Appl.	0.03	0.04	0.06	0.01
		Fortune Noded	0.00	0.05	0.10	0.05

Cluster 5

Site	Distance	Type	Minimum	Mean	Maximum	S.D.
Porter	0.16	Parkin Punctated	2.98	3.22	3.60	0.27
Jones Bayou	0.43	Barton Incised	0.07	0.27	0.45	0.16
Fullen	0.48	Kent Incised	0.00	0.03	0.06	0.02
		Ranch Incised	0.00	0.04	0.07	0.03
		Old Town Red	3.50	4.83	6.32	1.16
		Nodena R and W	0.06	0.15	0.21	0.07
		Rhodes Incised	0.00	0.00	0.00	0.00
		Walls Engraved	0.07	0.16	0.22	0.06
		Vernon Paul Appl.	0.00	0.04	0.07	0.03
		Fortune Noded	0.00	0.13	0.39	0.19

TABLE 7.2. CONTINUED

Cluster 6

Site	Distance	Type	Minimum	Mean	Maximum	S.D.
Castile Landing	0.52	Parkin Punctated	12.20	12.74	13.16	0.40
Nickel	0.59	Barton Incised	1.09	2.35	4.18	1.32
Chucalissa	0.71	Kent Incised	0.37	0.40	0.45	0.04
		Ranch Incised	0.15	0.43	0.69	0.22
		Old Town Red	0.29	2.00	3.44	1.30
		Nodena R and W	0.00	0.13	0.23	0.09
		Rhodes Incised	0.17	0.20	0.23	0.02
		Walls Engraved	0.00	0.22	0.67	0.32
		Vernon Paul Appl.	0.00	0.05	0.11	0.05
		Fortune Noded	0.15	0.23	0.31	0.07

Cluster 7

Site	Distance	Type	Minimum	Mean	Maximum	S.D.
Hollywood	0.30	Parkin Punctated	3.16	3.60	4.03	0.44
Commerce	0.30	Barton Incised	4.43	4.52	4.60	0.09
		Kent Incised	0.40	0.83	1.26	0.43
		Ranch Incised	0.00	0.07	0.13	0.07
		Old Town Red	1.08	1.66	2.25	0.58
		Nodena R and W	0.72	1.06	1.39	0.33
		Rhodes Incised	0.09	0.11	0.13	0.02
		Walls Engraved	0.18	0.35	0.53	0.17
		Vernon Paul Appl.	0.00	0.00	0.00	0.00
		Fortune Noded	0.00	0.00	0.00	0.00

Cluster 8

Site	Distance	Type	Minimum	Mean	Maximum	S.D.
Lake Cormorant	0.52	Parkin Punctated	5.40	6.30	7.61	0.81
Irby	0.47	Barton Incised	0.07	0.88	1.46	0.52
Woodlyn	0.45	Kent Incised	0.28	0.54	0.70	0.16
Walls	0.38	Ranch Incised	0.43	0.97	1.30	0.34
		Old Town Red	0.45	1.15	2.68	0.89
		Nodena R and W	0.00	0.05	0.14	0.05
		Rhodes Incised	0.22	0.36	0.60	0.14
		Walls Engraved	0.43	1.01	1.67	0.48
		Vernon Paul Appl.	0.00	0.00	0.00	0.00
		Fortune Noded	0.00	0.04	0.10	0.04

the fewest number of variables in discriminant analysis, identical clusters were obtained by K-means using only the types Parkin Punctated, Barton Incised, and Old Town Red. This is a critical point in considering validation of the K-means solution using discriminant analysis. I have included table 7.2 to illustrate the variability in all 10 decorated pottery types; but in the discussion below on validation, I will be referring to clusters defined using *only* the types Parkin Punctated, Barton Incised, and Old Town Red. The relative frequencies of these three types in the clusters are illustrated using box plots (figs. 7.3–7.5). Notice the overlapping percentages between many of the clusters.

Aldenderfer (1982) notes that discriminant analysis is often used to "validate" the results of cluster analysis. Using only the types Parkin Punctated, Barton Incised, and Old Town Red, discriminant analysis placed all site assemblages into the correct group (cluster). Although such a procedure is not uncommon in the literature, it is actually invalid (Milligan 1996:366–67). Baxter's (1993:204–6) warning, although appropriate, is not emphatic enough on this point. Therefore, this result is not particularly informative.

One acceptable method for assessing cluster validity is external criterion analysis "based on (exogenous) variables not used in the cluster analysis" (Milligan 1996:367). Recall that the eight clusters generated by K-means analysis were obtained using only three variables: Parkin Punctated, Barton Incised, and Old Town Red. To examine the validity of the clusters, a discriminant analysis was performed using only ceramic types *not* used to define the clusters. These included the decorated types Kent Incised, Ranch Incised, Nodena Red and White, Rhodes Incised, Walls Engraved, Vernon Paul Appliqué, and Fortune Noded, as well as Mississippi Plain and Bell Plain. All but a single site assemblage were placed into the "correct" group (table 7.3). Therefore, the groups obtained by cluster analysis appear to be valid within the limitations of the data set.

I also used discriminant analysis to test the validity of the traditional phase assignments of the 39 sites. As shown in table 7.4, discriminant analysis failed to place 10 of the 39 site assemblages into the "correct" traditional phase. Since traditional phase formulations included relative frequencies of Mississippi Plain and Bell Plain, I performed a second discriminant analysis, including plainwares as variables. Correct placement improved to 33 of 39 sites but remained inferior to results obtained by cluster analysis. Thus, the groups of sites derived through cluster analysis are demonstrably superior to the traditional phase assignments of the same sites, although the statistically derived groups do not, in most instances, represent radical departures from the traditional phases formulated for the study area.

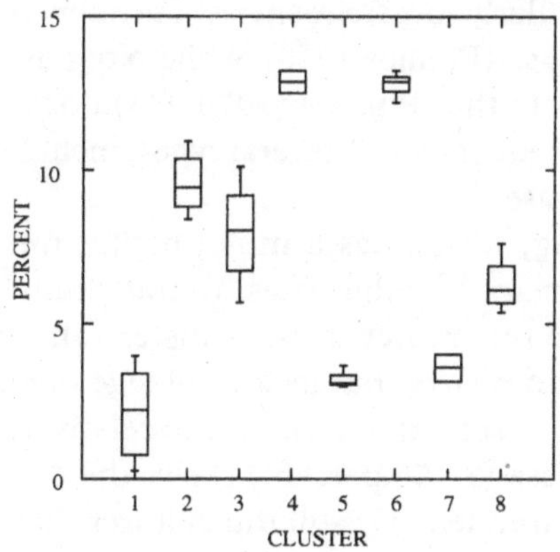

FIGURE 7.3. Box plot showing variation in the frequency of Parkin Punctated in clusters.

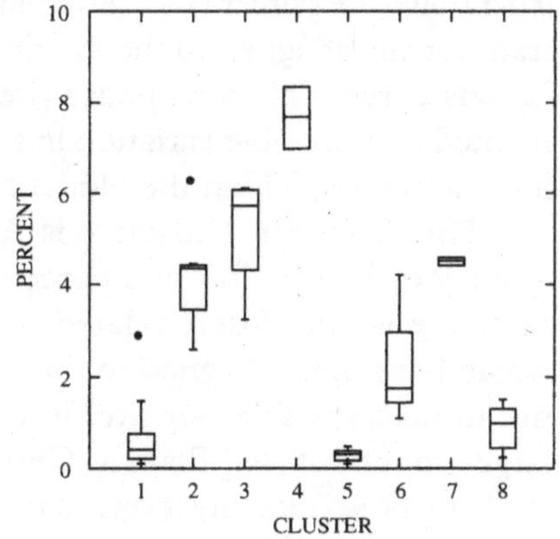

FIGURE 7.4. Box plot showing variation in the frequency of Barton Incised in clusters.

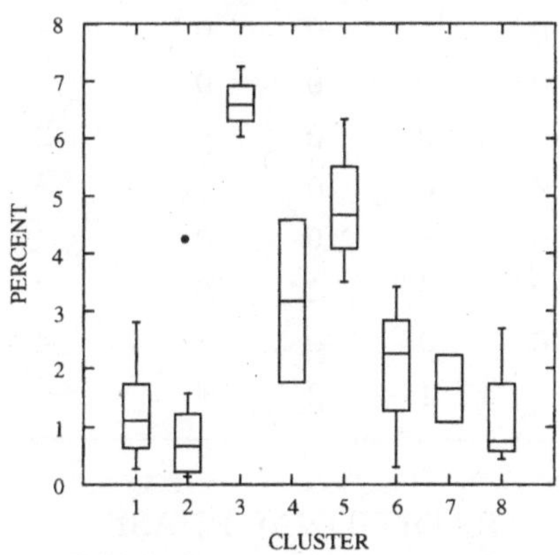

FIGURE 7.5. Box plot showing variation in the frequency of Old Town Red in clusters.

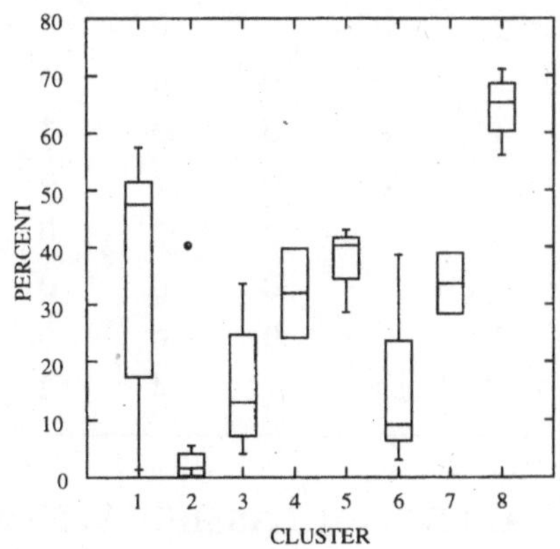

FIGURE 7.6. Box plot showing variation in the frequency of Bell Plain in clusters.

As discussed above, the relative frequencies of Mississippi Plain and Bell Plain may reflect synchronic social differences between groups of sites. Figure 7.6 illustrates variation in the frequency of Bell Plain between the group of sites generated by K-means analysis. Site assemblages included in Cluster 1 exhibit extreme variability in Bell Plain; collections from 40LA7 (14.8 percent), Notgrass (17.4 percent), and

Turnbow (0.3 percent) all have particularly low frequencies. Turnbow is traditionally assigned to the Parkin phase (Phillips 1970), while Notgrass is considered a Nodena phase site; note that Phillips (1970:935) documented considerable variation in the frequencies of several types, including plainwares, within the Nodena phase.

The outlier in Cluster 2 is Young, which has a much higher frequency of Bell Plain (39.8 percent) than the other sites; Young almost certainly is not closely related to the other sites in this cluster (all of which have been assigned to the Parkin phase), but its assemblage does not fit neatly with other sites in closer proximity. Finally, the relatively large amount of Bell Plain at Chucalissa (38.55 percent) skews the plot for Cluster 6; note, however, that this frequency is still much lower than

TABLE 7.3. CLASSIFICATION OF CERAMICS TYPES NOT USED IN DEFINING CLUSTERS

Cluster	1	2	3	4	5	6	7	8	Total
1	13	0	0	0	0	0	0	0	13
2	0	7	0	0	0	1	0	0	8
3	0	0	4	0	0	0	0	0	4
4	0	0	0	2	0	0	0	0	2
5	0	0	0	0	3	0	0	0	3
6	0	0	0	0	0	3	0	0	3
7	0	0	0	0	0	0	2	0	2
8	0	0	0	0	0	0	0	4	4
TOTAL	13	7	4	2	3	4	2	4	39

TABLE 7.4. CLASSIFICATION OF TRADITIONAL PHASE ASSIGNMENTS USING ONLY DECORATED CERAMIC TYPES

Phase	Nodena	Parkin	Kent	Tipton	Jones Bayou	Horseshoe Lake	Walls	Total
Nodena	3	0	0	0	0	0	0	3
Parkin	1	4	0	0	0	1	1	7
Kent	0	3	6	0	0	0	0	9
Tipton	0	0	0	5	0	0	0	5
Jones Bayou	0	0	0	1	4	0	0	5
Horseshoe Lake	1	1	0	0	0	2	0	4
Walls	0	0	0	1	0	0	5	6
TOTAL	5	8	6	7	4	3	6	39

the frequency of Bell Plain at any of the traditional Walls phase sites (Cluster 8).

It is obvious that the statistically derived groups of sites can be further refined. I only claim that my results are superior to earlier, intuitive efforts, not that the results are perfect.

Concluding Remarks

The Late Mississippian archaeological record of the Central Mississippi Valley exhibits enormous variation. This study represents an attempt to delineate underlying structures in a portion of that archaeological record, namely ceramic sherd collections from sites generally considered to have components postdating circa A.D. 1400. Attempts by previous researchers to order comparable data sets based on the dimensions of space, time, and content (i.e., the grouping of sites into phases) represent largely subjective comparisons of similarity between assemblages within "phases" and dissimilarities between assemblages from "different" phases.

Delineation of phases is complicated by numerous factors, including problems of sample size, representativeness, richness, and diversity. As emphasized below, current ceramic typologies do not adequately reflect variation in late period ceramics (e.g., Fox 1992; Teltser 1988). Robust chronologies are only now being developed (e.g., House 1991b; Mainfort 1996). Multiple components present at some sites also pose difficulties. While limiting interpretations presented here, these factors were faced by earlier researchers and therefore are not relevant to the present analyses, which sought primarily to assess the validity of previously defined phases.

Cluster and discriminant analysis of ceramic assemblages from 39 sites in the Central Mississippi Valley suggests that some previously defined late period phases represent relatively valid (or at least analytically defensible) units, while others are much less robust and some lack an objective basis. This partially contradicts O'Brien's (1995:35) recent assertion that "*no* amount of statistical manipulation can presently sort out proposed Parkin-phase assemblages from proposed Nodena-phase assemblages—a situation that can be extended to every late Mississippian-period phase defined for the tri-state area" (i.e., northeastern Arkansas, southeastern Missouri, and western Tennessee—author). In fact, not only can groups of sites be objectively derived, but most of these groups exhibit considerable spatial integrity. That is, many groups generally correspond to traditional notions of archaeological phases. Importantly, my analyses clearly demonstrate the superiority of site groupings generated using multivariate statistical methods to current, intuitively defined phases.

From the Spanish chronicles, it is evident that distinct political entities were present in the Central Mississippi Valley during the sixteenth century. Most researchers interested in this region believe that many, if not most, of the sites discussed here were occupied during or slightly prior to this time span and, therefore, were roughly contemporary (e.g., Morse and Morse 1983; Phillips 1970; Smith 1990).

Unfortunately, the chroniclers of the de Soto *entrada* do not provide us with commentary on stylistic or technological variation in ceramics within each of the "provinces" visited by the Spaniards. It is clear that there is considerable and significant technological variability in ceramics between some groups of sites in the Central Mississippi Valley. Sites in the traditional Parkin phase area of northeastern Arkansas are characterized by the overwhelming dominance of coarse shell-tempered ceramics (Mississippi Plain), while sites of the traditional Walls phase area in northwestern Mississippi exhibit very high frequencies of Bell Plain. This may suggest that the late period sites in these two areas were not part of the same political entity (e.g., House 1991b:313). But differences in ceramic technology are not so pronounced when comparing other site assemblages used in this analysis. Further, none of the ceramic assemblages under consideration have been subjected to rigorous technological analysis.

Of course, the groups of sites derived here are based on stylistic, not technological, differences, specifically relative frequencies of certain decorated pottery types. That such groups can be derived using multivariate statistical methods represents a major contribution to late period archaeology in the Central Mississippi Valley. Yet it remains unsettling that these groups of sites, some of which may partially correspond to some of the "provinces" traversed by de Soto, share virtually all of the current ceramic types used in this analysis and are distinguished by relatively small differences in type frequencies.[1] In short, the picture that emerges is one of considerable stylistic uniformity in ceramics throughout the study area.

In contrast, late period Caddo ceramics from southern Arkansas exhibit "extraordinary variability," which allows identification of numerous distinctive ceramic traditions within small regions (Schambach 1993a:80). Specific design motifs are readily attributable to individual traditions (Schambach, personal communication 1997), each of which represents a Caddo polity.

There seems to be, at least on an intuitive level, a seeming contradiction between the relatively uniform ceramics of the Central Mississippi

[1] It is important to note that the de Soto documents suggest that the inhabitants of the various "provinces" in northeastern Arkansas spoke dialects that were mutually intelligible.

Valley, which was home to several large, ranked polities with fortified towns (Morse and Morse 1983), and the distinct regional ceramic traditions of the Caddo, with their dispersed settlement pattern (e.g., Schambach 1993a). One might expect quite the opposite situation.

A partial explanation for this apparent problem may be found in analytical approaches to ceramic stylistic variability in the respective regions. The fine-grained stylistic analysis undertaken for the Caddo region (see Schambach 1981 for an early example) simply has not been accomplished in the Central Mississippi Valley. I strongly suspect that reanalysis of ceramic collections, emphasizing explicitly defined modes and motifs derived from complete vessels, would produce a data set from which much more pronounced stylistic differences could be identified between groups of sites in the study area.

Existing ceramic typology in the study area is simply inadequate for addressing even such basic issues as ceramic spatial and temporal variability, much less the nature of settlement patterns and political organization. The analytical methods used here provide hints of the potential information represented by the vast extant ceramic collections from the Central Mississippi Valley. Application of these methods to data sets not bound to existing ceramic typologies have the potential to significantly advance our understanding of the late period archaeological record in this region.

Acknowledgments

Ceramic counts from many of the sites used in this study were transcribed from copies of the original Lower Mississippi Valley Survey (Harvard University) records, copies of which are on file at the Department of Anthropology, University of Memphis. Several collections housed at the C. H. Nash Museum-Chucalissa were analyzed for use in this study; Shawn Chapman assisted with the analysis. Most of the western Tennessee data are derived from collections obtained and curated by the Tennessee Division of Archaeology. Charles McNutt, Mary Kwas, John House, and Mike O'Brien commented on previous drafts of this paper, although their much appreciated suggestions have not always been heeded.

CHAPTER EIGHT

SPIRO AND THE TUNICA: A NEW INTERPRETATION OF THE ROLE OF THE TUNICA IN THE CULTURE HISTORY OF THE SOUTHEAST AND THE SOUTHERN PLAINS, A.D. 1100–1750

FRANK F. SCHAMBACH

The Stranger, if he be not a trader, is an enemy.
—OLD ENGLISH PROVERB

Who were the Spiroans and how did they accumulate the hoards of prestige goods that, in sheer quantity, distinguish the Spiro site from all other Southeastern ceremonial centers? In 1978, after speculating without enthusiasm that they might have been the ancestral Wichita,[1] Phillips and Brown (1978:21–22) wrote: "Obviously it is not possible to pinpoint the descendants of the Spiroan people." Fifteen years later, citing circumstantial evidence, I proposed that they might be the Tunica (Schambach 1993b:221–24), although I did not see how that hypothesis could be confirmed archaeologically. Now Derrick and Wilson (1997) have published new bioanthropological data that, when interpreted within the framework of the new paradigm I have offered for the archaeology of the Arkansas Valley (Schambach 1993b, 1995), support my hypothesis that the Spiroans were ancestral Tunica. More importantly, they show what kinds of historical and bioanthropological data are needed to confirm it.

The Sanders Site and the Spiroan Trade Network

These new data come not from Spiro but from the Sanders site, located 150 miles to the southwest of Spiro in the Red River drainage in northeast

Texas (fig. 8.1). On the basis of a singular assemblage from 21 Mississippi period graves excavated by A. T. Jackson in 1931, Sanders has long been considered the type site for the Sanders "focus," an archaeological unit that supposedly represents a unique, Plains-oriented manifestation of Caddo culture on the western edge of the Eastern Woodlands in northeast Texas and southeast Oklahoma (Bruseth et al. 1995; Krieger 1946). But in recent years I have argued that the cultural and bioanthropological materials from the graves, most of the former so obviously Spiroan that Brown (1984:262) considers the Sanders focus a "regional variant" of his Arkansas Valley Spiro phase, represent a site unit intrusion (Schambach 1993b, 1993c, 1995, 1996, 1997). The intruders were Spiroan traders from the Arkansas Valley who established and maintained an entrepôt at Sanders for the purpose of obtaining Osage orange bows from the Caddo in exchange for Mississippian prestige goods. This interpretation rests on four sets of facts pertaining to the Sanders site and the natural history and ethnobotany of Osage orange (*Maclura pomifera,* or bois d'arc).

1. The Sanders site overlooks Bois d'arc Creek, near its confluence with the Red River. This 80 mile long creek was named toward the middle of the eighteenth century by French trappers operating out of La

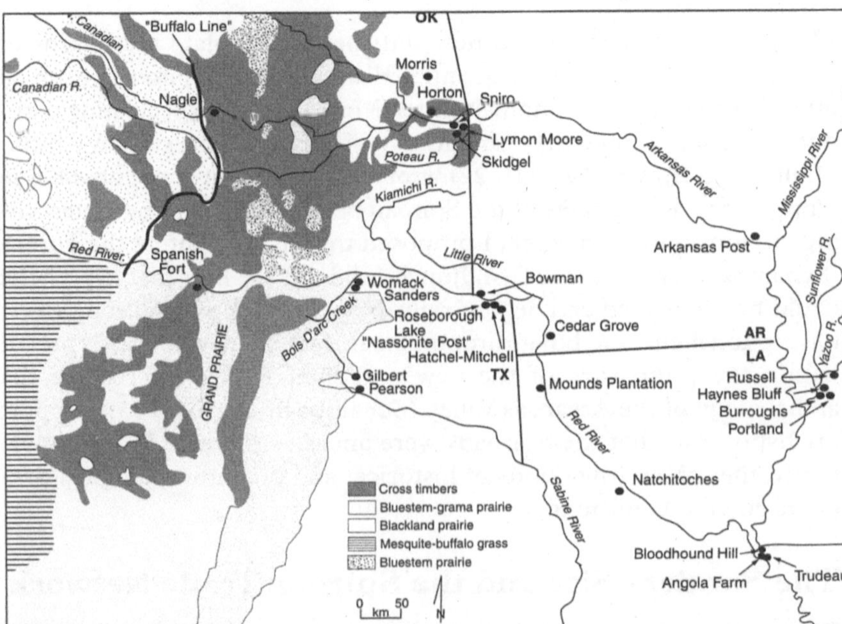

FIGURE 8.1. Sites and important biogeographical features discussed in the text.

Harpe's "Nassonite Post," located about 108 miles down the Red River (Wedel 1978). Seeing the Caddo cutting bow staves from a large stand of Osage orange trees that dominated the broad bottomlands of this creek, they called it "Bois d'arc" or "Bow Wood" Creek (Flores 1984:330 n. 14). These bottomlands lie directly in front of the Sanders site.

2. Osage orange is one of a small group of North and South American tree species that Janzen and Martin (1982:27; see also Delcourt and Delcourt 1991b:27) call "neotropical anachronisms." These are species that are or, in the case of Osage orange at the time of European contact, were, on the verge of extinction due to the extinction of the various Pleistocene animal species that ate their large, pulpy fruits and dispersed their massive seeds. Such species tend to have abnormally small modern ranges.

The modern range of Osage orange could not be called small, but it is a postcontact phenomenon. Because of its value to Euro-American settlers as a fast-growing hedge and windbreak plant, and as an exceptionally tough and durable hardwood (Burton 1973; Smith and Perino 1981; Winberry 1979), Osage orange was rapidly and widely planted throughout North America, particularly the Plains, the Midwest, and the Southeast (Smith and Perino 1981:29–30) soon after 1804,[2] the year Meriwether Lewis brought the species to the attention of science (Jackson 1962:170–71). Its range on the eve of European contact, however, was small, probably extraordinarily so. As of 1690, the year before horses were reintroduced to the Red River Valley (whereupon they would have resumed their role as one of the original Pleistocene animal vectors for the dispersal and propagation of this species, if such they were; see Schambach 1995:n. 27), its distribution was limited to a very small area in northeast Texas and southeast Oklahoma (Flores 1984:260–61 n. 224, 1985:114 n. 29; Weniger 1996:237–41). It is likely that the main, if not the only, stand was in the bottomlands of Bois d'arc Creek (Schambach 1995:11–[illegible]). Thus the Sanders site would have overlooked the best, possibly th[illegible], native stand of Osage orange in Holocene North America before 1[illegible]

3. Osage orange is one of the two best bow woods in the world, the other being yew, to which it is in all respects equal if not superior (Atwill 1992; Hamm 1989:22, 1992; Laubin and Laubin 1980:59; Peattie 1953: 480). It was by far the best available in native North America east of the Pacific Northwest, where Pacific yew was in use.

There is ample evidence from the historic period that its properties as a bow wood were appreciated and that Osage orange bows were widely distributed. Bows, or bow staves, of Osage orange—always apparently from the Kadohadacho country in the Great Bend region of the Red River Valley, which, as Swanton (1942:138) pointed out many years ago, "was famous for its bow wood, the Osage orange or bois d'arc"—were traded to tribes in the Mississippi Valley, the Southwest, and the Plains as far south as Sonora and as far north as Montana.

The earliest mention of Osage orange bows and the aboriginal bow trade is by Joutel, who, visiting the Kadohadacho in 1687 (Swanton 1942:41), reported that "Indians came to their country to get [bow wood] from distances of 50 or 60 leagues." While he was with the Kadohadacho, he met two Indians who had traveled to their territory in the Great Bend region of the Red River Valley for bows to take to the Quapaw living on the lower Arkansas in exchange for "products to be had along the Mississippi" (Swanton 1942:41).

Noting that in the nineteenth century the Tewa were using Osage orange bows evidently obtained in trade with the Comanche, or some other tribe east of them, who presumably had obtained them from the Caddo, Swanton (1942:37) speculated that the turquoises[3] and cotton blankets members of the de Soto expedition saw among the Caddo of northeast Texas in 1542 had reached that area in exchange for Osage orange bows.

The Tewa considered Osage orange wood "better for making bows than any which grew in the Tewa country," and the Pima also favored it (Robbins et al. 1916:68, 68n). The Osage orange bow that impressed Saxton Pope as the best of all the American Indian bows he examined and tested had been owned by a Yaqui Indian (Pope 1962:14–15), indicating that some Osage orange bows were traded to northern Mexico.

Early-nineteenth-century European travelers on the Plains repeatedly met Indians equipped with bows of Osage orange. In 1832 George Catlin (1973:32) found the Blackfoot using short, powerful, sinew backed bows of which he wrote: "The greater number of these bows are made of ash, or of 'bois d'arc' (as the French call it)." During his expedition of 1832–34, Prince Maximilian also recorded that the Blackfoot had bows of bois d'arc, noting that they were obtained in trade with tribes farther south (Peattie 1953:480). In 1853, on the Llano Estacado, a Lieutenant Whipple encountered a band of Kiowas who "carried superb bows of bois d'arc, ornamented with brass nails, silver plate and wampum beads" (Peattie 1953:480). Hamm (1989:21–22) states that "the people of the Missouri drainage, such as the Pawnee, Osages and Poncas, used osage orange for the most part, but occasionally used hickory." According to Otis T. Mason (1972:10): "The Pawnee warrior always preferred a bow of bois d'arc, and besides the one in actual use he would always have in his lodge a stick of the same material, which at his leisure he would be working into shape." Hamm (1989:21–22) reports examining Pawnee bows of Osage orange that were "unusually thick, powerful weapons pulling 70 pounds or more." He opines that: "On the Southern

Plains Osage orange was the overwhelming favorite for making bows since the dozen old Comanche and Kiowa bows belonging to museums and Indian families are all made of Osage orange." He also remarks, unfortunately without documentation, that "a few" bows of Osage orange were used by tribes such as the Potawatomi, Sac, Fox, and Chippewa residing around the headwaters of the Mississippi River (Hamm 1989:17).

4. Powerful, technically sophisticated Osage orange bows are well-attested archaeologically from two early Mississippi period Caddo sites in the Red River Valley in Louisiana and Arkansas. The most complete, best-described, and best-dated specimens are the remains of four bows from Mound 5, Burial Pit 5 (convincingly radiocarbon dated to circa A.D. 1050–1090) at the Mounds Plantation site in northwest Louisiana (see fig. 8.1; Webb 1984:18; Webb and McKinney 1975:104–8, figs. 5, 15). I have examined and photographed the remains of at least one and probably as many as three others in private collections from the Bowman site in southwest Arkansas (fig. 8.1). Excavated by relic hunters in the early 1960s, they are from mound burials similar in age and type to those Webb reported for Mounds Plantation.[4]

The most complete of the Mounds Plantation bows would have been 65 to 66 inches long, originally with a leather handgrip, recurved tips, and—judging from a replica of the original—a draw weight of approximately 70 pounds (Webb and McKinney 1975:104–5). The recurved tips, which show that Caddo bowyers had an impressive technical tradition behind them by A.D. 1050, would have made this a faster and flatter shooting weapon than a simple long bow (Baker 1992). The 70 pound draw weight, not unusual for Osage orange "self bows," significantly exceeds the 55 pounds modern archers consider adequate to kill any big game animal in North America (Baker 1992, 1994; Hamm 1994; Hardcastle 1992).

My interpretation of these four sets of facts is as follows: Because of the superiority of Osage orange as a bow wood and its extraordinarily limited natural range, powerful, expertly made Osage orange bows must have been a highly valued commodity in the economies of the Southern Plains and, as suggested recently by Lafferty (1994:201), the Southeast during the Mississippi period. More specifically, they were one of the two key commodities, the other being buffalo products, that circulated in a vast three-way Southern Plains and Mississippian exchange system (fig. 8.2) that involved Osage orange bows from the Red River Valley, buffalo products from the Southern Plains, and non-utilitarian Mississippian prestige goods such as shell cups, shell gorgets, and shell beads from the central Mississippi Valley and elsewhere in the Southeast (Schambach 1994, 1995).

The hub of this system was Spiro, not just one more Mississippian ceremonial center but the strategically located base of operations for long-distance traders who established and maintained entrepôts at the sources of supply of valuable goods (Schambach 1993b). At their Sanders site entrepôt they exchanged Mississippian prestige goods for Osage orange bows made by the Red River Valley Caddo. These they transported over a 150-mile-long natural route to Spiro (fig. 8.3; see also Schambach 1993c:15, 1995:10–11, fig. 4), whence some were carried east into Mississippian territory, while others were carried west into the Southern Plains. There, at other entrepôts such as the Nagle site (see below; Schambach 1995:19–20 n. 31, 1997:27–30) on the North Canadian River near present Oklahoma City (fig. 8.1), they traded them to Plains buffalo hunters for hides, dried

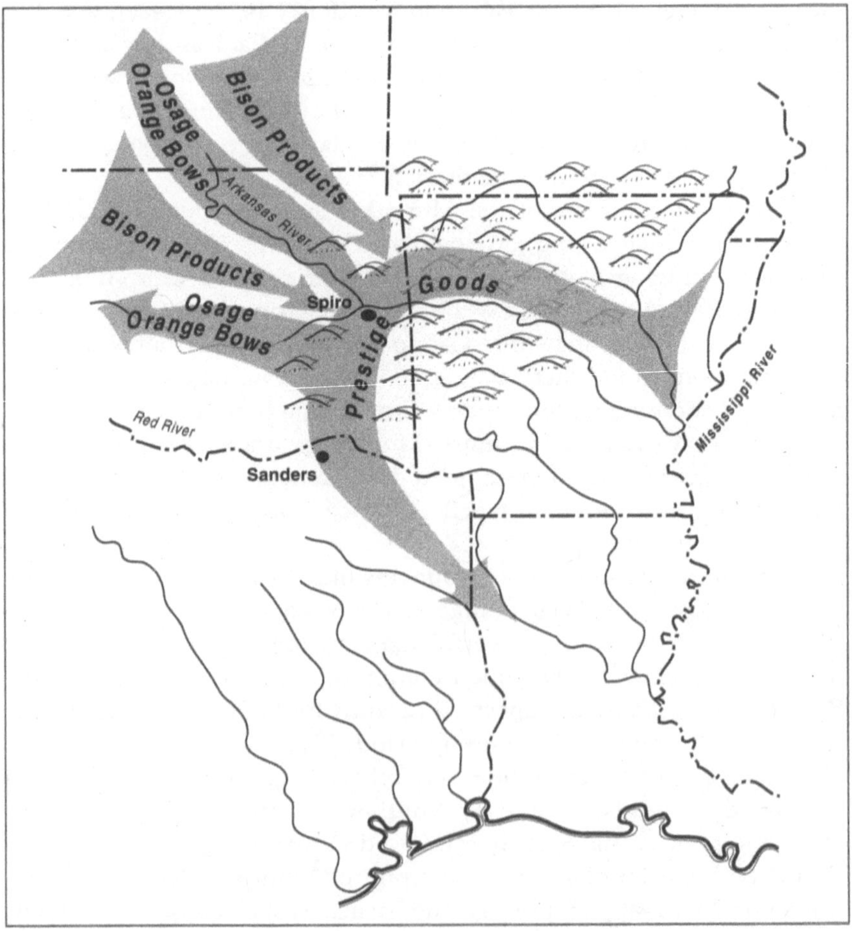

FIGURE 8.2. The Spiroan trade network.

meat, and tallow to be transported east to the Mississippi Valley via Spiro. The hoards of Mississippian prestige goods that accumulated at Spiro are a measure of the extent and importance of the activities of these traders in the economies of the Southeast and the Southern Plains between A.D. 1000 and 1350.

That is my solution to the riddle of Spiro, as posed by Phillips and Brown (1978:22; see also Brown 1996:31–34):

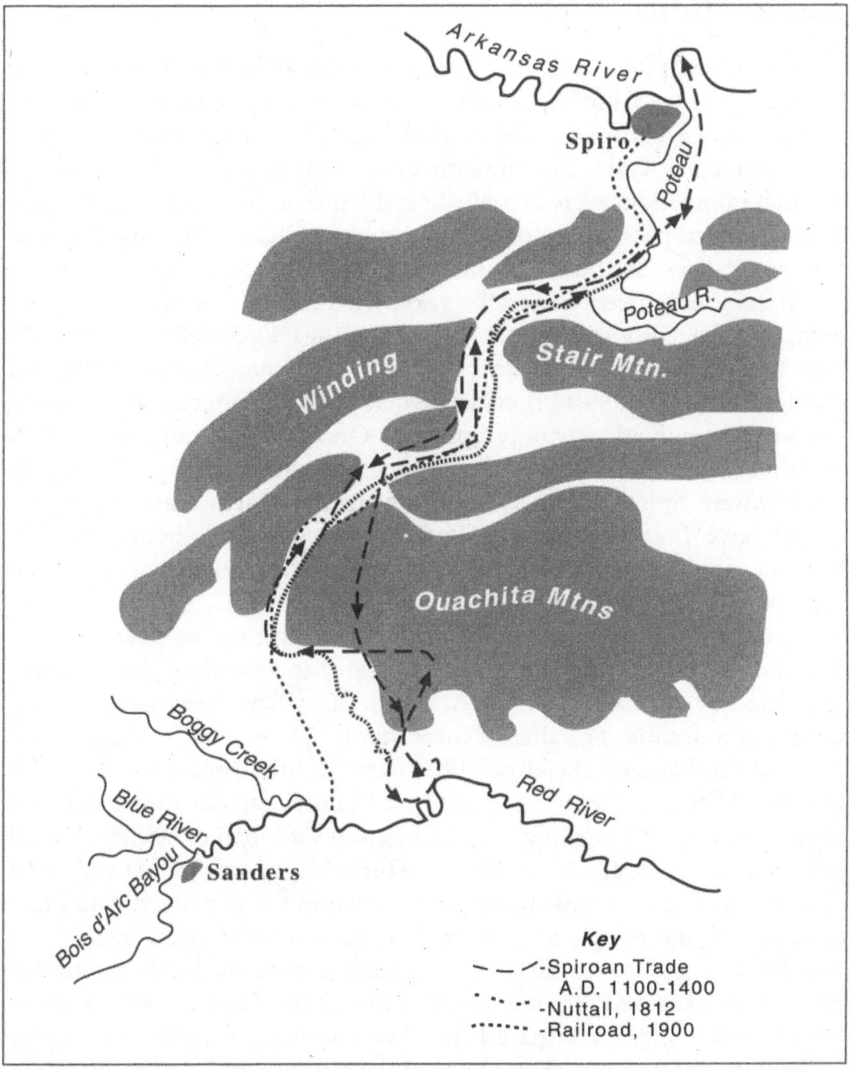

FIGURE 8.3. Use of the natural route from Spiro to Sanders through time.

> It is . . . assumed that the source of power of the ruling chiefs was control of the eastern gateway through which an extensive trade in raw and finished materials was passing at the time. From the nature and extent of exotic grave goods in the Great Mortuary burials, a strong import trade from eastern centers can be inferred, but what sorts of goods went the other way have not yet been determined.

The Bioanthropology of the Sanders Site and Its Implications

The evidence that the goods that "went the other way" were Osage orange bows and buffalo products obtained in exchange for Osage orange bows is circumstantial because these kinds of objects rarely survive archaeologically. But bioanthropological evidence that intrusive Spiroan populations were actually in residence at the Sanders and Nagle sites, the entrepôts where these goods were collected by long-distance Spiroan traders, has been accumulating for quite some time.

It has long been generally acknowledged on the basis of good archaeological (Brooks 1994:319–21; Griffin 1961:30; Shaeffer 1957:93–97) and bioarchaeological (Brues 1957:104, 1959:66; Owsley 1989:131; Owsley and Jantz 1989:140) evidence that the people buried at the Nagle site were foreigners, probably Spiroans. On that basis, coupled with its location (fig. 8.1), I interpret Nagle as a Spiroan entrepôt located precisely where Spiroan traders traveling up the North Canadian River would have first encountered buffalo *en masse* and, hence, buffalo hunters capable of supplying them with significant quantities of buffalo products (Schambach 1995:19–20 n. 31, 1997:28–30).

Bioanthropological observations suggesting that (as nearly all the cultural materials from the graves indicate) the Sanders site also was populated by intruders from the Arkansas Valley have been accumulating for about a decade. The first of these was by Dow (1987), who pointed out that the Sanders skeletons differ significantly from those from the Hatchel-Mitchell site, located about 100 miles farther down the Red River in northeast Texas (fig. 8.1) and clearly Caddoan on archaeological grounds (Story et al. 1990:340–41). Her ad hoc, archaeologically and bioanthropologically unsupported explanation for this unexpected discordance is that people at Sanders may have intermarried with Plains peoples. Burnett (1990b:393–99), analyzing unpublished data assembled by Jackson, observed that the infection rate in the Sanders skeletons was "dramatically high" compared to other populations in the Red River Valley, an observation that Diane Wilson (personal communication 1996) has confirmed. Furthermore, Burnett concluded that the Sanders skeletons are "markedly different" overall from Caddo skeletal populations from sites east of Sanders in the Red River Valley. Wilson (1993:11) added to the growing list of differences her observation that the Sanders skeletons evince an unusually high degree of degenerative joint disease of a type suggesting that the Sanders people may have regularly carried heavy loads on their backs or heads and might have done "a great deal of" traveling on foot.

As I argued some years ago, these peculiarities of the Sanders population relative to neighboring Red River Caddo populations are inexplicable according to the conventional hypothesis (Krieger 1946) that the people buried at Sanders were Red River Valley Caddo of long standing. But they are easily explained in terms of mine (Schambach 1993b:204–5, 1995:10–11). A group of traders from the Arkansas Valley would have been genetically different in ways detectable osteologically from people in the Red River Valley (Barnes and Rose 1990:12; Schambach 1993b: 190–93). Their skeletons could be expected to show, as some of the Sanders skeletons do, evidences of infections with diseases of childhood that are characteristic of the Mississippi period occupants of the Arkansas Valley (Brown 1984:259; Brues 1958, 1959; Burnett 1988: 212–14) but not of those of the Red River Valley. And the skeletons of long-distance traders regularly plying the 150-mile river and overland route between Spiro and Sanders could be expected to show the kinds of stress-induced degeneration that Wilson (1993:11) has identified in the Sanders site skeletons.

Confirmation that these are in fact the skeletons of long-distance traders from Spiro came with the publication of the aforementioned paper by Derrick and Wilson (1997; see also Wilson and Derrick 1996), a study of the styles of "cranial modeling"—that is, cranial deformation—exhibited by all skulls from presumed Caddo contexts in east Texas. Derrick and Wilson's crucial discovery was that two distinct styles of deformation, produced by different techniques, were used. The commonest was a "tabular," or frontal-occipital, style (fig. 8.4) that was also the norm for the Caddo throughout east Texas and (as Wilson has recently informed me) southwest Arkansas, because (except one specimen from a site in the Neches drainage) it is the only one represented at all but two sites—Sanders and an adjacent but much later *historic period* site called the Womack site (fig. 8.1), discussed later in this chapter. At these two sites a readily distinguishable "annular" style prevails (Derrick and Wilson 1997:142; Wilson and Derrick 1996:11–12).

The significance of this, although Derrick and Wilson do not discuss it, is that the annular style is characteristic of and essentially unique to Mississippi period and (as we shall see) later populations of the Arkansas Valley in eastern Oklahoma, particularly Spiro phase populations. It is the same as the "circular" style of deformation, "produced by a circular binding from the frontal region to the occiput," that according to Brues (1957, 1958, 1959), Stewart (1941:343–44), Neumann (1942:310), and Brown (1984:258–59) characterizes the substantial Spiro phase skeletal population from the Horton, Morris, and Spiro sites (fig. 8.1).[5] Predictably, it also is exhibited by all the males represented in the small collection of skeletons from the Nagle site (Brues 1957). It has not been identified elsewhere in the Southeast or the Plains, except a few possible isolated specimens from Missouri and northeastern Tennessee (Neumann 1942:310; Stewart 1941:343–44).[6]

Therefore, Derrick and Wilson's demonstration that the annular cranial deformation exhibited by the skeletons from Sanders and Womack is generally absent in other Mississippi period skeletal populations from the Red River Valley in Texas and Arkansas tips the scales in favor of my argument that, on what now amounts to comprehensive cultural and bioanthropological evidence, most of the people interred at the Sanders site were Spiroans from the Arkansas Valley.[7] Hence, I consider the Sanders site, the Nagle site, and (as I will argue presently) the

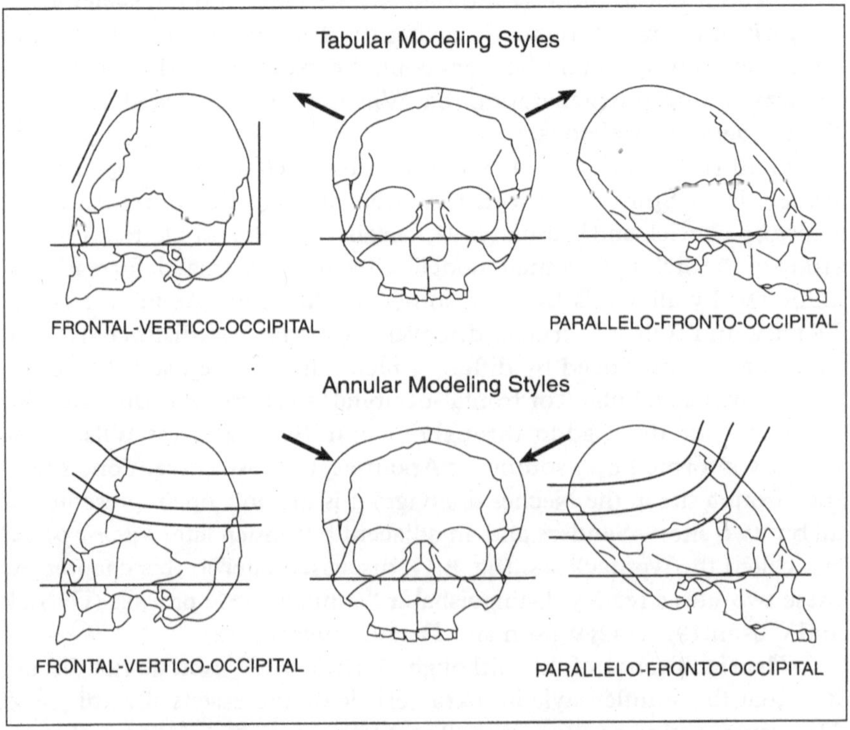

FIGURE 8.4. Tabular and annular styles of cranial deformation (after Wilson and Derrick 1996).

Womack site textbook examples of that phenomenon so rarely documented in the archaeological literature of the Southeast and the Plains, the site unit intrusion (B. D. Smith 1984a:29–30). Further, I consider the Sanders and Nagle sites, both populated with Arkansas Valley Spiroans and both strategically located with respect to resources that would have been of great value to Mississippian populations in the Mississippi Valley, compelling evidence that Spiro was the center for a Mississippian trade network that linked the Red River Valley, the Southern Plains, and the Central Mississippi Valley.

Cranial Deformation and the Ethnic Identity of the Spiroans

Did the Spiroans, a people whose descendants would be easily identifiable historically as well as archaeologically, provided they continued to practice annular cranial deformation, survive into the historic period? I have found only two possible references to this style of deformation in the Southeast during the historic period. Both appear to pertain to descendants of the Spiroans. The earliest and most explicit, Garcilaso's description of the people de Soto encountered in the province of Tula in 1541 (Varner and Varner 1951:457–58) is discussed here. The other, discussed later on, is a description by Father Gravier (see Shea 1861:134) of the Tunican practice of cranial deformation as of 1700 that only suggests the annular style.

According to Garcilaso:

> The people in this province of Tula differ from all those our Spaniards encountered previously; for, as we have said, the others are fine and handsome, whereas these, both male and female, have loathsome countenances. Even though naturally well featured, they render themselves hideous with devices wrought upon their persons. Their heads are incredibly long and taper off towards the top having been made this way by artifice; for from the moment they are born their heads are bound and are left thus until they are from nine to ten years of age.

This is a good description of annular deformation, which makes the head look very long, seen from the front or the side, and makes it "taper off towards the top" when viewed from the front (fig. 8.4). Tabular deformation also causes the head to look long from the front or side, but it does not cause it to taper above the ears. Because pressure is applied from the front and back only, it causes the head to bulge above the ears so that, viewed from the front, the person looks hyperbrachycephalic (see Lewis et al. 1995:fig. 11.7).

This is also a plausible description of how annular deformation was accomplished. Instead of binding an infant to a cradleboard during much of the first two years or so of life, as seems to have been the custom almost universally in the Southeast (Swanton 1946:539ff.), the people of Tula wrapped their children's heads with bands of cloth or leather, which they wore more or less constantly until they were eight or nine years old. The Spaniards must have seen this because, as is evident from Garcilaso's account, they found it difficult to communicate with the Tulans.

Since there is little doubt that Tula was in the Arkansas Valley, somewhere in the Fort Smith/Spiro area (Early 1993b:74–75; Hudson 1993:146–47), Garcilaso's account fits the bioarchaeological and historical data perfectly, and the Arkansas Valley in eastern Oklahoma was the one place on their route through the Southeast where the Spaniards could have seen people practicing annular cranial deformation. Also, since Early (1993b:73; see also Rogers 1996:68) equates the province of Tula with the Fort Coffee phase, and since the Fort Coffee phase ceramic assemblage differs from that of the Spiro phase only in nuances (Rohrbaugh 1984:279–81; Schambach 1993b:231),[8] Garcilaso's account affirms that the *Spiroans* were still in the Spiro locality about one hundred years after the supposed collapse (Brown 1996:200) of Spiro as a center for east-west exchange around A.D. 1450. And it informs us that they called themselves, or were called, the Tula.

The Fort Coffee Phase Tula as Traders

Garcilaso and the other chroniclers of the de Soto expedition also inform us that in 1541 the Tula, heirs to the Spiroan tradition of long-distance trading (Schambach 1993b:196–208, 1993c, 1995, 1997), were still importing buffalo products from the Southern Plains and trading them to people in the Mississippi Valley. The "corridor" for trade between the Southern Plains and the Mississippi Valley had not "shifted south to the Red River basin" after 1450 as Brown (1996:200) supposes.

Garcilaso (Varner and Varner 1951:457) reports that "In the town . . . our men found serving as bed covers a great number of cowhides which had been softened and dressed without removing the hair; and there were in addition many others waiting to be dressed. Moreover there was beef." Elvas (Quinn 1979:135) reports that after the battle of Tula, and after de Soto had sent to their cacique six captured Tulans "with their right hands and their noses cut off," Tulans began to come to the Spaniards bearing gifts of "cowhides." "After three days came an Indian whom the cacique sent laden with cowhides." The next day "three Indians came laden with cowhides, and three days after that twenty Indians came." Presumably, they too brought cowhides. Finally, the cacique himself came bringing "many cowhides as a gift, which were useful because it was a cold land."

The Spaniards realized that the hides and "beef" were imported. Garcilaso (Varner and Varner 1951:457) states that "no cows were to be seen in the fields, and it could never be learned from whence the hides had been brought." According to Elvas (Quinn 1979:135), they were told that "Nearby to the north there were many cattle," although the "Christians did not see them or enter their land, for the land was poorly settled where they were and had little corn." That "land" was the Southern Plains to the west and northwest of the Spiro locality, but the buffalo herds and buffalo hunting peoples that could have provided Tulan traders with hides, meat, and tallow in significant quantities were not "nearby," to judge from Voget's (1974:250, 252) discussion of the distribution of buffalo on the central and southern Plains in the late historic period. At that time, because of the distribution of various types of grasses in the territory that is now Oklahoma and Kansas, "buffalo *en masse* did not appear east of the 97th meridian" in the Arkansas River Valley. From there the "buffalo line," as I will call it, an imaginary line demarcating the approximate eastern edge of the range of the herds (fig. 8.1), curved northeastward in the direction of the Kansas River and "swept sharply to the southwest near the Canadian River." If that was also true in 1541, as seems likely, the closest source of buffalo products in quantity for the Tulans would have been Plains hunters living about 120 miles up the Arkansas River near its confluence with the Cimarron River. Or they could have obtained them from Plains hunters living about 170 miles west up the Upper Canadian River in the vicinity of the old Spiroan buffalo product entrepôt at the Nagle site (Schambach 1993b:207–8, 1993c:16, 1995:19–20 n. 31, 1997:28–30) near Oklahoma City.

Garcilaso's reference to the "many more" hides "waiting to be dressed" suggests that the Tula, like the Spiroans before them, were processing raw hides from the Plains before transporting them down the Arkansas River to northeast Arkansas, where the Spaniards also saw various buffalo products. These, all probably imported by the Tulans, included the "many heads of very fierce bulls" that Rangel (in Quinn 1979:180) saw over the door of the house of the "Lord" of Casqui; the "large quantity of dressed cow's tails[9] and others already cured" that Biedma (in Quinn 1979:184) reports at Coligua; the many "shields made of raw cowhide" that Elvas (in Quinn 1979:130) reported seeing in a town near Pacaha; and the "two cowhides" that he (Quinn 1979:133) saw at Coligua.

Garcilaso (Varner and Varner 1951:449) also describes a party of itinerant traders the Spaniards captured in the province of "Capaha," probably in Crittenden or Mississippi County, northeast Arkansas (Morse and Morse 1983:311), weeks before they got to the province of Tula. These were "eight Indians" who "were not natives of this place but strangers and merchants who in their trading passed through many provinces and included salt among the things they customarily brought to sell." Unfortunately, he does not say how the Spaniards, strangers there themselves and barely able to communicate via interpreters with the people of Capaha, recognized these men as "strangers and merchants." Perhaps it was because these "merchants" had hit upon an effective solution to what Richard I. Ford has called the paramount problem for anyone attempting to conduct extra-community trade in areas lacking a unifying hegemony, namely that in such circumstances "the stranger becomes trespasser no matter what his purpose may be" (Ford 1972:22). Assuming they were the suppliers of the buffalo products the Spaniards saw in northeast Arkansas, they would have been "merchants" from Tula, about 240 miles west of Capaha. If so, their solution—actually, that of their Spiroan forebears—to the problem of identifying themselves as traders rather than trespassing strangers, even if they happened to be caught stark naked, would have been the "incredibly long" tapered heads, that as Garcilaso wrote, distinguished the people of Tula from "all those"[10] the Spaniards had "encountered previously" (Varner and Varner 1951:457–58).

This historical evidence that the Spiroan trade network survived the "collapse" of Spiro as a center for east-west exchange circa A.D. 1450 is supported by archaeological evidence that organized trade between the Mississippi Valley and the Red River Valley via the Arkansas Valley continued after 1450. The most striking is an anomalous population of Mound Place Incised bird-effigy bowls centering in Cherokee, Harrison, Titus, and Red River Counties in northeast Texas, and in Miller and Lafayette Counties in extreme southwest Arkansas. These are the so-called "Fulton Aspect Effigy Bowls" of the *Handbook of Texas Archeology* (Suhm and Jelks 1962:47–49, plate 24), a populous category of obviously imported pots about which Caddo area archaeologists have exhibited remarkably little curiosity. Nonetheless, Phillips, Ford, and Griffin (1951:147–48) noted decades ago that "some of these are very close to St. Francis forms [that is, common in the St. Francis Basin in northeast Arkansas], indicating a northeast to southwest movement." Although a few specimens are reported from sites northeast of the Red River Valley in southwest Arkansas (Harrington 1920:plate 31a, b, 32a, b), their distribution in the Caddo area seems to be concentrated in a fan-shaped area south and southeast of the Sanders site and the mouth of the Kiamichi River in the Red River Valley. This, plus specimens from Fort Coffee phase contexts in the Arkansas Valley (Rohrbaugh 1982a:476–78) and from the Sanders site,[11] indicates that they were transported from northeast Arkansas via the old Spiroan trader's route between the Arkansas Valley and the Red River Valley (fig. 8.3).

The turquoise that occurs in Fort Coffee phase contexts in the Arkansas Valley (Rohrbaugh 1982a:78) and is abundant in what appear to be post–Sanders/Spiro phase contexts at Sanders and other nearby sites in the Red River Valley (Jurney and Young 1995:21–23) is additional evidence of this trade and indicative of the geographical and cultural areas that it encompassed.

Who Were the Tulans?

Who were the people of the Spiro phase–Fort Coffee phase tradition in the Arkansas Valley whom the Spaniards encountered in 1541 as the Tula and, perhaps, as itinerant "merchants" in northeast Arkansas? Granted they were not "Arkansas Valley Caddoans" supposedly related to the Caddo peoples living south of the Arkansas Valley in northeast Texas, southwest Arkansas, and northwest Louisiana (Schambach 1993b), could they have been the Wichita (Phillips and Brown 1978:21–22)? Or, could they have been, as Rohrbaugh (1982b) has hypothesized, that mysterious, possibly Wichita-related Plains tribe called the Kichai?

The Wichita can be ruled out because cranial deformation was neither a Wichita trait nor a Southern Plains trait (Bell 1984a:309, 323; Brooks 1989:78; Owsley 1989:133; Stewart 1941:349). Also, there is no plausible archaeological evidence that the Wichita were living as far south and east as the Arkansas Valley in eastern Oklahoma in 1541.

Rohrbaugh's (1982b) often-cited (see Story et al. 1990:346) hypothesis that they were the Kichai also can be ruled out. It rests not on ethnohistorical data, there being none for the Kichai, but on a few broad similarities between some decorated pottery of the Fort Coffee phase of the early seventeenth century in the Arkansas Valley and some aboriginal pottery from the early-eighteenth-century historic component at the Womack site in the Red River Valley, supposedly the earliest known component of the "Norteno focus" of northern Texas and southern Oklahoma (Duffield and Jelks 1961:69–75). On that basis, but without attempting to account for an apparent gap of about 80 years between what are supposed to be the latest Fort Coffee phase components in the Arkansas Valley at around A.D. 1620 (Brown 1996:27; Perttula 1992:142, 161; Rogers 1996:68) and the initial so-called Norteno focus occupation at Womack, dated by European trade goods to the period A.D. 1700–1720 (Harris et al. 1965:361), Rohrbaugh hypothesized that the Womack component was the result of a movement of Arkansas Valley Fort Coffee phase people south to the Red River Valley after A.D. 1600.

As I will argue in the next section, there is evidence of a relationship between materials attributed to the latest Fort Coffee phase occupations in the Arkansas Valley and those attributed to a so-called Norteno focus occupation at Womack, although it was much more indirect both spatially and temporally than the one Rohrbaugh proposes. So up to this point there is a germ of truth in his hypothesis. But his follow-up argument that the Fort Coffee phase is therefore protohistoric Kichai is untenable. It, he notes (Rohrbaugh 1982b:60), is dependent on Harris et al.'s (1965:360) admittedly tentative, unconfirmed identification of the historic component at Womack as the remains of the so-called "Kichai village of 1719" that La Harpe's lieutenant, Du Rivage, visited when he journeyed west up the Red River Valley from La Harpe's newly established "Nassonite Post." As I show in the next section, that identification is demonstrably wrong on historic grounds.

Who, then, were the people of Tula? Barring the possibility that they vanished soon after their encounter with de Soto, as did so many people in northeast Arkansas and elsewhere along the route of the de Soto expedition, that leaves only my suggestion (Schambach 1993b:221–24) that they were the Tunica.

The Womack Site and the Hypothesis that the Spiroans/Tulans Were the Ancestral Tunica

Until Derrick and Wilson's aforementioned work on the distribution of various styles of cranial deformation in east Texas came to my attention (Derrick and Wilson 1997; Wilson and Derrick 1996), I considered my suggestion (Schambach 1993b:222–24) that the people of the Spiro phase–Fort Coffee phase–historic Tula continuum in the Arkansas Valley were Tunica to be a cultural-historical interpretation rather than a hypothesis because, short of the remote possibility of using DNA data, I did not see how it could be tested. But their work contains an observation that raises the possibility that it can be tested against the archaeological and historical data; specifically, the observation that the annular style of cranial deformation (characteristic, as I have shown, of Arkansas Valley populations of the Spiro phase and of the sixteenth century) appears at two sites in the Red River Valley, Sanders *and* the nearby, early eighteenth century Womack site (Derrick and Wilson 1997:142; Wilson and Derrick 1996:11–12).

When I first read this, I was inclined to assume that the deformed crania from Womack would prove to be not from graves with the early-eighteenth-century French trade goods characteristic of that site, but from much earlier, Spiroan graves like those at the Sanders site. But Wilson assured me[12] that at least one of the annularly deformed Womack crania is from a grave containing European trade goods and Womack Engraved pottery. Therefore I was forced to deal with the puzzling fact that three or four hundred years after the Spiroan entrepôt at Sanders was abandoned, presumably, the same locality was occupied by people who must also have been intruders in the Red River Valley because they used essentially the same style of annular cranial deformation as had the Spiroans before them. Still more puzzling, they took up residence within a mile or so of the Sanders site.

Who were these intruders? On the evidence of their annularly deformed skulls, in addition to other bioanthropological evidence and comprehensive archaeological evidence, they were not Caddo people. Nor has anyone argued that they were. As I noted in passing above, the current (Harris et al. 1965:360; Perttula 1992:171; Story et al. 1990:346) interpretation of the main component at the Womack site is that it represents an A.D. 1700–1730 occupation by an "intrusive" Indian group, "tentatively" identified as Wichita or Kichai, which possessed a variety of French and Indian trade goods. But if the annular style of deformation exhibited by some Womack skulls means anything at all, it means these people were not Wichita—neither Arkansas Valley Wichita nor Red River Valley "Quidihai," aka Kichai—because there is no evidence that either the Wichita or the Kichai practiced cranial deformation.[13]

My argument that the people buried at Womack were not Kichai would crumble if Rohrbaugh's (1982b) hypothesis that the Kichai were not Plains people but immigrant descendants of the Fort Coffee phase people of the Spiro locality could be supported. That would make them descendants of the Arkansas Valley Spiro phase population in which, I contend, the trait of annular deformation originated in the Southeast, and to which it was confined. As just noted, however, Rohrbaugh's Kichai hypothesis depends on Harris et al.'s (1965:360) avowedly "tentative" identification of the historic component at Womack as Kichai, an identification that, because of two errors, is certainly wrong.

The first is the reference to a "village" in Harris et al.'s (1965: 357–58) identification of Womack as the site of "the early 18th century Quidehais (Kichai) village visited in 1719 by Du Rivage" of the La Harpe party. In fact, Du Rivage did not report seeing a Quidehais "village." According to La Harpe (Smith 1958:378), he reported of his contact with the Quidehais that "[t]hese people are nomadic, not having any fixed abodes; they follow the buffalo, which serves them as food, as their robe, for vestment." Perttula (1992:163) concurs that the "Kichai (or Quidehais)" Du Rivage encountered were "nomadic bison hunters." Thus the "village" to which Harris et al. refer is an unjustifiable extrapolation. The archaeological materials in evidence at the Womack site, described as "midden debris, burials and probable house remains"

(Harris et al. 1965:288), do not mark the site of an encounter with people described as "not having any fixed abodes."

The other error is that Harris et al.'s contention that Du Rivage's encounter with the Quidehais took place at the Womack site is based on the wrong league-to-miles conversion factor. Du Rivage reported 70 leagues as the distance he traveled as he made his way west up the Red River Valley from La Harpe's newly established Nassonite Post to the locality where he met the Quidehais. Using Harris et al.'s (1965:357–60) conversion factor, 1.59 miles to the league, the Kichai "village contacted by Du Rivage" would have been 111.3 miles west of La Harpe's post, compared to the 108 miles that now separate the Womack site from the probable site of La Harpe's post at Roseborough Lake (see Wedel 1978). But as Wedel (1971:44, 64 n. 31, 1978:2–3) has shown, and as Vehik (1994:254) has pointed out, the "common league" La Harpe and Du Rivage used was a 2.76 mile league.[14] So Du Rivage actually encountered the Quidehais about 193 miles west of La Harpe's post and 82 miles west of the Womack site. That is in better accord with the time (25 days) it took to make the trip out and back from La Harpe's post by horseback. It is also in better accord with the geography and the cultural ecology of the Red River Valley. Seventy of Wedel's 2.76 mile leagues place the encounter in the vicinity of "the great site known as Spanish Fort" (Bastian 1966; John 1992; Krieger 1946:161–64; Witte 1938). This site (fig. 8.1) is considered the remains of "a large 18th century Taovayas Village" (Harris et al. 1965:269; John 1992:197), but it is also thought to have been in use at least since the time of the late prehistoric "Henrietta focus," and apparently it was long a Southern Plains hub of trade and travel (Witte 1938:234). There Du Rivage could well have gone, drawn by trails and word of mouth, and there, where the wooded thickets of the "Cross Timbers" finally give way to the Plains[15] (Bastian 1966:1), he would have been likely to encounter nomadic buffalo hunters telling of Apache (?) living but 60 leagues farther west (Smith 1958:375–77).

It is not likely (even assuming he dawdled away 25 days making a 222-mile round-trip from La Harpe's post at Roseborough Lake to Womack on horseback) that Du Rivage would have found full-time buffalo hunters living and hunting in the vicinity of the Womack site.[16] There is no archaeological or historical evidence that buffalo frequented the Red River Valley that far east. Even the fertile Blackland Prairie, on whose northern edge the Womack site is located (fig. 8.1), seems to have supported few buffalo, a circumstance Lynott (1980:92) attributes to their nutritional preference for the short grasses of the Plains rather than the tall grasses of the Blackland Prairie.

Because Harris et al.'s interpretation of the Womack site as the locus of a Kichai "village" is invalid, Rohrbaugh's dependent hypothesis linking the Kichai with the Fort Coffee phase of the Arkansas Valley in eastern Oklahoma also is invalid. Part of his supporting argument, however, requires further consideration because it exposes a significant fault line in the concept of the Norteno focus (Duffield and Jelks 1961:69–75), thereby laying some groundwork for my argument that the so-called Norteno focus components at the Womack, Sanders, and Gilbert sites are neither Kichai nor Norteno focus, but the remains of early eighteenth-century Tunican entrepôts.

That part is Rohrbaugh's (1982b:51–52) well-documented contention that the historic period assemblages from the Spanish Fort, Stansbury, Stone, Vincent, Sanders, Womack, Gilbert, and Pearson sites —the assemblages traditionally assigned to the Norteno Focus (Duffield and Jelks 1961:69–75; Harris et al. 1965; Story et al. 1990:346–51)—have little in common other than European trade goods and stone tools of the aboriginal hide working complex. Traits of these two categories are of no value as phase markers because they were widespread in the Plains, the Southwest, and parts of the Southeast throughout the eighteenth century. These traits aside, the Norteno focus splits cleanly in two because of significant differences between what Rohrbaugh calls the "western Norteno focus sites" (the Spanish Fort, Stansbury, Stone, and Vincent sites) and an eastern group comprising the historic components at the Womack, Gilbert, Sanders, and Pearson sites.

The former are all Plains sites dating later than 1750 or so and are linked to the historic Wichita with a reasonable degree of certainty. But Womack, Sanders, and Gilbert[17] are all older, dating between 1700 and 1750 rather than after 1750. They are also in a different environment. They are not Plains sites but Woodland/Plains ecotone sites located some 80 miles east of the eastern edge of the Plains, precisely on the border between the Blackland Prairie of northeast Texas and the oak-hickory savanna to the east and northeast of it (fig. 8.1; Fenneman 1938:102, fig. 27). For the people responsible for the western Norteno focus assemblages, subsistence was based on the buffalo, whereas—predictably—there is scant evidence of buffalo hunting at Womack, Gilbert, and Sanders, although there is abundant evidence from Gilbert for heavy usage of deer (Rohrbaugh 1982b:54). There are predictable differences in settlement pattern as well. There is no evidence from Womack, Sanders, and Gilbert for the fortification ditches or the remains of circular, pit house–like structures reported from the western sites, particularly Spanish Fort. Not surprisingly, considering the proximity of these sites to early-eighteenth-century Red River Valley Caddo population centers, about 100 miles farther east, pottery of several Caddo types is comparatively well represented at Womack, Sanders, and Gilbert. But the western Norteno focus sites are almost without pottery,[18] and what little there is does not resemble the pottery from the eastern sites. Finally, Rohrbaugh (1982b:53) notes significant differences in mortuary customs, particularly in the orientation of graves, the positioning of the skeletons, and in the use of pottery in burials. Pottery, he notes, is poorly represented in the burials from Spanish Fort but well represented in those from Womack (Rohrbaugh 1982b:51–52).

Apparently, the people responsible for the historic components at the Womack, Sanders, and Gilbert sites were worlds apart temporally and culturally from those responsible for the historic components at the Spanish Fort, Stansbury, Stone, and Vincent sites.

Who Occupied the Womack and Gilbert Sites during the First Half of the Eighteenth Century?

According to Rohrbaugh (1982b:54–55), the many differences between the western and eastern Norteno focus sites show that the historic components at the Womack, Gilbert, and Sanders sites were not, although those at western sites probably were, the result of Wichita occupations. I agree. I agree also with his conclusion that some traits in these components hint at occupation by people "out . . . of the Arkansas Valley in eastern Oklahoma." Besides the ceramic traits he discusses, Derrick and Wilson's discovery that some occupants of the Womack site practiced annular cranial deformation points, as it does in the case of the Spiroans buried at the Sanders site, straight to the Spiro locality in the Arkansas Valley, the only place in the Southeast and the Plains where this style of deformation was the norm.

The trouble is, however, that the people buried at Womack could not have been, as were the Spiroans who used the Sanders site three centuries earlier, emigrants who had come directly from the Arkansas Valley. The consensus among archaeologists working with the Arkansas Valley data is that no one was living in the Spiro locality during the period between 1700 and 1729 when, according to Harris et al. (1965:360), the Womack site was occupied. The whole of the Arkansas Valley in eastern Oklahoma is thought to have been vacant by A.D. 1620 (Brown 1996:27; Perttula 1992:142, 161; Rogers 1996:68).

Who, then, were the people practicing annular rather than frontal-occipital cranial deformation who buried their dead at the Womack site between 1700 and 1730 if they were not, as Rohrbaugh and I agree, Wichita and if they were not, as I have been arguing, either Kichai or people who were in any sense Caddoan? Where did these people come from and what were they doing at Womack?

I think there is a plausible solution to this puzzle. It is complicated and roundabout, but since history tends to be complicated and roundabout, I see no reason to expect cultural-historical interpretations and explanations to be otherwise. I propose that the users of the Womack site were long-distance Tunican traders from the Red River mouth region in south central Louisiana who regularly sojourned there to trade guns and other French goods with visiting Wichita from the Arkansas Valley for buffalo products, horses, and Plains prestige goods.

Obviously, the key element in this proposal is my supposition that the only people who could have carried the ancient but rare Arkansas Valley custom of annular cranial deformation from the dawn of the historic period in this part of the Southeast in 1541 down to the early 1700s were the Tunica. In the next part of this chapter, I develop an argument in support of that supposition. Implausible though it may seem to readers accustomed to the standard interpretations of Caddo area prehistory, Arkansas Valley prehistory, and Tunican culture history, it is worthy of attention because it has the virtue of being a testable hypothesis. The discovery of some intact or reconstructible crania (presently there are none) from historically documented Tunica graves of the period between 1700 and 1730 is all it would take to confirm or falsify it.

Could the Tunica Be the Heirs to the Spiro Phase–Fort Coffee Phase Tradition of the Arkansas Valley?

If I am right about the identity of the people buried in the historic-period graves at Womack, the Tunica must have begun the series of moves that put them in the Red River mouth region circa A.D. 1706—not in northwestern Mississippi as Brain (1988:25) has proposed on flawed ceramic evidence,[19] but in the Spiro locality in the Arkansas Valley in eastern Oklahoma, as I have been arguing for the past few years (Schambach 1993b, 1993c, 1995). They would have been the Fort Coffee phase Spiroans whom Garcilaso and other de Soto chroniclers described as Tulans in 1541.

At that time, as I interpret the archaeology and the de Soto expedition chronicles, they still would have been living in the Spiro locality and their trade network, by then in place for more than 500 years, still would have been in operation. They still would have been transporting Osage orange bows, buffalo products, salt, pottery, and other commodities and prestige goods over long distances. This probably continued until about 1650, when the introduction of Spanish horses from the Southwest and French guns and other trade goods from the Mississippi Valley would have disrupted their ancient trade network. Suddenly, horse transport would have superseded human transport and guns would have superseded bows for warfare, thus putting them out of business as far as the vital western half of their trade network was concerned.

So, knowing what was going on everywhere in North America between the Pueblo area and the Mississippi Valley, as they would have if they were the long-distance traders I think they were, most of them[20] would have moved from the Spiro locality to the Yazoo River Basin (fig. 8.1) to try, unsuccessfully, to insinuate themselves into the hide trade that English traders based on the south Atlantic coast were operating there (Brain 1988:297; Holland-Braund 1996:28–29; Usner 1988:393).

Readers accustomed to the idea that the Arkansas Valley of western Arkansas and eastern Oklahoma was part of the Caddo area—as Arkansas Valley specialists would still have it (Brown 1996; Rogers 1996:53)—but unfamiliar with the Arkansas Valley material, might consider this hypothesis too bizarre to be taken seriously. It would be if the Mississippi period archaeological remains of the Arkansas Valley were similar to those of the historically documented Caddo area in the Red River Valley. Certainly, evidences of any kind of site unit intrusion by people with a Caddo material culture would be hard to miss in the Mississippi Valley. But, as I have shown elsewhere (Schambach 1993b, 1997), there is, for the most part, nothing even remotely Caddo-like about the Arkansas Valley material.

The exception, of course, is the artifacts of several categories that originally fooled archaeologists into thinking the Arkansas Valley was part of the Caddo area. These are the fairly abundant but clearly *traded* Caddo pots, pipes, and arrow points (Brown 1983:144, table 4; Schambach 1993b:206) that appear at Spiro and other important Arkansas Valley ceremonial centers along with much larger quantities of other traded goods, such as the "thousands of pounds of shell beads" and the three to four thousand conch shell cups (J. Brown 1975:151, 1984:255), that were moved into the Arkansas Valley from throughout the Southeast.

Apart from these traded goods, which appear in abundance only at ceremonial centers, the Mississippi period remains of the Arkansas Valley relate not to the Caddo area in the Red River Valley to the southwest, but to the Mississippi Valley to the east. Thus there is nothing fundamentally implausible about my hypothesis that the Tunica, who entered history in the Yazoo Basin circa 1690, had moved there recently from the Spiro locality rather than from northwestern Mississippi, as Brain (1988:285) postulates. There is no archaeological evidence that would prohibit this interpretation, and there is some that supports it. Let me begin with the ceramic evidence.

The four basic pottery types of the terminal Mississippi period Fort Coffee phase in the Spiro locality are the so-called "Northern Caddoan" types: Woodward Plain, Poteau Plain, Braden Incised, and Braden

Punctated. However, these are not called "Northern Caddoan" types because they resemble any of the late Mississippi period pottery types commonly found on Caddo sites in the Red River Valley, which they do not. They are regional varieties of several widespread Mississippian types[21] that Arkansas Valley specialists, operating provincially under the aegis of the misleading "Northern Caddoan Area" paradigm, have misclassified as independent Caddo area types (see Schambach 1993b:189, 208, 213).

Woodward Plain, a shell-tempered utility ware that accounts for about 90 percent of the average Fort Coffee phase ceramic assemblage (Rohrbaugh 1982a:415–20, 1984:280), is indistinguishable, except on the basis of vessel form, from Mississippi Plain (see Brown 1971:144, 1996:391; Schambach 1993b:212–13). If rim and body sherds of this type were found at a Lower Mississippi Valley site, they would be classified as Mississippi Plain. The only reliable indicator of its presence in sherd collections from Yazoo Basin sites supposedly occupied by the Tunica during the seventeenth century (Brain 1988:196–263) would be a high incidence of flat basal sherds from jars or flat-bottomed bowls, the predominance of jars and of flat-bottomed, as opposed to round-bottomed, bowls being the regional peculiarity of Mississippi-period pottery of most types in the Arkansas Valley.

Essentially the same is true of the second most common Fort Coffee phase type, Poteau Plain (Rohrbaugh 1982a:420–34). Because it intergrades with Woodward Plain/Mississippi Plain on the basis of paste (Brown 1971:184), and with Old Town Red on the basis of surface finish (Brown 1971:184–85), Lower Valley specialists probably would fail to recognize it as an intrusive Fort Coffee phase type unless confronted with a series of whole pots with their distinctive flat bottoms (see Brown 1971:fig. 27).

Similarly, unless good evidence for vessel form happened to be available, sherds of the minor Fort Coffee phase type Braden Incised (Rohrbaugh 1982a:456–60) that appeared in collections from Lower Valley sites would be sorted into one of the several similar varieties of Barton Incised (see Phillips 1970:43–47). Sherds of the other minor Fort Coffee phase type, Braden Punctate (Rohrbaugh 1982a:460–64), would be classified variously as Parkin Punctated, Owens Punctated, and as "Tunican Mode" rims. Whole pots or the right sherds of the type represented by the "Braden Punctate" pot Rohrbaugh (1982a:fig. 20, pot from LfMoI) illustrates from the Fort Coffee phase Lymon Moore site would be classified (see notes 19, 20) as Winterville Incised, *var. Tunica* (Brain 1988:388–89).

Thus, although Lower Valley archaeologists probably would not suspect it, due to the muddled taxonomic situation in the Arkansas Valley in western Arkansas and eastern Oklahoma, sherd collections from virtually any late Mississippi period site in the Lower Mississippi Valley from the Yazoo Basin south to the Red River mouth area could harbor unrecognized ceramic evidence of a substantial movement of Fort Coffee phase people from the Spiro locality to the Lower Mississippi Valley soon after A.D. 1620 because the same pottery types were in use in both areas.[22] Such intrusive assemblages would be detectable only if ceramic analysts paid close attention to indicators of vessel form, and then only if they also happened to have sherd collections from good contexts, a rarity at the suspected Yazoo Basin Tunica sites studied so far.

So much for the possibility that ceramic evidence of a movement of Arkansas Valley Fort Coffee phase people into the Mississippi Valley during the mid- to late seventeenth century could be going unnoticed by Mississippi Valley archaeologists. It could. But is there any evidence that such a move took place? I think there is.

Most obviously, the small collection of pots on record from documented or suspected Tunica contexts at Lower Mississippi Valley sites[23] exhibits a pronounced bias toward the flat-bottomed jar form characteristic of Fort Coffee phase assemblages in the Arkansas Valley. To me this suggests these are mostly pots of Arkansas Valley types that have been misclassified as Lower Mississippi Valley types. The only recorded historic period grave from the Haynes Bluff site, the most probable location for the village where the French first visited the Tunica in 1699 (Brain 1988:197), produced two aboriginal pots of interest. Judging from Brain's (1988:fig. 162) rather poor illustrations of them, these specimens, now classified as the Mississippi Valley types Barton Incised and Parkin Punctated (Brain 1988:201–2), could just as well be classified, on the basis of form, as the Arkansas Valley types Braden Incised and Braden Punctated. The "Barton Incised" pot is identical to many whole pots of the Fort Coffee phase type Braden Incised illustrated by Rohrbaugh (1982a:fig. 18–22). Except for the strap handles, the "Parkin Punctated" jar from the Haynes Bluff grave would be classified as Braden Punctated if found in the Spiro locality, where many pots of similar shape and design have been found in Fort Coffee phase graves (Rohrbaugh 1982a: fig. 20, vessel 4, fig. 21, vessels 2, 4, fig. 22). Indeed, it would probably be so classified despite the handles because, while they are not mentioned in the description of this type (Rohrbaugh 1982a:460–64), they appear occasionally on Woodward Plain bowls from Fort Coffee phase contexts (see Rohrbaugh 1982a:fig. 5, vessel F and fig. 20, vessels 1, 2, 1984:fig. 12.3z). Perhaps not coincidentally, the plain shell-tempered jar from the Russell site that Brain (1988:fig. 184h) identified as Mississippi Plain, *var. unspecified* and described as "a typical Tunica form" is of a form that is also typical of the Fort Coffee phase shell-tempered type Woodward Plain (Rohrbaugh 1982a:415–20, figs. 3–5). And is it not peculiar that the vessel form Brain considers typical of Tunica pottery is demonstrably typical of the pottery of the Fort Coffee phase of the Arkansas Valley but *not* of the pottery of the Parchman phase in northwestern Mississippi, the area from which he derives the Tunica (see Brain 1988:288–93)?

Evidence suggesting a generic relationship between Tunica culture in the Yazoo from 1680 or so to 1706 and the Spiro phase/Fort Coffee phase/historic Tula tradition of the Arkansas Valley is not limited to ceramics. Six additional lines of evidence pertaining to house types, subsistence, men's skills and activities, salt trading, cranial deformation and tattooing, and origin myths suggest the same thing.

House Types

The "round and vaulted" houses that Gravier (Shea 1861:135) reported for the Tunica in the Yazoo region in 1699 seem, as Brain (1988:296) notes, to have been unique for that time and place in the Mississippi Valley. He cannot derive them from the Parchman phase in the Upper Sunflower region in northwestern Mississippi, which he identifies as ancestral Tunican (Brain 1988:288–93, 296). They are, however, reminiscent of the circular houses that Rohrbaugh (1984:279) attributes to the terminal Fort Coffee phase occupation at Choates and other "late" (by which he means circa A.D. 1600–1620) Fort Coffee phase sites in the Spiro locality.

Subsistence

Gravier recorded that the Tunica on the Yazoo were growing sunflowers as well as corn (Shea 1861:132) and that they spent "a month" each year in the woods "with their families" harvesting and living on persimmons, "besides which they pound and dry great quantities which they preserve for a long time" (Shea 1861:135–36). These practices were not, of course, peculiar to the Tunica; still, it is worth noting that they accord well with Rogers's (1996:6; see also Brown 1996:31 and Fritz 1989:80–86, 1990: 9–11) recently published observation that the Spiro and Fort Coffee phase people of the Arkansas Valley had "a mixed economy of wild and domesticated plant foods with less reliance on maize in comparison to other areas of the Southeast." They do not accord quite so well with Brain's (1988:296–97) portrayal of the protohistoric Tunica as fully committed Mississippian farmers who "lived a sedentary life much dependent upon corn agriculture."

Men's Skills and Activities

Gravier recorded that Tunica men dressed "deer and buffalo skins . . . the best of all Indians that I have seen" (Shea 1861:134–35). Yet he also noted that buffalo, at least, were "very rare" in their country (Shea 1861:135), and La Source, who visited the Tunica the year before him, stated flatly that Tunica men "do not hunt" (quoted in Brain 1988:296).[24] This apparent discrepancy between the processing skills and the procurement activities of Tunica men calls to mind the "many cowhides . . . which had been softened and dressed without removing the hair" and the "many others waiting to be dressed" (Varner and Varner 1951:457) that the men of the de Soto expedition saw 160 years earlier in the province of Tula, a province where "no cows were to be seen in the fields, and it could never be learned from whence the hides had been brought" (Varner and Varner 1951:457). This suggests that Tunica were skilled in hide processing, although they did not hunt, because they were traders of hides, among other things, who had recently moved to the Yazoo from the Spiro locality, where a strong hide-working tradition can be traced from the Fort Coffee phase, which lasted at least as late as A.D. 1620 (Brown 1996:27; Perttula 1992:142, 161; Rogers 1996:68), back to around A.D. 1100 (Schambach 1993b: 196–99).

Salt Trading

My hypothesis that the Tunica Gravier and La Source described were traders recently moved from the Spiro locality makes sense of some very early references to Tunica activities west of the Mississippi that make little sense within the framework of Brain's (1988:296–97) hypothesis that the protohistoric Tunica were fully committed Mississippian farmers who "lived a sedentary life much dependent upon corn agriculture." "From the very first French contact," Brain (1988:296) writes, "the Tunica were specifically mentioned as being actively involved in the production and trade of salt" on the upper Ouachita River in Arkansas. "At that time," he concludes, they "were probably exploiting salt springs along the upper Ouachita River" and possibly also hunting "buffalo that came to the salt licks." But it is "unclear" to him "whether there was a western branch of Tunicans who maintained permanent residence on the Ouachita or whether these people were seasonal immigrants from the Yazoo." "Whatever might have been the case," he concludes, "the prehistoric Tunicans clearly were involved in the collection and trade of salt (witness the Tanico of the 'province of salt' described in the de Soto chronicles), and the Yazoo Tunica maintained a certain control, if not monopoly, of this basic commodity well into the historic period."

My explanation of the historically documented association of the Tunica with the saltworks on the "upper Ouachita," which are concentrated in the Arkadelphia-Malvern area,[25] is that they had an entrepôt there during the latter part of the seventeenth century, probably by then an old one established when they were still operating out of the Spiro area. There they obtained salt from local Caddo salt makers much the way their Spiroan ancestors obtained buffalo products from local Plains buffalo hunters at their entrepôt at the Nagle site in central Oklahoma and Osage orange bows from local Caddo bowyers at another entrepôt at the Sanders site in northeast Texas. In 1541 they probably had another salt procurement entrepôt at the place called Tanico in the "province of salt" described in the de Soto narratives (Varner and Varner 1951:454). However, according to the latest scholarship, Tanico was not in the Ouachita Valley as Brain thought. It was in the Arkansas Valley near Russellville (Early 1993b:70–71; Schambach 1993a:81–83), where the name seems to have been attached to a saltworks, or a small settlement near a saltworks, in the province of Cayas.

Elvas (Clayton et al. 1993:124) wrote of the salt being obtained there: "The Indians carry it thence to other regions to exchange it for skins and blankets." That is a passable description of a Tunican entrepôt in operation, provided the Indians doing the carrying were Tunica from the Spiro/Tula area, between two and six days travel farther up the Arkansas.[26] The documents do not reveal such details, although the archaeology of the place might, if it could be found. They do, however, indicate that Tanico was not a population center in the province of Cayas. Said center was a large palisaded town that the Spaniards were unable to find, according to Rangel (Clayton et al. 1993:304–5). Tanico was a very small settlement, if that, near a salt source, where the Spaniards spent considerable time making salt for themselves after the manner of the local people (and trying to find the cacique of "Cayas," who was not in residence at Tanico). This, too, matches my conception of what a Tunican salt-collecting entrepôt was probably like.

The best Brain's hypothesis permits him to do with these evidences of Tunicans west of the Mississippi[27] between 1541 and 1673 is to speculate, absent any archaeological evidence, that they might pertain to a "western branch of Tunicans who maintained permanent residence on the Ouachita" or that they might reflect the activities of "seasonal immigrants from the Yazoo" (1988:297). Neither alternative has much to recommend it. The first, if true, would vitiate his claim to have "positively identified" the "Upper Sunflower locale of the northern Yazoo Basin" as "the ancestral hearth of the Tunica" (Brain 1988:288). Why would that area have been "the ancestral hearth" if the Tunican population was spread, or scattered, from western Mississippi to the central part of the

Arkansas Valley in central Arkansas to the upper Ouachita Valley in southwest Arkansas?

The second is ad hoc guesswork. As he portrays them (Brain 1988: 296–97), the protohistoric Tunica were fully committed Mississippian farmers who "lived a sedentary life much dependent upon corn agriculture," had a culture history deeply rooted in northwestern Mississippi, and had no apparent predilection or motivation for long distance travel and trade. Why would such a people have also been "seasonal immigrants" to salt-boiling localities in the Ouachita Valley and the Arkansas Valley to the extent that their name would be linked with these places? And where is the archaeological evidence that they were?

Cranial Deformation and Tattooing

Like the Tulans described in the lengthy quotation from Garcilaso presented earlier (see Varner and Varner 1951:458), Tunica men and women exhibited both cranial deformation and tattooing at the time they were first contacted by Europeans (Brain 1988:295; Shea 1861:134; Swanton 1911:316–17). Also, the facial tattooing of the mid-sixteenth-century Tulans, which was "particularly on the interior and exterior of their lips, which they stain black" (Varner and Varner 1951:458) seems similar to the tooth blackening practiced by Tunica women of the early eighteenth century (Brain 1988:295). Therefore, as far as cranial deformation and tattooing are concerned, the documentary evidence does not contradict my hypothesis that the Tunica the French encountered in the Mississippi Valley in the early eighteenth century were the same people the Spaniards encountered in the province of Tula in the Arkansas Valley in October of 1541 (Clayton et al. 1993:304–5). Still, both practices were widespread among the Southeastern Indians of the early historic period (Hudson 1976:380; Swanton 1911:56–57, 345), so it is possible that the Spaniards also saw people with deformed heads and tattooing when they passed through the province of Quizquiz—Brain's (1988:288) hypothetical "ancestral hearth" for the Tunica—five months before they reached the province of Tula (Clayton et al. 1993:299). If so, the chroniclers of the de Soto expedition did not record it. They did, however, record that they thought the men of Quizquiz were "fine looking." (Elvas quoted by Brain 1988:289). Considering that the people of Tula struck them as "hideous" and "loathsome" (Varner and Varner 1951:458) because of their tattooing and their deformed heads, this could be considered an indication that the men of Quizquiz exhibited neither tattooing nor deformed heads. Or it could mean the people of Quizquiz exhibited styles of cranial deformation and tattooing that the Spaniards were used to seeing by then, and it was only the unique Arkansas Valley style of annular, as opposed to frontal-occipital cranial deformation, perhaps combined with a local style of tattooing around the mouth and on the lips, that they found "hideous" and "loathsome."

The clincher for my hypothesis would be documentary or archaeological evidence that the Tunica of the Yazoo practiced the annular style of cranial deformation peculiar to the Spiroans/Tulans of the Arkansas Valley rather than the frontal-occipital style favored elsewhere in the Southeast. To judge from Brain's (1988:295) comments on this subject, they did not. He writes: "Gravier reported that the heads of infants of both sexes were compressed in the cradle to produce artificial flattening," cradleboarding being the technique supposedly used to produce the frontal-occipital deformation commonly reported in the Southeast in the early historic period (Hudson 1976:31). But "compressed in the cradle" is Brain's *interpretation* of what Gravier had to say on this subject. What Gravier wrote was: "The women have a great tress of hair on the back which hangs down below the waist; they also make a crown of it around the head. Their head like the men's is flat. Mothers carefully put their children's heads in presses from birth to render them flat." (Shea 1861:134; see also Swanton 1911:316–17).[28] There is no mention of cradleboards, and it is questionable whether Gravier, who was only with the Tunica briefly and reported that he "saw hardly any children," had firsthand knowledge of how the deformation was accomplished. What he did see was that Tunica men and women had "flat" heads. It would be better for my hypothesis had he said their heads were "tapered" or "cone shaped," because that would all but confirm that the people of Spiro/Tula were the ancestral Tunica. "Flat," however, is good enough to keep it afloat. On the plus side, putting "children's heads in presses" sounds more like a description of the method for producing annular deformation, rather than frontal-occipital deformation, because the latter requires binding the whole child to a cradleboard.[29]

Brain goes on to say "archaeological evidence has failed so far to support" Gravier's observation that the Tunica had artificially deformed heads, and on that basis he concludes, "it must be inferred that the custom was rare even in Gravier's time and was soon dropped altogether, for it has not been found in contemporary or later Tunica burials."[30] But there is no documentary or archaeological justification for these inferences. Gravier did not write that "the custom was rare." The clear implication of his description of the practice is that all adults of both sexes exhibited cranial deformation and that mothers put the heads of all children of both sexes "in presses." Kniffen et al.'s (1987:182) observation that the modern "Tunica and Biloxi still mold an infant's head, massaging it with warm oil to make it round" suggests that the custom was not dropped soon after Gravier's time. The assertion (Brain 1988:295) that "archaeological evidence has failed so far to support" Gravier's observation is disingenuous, there being no archaeological evidence for or against the practice from any site in the Yazoo region, where no Tunica graves have been identified. Nor is there evidence from any of the graves from historically documented Tunica sites in the Red River mouth region, where the Tunica moved when they left the Yazoo Basin in 1706. None have yielded crania sufficiently intact to permit observations as to the presence and style of cranial deformation.

This leaves us with Father Gravier's observation that the Tunica did deform their children's heads and, I suggest, the viable possibility that they used bands of cloth or leather to produce annular deformation rather than cradleboards to produce frontal-occipital deformation.

Origin Myths

Finally, in this recitation of evidence favoring a Spiroan/Tulan ancestry for the Tunica, we come to Brain's admission that his placement of the "ancestral hearth" of the Tunica in the northern Yazoo Basin does not jibe with a Tunica origin myth "that refers to their emergence from a mountain near which they settled" (Brain 1988:22, 288). I do not suppose the "mountain" could not have been a mound, as Brain suggests, nor that the Mississippian people of the northern Yazoo Basin would not have known enough about the mountains east and west of their alluvial valley homeland to weave them into an origin myth. Still, such a myth would make better literal and historical sense (not that myths must do so) if the Tunica were recent immigrants from the Spiro locality, where substantial mountains are close by to the north and visible to the south.

Thus there is reason to take seriously the hypothesis that when the Tunica entered history on the Yazoo circa 1682 (Brain 1988:25, 294) they had not come from farther up the Mississippi Valley in the Upper Sunflower region as Brain (1988:266–77) claims; they had come, recently and possibly directly, from the Spiro/Fort Smith locality in the Arkansas Valley.

The Evidence That the Historic Component at Womack Is Tunica

I think my "Spiro locality" hypothesis for the place of origin of the Tunica whom the French found living on the Yazoo River at the end of the seventeenth century is robust enough to serve as the basis for a plausible, testable explanation for the puzzling historic period graves at the Womack site. The people with annularly deformed heads who were buried there between 1700 and 1729 (Harris et al. 1965:360) would have been long-distance Tunica (hence, originally Spiroan/Tulan) traders who had reactivated their old, northeast Texas entrepôt soon after they moved from the Yazoo to their new homeland in the Red River mouth region around 1706.

If so, there should be evidence of some kind of cultural connection between the Womack site and the historic Tunica sites in the Red River mouth region. In fact, there is, and I am not the first to notice it. Harris et al. (1965:360) pointed out that there is archaeological evidence of "a definite connection" between the Womack and Angola Farm, a Tunican site excavated by Ford (1936:129–40) and occupied, according to Swanton, from "about 1709 until 1729" (Harris et al. 1965:358). That conclusion is based mainly on their (Harris et al. 1965:315) observation that 47 of the 56 bead types found at Womack are also found at the Angola Farm site. Nor were beads the only artifact category in which correspondences between Womack and Angola Farm were apparent. Harris et al.'s (1965:327–43) 1700–29 date for Womack is based primarily on many close similarities between gun parts found there and at the historically dated Angola Farm site.

The conventional interpretation of these similarities is that they have no ethnic significance; they merely reflect the fact Benard de La Harpe (Wedel 1978) and other French traders operating out of New Orleans were supplying the same kinds of goods to whomever was living at Angola Farm and at Womack between 1700 and 1729. Normally that would be the right interpretation; protohistoric sites from east Texas to Labrador tend to yield remarkably similar assemblages of European trade goods, provided they are contemporaneous. However, there is no hard evidence that the French were responsible for the movement of these trade goods and, while that possibility cannot be ruled out completely, there is evidence of several kinds that they were not involved.

To be specific, and to begin with the obvious, Harris et al. (1965: 360) have argued, conventionally, that "some of the items common to these sites (i.e., Angola Farm and Womack) represent goods distributed by the La Harpe party," meaning mainly the "fifteen hundred livres of merchandise" (Smith 1958:372) that La Harpe's emissary, Du Rivage, gave to the Kichai. But, as I have shown, Du Rivage did not visit the Womack site and distribute goods to "Kichai" people there. The people he visited were more than 80 miles farther west.

Not surprisingly, two other sets of circumstances also belie the argument that the European goods at Womack reached there as a result of the La Harpe expedition. One is the range and quantity of European goods represented by the recorded artifacts found.[31] Judging from the reported number of trigger guards, which are items not likely to have been brought to the site as spare parts, there were least 17 guns (Harris et al. 1965:307–57), and those probably represent but a fraction of the guns brought to the site. This indicates sustained trade rather than a single distribution of "1500 livres of merchandise" (Smith 1958:372). Since the price for muskets at that time seems to have been 75 to 100 livres each,[32] just the guns that are represented archaeologically at Womack would probably have been worth more than 1500 livres. And it is unlikely that the merchandise Du Rivage distributed consisted mostly of guns, assuming he distributed any guns at all.

Second, the time span Harris et al. (1965:36) assign to the European trade goods (1700–30, with a few possibly manufactured between 1675 and 1718) also indicates sustained contact rather than a single distribution of goods in the year 1719. European goods could have begun reaching the Womack site more than twenty years before La Harpe established his post downriver.

What was the source of these goods, if not the Du Rivage party? The next best possibility might seem to be La Harpe's Nassonite Post (Wedel 1978). However, there is no documentary or archaeological evidence that it functioned as a center for significant French trade with the Indians living close to it in the Red River Valley, much less those living 108 miles to the west at Womack. Nor should that be surprising, since it was not established for trade with the Indians. La Harpe established it with the misguided intention of trading illegally with the Spanish and when, within weeks of his arrival, it became apparent that this was impossible, he abandoned it, physically and financially (Smith 1958:256–58; Wedel 1971:42–47, 1978:1). According to recent work by Usner (1992:34–35), he was also "forced to abandon his people who were sick and dying of fever and exhaustion due to lack of proper supplies." Of the "nearly forty" he started with, he left "only seven or eight on the Red River" and took ten others back downriver with him. Those that remained (they had come equipped with a set of mill stones and other agricultural implements) apparently married Caddo women and took up farming, trapping, and hunting for a living. As Wedel (1971:38) concluded: "The commercial possibilities indicated by La Harpe's explorations were never pursued. This may be attributed to circumstances relating to the general desperate condition of the colony at the time, as well as the certain lack of vision and jealousies on the part of many officials both in Louisiana and in France."[33]

If the European goods found at Womack did not reach there because of La Harpe's activities, can their presence be attributed to any other European agency or activity? On this point the conventional answer would be "yes." Historians (Bolton 1915:34–36, 1970:44, 49) and archaeologists (Gregory 1973:12; Jelks 1967:244; Perttula 1992:150) alike have long maintained that between 1685 and 1750 the Louisiana territory was home to "indefatigable, omnipresent, French *chasseurs*" (Bolton 1970:49) engaged, among other things, in an extensive independent trade with the Indians. Yet here, again, there is no historical or archaeological evidence for the existence of these traders. If anything, the documentary evidence contradicts this thesis.

According to Mildred Wedel (1971:37), "there is no certain or direct evidence" that significant numbers of French *coureurs-de-bois* had penetrated the interior of French Louisiana and were trading extensively with the Indians before La Harpe's expeditions up the Red River and the Arkansas beginning in August 1718. Brain (1988:328) makes the same point: "It is true that the French in Canada, few in numbers, adopted a trading relationship with the Indians that contrasted with the territorial demands of the many English colonists in the Northeast." However, "[i]n Louisiana, the roles were reversed; it was the French who were moving in as a large colonial presence and the English were distant traders." More specifically, John (1975:199) notes that "the Kadohadachos remained so isolated from the French traders in Louisiana that as late as 1711 they obtained French merchandise principally by bartering horses to the Illinois." That is a particularly telling observation. If these supposedly numerous independent French traders were not serving the populous and well-off Kadohadacho by 1711, it is not likely that they were reaching peoples 100 miles west of them on the Red River either.

The generally held assumption among archaeologists, as expressed recently by Perttula (1992:150), is that the lack of historical documentation of the activities of the many "traders, adventurers and coureurs de bois" who were supposedly living among the Caddo in the period between 1675 and 1750 is due to the "general illiteracy" of these people. But it is wrong to suppose that all these men were illiterate. La Harpe was literate. So was Anthony Glass, who traded and adventured in the Red River Valley between 1790 and 1810 (Flores 1985). And, assuming there were some illiterate French traders in the Red River Valley between 1675 and 1750, their illiteracy would not have prevented other people from recording their activities. Had those activities been extensive enough to have a significant impact on the economy of French Louisiana, it is practically inevitable that there would be some records of them. But none seem to exist.

What the records do show is that there were very few Europeans in French Louisiana during the whole first quarter of the eighteenth century.[34] In 1708 there were only 122 soldiers and sailors and 77 settlers (24 men, 28 women, and 25 children). By 1718 there were "no more than three hundred and fifty to four hundred people" (Usner 1992:25). That is not a pool from which large numbers of "traders, adventurers and coureurs de bois" could have been drawn.[35]

La Harpe himself, literate and observant as he was (Wedel 1971:59, 1974), did not mention encountering such men during his two lengthy explorations of the Red River Valley and the Arkansas River Valley between August 1718 and May 1722 (Wedel 1971). Except an unsurprising meeting, since it was on the Red River below Natchitoches, with a Frenchman named Beauleiu, "resident of Natchitoches, who was going down to New Orleans loaded with corn, bear oil and tobacco" (Smith 1958:82), he seems to have met no European traders, travelers, or hunters during his long journey up the Red River to the Texarkana area and thence overland to the Arkansas River in eastern Oklahoma. He does, however, describe witnessing, while he was among the Wichita on the Arkansas, the arrival of "a savage of the Chickasaw nation with merchandise who had come from the 'Yasous' (i.e., Yazoos) and appeared troubled at seeing me in these villages." The "merchandise" the Chickasaw carried probably was supplied by the English on the south Atlantic coast (see Brain 1988:30–31 and Waselkov 1989:328), another indication—as is La Harpe's observation that the Chickasaw "appeared troubled" at seeing him—that if independent French traders were abroad in the Louisiana territory, they were not very active as far north as the Arkansas Valley. Nor, it would seem, were they active in the Yazoo region.

There also should be direct and indirect archaeological evidence of these French traders. Yet, strangely, considering their supposed ubiquity in the Louisiana territory during the late seventeenth and early eighteenth centuries, none has emerged. Except the Roseborough Lake site, the probable site of La Harpe's failed post (Wedel 1978), there are no habitation sites or cemeteries attributable to them, nor are there graves or other features attributable to them at aboriginal sites such as Womack, Gilbert, and Sanders. All we have are the European goods that they supposedly transported into the interior.

Yet here, too, the evidence fails to support the supposition that they were present, let alone numerous. The facts are that eighteenth-century European trade goods are astonishingly scarce in the Red River Valley (and adjacent areas) north of Natchitoches and their distribution is oddly restricted geographically. The only early eighteenth-century sites in and around the Red River Valley at which European goods appear in quantity, other than Roseborough Lake, are Womack, Sanders, and Gilbert (fig. 8.1), all of which must have been on the extreme western edge of the main centers of Caddo population in northeast Texas, northwest Louisiana, and southwest Arkansas at that time. If French traders were operating within the Caddo territory, rather than just along the western edge of it, significant archaeological evidence of their activity has yet to emerge.

What seems to be emerging instead is archaeological evidence that they were not there. There is a short but, apparently, growing list—Bob Williams (Perino 1980), Cedar Grove (Trubowitz 1984:30–43), McLelland and Joe Clark (Kelley 1997; Kelley et al. 1996), and Beene Plantation (Kelley 1997:16)—of carefully investigated seventeenth- and early-eighteenth-century Caddo sites in the Red River Valley that have produced few if any of the European goods that should be abundant if independent French traders were as active as they are supposed to have been.

So the ubiquitous, independent French trader of the Louisiana Territory before 1750 is a myth created because no one has suspected there might be another explanation for the presence of European goods at sites like Womack. But there is. Tunica traders could have moved European goods from Angola Farm to Womack, just as the "savage of the Chickasaw nation" whom La Harpe encountered was moving "merchandise," presumably European merchandise, up the Arkansas Valley to eastern Oklahoma. And, in fact, the assemblages from the middens and the otherwise inexplicable graves at Womack are replete with hitherto misinterpreted clues that they did.

Most significantly, the assemblage of eighteenth-century artifacts includes imported *Indian-made* goods that French traders probably would not have brought to the site, most of which—like the European goods—point down the Red River to Angola Farm and other Tunica sites. The Natchitoches Engraved, *var. Natchitoches* bowl (Harris et al. 1965:fig. 4B; Schambach and Miller 1984:124, fig. 11-11) from Womack is an import from down the Red River, probably from south of the Arkansas line, since pottery of that type and variety is rare in the Great Bend region.[36] Apparently the Tunica used Natchitoches Engraved, *var. Natchitoches,* probably obtained by trade from the Natchitoches Caddo, because it appears in sherd form at Angola Farm (see Brain 1988:fig. 137e).

The aboriginal conch shell beads and pendants from Burial 6 at the Bloodhound Hill site,[37] a Tunica cemetery located a short distance from Angola Farm, with which it appears to be contemporaneous (Brain 1988: figs. 126, 146, 173), resemble the conch shell beads and gorgets from the graves at Womack (Harris et al. 1965:305–6, fig. 7).[38]

Although the snub-nosed end scrapers that are so extraordinarily abundant at Womack (Harris et al. 1965:294–95 report 872 specimens, a record number, surely, for any site in the Southeast) are a standard tool in the widespread Plains hide-working complex, it is noteworthy that they have their counterparts at the Tunican Haynes Bluff, Russell, and Bloodhound sites (see Perttula 1992:172–73). At Bloodhound one was found next to the left hand of an adult male in Burial 7 (Brain

1988:398), an indication, presumably, of one of his major interests and activities in life.

The graves excavated at Womack yielded considerable circumstantial archaeological and bioanthropological evidence that they are mostly, if not entirely, the graves of Tunica traders from the Red River mouth region. Partly, this is negative evidence ruling out other possibilities. The annular deformation exhibited by most of the crania from these graves (Derrick and Wilson 1997:142; Wilson and Derrick 1996:12) means, as I argued earlier, that these people were not Red River Valley Caddo, for whom frontal-occipital rather than annular deformation was the mode. It also means that they were not Wichita or Kichai since the Plains tribes eschewed cranial deformation throughout the prehistoric and historic periods.

On the other hand, these could be considered historic Tunica graves—indeed, classic historic Tunica graves—because they contained the same omnium-gatherum of European goods and aboriginal goods, all apparently obtained in trade from far-flung sources, that characterizes the graves at all historically documented Tunican sites. The one distinctive trait that all Tunica graves identified so far have in common is that the mortuary furniture consists mostly of traded goods (which is also true of the Mississippi period mortuary assemblages from the Craig Mound at Spiro and the Sanders site). As I have tried to show, the Tunica probably did not have a ceramic complex of their own by the time of their move to the Red River mouth region circa 1706. Tunica graves from that time onward (and no earlier Tunica graves have been identified) contain nothing that is obviously Tunica made. They stand identified as Tunica solely because they were interred at historically documented Tunica sites and they contain European and aboriginal goods of the right period. This is not entirely a new observation. Ford (1936:140) noted more than 60 years ago with respect to Tunica pottery that the Tunica at Angola Farm had "taken over the pottery of the Caddo and Natchez rather thoroughly."

Finally, there is a bit of hearsay historical evidence, provided by La Harpe but heretofore missed or ignored by archaeologists and historians, that suggests that Tunica travelers were abroad in the Great Bend region in the Red River Valley in 1719 and that their presence was not unusual. On October 28 of that year, while en route to New Orleans via the Red River after his arduous journey to contact the Wichita in the Arkansas Valley, La Harpe met, at a point ten days travel downriver from the "village of the Cadodoquious . . . three pirogues of our savages, coming from buffalo hunting" who told him "of having encountered, near the little river[39] several *cajeux* [or cane rafts][40] newly made, constructed by the Tonicaus, who are the Yasous."[41] Two days later La Harpe himself "saw the cajeux upon which the Tonicaus had crossed the river" (Smith 1958:538).

The most interesting thing about La Harpe's references to these cane rafts is that his "savages" recognized them as the work of the Tunica without having seen the Tunica themselves. Whether or not they were right about the Tunica making those particular rafts, this suggests that the Tunica traveled through the Great Bend region frequently enough that they were known for the practice of making cane rafts to cross rivers. Although there may be other possibilities, my explanation for this evidently frequent travel[42] is that they were operating an entrepôt at the Womack site—an entrepôt that had already been in use for some 20 years when La Harpe crossed their trail in 1719. La Harpe's observation that the cajeux were newly made, as of October 28, 1719, suggests they were en route to or from what was, to anticipate my forthcoming discussion of the raison d'être for this entrepôt, probably an annual fall hide and horse-trading session with visiting Wichita at the Womack site.

With these various lines of circumstantial evidence in mind, I conclude that the graves excavated at Womack are Tunica graves, and that the site itself represents a site unit intrusion of Tunican traders from the Red River mouth area. Confirmation of this must await the discovery of crania from historically documented Tunica graves that are sufficiently intact to permit observations on what, if any, style of cranial deformation the Tunica were using between 1700 and 1750. Verification of my hypothesis that they were using the annular style would link them to the Womack site and, more important, to the Tulans of 1541 and the Spiroans of the Mississippi Period.

Was the Gilbert Site a Tunican Entrepôt?

One thing leads to another. If the historic component at the Womack site represents a site unit intrusion from the historic Tunica Angola Farm site, then the obviously related historic component at the other major so-called "Norteno focus" site in northeast Texas should be one also. This is the Gilbert site (Jelks 1967), located about sixty miles south of Womack on the upper Sabine (fig. 8.1). It too has yielded significant quantities of both European and Indian-made goods that probably came from the Red River mouth area.

We do not have the benefit of Harris and Blain's scholarship when it comes to comparing the Gilbert site assemblage (dated to approximately 1750, mainly on the basis of European bead types and various gun parts; see Blain and Harris 1967:41–81; Harper et al. 1967:104), with the assemblage from the Trudeau site (dated historically to 1731–64; see Brain 1988:65), where the Tunica were living when the Gilbert site was in use. Yet it is obvious that there are correspondences. At least 17 of the 28 bead types recognized at Trudeau also appear at Gilbert (Brain 1979:116–31) and there are some very specific similarities between the gun parts from Gilbert and the guns from Trudeau (Brain 1979:214–16).

Also, as Miller and I pointed out in 1984 (Schambach and Miller 1984:121–22), the "Emory Punctated" pottery reported from Gilbert (Story et al. 1967:135–39, fig. 57g, h, i) looks identical to the Winterville Incised, *var. Tunica,* from Trudeau (Brain 1979:234–37). Hence those who accept Brain's (1979:234, 1988:393) hypothesis, fallacious in my opinion, that Winterville Incised, *var. Tunica,* is an "ethnic" marker for the Tunica would have to consider the possibility that this pottery signals a Tunica occupation at Gilbert. I think it does, but not for that reason. I suspect that it, and the Natchitoches Engraved pottery from Gilbert (Story et al. 1967:125–29), is pottery the Tunica obtained from the Red River Caddo in the Natchitoches area[43] and brought to the Gilbert site as trade goods or for their own use. The latter seems most likely since, as I have just argued, they probably had no ceramic complex of their own after about A.D. 1700.

While these correspondences are important, the crucial piece of circumstantial evidence that this was yet another Tunican entrepôt has to do, not with the artifacts from Gilbert, but with the location of the site itself. To explain why this seems to be the case, I must consider two related questions: How did the Tunica amass the wealth in trade goods, the so-called "Tunica treasure," that Leonard Charrier looted from about 113 of their graves at the Trudeau site (Brain 1979:276)? And, how might the operation of entrepôts in northeast Texas have been involved in that process?

Current thinking on the source of the "Tunica treasure" is that it came from trade in "salt and horses" (Brain 1979:282), with the Tunica functioning as "middlemen" between the French in New Orleans and the Indians to the north. It is supposed that the Tunica profited from this trade because of their strategic location in the Red River mouth area between the French in New Orleans and the Caddo, Wichita, Osage, Quapaw, and other tribes living upriver in Louisiana, Mississippi, Arkansas, Texas, and Oklahoma (Brain 1979:280–82; Kidder 1993:237; Perttula 1992:201). Although this interpretation sounds plausible, since the Tunica were living athwart the main river route between the French and these tribes, it has two flaws.

First, as I pointed out earlier, there is no historical or archaeological evidence to support the supposition that the French were trading extensively with the Indians upstream from New Orleans before 1750, particularly those up the Red River Valley, which was blocked by the Great Raft beginning not far above Natchitoches. Second, no one has explained how location alone would have enabled the Tunica to profit—handsomely, it seems—from this putative trade between the French downriver and the various tribes upriver. Were they, perhaps, collecting tolls from passing French traders?

I doubt their role was that passive. I suggest they profited because, as had been their practice for 500 years with bow wood, buffalo products, and salt, they were running the trade with Indians upriver rather than merely feeding off a French operation. They controlled the supply of Indian goods to the French, and of French goods to the Indians, by establishing their own entrepôts at the sources of supply of valuable commodities, specifically the Womack and Gilbert sites, and moving goods to and from them.

The goods moving through these entrepôts probably included all the important commodities of the eighteenth-century French-Indian frontier (Gregory 1973:289): salt, hides, Osage orange bows, European guns and ammunition, other European goods ranging from axes to ornaments, and, particularly—I think—horses. Horses, generally considered one of the main sources of Tunica wealth (Brain 1979:282; Gregory 1973:11; Swanton 1911:312), were probably also one of the main reasons, if not *the* main reason, for Tunican interest in the Womack and Gilbert sites. Indeed, as I will try to show, they probably account for the locations of these sites as well.

Were the Womack and Gilbert Sites Tunican Horse and Hide Trading Entrepôts?

There is no doubt that the Tunica were horse traders. The Tunica chief, Cahura-Joligo, was "renowned for his involvement in the horse trade" and a wealthy man by European standards for that time and place because of it (Brain 1979:282; Gregory 1973:11; Usner 1992:63; Swanton 1911:312). Because he was a chief, he was probably not in this enterprise alone; the whole tribe would have been involved and profiting from it. The key question about this horse trade, the mechanics of which are unknown, is where did the Tunica get horses between 1700 and 1760, the period within which the "Tunica treasure" was accumulated?

Conventional thinking on the horse trade in Louisiana during this period is that, despite Spanish opposition to trade between the Caddo and the French in Louisiana, particularly if it involved guns and ammunition, horses were filtering into the French territory in the Mississippi Valley from the Spanish settlements in the Southwest via the Hasinai and the Natchitoches (Gregory 1973:281). Perhaps some were,[44] but that does not explain the Tunican involvement in the horse trade. Had they managed, somehow, to insinuate themselves between the French and the Hasinai?

Nor does it account for all the horses that were coming into Louisiana. By 1720, according to Wedel (1981:36–37), the Spaniards were making it "more difficult" for the French to get horses "through Hasinai Caddo middlemen" (she does not mention Tunica middlemen), and the French were exploring the possibility of getting them from the Wichita or the Osage. One reason for Bienville's interest in La Harpe's second trip to the Wichita, according to Wedel (1981:37–38), was "the fact that the Tawakoni [Wichita] were reported to have large numbers of horses," although the French did not know where they were getting them.

I think there is good historical and circumstantial evidence that the Tunica, by virtue of their long and continuing familiarity with the Red River Valley in the vicinity of their old entrepôt at the Sanders site and with their old homeland, the Arkansas Valley, knew about the Wichita's horses long before the French heard about them. Specifically, I think there is circumstantial evidence that they knew the Wichita were getting horses from a significant and growing feral herd in northeast Texas that was unknown to Europeans of that era and has remained unknown to archaeologists and most historians of this one. I also think there is circumstantial evidence that they were involved with the Wichita in the procurement of horses from this herd, some of which they traded to the French in Louisiana, bringing them in via Natchitoches, thus giving the French the impression they were coming from the Hasinai country.

This hypothesis came to mind when I began thinking about why the Gilbert site, located near the headwaters of the Sabine River (fig. 8.1), should, like Womack, located 60 miles to the north on the Red River, be loaded with French and Indian-made trade goods. It seems likely that whatever the people who frequented the Womack site did to get these goods in quantity, those frequenting the Gilbert site a few decades later probably did too. But unlike Womack, which is obviously well situated to command what trade and travel there was up and down the Red River Valley, Gilbert seems to have been off the beaten path, an unlikely spot for trade goods to accumulate in any noteworthy quantity. There is, however, one important common element in the locations of these sites. Both are *precisely* on the edge of the Blackland Prairie (fig. 8.1; see also Fenneman 1938:102–8, fig. 27, plate 7),[45] as are the two other northeast Texas sites with so-called Norteno focus components, Sanders and Pearson (fig. 8.1).

I doubt that this is just coincidence. Something was attracting people and significant quantities of European and Indian trade goods to the edge of the Blackland Prairie between 1700 and 1760. But what? It was not buffalo hunting, considering the dearth of buffalo bones in the faunal remains from the sites themselves and Lynott's (1980) argument that the grasses of the Blackland Prairie were not attractive to buffalo. It was, I suggest, feral horses from the Blackland Prairie.

According to the environmental historian Dan Flores (1985:102 n. 8), when Domingo Teran de Los Rios traveled to the Upper Nasoni village on the Red River in northeast Texas in 1691 with the intention of establishing a mission, he brought "more than 1000 horses and mules . . . at least 200 of which were lost." Apparently some of these animals colonized the Blackland Prairie so successfully that they increased into a large feral herd whose existence remained unknown to Europeans until American "mustangers" discovered it around 1800.[46] It then became an important source for the feral horses they brought into the Southeast. In 1802 alone, according to Flores (1985:102 n. 9), "an estimated 7,300 Texas horses," most of them apparently from the Blackland Prairie herd, "passed through Louisiana to eastern markets."

Despite what must have been heavy pressure from the mustangers, this herd seems to have survived until about 1820, at least. When the trader Anthony Glass ascended the Sulphur River en route from Natchitoches in 1808, he began to see feral horses immediately upon entering the Blackland Prairie. Seven days later, on Bois d'arc Creek about "75 miles from its mouth" (and from the Sanders and Womack sites), he "saw great numbers of Wild horses" (Flores 1985:43–44). When Thomas Nuttall visited the Red River Valley in 1819 he found the first "native stands" of bois d'arc growing on "the Horse-prairie 15 miles above the mouth of the Kiamesha" and directly across the Red River from the Womack and Sanders sites. This prairie, Nuttall explained, "derives its name from the herds of wild horses, which till lately frequented it, and of which we saw a small gang" (Nuttall 1980:173).

Granted that the Blackland Prairie horse herd was of a size to be economically important around 1800, could it have been an important source of horses for the Wichita and the Tunica about a hundred years earlier? Probably. Particularly when we consider that the Tunica horse trade must have been on the scale of penny capitalism; the number of horses coming into the French settlements from all sources during the first few decades of the eighteenth century was very small. By 1718, according to Usner (1992:176), French colonists in Louisiana possessed only "four hundred head of cattle and two hundred horses."

In any case, between 1691, the time of the Teran expedition, and 1701, the time horses started appearing in Tunica villages in the Red River mouth area, according to Gregory (1973:281),[47] and the time my putative Womack entrepôt was probably established by the Tunica, the horses lost by the Spaniards could have increased—assuming 50 to 100 animals to start and the exponential growth[48] characteristic of such situations (Crosby 1972:82–84)[49]—to several thousand animals or more.

By 1719, the year La Harpe tried to establish his doomed trading post on the Red River and the approximate time the Womack entrepôt was abandoned, there could have been 20,000 to 50,000 horses on the Blackland Prairie. By 1750, the generally agreed upon mean date for the occupation of the Gilbert site, this herd could have numbered a million or more animals, mathematically speaking. Ecologically speaking, it had probably stabilized at the maximum carrying capacity for the Blackland Prairie. Considering the number of square miles involved, and the apparent scarcity of buffalo (Lynott 1980), which otherwise would have competed with the horses for food, that could have been in the hundreds of thousands.[50]

According to my hypothesis that the Sanders site was a Spiroan, hence proto-Tunican, entrepôt, the Tunica would have been exploiting the trade potential of the Osage orange of the Blackland Prairie for 500 years. Therefore, they would have known about this growing horse herd early on. So, I suspect, would the Caddo of the western reaches of the Red River beyond the Great Bend, because they had to go to the Blackland Prairie to get their Osage orange bow wood (Schambach 1995). So, by 1719, might the Osage[51] because in that year La Harpe (Smith 1958:383) met a party of twenty of them coming down the Kiamichi when he traveled from his newly established Nassonite Post on the Red River to the Arkansas Valley.[52]

More important, as far as the question of the function of the Womack and Gilbert sites is concerned, the Wichita must have known about the Blackland Prairie horse herd. I suspect that it was an important source, if not the main source, for the "large number of horses" (Wedel 1981:37) the Wichita had—many more, apparently, than the Osage or the Red River Valley Caddo, the horses that attracted the attention of the French in New Orleans, circa 1720. Although the crania with annular deformation from the graves at Womack show that someone other than the Wichita "owned and operated" the Womack site, there is archaeological evidence that Harris et al. (1965:360) were right in associating the Wichita with the Womack site in some way. End scrapers of Kay County, Oklahoma, chert,[53] a catlinite pipe fragment (Harris et al. 1965:291–92, 294, 298) and, less specifically, triangular arrow points (Harris et al. 1965:fig. 1B–E) and clay elbow pipes found at Womack (Harris et al. 1965:fig. 6I and J), indicate contact with people in north central Oklahoma. Artifacts from the historic Wichita Bryson-Paddock (Hartley and Miller 1977) and Deer Creek (Wedel 1981) sites on the Arkansas River in north-central Oklahoma that must have come from the Red River Valley, particularly sherds of Womack Engraved pottery from Bryson-Paddock (see Bell 1984b:fig. 17.3h), and European trade beads of the same types found at Angola Farm and Womack[54] are additional evidence of trade between central Oklahoma and northeast Texas during the early historic period.

On the basis of this evidence, I surmise that soon after 1700 the Wichita began bringing buffalo hides and other buffalo products, deer hides, catlinite pipes, and locally obtained and halter-trained feral horses to the Tunica entrepôt at Womack to exchange for the French guns and ammunition they needed to fight their battles with the Apaches and to keep their neighbors to the northeast, the Osage, off their backs. Thus the Tunica would have obtained their "treasure" mostly by exploiting between 1700 and 1760, in cooperation with the Wichita of north-central Oklahoma, a supply of feral Spanish horses on the Blackland Prairie that the Europeans did not know about. Their first entrepôt was at Womack, with some occupation of the nearby Sanders site, the site of their original Red River entrepôt about 500 years earlier. Considering that some of the European trade goods indicate the Womack site could have been occupied as early as 1675 (Harris et al. 1965:360), and considering Gregory's (1973:281) observation that the Tunica were obtaining horses from somewhere up the Red River as early as 1701, I estimate that the entrepôt at Womack had been in operation for about 20 years when La Harpe established his Nassonite Post 108 miles down the Red River from it in 1719.

The trade goods at Womack indicate occupation there ended before about 1729 (Harris et al. 1965:360). Those from the Gilbert site (Jelks 1967:243) show occupation began there about the time Womack was abandoned. This suggests the Tunica moved their entrepôt south to the headwaters of the Saline soon after La Harpe opened his post in 1719. Their main reason may have been to avoid bringing horses down the Red River past the newly established French post, thus blowing the cover on the Blackland Prairie horse herd. Increasing pressure from the Osage may have been another factor. Or, maybe the Tunica just found the Gilbert site more convenient to their home base at the mouth of the Red River.[55]

Considering that the snub-nosed end scrapers found in such astonishing numbers at Womack (872 specimens; Harris et al. 1965:294–95) and Gilbert (418 specimens; Jelks 1967:197–98) were probably not butchering tools but tools "used to remove hair and reduce hide thickness, later steps in hide processing" (Creel 1991:42–43), these sites must have been hide-collecting as well as horse-collecting entrepôts, places where the Tunica received raw hides from the Wichita and prepared them for transport and trade to the east and southeast in Arkansas and Louisiana. The time-consuming work of processing the raw hides brought to these sites was probably best done as soon as they were obtained, both to lighten them for transport and to prevent spoilage.

This work, at which Tunica men were expert (Shea 1861:134–35), would have kept them in residence at these entrepôts for substantial periods each year.

Conclusions

My contention that the Tunica maintained horse- and hide-trading entrepôts in northeast Texas throughout the first half of the seventeenth century is a logical extension of current thinking on the subject of the Tunica and their trading. I agree with Brain (1988:324) that the eighteenth-century Tunica were traders par excellence, people who "consciously or unconsciously . . . played their entrepreneurial role according to European rules." I also agree with Gregory (1973:v, 275; see also Jeter et al. 1989:238–39) that when Europeans began moving into the Lower Mississippi Valley, the Trans-Mississippi South, and the Southern Plains, they did not have to go to the trouble of finding out for themselves what the resources of this vast area were and of establishing the complex system of trade relationships with dozens of different tribes that was necessary to obtain them. They simply took advantage of "an established Indian trade network" (Gregory 1973:275), which was easy to do because the Indians welcomed the goods they had to offer. I am convinced that this Indian trade network was, as Gregory claims, "a very complex system of barter extending from the Mississippi River to eastern New Mexico . . . and from the Arkansas River to the Gulf" and that, as he also claims, "Items exchanged included ceramics, salt . . . hides, Osage orange (bois d'arc) wood for bows, and horses and Native American slaves from the Plains and Southwest."

All I am doing in my reinterpretation of the Spiroan phenomenon, of the Sanders and Nagle sites, and now of the Womack and Gilbert sites, is marshaling evidence that this was a "system," that it was extensive and complex, that—as we might expect of a complex phenomenon—it had roots deep in the past, and that it was the creation of the ancestors of the Tunica of the historic period. I think I have presented good, if largely circumstantial, evidence that these ancestral Tunicans established it—as the Spiroans—around A.D. 1000; that they were operating it—as the Tula—when the Spaniards invaded the Mississippi Valley in 1542, and that they were still operating it—as the Tunica—160 years later when the French arrived in Louisiana.

The discovery of historical or bioanthropological data showing that the Tunica practiced annular cranial deformation in the period between about 1670 and 1750 would confirm that this was their role in the culture history of the Southeast between A.D. 1100 and 1750.

Acknowledgments

I thank Jeffrey Brain, Darrell Creel, Bill Day, Tom Green, David Jeane, David Kelley, Robert Mainfort, Diane Wilson, and Stephen Williams for their comments on earlier drafts of this chapter. Except Mainfort, none of these reviewers has read this version or would necessarily endorse any, much less all, of the ideas I present. I also thank Darrell Creel, curator of collections at the Texas Archeological Research Lab, University of Texas, Austin, for permission to examine the records and collections from the Sanders site held at that institution. I am grateful to Mike Evans for creating figure 8.1 and to Jane Kellet, the Arkansas Archeological Survey's artist and photographer, for figures 8.2 and 8.3. Finally, I thank Donna McCloy of the Magale Library, Southern Arkansas University, for the scores of interlibrary loan requests she made on my behalf while this chapter was in preparation; the work it represents would not have been possible without her competent and unfailingly good-humored assistance.

ENDNOTES

1. A possibility Brown (1996:200) now apparently rejects.

2. It was transplanted to the Old World around 1820 and can now be found from the British Isles to Australia (Smith and Perino 1981:29–30).

3. Predictably, the Sanders site and the nearby Goss site are among the four sites in northeast Texas that have yielded significant numbers of turquoise beads and pendants (Jurney and Young 1995:21–23).

4. There are three reasons for the survival of these 900 to 1,000 year-old bows. One is that the heartwood of bois d'arc "is the most decay resistant of all North American timbers, mainly because it contains an antifungal agent" (Burton 1973:5). Another is that the very deep grave pits that are generally found in the mounds at early Caddo ceremonial centers sometimes penetrated the water table, as did Burial 5 in Mound 5 at Mounds Plantation, creating a favorable environment for the preservation of wood. Third, the almost routine occurrence, in graves, of clusters of arrow points that apparently represent arrows in bundles or quivers suggests that most Caddo males were buried with bows and arrows.

5. Rumor has it that two of the four skulls from the Craig mound that are complete enough to permit such observations exhibit frontal occipital deformation and two exhibit "circular," or annular, deformation. There is nothing in print on this, but we do have Brown's (1984:258–59) statement that "Uniting this population"—by which he means the Arkansas Valley population represented by skeletons from the Horton, Morris, and Spiro sites—"was the practice of cranial deformation among some of the adults (both male and female)." "This deformation," he goes on to say, "is the circular (i.e., annular) type."

Most of the human heads depicted in the shell art from Spiro are shown in profile, so it is impossible to tell if the cranial modeling that is obvious in many cases was annular or frontal-occipital. The few shown in full face (Phillips and Brown 1978:fig. 7, specimens 216, 281, 283) appear to be depictions of people with annular deformation, because of the decidedly abnormal way the heads narrow from the ears up. Significantly, all of these are of the "Craig" style, which Phillips and Brown consider indigenous to Spiro.

6. For reasons adduced later in this chapter, we also can expect to see this style in crania from any early-eighteenth-century graves that might be found at the Gilbert site (Jelks 1967), located about sixty miles south of Sanders and Womack on the upper Sabine River.

7. Absent published archaeological and bioarchaeological analyses of the Sanders site mortuary data (when I examined them in 1995 I found them remarkably complete and detailed, particularly for work done in 1931), we cannot be sure that all of the graves are related to the Spiroan entrepôt, or that all the individuals in them were Spiroans. Possibly some of the females were from local Red River Valley populations. There is also some possibility that slaves drawn from other populations were interred with or near their Spiroan masters.

8. It would be helpful to know whether annular deformation is represented among the crania from the Lymon Moore cemetery and the Skidgel site (Rohrbaugh 1982a), the type sites for Rohrbaugh's (1984:271) newly defined Fort Coffee phase. Unfortunately, there are no descriptions of this material that I know of. Nor are there any for the skeletal material from the various WPA excavated cemeteries in the Spiro locality that Rohrbaugh has recently shifted from the old Fort Coffee focus to his newly defined Spiro phase. If there are any intact crania exhibiting deformation from these sites, the annular style should prevail.

9. "Dressed cow's hides *with tails attached*" would make better sense ethnohistorically. See Swanton 1946:plate 64, 70, no. 21.

10. Not *quite* all, obviously, if the little band of eight itinerant traders had annularly deformed heads as I am suggesting; but I do not take Garcilaso's statement that literally.

11. In December 1995 I examined one excellent specimen of this type, consisting of most of a single pot in fragments, in the Texas Archeological Research Laboratory collections from the "midden area" at the Sanders site.

12. The skeletons are from eight graves excavated at Womack by the University of Texas in 1931 (Harris et al. 1965:288). Neither the skeletons nor the graves have been described in print.

13. During the discussion following my presentation of the original version of this chapter at the 38th Caddo Conference (Schambach 1996), Hiram Gregory reasserted that they were the Kichai, arguing that we do not know whether or not they practiced annular cranial deformation.

The latter is true, but only because the Kichai have never been satisfactorily identified archaeologically or historically—which, of course, is why they have made such a handy *deus ex machina* for those trying to puzzle out the tribal identity of the occupants of Womack and other so-called Norteno focus sites. If, however, they were a Wichita subtribe (Newcomb 1961:13), it is all but certain that they did not practice cranial deformation because, as I noted in the discussion of the identity of the Tulans, it was not a Plains trait and not a Wichita trait. Nor did they if, as Hartley and Miller (1977:252)—citing unpublished work by Jack T. Hughes—suggest, they were a separate tribal group, more closely related to the Pawnee than the Wichita, that developed in situ "along the Trinity and middle Red River headwaters out of the Henrietta-Washita River-Custer complex." This is apparent from good skeletal evidence (Owsley 1989:127) from the Harrel site (type site for the "Henrietta focus"; see Suhm et al. 1954:50) and from the McLemore site (Brues 1962:75; Owsley 1989:130–33), one of the key sites in the Washita River phase. Neither population shows evidence of cranial deformation.

14. This can be confirmed using figures that appear elsewhere in La Harpe's journal. La Harpe states that the distance "by land in direct line" (Smith 1958:85) from "the entry of the Red River, situated at the thirty-first degree of latitude" (Smith 1958:78), to Natchitoches "would be only thirty-eight leagues of road, or thereabout" (Smith 1958:85). That would be 104.8 miles, using Wedel's conversion factor, or 60.4 miles using Harris et al.'s. According to the Louisiana Department of Transportation and Development's "Official Highway Map," the straight line distance between these points is 94 miles. According to my 1994 Rand McNally Road Atlas it is about 107 miles. In either case, it is clear that Wedel's conversion factor is the right one.

15. Krieger's (1946:172) erroneous notion that the Sanders and Womack sites are "approximately on the border between eastern forest and open plains" may have contributed to Harris et al.'s misconception of Womack as a place frequented by Plains buffalo hunters. In any case, these sites are not on the edge of the "open plains." They are more than 80 miles east of them on the edge of the Blackland Prairie, which is separated from the "open plains" by two north-south oriented bands of savanna, called the Eastern Cross Timbers and the Western Cross Timbers, and by the Grand Prairie, which lies between them (Fenneman 1938:102, fig. 27; see also fig. 8.1, this chapter).

16. That is not to say he couldn't have encountered buffalo *hunters* visiting the Womack site to trade. The implications of my conclusion (see below) that Womack was a Tunican entrepôt established for trade with the Wichita are that he might have, had he made his trip in the late fall rather than in June, and had he visited the Garret's Bluff locale where the Womack site is located.

17. I exclude the Pearson site, the latest of the "eastern group" and the most divergent in other respects as well, because it seems likely that it represents a Norteno focus (or Wichita) occupation in northeast Texas around 1760 (Duffield and Jelks 1961:76–79).

18. Blain (1992:193) has commented on the "startling" difference "in quantity alone" between the pottery from Gilbert and the pottery from the "more westerly . . . Norteno sites at the Spanish Fort locale." Partly on that basis he now questions (1992:177) the original assignment of the Gilbert site to the Norteno focus (Jelks 1967:244), stating: "However probable it might appear, a Norteno affiliation in the ethnohistorical sense is less secure" than it once seemed.

19. Brain's (1988:273) identification of the Upper Sunflower region Parchman phase as prehistoric Tunica—and hence his claim to have

"positively identified" the "Upper Sunflower locale of the northern Yazoo Basin" as "the ancestral hearth of the Tunica"—is triply flawed.

First, it rests on suspiciously small numbers of suspiciously small body sherds said to be of his allegedly diagnostic Tunica type Winterville Incised, *var. Tunica,* and of a few rim sherds supposedly bearing the allegedly equally diagnostic "Tunican Mode." These are the kinds of ceramic identifications that are only convincing to the true believer and, as Jeter (1990a:147–48) has observed regarding them: "Some of us are not convinced." One could probably find a few small sherds that might possibly have come from so-called Winterville Incised, *var. Tunica,* pots in surface collections from almost any Mississippi period site in the Lower Mississippi Valley. All this means is that this variety and type, like so many Caddo area and Mississippi Valley types (Schambach and Miller 1984:113–14), cannot be reliably identified from small sherds, particularly sherds that do not show both the rim and the body decoration.

Second, granting the slim possibility that the identifications are right, there is, as Jeter (1990a:147–48) also notes, the serious methodological problem inherent in assuming "a one-to-one correlation between alleged 'diagnostic' or 'marker' artifact types/varieties/modes (or "sets" of them) and ethnic groups." I agree with Jeter that the correlation is usually apt to be "significantly less than one to one." In this case, I doubt there is one. There are other reasons, particularly trade, why a few sherds of Winterville Incised, *var. Tunica,* might show up in a collection from a site in northwestern Mississippi.

Third, it is, as Jeter (1990a:147–48) states, always "a very questionable systematic procedure to give ethnic names to artifact types, varieties, modes or other archaeological concepts such as phases." The reason this procedure is questionable is that one is so apt to be wrong, in which case the result is obfuscation and confusion without end. In this case, it is clear that Brain is wrong. Because the pottery he calls Winterville Incised, *var. Tunica,* is the dominant type and variety at the Trudeau site, he has jumped to the mistaken conclusion that an eighteenth-century variety of a pottery type with a long history of development in the Caddo area (and none that he can demonstrate in the Lower Mississippi Valley) can be used as an ethnic marker—indeed, "a prime . . . diagnostic" (Brain 1988:394)—for the Tunica from the mid-sixteenth century through the eighteenth century. But, as Miller and I demonstrated many years ago (Schambach and Miller 1984:121–22, fig. 11-10; see also Perttula 1992:table 9), and as Brain (1988:394) concedes, his Winterville Incised, *var. Tunica,* probably is derived from what we call the *Shaw* variety of the Caddo area type Foster Trailed Incised. This variety is traditionally classified as Emory Punctated by Caddo specialists. That is how Brain should have classified it as well. But he (1988:394) argues that his *Tunica* variety "developed in northwestern Mississippi, drawing decorative inspiration from *Shaw* directly" (how Tunican potters in northwestern Mississippi might have drawn "inspiration" from Caddo potters about 250 miles away in southwest Arkansas he does not say) and then was taken first to the Yazoo and finally to Trudeau (where it is the dominant decorated variety), whence it was taken up the Red River to Los Adaes and Gilbert.

The fatal flaw in this argument is that according to the Red River Valley ceramic chronology, which is arguably one of the most fine-grained and secure chronologies in Southeastern archaeology (see Perttula 1992:119–20; B. D. Smith 1984b:275), the *Shaw* variety of Foster Trailed Incised did not appear until A.D. 1700–25 (Perttula 1992:tables 9, 14; Schambach and Miller 1984:122). Hence, its acknowledged derivative, Winterville Incised, *var. Tunica,* would not have appeared in the Mississippi Valley prior to the second quarter of the eighteenth century. Not surprisingly, there is no convincing evidence (by which I mean whole pots or good-sized sherds from *dated contexts*) that this variety was being made anywhere, least of all northwestern Mississippi, as early as the mid-sixteenth century, when Brain's protohistoric Tunicans were supposedly using it there.

So here we have another instance where, as is the case with the archaeology of the Arkansas Valley in general and Spiro in particular (Schambach 1993b:208–13), and as is the case with the Sanders site in northeast Texas (Schambach 1993b:203–6, 1995), the penchant of the Tunica and their Spiroan forebears for transporting significant quantities of pottery over considerable distances has led archaeologists astray.

20. Contrary to the conventional wisdom, I consider the pottery of the types Womack Engraved and Emory Punctated (the latter aka Foster Trailed-Incised, *var. Shaw,* according to Schambach and Miller 1984:121–22; aka Winterville Incised, *var. Tunica,* according to Brain 1979:234–37; and aka Braden Punctate according to Rohrbaugh 1982a:461) that occurs at various Fort Coffee phase sites in the Spiro locality (Rohrbaugh 1982a:487–92, figs. 26, 27 for Womack Engraved, and for Emory Punctated 460–64, fig. 20 "LfMoI, Isolated find") evidence that the area was not completely abandoned until after 1700.

Certainly, these pots were made after A.D. 1650 and they could have been made as late as the 1720s and 1730s. The Emory Punctated pot Rohrbaugh illustrates (1982b:fig. 20, lower right-hand specimen labeled "LfMoI isolated find, Braden Punctated") indicates that someone with close ties to northeast Texas and the Red River Valley, including the Red River mouth region, was doing something at the "Fort Coffee phase" Lymon Moore site (LfMoI) as late as 1730.

In terms of the hypothesis I am developing here, this suggests that the Tunica continued to operate an entrepôt in the Spiro locality, probably for the purpose of collecting buffalo hides, for some decades after most of the population moved down the Arkansas to the Yazoo. The Emory Punctated pot from Lymon Moore indicates that they continued using it after they moved to the Red River mouth region.

21. This presents the possibility that the Tulans/Tunicans of the Arkansas Valley in eastern Oklahoma were a linguistically and culturally divergent western branch of a much larger Tunican speaking population that had long occupied the Mississippi Valley in northwestern Mississippi, western Tennessee, and northeast Arkansas (see Hoffman 1993:134–40; Rankin 1993:213–18). That, however, is a topic too complicated to be taken up here.

22. Another possibility is that there might be no ceramic evidence whatever of this move. When they left the Fort Smith area, the Tunica might have abandoned their own already weak ceramic tradition (Schambach

1993b:208–10) and relied thereafter on traded pottery, as they had already been doing to some extent for several centuries, judging from the large quantities of traded Caddo area and Lower Mississippi Valley at Spiro and other sites in the Spiro locality (Brown 1983:144, table 4; Schambach 1993b:210–12, 1993c:15).

This possibility is not as far-fetched as it might seem. The Tunica were relying heavily, if not entirely, on traded pottery for mortuary offerings by the time they reached the Red River mouth area circa 1706. None of the five aboriginal pots from the graves at Angola (Ford 1936:fig. 27) appears to be Tunica made. Ford (1936:139–40, fig. 27) identified one (fig. 27e) as "a Natchez type vessel." That specimen has since been classified as Leland Incised, *var. Fatherland,* by Phillips (1970:106), who, without equivocation, calls it "a Natchez phase type." Ford apparently thought the pot he illustrated as figure 27a was Natchezan also, as did Quimby (1942a:266). Phillips (1970:154) has reclassified it as Pocohontas Punctated, a type, he says, of "the Lower Red River-Natchez region." The engraved, so-called "Caddoan" bottle from Angola (Ford 1936:fig. 27c; Brain 1988:fig. 129c) could be that, although, to me, it looks more like a Walls Engraved bottle from northeast Arkansas. The remaining pots (Ford 1936:fig. 27b, d) could be Natchezan or, as I suspect, Koroan; however, no one has ever identified them as Tunica.

23. Judging from Brain's (1988:196–263) overview, only eleven whole pots are recorded for the four Yazoo Basin sites (Haynes Bluff, Portland, Burroughs, and Russell) that might have been occupied by the Tunica during the seventeenth century. Five are from Haynes Bluff (Brain 1988:fig. 160a, b, c, fig. 162) and six are from Russell (Brain 1988:fig. 184a, b, c, d, g, h).

24. Brain (1988:296) suggests that La Source's observation that Tunica men did not hunt, and Gravier's that "[t]he men do here what peasants do in France; they cultivate and dig the earth, plant and harvest the crops," are evidence of a cultural-historical link with the sixteenth-century province of Quizquiz because the men of the town of Quizquiz were "away tending the fields" when the Spaniards arrived, leaving the women defenseless.

Perhaps it could, but only if the unfortunately timed absence of the men of Quizquiz could be considered evidence that "these people, almost alone among eastern tribes, had made the transition to an agricultural strategy wherein the men performed the primary function of working the fields" (Brain 1988:296). But it was a common practice in the early prehistoric Southeast for men to handle the heavy labor of clearing and preparing the fields for spring planting, while men and women shared the lighter work of planting, tending, and harvesting (Hudson 1976:267–68; Usner 1988: 393–94). Considering that the Spaniards probably reached Quizquiz on May 8, 1541 (Dye 1993:41), about the time for spring planting in the mid-South under the cooler than normal Little Ice Age climatic conditions that prevailed then, it would seem that the men of Quizquiz were not doing anything out of the ordinary.

Even if they were, Brain's point would still be questionable because the latest reconstructions of the de Soto route (see Dye 1993:40–41) convincingly place the province of Quizquiz well to the north of the Upper Sunflower region in the Memphis area and link it, not with the Parchman phase, but the Walls phase (see Jeter et al. 1989:225 and Morse and Morse 1983:308–9).

25. There is no evidence a "western branch of the Tunicans" maintained "permanent residence" in this area and no realistic possibility that such will be found. Nor is there any archaeological or documentary evidence of the buffalo Brain imagines the Tunica hunting at the Ouachita Valley "salt licks" (see Early 1982b, 1993c; Schambach 1970, 1998; Schambach and Early 1982).

26. Elvas says "a day and a half" from Tanico (Clayton et al. 1993:125). Rangel says they "left from the site of Tanico or Cayase" on a Wednesday and reached Tula on Friday (Clayton et al. 1993:305). Garcilaso says they traveled two days to reach the border of the province of Cayas and four more through "uninhabited lands" to reach the principal town of Tula (Varner and Varner 1951:454). Elvas, unfortunately, says Tula was "south" of Tanico, which makes no sense, but Biedma says it was "upriver" from Tanico (Clayton et al. 1993:125, 242).

27. Speaking of "Tunicans west of the Mississippi," I do not accept Jeter's (1986:58) argument that "Tunicans (including the Tunica and/or Koroa) were the principal occupants of the southeastern quadrant of Arkansas and adjacent portions of northeastern Louisiana, possibly for several hundred years before the De Soto *entrada.*" One problem with that argument is it rests heavily on Swanton's (1939) discredited reconstruction of the de Soto route through Arkansas (see Young and Hoffman 1993 and Schambach 1993a:101–2).

Also, Jeter's (1986:42) conflation of the Koroa with the Tunica is based entirely on the fact that "Swanton (1911:33) tentatively classed the Koroa as speakers of a Tunican language." That he did. But he did so (Swanton 1919:7) "on the grounds of historical association and a few statements of early writers, especially Du Pratz's affirmation that Yazoo and Koroa shared with Tunica the peculiarity of employing a true *r* which the surrounding peoples could not even pronounce." Neither one, nor both, of these lines of evidence which Swanton himself (1911:33) disparaged as "merely circumstantial," would be sufficient reason for conflating Tunican culture with Koroan culture. Some of the southeast Arkansas material is probably Koroan (Schambach 1981:106), but none of it is demonstrably Tunican.

28. Swanton's version of the latter sentence is "Mothers carefully put the heads of both boys and girls under pressure from birth to render them flat."

29. Compare this to Garcilaso's "from the moment they are born *their heads* are bound" (Varner and Varner 1951:456, emphasis added).

30. Brain buttresses this conclusion with the observation that head deformation "is not depicted in the DeBatz watercolor sketch of prominent Tunica (said to be Bride les Boeufs and his wife and child; see Bushnell 1927:plate 2 and Swanton 1946:plate 48), which he presents as figure 208 in *Tunica Archaeology* (Brain 1988) and on the cover of *Tunica Treasure* (Brain 1979).

Maybe so. But can we be sure the man depicted was a Tunica? Swanton (1946:plate 19; see also Bushnell 1927:plate 5) presents a sketch captioned "Choctaw Indians, From The Sketch By DeBatz" featuring a nearly identical male figure that looks like the same man. He is in almost exactly the same pose, seems to have the same design tattooed on his chest and throat, and is accoutred with the same breechcloth, knife, powder horn, and staff with three scalps attached. Only his hairstyle and facial painting or tattooing are a little different. Was the original model for this figure a Choctaw or a Tunica?

It would seem that he was a Choctaw because DeBatz made the sketch for the "Choctaw Indians" or "Choctaw Warriors" painting in late January of 1730 (Bushnell 1927:11), and he made the sketches for the drawing of Bride les Boeufs, or "Buffalo Tamer," immediately after the death of his chiefly predecessor, Cahura-Joligo, on June 14, 1731, and then redrew them in New Orleans on June 22, 1732 (Bushnell 1927:5–6).

Also, the extraordinary breadth of the head of this man and the positioning of his ears suggest that, *contra* Brain, he has a deformed cranium. But the deformation is of the frontal-occipital style (see Lewis et al. 1995:fig. 11.7 for an artist's conception of a full face view of a person with frontal-occipital deformation) so characteristic of the Choctaw that the English traders called them "Flat Heads" (Galloway 1995:168; Swanton 1946:539), and Swanton (1946:817) describes them as "addicted to the custom of frontal head deformation."

The woman in the DeBatz watercolor of prominent Tunica is said to be the wife of Cahura Joligo (Brain 1979:cover illustration, 1988:fig. 208). Probably so, since she wears her hair in a style fitting Gravier's description (Shea 1861:134) of the "great tress of hair on the back which hangs down below the waist" favored by Tunica women. I think she has a deformed cranium as well, but it is impossible to tell whether the style is frontal-occipital or annular because her head is shown in profile. To my biased eye it seems to taper above the ears in a manner suggesting annular deformation.

To turn briefly to another point, why would a man born into a society of fully committed Mississippian farmers living in a part of the Lower Mississippi Valley where buffalo were, at best, "very rare" (Shea 1861:135) be named "Bride les Boeufs," or "Buffalo Tamer"? What would such a man have had to do with buffalo? I suspect this was a French rendition of a traditional Tunica name, perhaps a chiefly title, that was part of the cultural baggage the Tunica brought from the Spiro area.

31. Harris et al. (1965:287) were not the only persons who collected from the site, nor the only ones who dug there, so the collection they report is probably but a part of the European artifacts that have been found there.

32. I extrapolated this figure from data presented by Surrey (1968:301–2), who relates that "[i]n 1719 a trader exchanged three muskets, some powder, knives and a few trinkets with the Osage Indians on the upper Missouri for two horses and a mule." Shortly thereafter the same trader lost "six horses and a colt in attempting to cross a stream, a loss estimated at more than 900 livres." Thus, in this particular trader's eyes, at least, the going rate for a horse, which could be gotten in trade for one musket, seems to have been about 150 livres.

33. The post—Arkansas Post—that de Tonti established at the mouth of the Arkansas in 1682 does not seem to have functioned effectively as a center for French trade with the Indians either. Wedel (1981:30) relates that "French Canadian traders received beaver skin said to be of mediocre quality and deer hides from the Quapaw . . . for a few years at least" after its founding. However when Le Sueur visited there in 1700, he "found no Frenchmen . . . but instead an English trader from Carolina who had provided the Indians with fusils and swords."

Wedel ends her discussion of Arkansas Post with the cryptic statement that "[n]o record of the French traders who made this their headquarters during the next two decades has been found." Surely she intended to say "the French traders who *supposedly* made this their headquarters during the next two decades," for if "no record of the French traders who made this their headquarters has been found," how could it be known that they did so? Suffice it to say that, as with the Nassonite Post, there is little evidence that Arkansas Post was the center for French trade with the Indians that archaeologists seem to think it was during the first few decades of the eighteenth century.

34. They also show that there was a shortage of goods that small-time French entrepreneurs might have traded. Usner (1992:78) writes that "in quality as well as quantity of merchandise, Louisiana suffered a chronic shortage in its supply of imported goods available for the Indian trade." Hence the Indians came to believe that the French were "entirely poor" compared to the English and "unable to manufacture goods as well as the English did" (Holland-Braund 1996:36–37).

35. There was a significant population surge between 1717 and 1721 when the Company of the Indies transported 7,000 Europeans and 2,000 West African slaves to the Gulf Coast (Usner 1992:32). But by then activity at the Womack site was probably drawing to a close.

36. Significantly, the locally exotic aboriginal mortuary pottery from Womack has long been considered "pottery like that of Glendora focus, representative of historic Caddo in the Lower Red River Valley" (Krieger 1946:164 n. 80; Suhm et al. 1954:222).

37. Brain (1988:172, fig. 146) identifies from Burial 6 at Bloodhound Hill "a crushed vessel of native Caddoan manufacture . . . probably belonging to the upper Red River type Avery Engraved." I cannot be sure it is Avery Engraved, judging only from his illustration, but it certainly could be, and it could be from "the upper Red River," given my interpretation of Womack.

38. Although the three beads from Womack are not illustrated, two are described as "tube-shaped" and one as "barrel-shaped" (Harris et al. 1965:305), which sounds like the beads from Bloodhound. One of the two "gorgets" from Womack (Harris et al. 1965:fig. 7B) is not a gorget, but a disc with a central hole like those from Burial 6 at Bloodhound (Brain 1988:fig. 146b).

39. Apparently this was the Little River, which joins the Red River just west of the "Great Bend" near Fulton, Arkansas.

40. *Cajeux,* according to Le Page du Pratz (in Tregle 1975:362; see also Surrey 1968:58–59), were rafts made of bundles of cane: "They cut a great number of canes, which they tie up into faggots, part of which they fasten together sideways, and over these they lay a row crossways, binding all close together, and then launching it into the water." I am indebted to David Kelley for this reference.

41. "Tonicaus" is close enough to "Tonicas," la Harpe's rendering of "Tunica" at the time he visited the Tunica village near the mouth of the Red River on his way up the Red River in January 1719 (Smith 1958:78–80), to leave little doubt that the builders of these *cajeux* were the Tunica. However (and not surprisingly, since La Harpe was sick and drifting in and out of

coma during this leg of the trip; see Wedel 1971:45), the phrase "who are the Yasous" makes no sense. There is no evidence, nor is it likely (see Swanton 1911:34), that the Yazoo were ever called the "Tonicaus." It is probably a garbled reference to one or both of the related facts that for some years prior to 1706 the Tunica had lived on the Lower Yazoo River, where they were closely associated with the Yazoo people (Brain 1988:25–30). My guess is that La Harpe's "savages," who were probably the same Natchitoches guides he engaged on the trip up the Red River, still considered the Tunica a people "from the Yazoo" because they had moved from there to the Red River mouth area only 10 to 13 years earlier, between 1706 and 1709 according to Brain (1988:31). In that light, the phrase "the Tonicaus, who are the Yasous" would make sense if simply amended to "the Tonicaus who are from the Yasous."

Swanton (1911:34) thought the opposite: that La Harpe meant "that the Tunica of whom his men told him at this time were really Yazoo." I reject that because there is no other evidence that the Yazoo were ever in the Red River Valley, nor is there any reason to suppose they would have gone there.

42. Travel and transport up and down the Red River by canoe would not have been feasible because of the Great Raft, an ancient 140-mile-long log jam that plugged the river from the vicinity of the mouth of Loggy Bayou in Louisiana almost to the Arkansas state line, turning the valley on either side into a patchwork of lakes and swamps (Bowman 1911:534–38). It took La Harpe 26 days to travel by boat up the Red River from Natchitoches to the mouth of the Sulphur River (Smith 1958:246–49; Wedel 1971:43, 1978:2), a straight-line distance of about 130 miles.

43. According to Avery (1996:14), this pottery, which he calls Emory Incised, "dominates" the aboriginal ceramic assemblage from Gregory's excavations at Los Adaes.

44. Or perhaps that is only where the French *thought* these horse were coming from.

45. According to Fenneman (1938:108), the Blackland Prairie comprises a long, narrow band of "very stiff calcareous clay, the soil on which is called 'black waxy,'" that stretches from the Red River Valley in the vicinity of the Sanders and Womack sites southwestward to Austin, San Antonio, and beyond and supports a fertile prairie. It was, as of 1938, "the foremost agricultural district of Texas."

46. Europeans did not learn about the Blackland Prairie horse herd until about 1800 because they rarely visited that part of Texas during the first three-quarters of the eighteenth century. According to Gregory (1973:281), the Kadohadacho villages were as far as Bienville and St. Denis got in 1701. To have seen horses on the Blackland Prairie, they would have to have traveled about 100 miles farther west. As Duffield and Jelks (1961:73–74) point out, the next eighteenth-century European explorer of record to push up the Red River beyond the Kadohadacho villages in the Great Bend was La Harpe in 1719, but he established his Nassonite Post about 108 miles east of the Womack site (Harris et al. 1965:359) and the Blackland Prairie. Since he traveled "on horseback" on "an Indian trail along the north side of the river" (Wedel 1971: n. 3), Du Rivage should have seen horses on Nuttall's "Horse Prairie" (Nuttall 1980:173) in the Red River valley west of the mouth

of the Kiamichi when La Harpe sent him west from the newly established Nassonite Post to look for "nomadic tribes." But he did not, perhaps because—assuming they were there—the trail kept to the high ground north of the river bottoms and of the "Horse Prairie," and perhaps also because his Indian guides made it their business to keep him from seeing them.

47. Brain (1988:31) states that the date of the "Tunica migration from the Yazoo" to the Red River mouth area "was probably 1706," which does not jibe with Gregory's 1701 date for "Tunica villages" in—I presume—the Red River mouth area.

48. Horses have the potential for exponential population growth when introduced to a new, favorable environment. According to Waring (1983:58), "Fillies can come into estrus as early as their second summer when 14 to 17 months of age," although conception is very low in yearlings. The gestation period is 340 days (Waring 1983:46), and in free-ranging herds mares foal annually, weaning the last foal just weeks or days before the next is born (Waring 1983:58).

49. When horses were introduced to areas with favorable environments in the New World their natural increase often approximated a "biological explosion" (Crosby 1972:82–84). Bearing in mind the size and economic importance of the Blackland Prairie herd in the early 1800s and considering that in modern times the Blackland Prairie between Austin and the Red River Valley was rated "the foremost agricultural district of Texas" (Fenneman 1938:108), it is likely that a biological explosion of horses occurred there around the beginning of the eighteenth century.

50. Obviously, these horses would have been valuable to the Indians who found out about them. I suspect they also had an effect on the ecology of the Blackland Prairie that was of equal economic importance to the Plains Indians. As I argue earlier in this chapter and elsewhere (Schambach 1995:19 n. 27), by the year of the Teran expedition the range of Osage orange had shrunk (for want of the extinct Pleistocene species, probably horses, that once propagated it) to a few streams, particularly Bois d'arc Creek, that traversed the Blackland Prairie. All the Osage orange in the world was growing along those streams, probably not the supply that would be needed to furnish Osage orange bows to every Plains tribe as far north as the Blackfoot during the next century and a half.

But when horses were reintroduced to the area, they would have begun spreading Osage orange—as they still do—in and around the Blackland Prairie. So the ecological effect of the "failed" Teran expedition may have been to turn the Blackland Prairie into a generator of the two species that would prove vital to the Plains Indians horse/buffalo hunting culture of the eighteenth and early nineteenth centuries: horses and Osage orange.

51. Haas (1950:131) has translated and published a Tunica text describing the capture and torture of a man who was probably an Osage. She comments that although the Tunica word for this man "seems to be practically identical with the name the Osage apply to themselves . . . it might seem that the Tunica were too far south to render it likely that they would capture an Osage Indian." Perhaps not, if the Tunica and the Osage were in competition for horses and bow wood on the Blackland Prairie.

52. The traditional enmity between the Osage and the Caddo may date

from this time. It was most likely based not on the "bellicosity" of the Osage, but on their economic interest in the horses and Osage orange of the Blackland Prairie.

53. The Gilbert site yielded two Indian-made gun flints and some debitage of Kay County chert (Jelks 1967:84, 208).

54. Brain's (1979:116–31) series of maps showing the spatial and temporal distributions of bead varieties found in the "Tunica Treasure" collection suggests that there was a direct trade relationship between the Angola Farm site, Womack, and the Deer Creek site.

55. The most direct route from the Tunica Bayou area, where the Tunica were living between 1730 and 1764 (Brain 1988:34), to the Blackland Prairie is not up the Red River Valley all the way to the Great Bend, but up the Red River to Natchitoches, then cross-country to the Sabine, and up it to the Gilbert site, near Emory, Texas.

CHAPTER NINE

FROM FAMOUS FORTS TO FORGOTTEN FARMSTEADS: HISTORICAL ARCHAEOLOGY IN THE MID-SOUTH

Leslie C. Stewart-Abernathy

There are many points at which one might begin the story of historical archaeology in the Mid-South. Here is an early example of one major theme in the field, the examination of historic Native Americans. Frederich Gerstacker, a German sportsman and later author, was bear hunting in Newton County, Arkansas, in the early winter of 1843. He and some companions were exploring a cave, hoping for bear.

> An unexpected sight suddenly arrested our progress,—the skeletons of a man and of a bear, lying peaceably within three feet of each other. A rifle, thickly covered with rust, and a corroded knife, lay by the side of the first, and some glass beads convinced us that it was the skeleton of an Indian, who had bravely attacked the bear single-handed, and had fallen in the struggle, the skeleton of the bear proving that he had sold his life dearly (Gerstacker 1968:337–38).

One of the party noted the Native American skeleton was complete except for some small bones of the hand, probably removed by small animals. They also noted the left arm was broken, and the knife was lying on the right side of the skeleton. These are detailed observations to be sure. The party left the scene untouched (Gerstacker 1968:338). It is noteworthy that in January 1838 Gerstacker wanted to investigate some "sepulchral monuments on the banks of Spring river," but was unable to arrange a trip with his overnight host. Gerstacker (1968:84) was disappointed, since his almost-guide had found "urns and weapons in the graves, but he had none to show me, for these people have no regard for anything that does not offer some immediate prospect of gain."

Four decades later, another visitor to Arkansas sounded a second major theme of historical archaeology in the Mid-South, the study of forts. In December 1882, Edward Palmer was examining mound sites along the Arkansas River in Arkansas and Desha Counties as part of the great Mound Survey conducted by the Smithsonian Institution Bureau of Ethnology (Jeter 1990b:217–240). Though his concern was with Native American earthworks, Palmer's notes indicated that he was also alert to early historic sites:

> On what is known as the Turner Place & now owned by the widow of Thomas Bizzell are the outlines of an old fortification . . . This fort was made very probably to protect a French trading post. As Mr. Oliver Bizzell says, numerous thimbles, pipes, broken dishes, parts of revolvers, guns & pieces of silver coin have been found, as if the center [of the coin] had been used for gun sight. The remains of an old Forge were uncovered a short time ago and Chinese & other coins were found with broken articles of Indian origin. A chinese coin and part of a pistol (stone) were presented to that gentlemen, who also says that stone bullets moulds have been found . . . Not far from the Fort is a ridge that appears to have had houses of European origin upon it. At one corner of the fort is a hole 16 ft. deep, supposed to have been a magazine (Jeter 1990b:240).

This fortification was some four feet high according to Palmer, with a ramp or path leading down to the Arkansas River. We now suspect the fort and the accompanying house sites were remnants of Arkansas Post, or at least the second location of the post, occupied 1756–79 (Arnold 1983, 1991). During the period it was actually legally Spanish. The site, 3DE23, was relocated by Burney McClurkan in 1971 (McClurkan 1971, 1972), but even then it was mostly gone; it was completely obliterated by the 1980s.

A human skeleton diagnosed as Native American because of the presence of trade goods and a colonial fort: these are precisely the research areas sounded by Hodges and Hodges (1942) as "Possibilities for the Archeologist and Historian in Eastern Arkansas." Twenty years later, Williams (1962) made the same call for the wider region. His paper is indicative of the way the field was then defined—Contact and Colonial. Look for trade goods that are then used to approximate a date for contact, or at least document nationality of European colonial power (but see Brown 1979a for a frequently ignored warning). Go after the central places of the colonial experience, forts and associated Europeans or Native American hamlets. Williams provided a useful summary of work to date and a call for action. He noted seventeen Native American sites with trade goods, from Campbell (southeastern Missouri) to Menard-Hodges (Arkansas) to Oliver, Haynes Bluff, and Fatherland (all Mississippi), and Trudeau (Louisiana). He also called attention to several colonial settlements and forts, from Arkansas Post to Fort St. Pierre in Mississippi.

Today, some three and a half decades later, many of the sites Williams pointed out have been further studied—Fatherland (Neitzel 1965, 1983) and Trudeau (Brain 1973, 1979), of course, but also Fort St. Pierre (I. Brown 1975a, 1975b, 1976a, 1978) and a whole series of Contact sites (e.g., Brain 1988; Brown 1976b, 1979b, 1985; Hogue et al. 1996; and see also Davis 1991 and Galloway 1982). The field of historical archaeology has changed since Williams wrote in 1962, not least with the founding of the national Society for Historical Archaeology in 1967. The Old Reliables have not been forgotten—in the summer of 1997 two seasons of fieldwork began at the Quapaw village of Osotouy at Menard-Hodges and what is apparently the adjacent Colonial site of the first Arkansas Post (1686–99) (House 1997, 1998; Stewart-Abernathy 1998a; Stewart-Abernathy and Farmer 1997). The field has also grown, however, in the topics considered suitable for examination, beyond the exotic Otherness of Colonial and Contact, and 200 years' distance in time, all the way to forgotten farmsteads from the beginning of the twentieth century. This chapter examines of some of the ways the field has grown in the Mid-South.

Defining Historical Archaeology

One must start with definitions, to set boundaries in time and space, keeping in mind that an effort to define can also introduce substantive and theoretical problems. To begin with, fledgling historical archaeologists learn in their college classes today that the field they are seeking to understand is concerned with three related sets of phenomena: first, the expansion of Europeans to the rest of the world after the sixteenth century; second, the impact that expansion had on those living in the areas to which Europeans were moving; and third, the transformations in European and postcolonial cultures in the ensuing centuries. This is a fairly broad definition, as it covers some 400 years of remarkable cultural and demographic change, along with the rise of industrial civilization as we know it. It might be simpler if we define the field in a practical way, as what it is that historical archaeologists do and have done. There are advantages to a practical perspective, but the chief problem is that most of the historical archaeology done in the Mid-South, at least until the last decade or so, has been conducted by people who were not trained as historical archaeologists but as prehistorians. These folks found themselves on historic sites, or at least encountering European artifacts, as result of cultural resource management projects, or because somebody needed to do something about a site in danger, or just because of the image of the archaeologist as capable of handling any sort of site, from Archaic lithic scatter to Woodland hamlet to Civil War battlefield. They then taught themselves how to deal with documents and artifacts.

Unfortunately, historic sites are different from prehistoric ones in many ways, including issues of significance, opportunities for research, advantages in terms of efficiency of data gathering, and scope. Perhaps the least complicated is that most of the portable material culture was made hundreds or thousands of miles away by people with different ideologies, if not even different languages, than the ultimate users and discarders. The context is always the world system and how the particular users of those objects fit into that system. In such situations, too often prehistorians bring to the field all their conceptions drawn from the local and regional scale of most prehistoric sites. Regardless of the best of intentions, there has often been damage to the sites studied through incompetence. To put it briefly, a lot of historic sites, or at least features on those sites, have been poorly handled by professional archaeologists with poor formal or self-training. Indeed, larger problems remain from the history of historical archaeology in which sites were poorly handled theoretically, analytically, and managerially. Unfortunately, when the documents and oral history are rich, the archaeologist often looks superfluous when the questions asked are naive, as they often are when transferred from prehistory. It is possible, for example, to understand the continued hesitation by managers to expend CRM resources on twentieth-century sites, as the direct result of the superficial way many of those sites have been handled in the past by archaeologists.

Defining the Mid-South

A second definition has to do with the area considered as the Mid-South. There are many definitions one might use, from drainage networks to state boundaries to a list of agreed-upon cultural traditions. Certainly geographical bounds are useful, but they are subject to ethnocentrism. Participants in the Mid-South Archaeological Conferences might consider the Mid-South as focusing on Memphis and extending south to about Natchez, north to the mouth of the Ohio, west into Arkansas and Louisiana perhaps as far as Little Rock and Alexandria, and east to the Tennessee River and the Mississippi hills. (Residents of Alabama, the self-styled "Heart of Dixie," might disagree, though.)

With historic sites, however, one is always by necessity dealing with issues of the world framework of interaction. For example, the factories of Staffordshire touched every fort and farm from the middle of the 1700s onward, and political and economic events in London, Paris, Madrid, Philadelphia, and New York found expression in the archaeological record of the Mid-South. Ironically, given this wider scale, one might easily define the Mid-South as an ignored backwater, surrounded by Ph.D.-granting institutions to the north, south, east, and west, but with no such institutions in the region itself.

With Ph.D. programs come graduate students who need thesis and dissertation topics, and with those research efforts come site reports and special analyses. This has been a problem with prehistoric sites that have at least drawn the attention of outsiders to such obviously necessary targets as Late Mississippian village and mound sites in the Mid-South, but it is certainly true with historic sites. It is no accident that so much of academic historical archaeology takes place on the East and West Coasts, in the upper Midwest, and in the Southwest, where graduate schools sitting cheek by jowl are turning out scores of theses and dissertations on colonial Anglo, Spanish, and plantation topics. For obvious reasons one need not also wonder that eastern Tennessee has been so well covered, or southern Illinois, or Georgia, or Florida.

A key element in the history of historical archaeology in the Mid-South is thus a lack of local trained talent, leading to one of two situations. One is the convert, someone who discovers that historic sites can be so much more productive and downright interesting than the lithic scatters or type-variety classifications in which they were brought up. Some of the costs of on-the-job-training previously have been noted. The second situation brought about by the lack of an institutional base is the expedition mentality, in which raids were made by outsiders to a select few sites, and the great hinterland of those sites were left unexplored until mid-southerners began to take responsibility for their own backyards. The long-term commitment by the Lower Mississippi Valley Survey was one exception, but many times the natives have been surprised by quick projects conducted on important sites in our territory by National Park Service archaeologists from Santa Fe, Lincoln, Atlanta, or Harpers Ferry, not to mention the mercenary elements within the world of contract archaeology.

But if we do go to geographical boundaries, that also can be confining in a multitude of unpleasant ways, not to mention that it can reinforce the image of the Mid-South as an empty quarter where not much of significance ever happened in either the historic past or the study of that past. For example, eliminating southern Louisiana takes away all the work done by people in New Orleans, by Shenkel, Hudson, Castille, and others (e.g., Castille et al. 1982; Castille et al. 1986; Hudson and Hudson 1974; Shenkel 1971; Shenkel and Hudson 1972; Shenkel et al. 1979), and even the work of Quimby (1942b, 1957), who was looking at Contact period sites south of Baton Rouge more than 50 years ago. We should not even think about the extraordinary work in documenting riverine heritage by Saltus around Lake Pontchartrain and vicinity (e.g., Saltus 1986, 1988; cf. Pearson 1981), not to mention all the lower Mississippi River watercraft and plantation research supported by the New Orleans and Vicksburg District Corps of Engineers (e.g., Castille 1979; Castille and McCloskey 1981; Castille and Weinstein 1986; Goodwin et al. 1985; Goodwin, Gendel, and Yakubik 1983; Goodwin, Yakubik, and Gendel 1983; Goodwin, Yakubik, and Goodwin 1983; Hahn, Saltus, and James 1994; Yakubik 1988; Yakubik and Mendez 1994; Yakubik et al. 1985, 1986).

Eliminating western Louisiana and the Red River country makes us forget the Borderlands work by Webb, and Gregory and his students on Spanish Los Adaes and regional Contact sites, not to mention Civil War sites (Gregory and McCorkle 1981; Gregory and Webb 1965; Gregory et al. 1982; Gregory, Eschenfelder, et al. 1984; Gregory, Lee, et al. 1984; Webb 1962). For that matter, 15 years of archaeology conducted by Stewart-Abernathy and others at the major Arkansas antebellum town in the Red River, Old Washington Historic State Park, also disappears from the screen (e.g., Ewen 1992; Guendling 1993a; Stewart-Abernathy 1982a, 1983a, 1986a, 1986b, 1988a, 1992a, 1995, 1997a; Stewart-Abernathy and Farmer 1988; Stewart-Abernathy and Ruff 1986, 1989).

How far above the mouth of the Ohio can one go? There has been interesting historical archaeology just north of the Mid-South—for example, at French colonial settlements (see Walthall 1991a) including, on the Mississippi, Ste. Genevieve in Missouri (Norris 1991; Thurman 1984; Wesler 1998) and Fort Chartres across the river in Illinois (summarized by Keene 1991), and at Fort Massac on the Ohio (Walthall 1991b) (and see also the published volumes of papers from the Symposium on Ohio Valley Urban and Historic Archeology for additional work on the northern periphery).

Problems continue. Certainly by stopping at the Tennessee River all the fine work by the Tennessee Division of Archaeology at such sites as the Hermitage and others in the Nashville vicinity cannot be counted, though that work extends back into the early 1970s (e.g., S. D. Smith 1974a, 1976).

Further south, if the Mid-South does not continue into Alabama, the remarkable work by Derry (1992, 1997, 1998) at Old Cahawba must be ignored, not to mention recent work on the French Alabama coast (most recently, Gums 1997; Gums and Waselkov 1998; Waselkov 1997).

If the western edge of the region lies somewhere around or west of Little Rock, that eliminates over three decades of archaeology at Fort Smith, both at the actual "Forts" complex that is now a National Historic Site (Coleman 1990; Dollar 1966a, 1983; Moore 1962, 1963a, 1963b, 1963c) and in the adjacent town—for example, at the 1840s Tilles

House (Jurney 1975) and the 1870s Clayton House (Sabo and Hilliard 1980; Stewart-Abernathy 1980a). Not to mention nearby Fort Chaffee, an enormous U.S. Army base established at the beginning of World War II on top of a complex rural settlement landscape (Bennett et al. 1993; Blakely et al. 1990; Sierzchula et al. 1995). That boundary also means we cannot look at work 25 and 30 years ago along the Arkansas River corridor west of Little Rock, in search of such early 1800s sites as Spadra Fur Factory (Dollar 1966b; Westbury 1971) and Cadron (S. D. Smith 1974b). It also eliminates some interesting work at yeoman and tenant farmsteads led by Santeford in the Ozark foothills in Conway County (Martin and Jones 1978; Santeford 1982; Santeford et al. 1985), and work by archaeologists with the Ozark-St. Francis and Ouachita National Forests (Coleman 1996; Etchieson and Coleman 1996; Pfeiffer 1993). For that matter, one cannot talk about historical archaeology in most of the Ozarks in northwestern Arkansas and southern Missouri at Anglo-American sites (Abernathy and Jones 1979; Hilliard and Sabo 1984; Stewart-Abernathy 1985a, 1985b, 1986c, 1986d, 1987a, 1992b; Cande 1992, 1995a; cf. Sabo et al. 1982; see Cande 1995b for a more complete list of citations), and African American farmsteads in the Ozark foothills (Santeford 1980a, 1980b), and even testing at George Washington Carver's boyhood home in southwestern Missouri (Neuman 1958).

Fortunately, even with the omissions I noted and confining the discussion to the conventionally understood Mid-South, there is a rich history of historical archaeology left to discuss. This chapter will do so, in two parts: first the history of the field to the mid-1960s and then up to about the present.

Historical Archaeology in the Mid-South to the Mid-1960s

Although Frederick Gerstacker may have been an early pioneer and Edward Palmer pointed the way, for decades the history of historical archaeology in the Mid-South was primarily the accidental result of someone who suddenly encountered glass beads while going after Native American grave goods. Williams's (1962) paper summarizes the contributions of C. B. Moore (1908, 1911) and others more reputable in this regard. Sam Smith (1996a and see 1996b) has done this specifically for Tennessee. When historical archaeology in the Mid-South was extended to Euro-Americans, the targets for decades were famous forts. Sam Smith noted one of the earliest instances, the testing in the 1930s of Civil War Fort Donelson on the Tennessee River (Luckett 1937; Smith 1996a). And the support, need one add, was federal.

The pattern continued after World War II, when, one might argue, the wider cultural context of the Cold War encouraged extensive support of matters American. For example, one of the locations of peripatetic Arkansas Post had been preserved initially as a state park, but it was passed to the federal government and archaeological work got under way in the mid-1950s (Coleman 1987; Holder 1957; Mattison 1957). Related to this work, Ford examined the nearby Menard-Hodges site for the National Park Service, searching for the Quapaw village of Osotuoy, where Arkansas Post was first established in 1686 (Ford 1961; Ford and Neitzel 1958). And except for work noted elsewhere, as at Fatherland in the 1960s and a very few other places, that was about it. Even as the field of historical archaeology was getting well under way from the 1930s on in such places as New England, Colonial Williamsburg, St. Augustine, and the missions of California and Arizona, and even closer at hand at Fort Toulouse in Alabama (Chase 1966; cf. Heldman 1973), archaeology in the Mid-South was largely concerned only with prehistory. Even the Smithsonian River Basin Survey program, which had done important work in the 1950s at fur-trade posts along the Missouri River, accomplished no historical archaeology when the survey was carried out for Dardanelle Reservoir on the Arkansas River west of Little Rock (Greengo 1957).

There was at least one remarkable exception to the concern with famous forts and contact sites. That was the appearance in 1964 of a report on an early-nineteenth-century farmstead site in Stewart County in western Tennessee. This report, on a log cabin known as the Brake Site, was one of the first publications in the entire Southeast, much less the Mid-South, on such an ordinary place. The authors were Dan and Phyllis Morse (Morse and Morse 1964).

Historical Archaeology in the Mid-South after 1967

Several developments in the mid-1960s opened a new era for archaeology in general in the Mid-South, and historical archaeology benefited greatly. Certainly the continuation of research by the Lower Mississippi Valley Survey permitted attention to the colonial and contact sites (e.g., work by Brain and Brown noted above). One new trend was the growth of the Conference on Historic Site Archaeology and the regular publication of the conference papers. The conference had been founded in the early 1960s by Stanley South to encourage discussion about historical archaeology in general, but it was to be a long time after Williams's (1962) call for action that articles on the Mid-South began to appear (e.g., I. Brown 1975a; House 1977a, 1977b; Price and Price 1978a; and see below).

At least mid-southerners had a forum for discussions by fellow travelers and models to show one's skeptical colleagues and superiors.

A second development was the founding of the national Society for Historical Archaeology in 1967. Soon the shiny green paper covers of the society's journal, *Historical Archaeology,* began to show up on desks across the Mid-South. In fact, all regions of North America were represented in the 1967 inaugural issue—except the Mid-South. In fact, the region's first appearance was not until 1985, with Cynthia Price's article about her and James Price's work at the antebellum Widow Harris Cabin site in southeastern Missouri, about which more will be said later (and note Stewart-Abernathy's article based on Old Washington archaeology, 1986a).

Perhaps the most important of these developments were two others: first, the creation of regional archaeology programs, and second, federal environmental impact legislation (e.g., Davis 1988; McGimsey 1997; Thorne 1988; and see Bense 1994, 1997). The regional programs at last began to make up for the absence of graduate schools by supporting professional archaeologists permanently in the Mid-South tasked with basic goals of research and public interaction. A number of states even instituted planning to deal with historic sites (Abernathy 1982; Smith et al. 1983; Stewart-Abernathy and Watkins 1982; cf. S. D. Smith 1990), although to date only Louisiana has formally considered underwater sites (Terrell 1990). In turn, the federal legislation provided the money and the focus on all cultural resources within the scope of a particular construction project. This was an opportunity, though it has not always resulted in deep insights, or even in adequate copies of reports to make whatever insights were achieved more widely known.

Regional Archaeology Programs

The Arkansas Archeological Survey

One of the first regional programs was the Arkansas Archeological Survey, which was established in 1967. The key principle of the Survey is that archaeologists are placed in each part of the state, charged with conducting basic research and monitoring work of all kinds in their territories. Solving "History's Mysteries," to quote one of the founders of the survey, was an important part of the work (Davis 1967).

The station archaeologist placed at Jonesboro was Dan Morse. Over a period of 30 years, and in spite of their deep commitment to Dalton and Mississippian archaeology, the Morses made many contributions to historical archaeology in their area. This has ranged from the excavation of historic graves (Morse 1971b), to encouraging amateur archaeologists in historic archaeology projects (Bonow 1976), to assisting in documenting Mississippi River wrecks such as the Civil War–era *South Bend* (Morse and Morse 1983:329–31). They also argued successfully that official Arkansas state site numbers should be issued to loci such as fields and houses mapped on the General Land Office plats from the antebellum period, an act crucial to understanding settlement pattern and the cultural landscape regardless of whether one could actually find any historic artifacts at those sites.

The Morses also were active in incorporating historical archaeology into the occasional contract project. P. Morse (1986), for example, turned a water-line project into a search for an antebellum town site in Craighead County. An important milestone in historical archaeology in northeastern Arkansas in fact was the Zebree archeological project. This work is well known for its investigation of a Mississippian farmstead, but part of the occupation at the location included a pioneer homestead. This historic occupation, represented particularly by a cypress-lined square well with trash fill, was treated as significant and given due care in excavation and analysis (Morse and Morse 1977; P. Morse 1977a and 1977b). Perhaps an important part of this analysis is the suggestion by P. Morse of the "Bedroom Artifact Pattern," following Stanley South's lead regarding such objective statistical constructions as the Kitchen Artifact Pattern and the Frontier Artifact Pattern. The recovery from the well of three sections of a bed rail at least provided P. Morse (1977b:27-3) the underpinnings of the Bedroom Pattern. This might be the kind of trend to follow in searching for the dimensions of everyday life, not to mention nightlife. One might add that P. Morse (1977b:27-5) also suggested a "Barn Artifact Pattern," but there is uncertainty as to how serious this was because that putative "pattern" was based only on such finds as a wagon tire fragment, a hoe, a bit from a bridle, and a buggy brace. Perhaps this should be renamed the Wagon-Garden-Stable-Carriage Pattern. Or perhaps not.

The Morses also encouraged others, including Sam Smith, who served as station assistant at Jonesboro in the early 1970s. The Morses and the survey leadership encouraged, or at least permitted, Smith to initiate a variety of historic projects, including developing historical site leads on many of Arkansas's counties, taking advantage of needs of the Arkansas Department of Parks and Tourism to conduct research at such places as the early 1800s town of Davidsonville and other extinct towns (S. D. Smith 1972a, 1978; Smith and Davidson 1975), and even looking for historic pottery-making sites (S. D. Smith 1972b). Smith was also available for contract projects on historic sites, including at Cadron (S. D. Smith 1974b), as mentioned above.

Other station archaeologists also soon conducted historic projects.

The first station archaeologist at Pine Bluff, for example, was Burney McClurkan. He had experience in the long tradition of historical archaeology in Texas, and he soon initiated a variety of projects targeting historic sites, including Civil War Fort Curtis in Helena (McClurkan 1968), the lost locations for Arkansas Post (McClurkan 1971, 1972), and further fieldwork at the Cadron site in advance of construction of a replica blockhouse (unpublished, but carried out in 1976).

The first decade of the Survey brought in a number of M.A.-level graduate students with historical archaeology experience. Although many of them focused on western Arkansas near the Survey base at the University of Arkansas at Fayetteville, they also were available for projects elsewhere. For example, Westbury and Martin carried out additional fieldwork at Arkansas Post (Martin 1978; Westbury 1975, 1976) as part of the ongoing consideration there (e.g., Cobb et al. 1971; Stewart-Abernathy 1980b; Walker 1971; Walthall 1991c). Given the increasing importance of historical archaeology in Arkansas by the late 1970s, the Survey created the position of de facto state historical archaeologist with the hiring of Stewart-Abernathy in 1977 (then surnamed Abernathy) as the second Pine Bluff station archaeologist (later transferred to Russellville in 1989).

The multiple responsibility of a station territory and a state territory has had mixed results in the last two decades, but without doubt historical archaeology became something everyone was supposed to do. Stewart-Abernathy conducted a wide variety of projects, including numerous cooperative efforts with Arkansas State Parks, such as further work at Davidsonville (Stewart-Abernathy 1980c, 1983b, 1994a; and see Dollar 1977, Klinger 1976), at the mid-nineteenth-century Black River town of Jacksonport (Abernathy 1978a), and of course at Old Washington (see above). Numerous small projects were carried out as well. These remain mostly unpublished but include test work at the site of an antebellum detached kitchen near Arkadelphia; a survey of late-nineteenth-century historic properties encompassed by the construction, during the world wars, of Camp Pike and later Camp Robinson in North Little Rock; nineteenth-century urban archaeology in Little Rock; salvage of an 1830s cellar deposit near Pine Bluff; test excavations at an 1840s two-story log plantation house near Dumas; documentation of an African American sawmill community and its aftermath in Parkin; and even data recovery at an early-twentieth-century complex of wreckage of large Mississippi River watercraft at West Memphis (Ernest 1994; Stewart-Abernathy 1980d, 1981, 1982b, 1982c, 1984a, 1987b, 1987c, 1988b, 1990, 1991, 1992c, 1992d, 1994b, 1994c, 1996a, n.d.). Stewart-Abernathy's position as advocate also resulted in a wide variety of talks to preservation groups and professional archaeologists in Arkansas (e.g., Abernathy 1978b; Stewart-Abernathy 1980e, 1982d, 1984b, 1985c, 1994d, 1994e), as well as synthesis papers to professional groups (Stewart-Abernathy 1980f, 1982e) and symposia on Arkansas historical archaeology at national meetings that featured a variety of practitioners in the state (Stewart-Abernathy 1980g; Swanda 1980; Watkins 1980a, 1980b).

Tennessee

Other states have not been as successful in starting statewide programs that include ongoing historical archaeology in the Mid-South, but Tennessee has had a leader in Sam Smith, who joined the Tennessee Division of Archaeology in 1974. Although much of Smith's work has concentrated on central and eastern Tennessee (e.g., S. D. Smith 1996b), he instituted an important series of topical site surveys that did much to point to a rich archaeological heritage, including pottery-making sites, gun making, and sites associated particularly with the Civil War (Prouty and Baker 1996; S. D. Smith 1990; Smith and Rogers 1979; Smith et al. 1991). He also went looking for forts in the heart of downtown Memphis (S. D. Smith 1980, 1982). Other archaeologists working on historic sites within the framework of the Division of Archaeology included Mainfort, who undertook three field seasons at Civil War Fort Pillow (Mainfort 1980; see also G. P. Smith 1977), as well as extensive archival research (e.g., Cimprich and Mainfort 1989). The Tennessee SHPO and Division of Archaeology have also been working closely with government agencies and archaeologists in Memphis, one of the faster growing cities in the state.

Missouri

In the absence of a statewide program, James and Cynthia Price have been carrying out their own regional program in southeast Missouri since the mid-1970s. Using funding from a variety of sources, including the National Endowment for the Humanities, the National Park Service, and the U.S. Forest Service, the Prices have explored a variety of sites and issues, ranging from the specifics of British ceramic availability (C. Price 1979) and faunal distribution on single sites (C. Price 1987a), to specific studies of individual antebellum and postbellum farmsteads (C. Price 1981a, 1993; J. Price 1976a, 1978b), to town sites with great names such as Eminence (C. Price 1980, 1984a; J. Price and C. Price 1979), and to wider studies of river valleys and environmental zones (C. Price 1977, 1981b, 1984b, 1985, 1987b; C. Price and J. Price 1981; J. Price 1975, 1976b; J. Price and C. Price 1978a, 1978b, 1981). Their body of work represents an unmatched database, drawing as it does on more than two decades of research in just a few counties in the Missouri Bootheel and the adjacent eastern Ozarks.

Kentucky

Kentucky does not have a formal regional archaeology system, but interesting work has been under way in Kentucky west of the Tennessee River for quite some time by archaeologists based at Murray State. That area may or may not be part of the Mid-South (at least concerning historical archaeology, since Wickliffe Mounds seems to belong [and see Wesler 1993a]); regardless, interesting work has long been under way near the Land Between the Lakes at both urban and rural domestic sites. Wesler has been active in Paducah at the mouth of the Tennessee River (Wesler 1983, 1984a, 1984b, 1987, 1993b, 1997), and Carstens has been looking closely at Smithland at the mouth of the Cumberland, including both antebellum urban sites (Carstens 1997) and Civil War forts (Carstens n.d.a). There has even been a search for George Rogers Clark's Fort Jefferson, built in 1780 at the mouth of the Ohio River (Carstens 1984; Stein et al. 1983; and see Carstens n.d.b).

Louisiana

Louisiana has seen an enormous amount of historical archaeology south of Baton Rouge and on the colonial Red River frontier (see above), but until recently it has lacked a regional archaeology program that might bring attention to important historic sites elsewhere. Historical archaeologists at Louisiana State University and elsewhere occasionally have been active in or near the Mid-South. For example, Orser, well known for plantation work in the far Southeast (e.g., Orser 1990), conducted fieldwork in urban archaeology in Shreveport in 1986 (Orser and Holland 1986), and Holland (1986) examined tenancy in central Louisiana.

Mississippi

Mississippi has had an archaeological survey since 1968, but an understandable focus on the extraordinary prehistory in the state has limited the amount of work conducted on historic sites except in the context of cultural resource management (see below). There has been much concern, for example, by a number of regional archaeologists with the Mississippi Department of Archives and History, including sites ranging from the Contact period (e.g., Connaway et al. n.d.) to remarkably well-preserved historic fishweirs (Connaway n.d.; Sims and Connaway 1998). There is due attention to such spectacular sites as the Confederate gunboat *Cairo* (Hon 1988) and surprisingly sometimes even to lesser vessels such as gasoline-powered stern-wheelers (Gramling 1980). There has also been attention to sites along the Natchez Trace (Atkinson 1985b, n.d.; Jack Elliot, personal communication 1994), and sometimes significant discoveries elsewhere (e.g., John Milner Associates 1978; Kaye 1988).

Jack Elliot, in his position of archaeologist with the Mississippi Department of Archives and History, has been for two decades an active proponent for many aspects of historical archaeology in the nineteenth century (e.g., Elliott 1987, 1994). He has worked closely on test excavations with local chapters of the Mississippi Archaeology Association, such as the Gulf Coast and Pearl River chapters (although these two groups in particular are outside the "Mid-South"). Elliott has also focused on the Natchez area and Fort Rosalie (Elliott 1989, 1998a). Much of Elliot's fieldwork in historical archaeology remains unpublished, a situation that parallels that of Stewart-Abernathy and other regional archaeologists who have much to do, little time to do it, and frequently minimal resources for follow-up analysis and publication.

Historical archaeologists in Mississippi who work on more recent historic sites, however, often remain at a disadvantage because of the unusual policy of state officials to generally refuse to issue official site numbers to sites whose occupation happen to date after 1900. This extraordinary policy questions the legitimacy of those historic sites, and it also lessens our opportunity to understand the lives and contributions of those who occupied those sites. Debate about this policy continues (most recently, Elliott 1998b; Stewart-Abernathy 1998b).

Some have drawn attention to the possibilities for a more inclusive historical archaeology in Mississippi—for example, for African American archaeology (Ferguson 1992; Singleton 1989, 1990, 1991; and see Ponder 1998). Amy Young recently has begun a vigorous program of historical archaeology at the University of Southern Mississippi, and the results are already starting to appear at national meetings (e.g., Cherry 1998; Kidd 1998; Ponder 1998). U.S. Forest Service archaeologists, such as Sam Brookes, have actively supported consideration of historic sites in the late 1800s and into the 1900s on National Forest lands in Mississippi (e.g., Abraham 1998; Peacock 1992, 1994; Reams and Cramer 1998).

Federal Legislation

The extension of cultural resources management considerations to historic sites has had a dramatic impact in increasing the amount of archaeology conducted at historic sites. Much good work has resulted, but the addition of an enormous new source of funding has not necessarily resulted in long-term benefits either to the archaeological resources or to our knowledge of the past. Who knows, for example, what is in the hundreds of small CRM reports accumulated in the National Archeological Data Base of citations or the scores of reports for the Mississippi Soil Conservation Service and State Highway Department; or all those "Archeological and Historical Assessments" for east Tennessee bridges and highways near Memphis or in southeast Missouri; or all those other unsung, short-duration, limited-scale efforts? With no syntheses written and usually no essay explorations presented by their authors in regional and national archaeological professional meetings, one wonders at the return on the investment. The optimist hopes that if anything significant had been found, more detailed work would have ensued.

Certainly this is the case in many projects, where the necessity for an environmental impact statement has resulted in surveys, testing, mitigation, and overviews. Such projects have documented moonshine still sites and family farmsteads in the eastern margins of the Arkansas Ozarks (House 1977a, 1977b; Santeford et al. 1993), and antebellum cellar deposits potentially associated with African Americans in highway rights-of-way on the eastern edge of the Gulf Coastal Plain south of Little Rock (Santeford and Spears 1994; and see Cande 1991).

Historic cemeteries in the Mid-South also have been considered, following on the pioneering work of Rose (1985) and others just outside the region at the Cedar Grove African-American Cemetery in the Red River Valley. There is increasing appreciation that historical archaeologists are well qualified to deal with historic human remains—for example, in national and Confederate cemeteries in central and eastern Arkansas (Guendling 1989a, 1989b, 1990) and in family and community cemeteries in southwestern Tennessee and northeastern Mississippi (Weaver 1994a, 1997a; Wilson 1998).

The Memphis urban area has seen some archaeological work in the past at recognized historic properties, funded by traditional nongovernmental means, including the Memphis Chapter of the Association for the Preservation of Tennessee Antiquities (Weaver 1990a) and Memphis Museums (L. Weaver et al. 1997).

Those projects, however, are tiny compared to the scale of recent EIS-based archaeology. Local archaeologists have made great progress in understanding Memphis as an urban archaeology locale by aggressively ensuring that many large-scale development and planning projects in Memphis include a consideration of cultural resources (e.g., Childress et al. 1995; Council 1985; Kern 1979, 1980, 1981a, 1981b; G. P. Smith 1985, 1987, 1991; Weaver et al. 1994; Weaver et al. 1998). The intensive archaeology conducted as part of the redevelopment of downtown, including Beale Street and the waterfront, has been particularly notable, with much good work and important data recovered under the auspices of such projects as the Memphis Area Transit Authority North Terminal, the AutoZone Complex, the Peabody Place complex, and the "Rum Boogie" site (Collins et al. 1997; Garrow et al. 1998; Jolley 1984; Joseph 1986; Weaver 1988, 1990a, 1990b, 1992, 1994b, 1996a, 1997b, 1998; Weaver et al. 1990; Weaver et al. 1991; Weaver et al. 1994; Weaver et al. 1995; G. Weaver et al. 1997) (and see Weaver 1998 for a recent thorough bibliography with references organized by theme). Archaeologists have even examined an orphanage via two privies and a cistern that were filled with trash in the late 1800s and early 1900s (G. P. Smith 1992).

Though on a much smaller scale, Little Rock has also seen quite a bit of work under the umbrella of EIS projects (e.g., Guendling 1993b), although by far most of the contracted historical archaeology has been directed at important historical buildings undergoing restoration, including the 1830s Old State House (Guendling and Kwas 1997) and the remarkably preserved antebellum block at the Arkansas Territorial Restoration (J. Stewart-Abernathy 1989; Kwas and Guendling 1999).

Rural contexts have not been neglected. Contract funds have paid for intriguing work at a number of African American and multioccupant tenant and owner-occupied farmsteads in the delta country of east Arkansas (Buchner 1992; Buchner and Childress 1991; Buchner and Weaver 1990; Childress 1990; Harcourt 1993; Kelley 1981; Klinger, Cochran, and Dollar 1983; Klinger and Kandare 1988; Weaver 1991, 1997b; Weaver and Hopkins 1998; cf. Stewart-Abernathy 1985c). Much progress has been made in developing methods to deal with landscapes of dozens or scores of tenant sites as part of projects involving large-scale drainage ditches and other watershed improvements (e.g., a series of projects conducted by Mid-Continental Research Associates, including Lafferty et al. 1984; Lafferty, Santeford, et al. 1985; Lafferty, Spears, et al. 1985; Lafferty et al. 1987; Lafferty et al. 1993; Lafferty and Hess 1995; see also Anderson 1989).

Plantation sites in western Tennessee and Mississippi are also beginning to be addressed (Allen and DuVall 1995; Hahn, Crawford, and Pearson 1994; Kline 1991; Starr 1996; Weaver et al. 1990). Industrial sites have come under attention; for example, an early-twentieth-century African American sawmill community in Louisiana (Whelan and Pearson 1988).

Without this context of EIS work, underwater resources might have continued to be neglected, but U.S. Army Corps of Engineers proposals for a variety of channel maintenance and improvement projects led to significant projects in Mid-South waters, including survey in the Yazoo (Britt 1998; Owens 1979), discovery of the Civil War wreck the *Homer* in the Ouachita (Pearson and Saltus 1993), and searches in the Felsenthal region at Lake Jack Lee, just north of the Arkansas/Louisiana border (Watkins 1980a, 1982, 1984). In addition, riverfront development in Memphis, Helena, and elsewhere has led to some interesting historical archaeology exploration projects at sites whose purpose was to serve watercraft or the water-to-rail transition (e.g., Weaver 1996b, 1997c; Weaver and Hopkins 1993; Weaver et al. 1996).

The most important epoch in historical archaeology in the Mid-South (or at least in the vicinity), however, came in the late 1970s and early 1980s with the Tennessee-Tombigbee Waterway Project. This was a remarkably arrogant effort to construct a second Mississippi River, parallel to the first but running southward down eastern Mississippi and southwestern Alabama. Given the unbelievable scale of earthmoving envisioned, archaeology had a major role to play. A great variety of entities were involved, including Mississippi State University, Commonwealth Associates, Coastal Environments, the University of West Florida, the University of Alabama, the University of Michigan, and Michigan State University. The Mississippi Department of Archives and History was a particularly strong local advocate early in the planning for due consideration of historical archaeology at funding levels approaching that of prehistoric sites (Atkinson and Elliott 1978; Jack Elliot, personal communication 1997).

The Tennessee-Tombigbee project produced almost 60 reports on historic and prehistoric cultural resources according to one estimate (Thorne 1988:31). The key to the success of such a massive effort was unity in planning. According to one author, management of the various cultural resources along the Tennessee-Tombigbee Waterway provided the opportunity to develop a management plan for resources that were spread over a large geographical area (Thorne 1988:31). The plan included a National Register district (Tennessee-Tombigbee Multiple Resource District) over the entire 135 miles of waterway, and a flowchart for site selection for management options. The unity of results was also ensured by a unity of analytical design; for example, in the analysis of historic ceramics (Cleland 1983a; Donahue 1983; Minnerly 1983a). Historic projects undertaken included the investigation of townsites at Barton, Colbert, and Vinton (Minnerly 1982, 1983b), plantation landscapes at Waverly (Adams 1979, 1980; Riordan 1980) and Sharpley's Bottom (Kern et al. 1981; Tordoff and Kern 1981), yeoman farmsteads at Bay Springs (Hubbert 1977; Smith et al. 1982), and even industrial sites (Adams et al. 1981; Hambacher 1983). Underwater archaeological research also was conducted along existing channels of the Tombigbee River (Gulf South Research Institute 1977; Purdy 1982).

Given all the work performed, it is a tragedy that almost all of it has been forgotten except in the memories of the many participants currently practicing historical archaeology in such diverse and non–Mid-South locations as Kentucky, South Carolina, Michigan, and elsewhere (for similar concerns, see also Bense 1994 and Jeter 1996). Excellent and not so excellent work was published, but only in the limited distribution reports filed with the U.S. Army Corps of Engineers and the National Park Service. A synthesis was published on the prehistory (Jenkins and Krause 1986), and a project overview book mentions historical archaeology (Brose 1991), but for any detail on the historical archaeology one has to either find the rare reports or dig data out of scattered professional papers (e.g., Adams and Smith 1985; Cleland 1983b; K. McBride 1984; S. McBride 1984, 1987, 1994). Then again, if the only place to find references on historical archaeology is in the gray literature, what does that say about the importance of historical archaeology as funded by CRM? (Unfortunately, the same difficulty of access is also true for the reports on prehistoric sites.)

Conclusion

I will conclude this overview of the history of historical archaeology in the Mid-South by pointing to some trends. One is that while due consideration is still given to the famous forts, it is no longer automatically a struggle to argue for fieldwork at the more-or-less forgotten farmsteads. There is now even a constituency for tenant and plantation sites, thanks to the work elsewhere in the Southeast (cf. Orser 1990; Singleton 1990, 1985) and the demonstration that useful results can be gained here in the Mid-South—for example, at Doro Plantation, Mississippi (Hahn et al. 1994).

It is also intriguing to note that interest is building in historic Native Americans again, not early in the Contact period but later in the eighteenth and nineteenth centuries as they struggled to create a new way of life surrounded by Anglo-Americans. This consideration is timely, though in some cases perhaps too late. For example, in the late 1970s some pot hunters in northern Mississippi destroyed an important locus for understanding historic Chickasaw interaction when the looters went after Chickasaw graves that included flintlock rifles, silver ornaments, metal axes, and thousands of glass beads as burial furniture.

There have been successes. There is now more than two decades of examination of the Chickasaw and Choctaw in their homelands in Mississippi, tracking the dynamics in their way of life from the seventeenth to the nineteenth century (Atkinson 1975, 1979, 1985a, 1986a, 1986b, 1987a, 1987b; Ball 1976; Blitz 1985; Galloway 1995; Johnson et al. 1989; Johnson et al. 1991; Mooney 1994; Penman 1983; Voss and Blitz 1985, 1988; and see Collins 1927; Haag 1953; Ward 1984). Consideration of the emigrant Cherokee in Arkansas is still relatively new (Davis 1987;

Stewart-Abernathy 1996b, 1997b; see especially for eastern Arkansas Meyers 1997; for other emigrants on the far western margins of the Mid-South, see McCrocklin 1985, 1992a, 1992b). There is an increasing appreciation that those Cherokee actually were the pioneers who created much of the European-style frontier landscape in eastern and northwestern Arkansas, including many of the roads, fields, settlements, and mill sites that were so happily taken over by the Anglo-Americans who effectively erased the preceding occupants from the records.

One new development is another regional conference, the South Central Historical Archeology Conference, whose as-yet-vague boundaries at minimum encompass the Mid-South. The recent inaugural meeting in Jackson, Mississippi, featured papers on a variety of topics, including fishweirs, African American concerns, watercraft, and urban archaeology issues (Derry 1998; Pietak 1998; Sims and Connaway 1998; Weaver and Kowaleski 1998; Young and Crowe 1998).

This chapter began with a passage from sportsman and author Frederich Gerstacker about a Native American skeleton found in a cave with a bear. Let me conclude with another passage from Gerstacker, this time concerning his part in actually creating a historic site somewhere in the Cache River lowlands. In June 1839, Gerstacker and a fellow German agreed to serve as herdsman for cattle over the summer, but they needed some sort of shelter. Consequently, on the morning of June 10, "we began to build our house; we pulled down an old block-house [a log house], standing about three miles from the site we had chosen, and carted the logs to our prairie where we could easily rebuild it. . . . Ours being an old house rebuilt, the logs all fitted each other, and door and chimney were already cut . . . we soon had the house up all but the chimney, which being summer, was not so necessary" (Gerstacker 1968:143–44). The whole task was actually completed in one day. Note, however, how quickly he dismissed the achievements and successes, and failures, of whoever had built that old log house. He says no more about the original site.

Once upon a time, two prominent archaeologists in northeastern Arkansas suggested the notion of the Davidsonville Phase as a way of easing the acceptance of considering early-nineteenth-century historic Euro-American sites (Morse and Morse, personal communication 1982; but note its omission from Morse and Morse 1983). Perhaps now we can consider the site created by Frederick Gerstacker and his partner on its own terms, without the awkward baggage of narrow viewpoints that get in the way of understanding that site as part of a worldwide system of trade and travel. If so, then perhaps we can thank some of the post–World War II generation of scholars practicing historical archaeology in the Mid-South. Thank you for making my own work possible.

Acknowledgments

I want to thank Dr. Charles R. McGimsey and Hester Davis, who brought me into the Arkansas Archeological Survey and provided a supportive framework for years. I also want to thank Dan and Phyllis Morse, who have encouraged me and others to undertake historical archaeology in as many settings as possible. Since a key purpose of this chapter is to document historical archaeology in the region, I apologize for omitting references that should have been included. References were sought from a variety of sources, including the historical archaeology library at the ATU station, Russellville; the Survey library at the Coordinating Office, Fayetteville; the journals *Historical Archaeology*, *Southeastern Archaeology*, *Mississippi Archaeology*, and others; the National Archeological Data Base; and colleagues who generously offered bibliographies, including John Connaway, Bob Lafferty, Bob Mainfort, Dan and Phyllis Morse, Martha Rolingson, Sam Smith, Mary Evelyn Starr, Guy Weaver, and Kit Wesler. Part of the goal of any "comprehensive" study is to stimulate others to note omissions and bring them to the attention of colleagues. I urge other historical archaeologists to make sure complete bibliographies of historical archaeological work exist for their states and to publish those bibliographies in state journals.

CHAPTER TEN

ANCIENT RACES OF GIANTS, MOUNDBUILDERS, AND HERO COLLECTORS: NEWSPAPER ACCOUNTS OF ARKANSAS ARCHAEOLOGY, 1870–1930

MICHAEL P. HOFFMAN

> *PETRIFIED WOMAN IS FOUND NEAR JASPER. Special to the Gazette.*
> *Jasper, Aug. 8—Charles Edwards and J. T. Sexton of Mount Judea are exhibiting a perfect likeness of a human form in solid rock. It was taken from the ground by Ed. Pierce on his farm eight miles southeast of here, which is said to have yielded more than 12 skeletons. That now being exhibited resembles a woman. The hands rest on the stomach.*
>
> —*Arkansas Gazette,* AUGUST 9, 1925

Introduction

Local newspaper accounts are potentially useful sources of archaeological information that are commonly overlooked in research. While these accounts may provide useful factual information about site locations and finds, much of their value relates to their expression of public attitudes toward prehistory, archaeology, and archaeologists at the time they were written.

There are several reasons why newspaper accounts about archaeology are underutilized. One is that they are scattered, and usually there is no easy way of systematically retrieving them except by laborious reading of originals or microfilm files. Another is that newspaper accounts often were written by gullible people who favored naive or sensationalist perspectives. A researcher who uses them as sources of empirical information must sort out factual data such as locational information from interpretative accounts that often reflect the current local fantasies. Interpretative accounts, however, reflect the areal and popular attitudes of the time and as such are useful for tracking public perceptions of archaeology.

About 10 years ago the University of Arkansas library undertook a project to copy extant issues of every Arkansas newspaper, including rural weeklies, for its collections. A small, dedicated staff spent about two years visiting county seats and historical societies to make copies. Fortunately for this paper, one of the staff, Robert Myers, was a B.A. anthropologist with an enthusiastic eye for detail. Myers made copies of all articles and notes that dealt with prehistory, archaeology, and Native Americans and gave them to me. His sample is not a complete one because it does not include the newspaper files that the university library already possessed. Nevertheless, it is a formidable collection of several hundred articles, which forms the data source for this paper. Robert Myers's labors made this paper possible, and I thank him.

Here, I will demonstrate the research value of Arkansas newspaper accounts in the 1870–1930s era (plus or minus). The beginning of the era was chosen because the newspapers began to include relatively frequent notices of archaeology then. It ends during the time of establishment of an Arkansas-based professional archaeology, after Samuel C. Dellinger, curator of the museum at the University of Arkansas, began a program of scientific research in the state (Hoffman 1981). Williams (1991:61) has termed the early part of the era "the golden age" of American archaeology, in which federal agencies, eastern museums, and local gentry excavated Native American sites and debated issues like "who built the mounds?" The topics I discuss are sites and their contents, history of archaeology, and popular beliefs and attitudes about archaeology.

Sites and Their Contents

Much of what appears in Arkansas newspapers about archaeology in the period is of limited empirical value because descriptions are often nonspecific and inadequate. A major exception is a series of 20 brief notices of discoveries reported between 1909 and 1927, primarily in the *Baxter Bulletin* of Mountain Home, but also including articles from the *Cotter Record* and *Marshall Republican.* All three of these were small-town weeklies in the middle White River drainage of the Ozark Mountains. For at least some of the period, the *Baxter Bulletin* was operated by the Shiras brothers, an energetic, literate, multigenerational newspaper family that was highly regarded in the community. The region served by the newspapers was so small that virtually every bit of news in the countryside was reported to them and published. Most of the short articles are unadorned and factual. They report farmers who plowed up burials and local people who excavated them. Importantly, locations are included. For instance, the October 8, 1909, *Baxter Bulletin* reports that excavators found skeletons and pottery in a field just north of Lead Hill. In 1911 another cemetery on the Hutcheson Farm just downstream and opposite Norfork yielded skeletons (February 24 and April 21:1). There, "[t]he Indian pots were made of red clay and mussel shell. The shell had evidently been beaten up and mixed with the clay." The shapes of the pots included a bottle form. Obviously this was a Mississippi period cemetery. Reports of skeletons and cemeteries total at least 13 locations in the bottomlands of the White and Buffalo Rivers, an area that now is largely uncultivated and poorly known archaeologically. The reports provide evidence of an important Middle Mississippian occupation in the broad flood plain of the White and Buffalo Rivers in the Arkansas Ozark Mountains. This is a picture contrary to most modern archaeological appraisals there. A check of the Arkansas Archeological Survey Site files reveals that at least two sites (3ST26, Sylamore Ferry, and 3BA1, Buffalo City) are listed in the described locations but contain no records of the early 1900s activities described in the articles. The newspaper accounts both give information on where these sites were and some indication of their spacing. Many have now been destroyed by developments or washed away by the great floods of the pre–White River reservoir days, so the skimpy, factual references in the *Baxter Bulletin* are among the few surviving sources of information of the Middle Mississippian presence in the heart of the Arkansas Ozarks.

Another very useful factual newspaper account that I have found valuable in my research—although I didn't obtain it from the university library project—is the report of a cemetery on the Arkansas River near Fort Smith that was exposed by a flood in 1937 (*Fort Smith Times-Record,* October 9, 1937). It was located at the mouth of Frog Bayou in an area that has since been land leveled. The newspaper account was enriched by interpretative quotes from Ken Orr, then a graduate student at the University of Chicago and fresh from participation in the professional excavations at Spiro. Photographs and Orr's statements document the site as one of the Spiroan culture. It is the easternmost known site of the culture and is known solely by the newspaper account.

These two specific examples demonstrate the usefulness of newspaper records as data sources in archaeology. There have to be many more such cases. With few exceptions, cultural resource management and other archaeologists are unaware of the potential of newspaper records or do not have the energy, time, or money to spend going through them issue by issue seeking out gems of information. Similarly, most modern archaeologists fail to interview local collectors and record their materials as a routine part of an investigation. Current state site survey files rarely and unsystematically contain newspaper accounts. I suspect that only a major focused effort to record and index newspaper information about Arkansas archaeology by the staff of the Arkansas Archeological Survey will make such data easily available.

History of Archaeology in Arkansas

An Arkansas-based professional archaeology dates to 1925, when S. C. Dellinger, the first curator of the University of Arkansas museum initiated state-sponsored research and collection. Before that date, beginning in the Reconstruction era, investigators for various eastern and northern institutions made forays into the state to excavate sites and recover artifacts. Most decent-sized Arkansas towns also had members of the local elite—doctors, lawyers, clergymen, judges, and former Civil War officers—who engaged in avocational excavations. The newspapers reflect local impressions of these early investigations.

An early impetus to the development to archaeology in the state was the 1876 U.S. centennial exhibition at Washington. Each state had an exhibit at the event, which included archaeological finds. It was an opportunity to demonstrate state pride, and citizens of Arkansas eagerly participated, perhaps as part of the post–Civil War healing process. The *Arkansas Gazette* of August 4, 1875, reported that "H. W. McMillan, of Arkadelphia has been appointed archaeologist in the state centennial movement." McMillan, a Civil War general, was replaced soon by William Barry II of Hot Springs, who elicited artifacts for the exhibition in the *Booneville Enterprise* on November 12, 1875. He promised that collections would become part of "the (national) archives." The *Arkansas Gazette* (September 27, 1876:2) confirmed that an exhibit did occur and that "mound builder relics" were an important part of it.

Notice of the Smithsonian Institution Bureau of American Ethnology mound investigations of the latter nineteenth century was minimal and is discussed by Jeter (1990b:359–61). The explorations of C. B. Moore for the Philadelphia Academy of Natural Sciences also received notice in the Arkansas press. The *Marked Tree Gazette* in 1910 (March 25) observed that:

> Capt. J. S. Raymond and R. M. G. Miller of Philadelphia, Pa. were here one day last week in the interest of the Academy of Science of Philadelphia and for the National Museum of Washington, hunting Indian relics . . . At the Cummings place, . . . they found several pieces of valuable pottery, but as their records showed the academy had such pieces, they were given (to) Mr. Cummings.

In spite of such generosity, the work of Moore for the Philadelphia Academy was perceived as an alien threat to the state's heritage as both the *Arkansas Gazette* of January 25 and the *Huttig News* of January 30, 1909, indicate. The article entitled "To Keep Indian Relics in State" and subtitled "Senator Rasco to Introduce Bill Prohibiting Nonresidents from Excavating and Carrying Away Archeological Finds" lauded the effort "to preserve the historic relics and the valuable archaeological finds of the state." Moore's work generated a sort of Arkansas-first movement that was led by H. L. Stoddard of Stuttgart who was quoted as saying:

> Last Spring an expedition was sent into Arkansas by the Academy of Natural Sciences of Philadelphia to excavate and carry away aboriginal and Indian relics and remains. They made considerable finds and have recently built a gasoline boat at Monroe, La. and press reports state that the expedition is now on its way up the Ouachita for Arkansas points and will rendezvous at Camden . . . It is planned to place a prohibitory tax on nonresidents and foreign expeditions entering the state for the purpose of securing and carrying away these relics.

Nothing seems to have come from the bill, but the antipathy toward archaeological carpetbaggers continued well into the middle of the twentieth century, and in a positive sense it stimulated the beginning of a homegrown professional archaeology in 1925.

While hackles rose quickly when institutions outside the state did archaeology in Arkansas, paradoxically there was local pride that the state was so rich in prehistory that outsiders were interested. The southwest Arkansas *Washington Telegraph* (December 22, 1916:1) headlined that Mark Harrington of the Heye Foundation (Harrington 1920) found Hempstead County "rich in ancient relics." According to that article,

> A number of men from New York have been at work on a group of mounds three miles east of Washington for several months, and they have been wonderfully successful in unearthing relics of this prehistoric race of whom practically nothing is known . . . The mound diggers are employed by a New York City museum and the curios found are shipped there each Monday.

Warren King Moorehead (Moorehead 1931) of the Phillips Academy in Andover also got generally positive press in Arkansas. In 1902 (July 19:2), the *Osceola Times* published a letter from him asking for artifacts from the state so that they could be "preserved in fireproof buildings." He offered to pay express charges on them. In 1903 (April 3), the *Baxter Bulletin* reprinted a *St. Louis Globe-Democrat* article by Moorehead describing the first archaeological expedition of the Phillips Academy, which was to the Ozarks. Moorehead thought it possible that this region would yield primitive "cave men." He gave an interview to a reporter for the *Arkansas Gazette* when he visited in 1934 (February 28). In the interview he urged the establishment of many small museums to display the "wonderful culture here" and preached against pot hunting and professional trespass: "It is wrong . . . for Alabama to trespass on Arkansas territory in search of relics. . . . Taking away from a state its heritage is . . . nothing short of sacrilege." He urged the passage of a state antiquities act based on the permit system. During his Arkansas visit, Moorehead visited several private museums around the state and the History Commission, but seems not to have come to the museum at the university, where he was probably held in some hostility by its Arkansas-first curator, Sam Dellinger.

Archaeological excavation of dry deposits in caves and bluff shelters of western Arkansas gained popularity in the early 1920s with the work of Mark Harrington (1960). Although there was little newspaper commentary on his work at the time he was in the field, it was one of the "outside agitator" catalysts that began the archaeological career of S. C. Dellinger for the University of Arkansas. The first archaeological expedition of the University of Arkansas, however, was described in two 1925 articles in the *Arkansas Democrat* (January 4:6) and the *Southwest-Times Record* (April 5:8). Eight undergraduates were led by a geology professor in excavation of a cave in the western Arkansas Ozarks. In 1925, Dellinger was appointed curator of the university museum and began a 35-year control of the professional archaeology of the state (Hoffman 1981). In 1926, the *Arkansas Gazette* (May 22) reported that an expedition from the Oklahoma Historical Society was excavating bluff shelters in western Arkansas. In response to such invasions from outside Arkansas, Dellinger had this to say:

> Imagine my chagrin when I visited such museums as Peabody at Harvard, the National at Washington, D.C., the one at the University of Michigan, the Heye Museum of the American Indian at New York and found that their finest and most valuable Indian displays had been sent from Arkansas. Specimens are there that can never be found again in our state. They were sold to the big museums for a nominal sum. They are not like a crop of cotton or corn that can be grown again but when these go out of state they are lost forever. In many instances they were simply collected by expeditions of the sort that are sent into more backward states or countries . . . Many savage tribes considered it a high honor to give their wives to visitors from other countries. Our native Arkansans seem to consider it a similar honor to bestow our archeological relics upon any outsider who happens to be in our midst (*Arkansas Alumnus,* January 1930:5).

The state's leading newspaper, the *Arkansas Gazette,* rallied to Dellinger's attitude:

> Time and again, like Paul Revere, we have carried the warning to the noble Arkansans of the looting of valuable Arkansas Indian relics by archeologists from other states. Professor Dellinger is the authority for the statement that within the past two years the representatives of no less than eight other states have roamed over Arkansas carting off specimens of ancient art that can never be recovered (March 7, 1926:5).

The newspaper suggested a slogan for a campaign—"Arkansas for the Arkansans."

Even much later in his career, Dellinger was reluctant to tolerate outside scientific archaeological research in the state that was unconnected to the museum at the University of Arkansas. A particularly brusque exchange occurred when Philip Phillips of Harvard's Peabody Museum, along with James Griffin of the University of Michigan and James Ford of the American Museum of Natural History, wished to conduct site survey work in 1939–40 in eastern Arkansas. Dellinger fumed about this because outsiders were again entering the state and because he had not been contacted in advance. He wrote letters in opposition to Phillips, Ford, the Peabody Museum, and the Smithsonian Institution claiming: "It appears to be that I will be forced to take a very definite stand against any parties coming into Arkansas who are not working in collaboration with the University" (Dellinger 1940a), and "I regret that any group would come in here and skim off the remainder of the cream without even considering our desires in such matters" (Dellinger 1940b).

Phillips et al. (1951:40) retorted, "The cream . . . had long been skimmed and safely removed to the collectors' shelves." Griffin later told me that they (Phillips, Ford, and Griffin) had formed a pseudo-organization called "the cream-skimmers."

Forays into Arkansas by outsiders prompted Dellinger to begin his own program of excavation funded by a Carnegie Foundation grant five years later. Dellinger's career and impact on Arkansas archaeology were well chronicled by the Arkansas press and have been the subject of previous research (Hoffman 1981).

There were several important, scholarly avocational archaeologists in the first half of the twentieth century who were profiled by the press. The *Arkansas Democrat* in 1929 (November 10:1, 5) gushed over the collection and archaeological potential of a Prescott youth newly graduated from high school:

> In these rooms there is arranged for display the second largest collection of Indian relics in Arkansas . . . Dorris Dickinson of Prescott is the owner of these relics. Last spring Dorris graduated from the Prescott High School and this year plans to enter the University of Arkansas. There are a great many people who while they can't see a particle of sense in all these relics are quite willing to expect great

> things of Dorris, for the thing he has accomplished has won the admiration of archaeologists, persons interested in archaeology and Prescott in general.

Dickinson, who became known as Samuel Dorris (or S. D.), went to the University of Arizona instead of Arkansas and became the second anthropology graduate in the history of the state. During the late 1930s and early 1940s he authored and co-authored archaeological articles (Dickinson 1936, 1941; Dickinson and Dellinger 1940) and was director of the WPA archaeological laboratory in the early 1940s. From that time on, however, his career turned to journalism and he was a newspaperman in Arkansas and Louisiana until his retirement in the 1960s. His avocational interest in archaeology and Arkansas colonial history continued, however, and he writes and publishes to this day.

Also in 1929 (March 3), the *Arkansas Democrat* featured the archaeological endeavors of Harry Lemley of Hope, Arkansas, then an attorney and later a judge:

> For many years, the collection of Indian and moundbuilder relics has been his favorite hobby. He and his brother . . . have accumulated one of the largest and most valuable collections in the United States. They have donated or sold to American or foreign museums hundreds of specimens.

The paper published an accompanying article by Lemley, which he claimed was prepared at the request of the American Anthropological Association for publication. Lemley continued to be the major avocational archaeologist in southwestern Arkansas until after World War II, sponsoring excavations and authoring and co-authoring professionally competent articles (Lemley 1936, 1942; Lemley and Dickinson 1937; Dickinson and Lemley 1939). Informally, archaeological research in the southwestern part of the state became his domain, and Sam Dellinger, representing the state from the university, largely did not work in that area because of that understanding.

Lemley and Dickinson were but two of several other avocational archaeologists of the 1930s and 1940s who came from the local elite and published in regional journals. Dr. and Mrs. T. L. Hodges of Bismarck were other good examples of such persons (Early 1986).

The Moundbuilders

Not surprisingly, in my sample there were 15 pre-1930s articles that emphasized the mysterious Moundbuilders. Over half of these (8) were published before 1900, which may indicate that the popularity of such an idea peaked in Arkansas before the turn of the century and the publication of Cyrus Thomas's (1894) monograph refuting the idea. The moundbuilder myth died slowly in Arkansas in the popular imagination—but it did die—and Dellinger, to his credit, did not contribute to it.

However, according to an early correspondent who wrote to the *Arkansas True Democrat* in 1859, "It is evident that this western country was inhabited by a race of people long before the Indians came, of whom they know nothing whatever. . . . They have left monuments of their labors to tell that they once existed." The correspondent then discussed excavations of mounds in which he participated on White River in eastern Arkansas. This is a very early reference to excavation.

The *Osceola Times* of 1873 (August 9) described a very large moundbuilder "musical instrument" fit for a race of giants. An extensive four-part series in the *Arkansas Gazette* published in 1880 (April 20–24) by Rev. Dr. W. C. Stout on "The Mound-Builders of Arkansas" was surprisingly erudite and rational, and it presaged Cyrus Thomas's (1894) conclusions about who built the mounds and other modern issues. After detailing 19 points of argument, Stout concluded:

> First, the mounds were in use by the people who dwelt here three hundred years ago; and . . . these people were the builders: Second, that between the middle of the sixteenth and the end of the seventeenth centuries the mound builders perished from the land as a people, by war, pestilence or famine, or all combined, as all these agencies have been shown to have been possible.

He relied on the de Soto narratives to confirm that the native people then were building mounds.

Another surprisingly prescient *Arkansas Gazette* communication by Capt. H. M. McVeigh in 1888 (April 14) used de Soto's chronicler Biedma to document the following:

> The race of people living here at that time . . . were an agricultural people, living in walled towns, and cultivating immense fields of Indian corn.
>
> They were subsequently driven out by the fiercer tribes of the north who came out of the Ohio and descended the Mississippi.

Unfortunately, the scholarly efforts of Reverend Stout and Captain McVeigh did little to deter Arkansas newspapers in the early 1900s from subscribing to the mysterious non-Indian moundbuilder idea, so that even on May 25, 1927, the *Arkansas Democrat* could say:

> The builders of the so-called "Indian " mounds scattered throughout the Mississippi valley, including the mounds of Toltec, are believed to have been migrants or at least the descendants of migrants, driven from their long accustomed habitation in the fertile valleys of southern Mexico by conquering hordes of invaders of Maylay *[sic]* origin.

A Race of Giants

A persistent folk belief evidenced in the newspapers was that the skeletons unearthed represented a race of giants. The widely publicized fraudulent "Cardiff Giant," "found" in New York in 1869 (Williams 1991: 87–89), may have reinforced the prehistoric giant image. The belief probably relates to the idea that the moundbuilders had unique and superior qualities generally including size. In Arkansas, reports of large bones and footprints found by local citizens provided the "proof."

Between 1873 and 1943, there are 11 references to the ancient race of giants. On August 9, 1873, the *Osceola Times* reported that one human skeleton was thirteen feet in height, and that of a child was "as large as a full grown man of our day at birth." According to an article in the *Fort Smith Elevator* (July 4, 1884:1), a Captain Hanna unearthed a skeleton in southwestern Arkansas that had a skull of

> huge proportions, receding from the eye-brows so as to make the impression of a brutal nature, like that of a gorilla . . . It denoted ferocity and great strength. The opinion of our local anatomists . . . was that the man could not have been less than eight feet in height. It was probably more, for the skeleton measured six feet from the knee to the top of the skull.

The *Arkansas Gazette* of February 8, 1891, reported that, "While opening out a large ditch on his farm five miles south of Okolona one day this week, Capt. J. Hays unearthed the remains of a monster member of some prehistoric race." A March 20, 1921, article in the *Baxter Bulletin* entitled "Remains of Giants Found by Savant in Ozark Cave" reported "a race of cave dwellers, undoubtedly Mongoloid, but much larger than modern man, is believed to have populated the region." In 1927, the May 25 *Arkansas Democrat* asserted that the moundbuilders were " a race of giants, averaging between seven and eight feet in height." A few years later, in 1930, it reported that skulls found at Corning were one-quarter larger than those of modern humans and that "a race of people who may have been at least more than eight feet in height" were present. These people were not Indian.

On November 6, 1932, the same newspaper, in a piece entitled "What a Man of the Aborigines," described a footprint in stone 15 inches long and 5 inches wide. On November 11, 1932, the most archaeologically rational of the Arkansas newspapers, the *Baxter Bulletin,* discussed a skeleton of a man seven feet tall, but the editor had taken the trouble to read accounts of the large size of men in the Osage tribe who frequented the Arkansas Ozarks in the colonial period. Mysterious non-Indian prehistoric giants were abandoned. By 1943 its editor, Tom Shiras, could characterize a prehistoric man "(who) was over seven feet tall, a very large young man" as an Osage Indian.

Hindoo Idols, Slate Tablets, and a Jonesboro Eccentric

The "golden age" of American archaeology was also a time of many archaeological frauds or hoaxes (Williams 1991:77–97) of varying levels of sophistication. There are several Arkansas examples in the literature, including the notice quoted at the beginning of this chapter of the petrified woman found near Jasper (*Arkansas Gazette,* August 9, 1925).

An early reference in the *Pine Bluff Commercial* (February 26, 1885) relates a find of a thirty-feet-long "Hindoo idol" carved out of petrified wood unearthed in the piney woods of Jefferson County in southeastern Arkansas. It was viewed by the newspaper reporter and described as having "clear cut and prominent female features . . . the head crowned with what appeared to be serpents intertwined." Perhaps the possibility of such an artifact was placed in the reporter's mind by the writings of Caleb Atwater, who advocated that people from India built the mounds (Williams 1991:41). An equally fantastic find of "212 slate tablets with three pictures on each" was said to have been found by an English miner in Scott County.

> The pictures portray a history of the Quapaw Indians during the reign of Queen Singing Bird the First of the good queen, etc. Also [shown was] the appointment of the great young chieftain Silent Tongue to the office of ambassador to frame a treaty of peace with the Chickasaws . . . It gives the manners and customs of the Quapaws, their religion and form of marriage . . . Their government was a constitutional monarchy . . . the sun chiefs were not Indians, but Aztecs.

According to the clipping, which must date to the late nineteenth century, but which has lost its context, a Dr. LaRue was translating these tablets. The tablets sound similar to fraudulent nineteenth-century tablets found at the Grave Creek Mound in West Virginia and in mounds near Davenport, Iowa (Williams 1991:80–97), which were hotly debated in the literature of the "golden age." Both the Hindoo idol and the slate tablets, if they could be studied today, could revolutionize our interpretation of Arkansas archaeology!

A delightful player in fantasy and Arkansas archaeology was an elderly Jonesboro man, profiled by bemused newspapers no less than six times between 1924 and 1930 (Morse and Morse 1983:330–33). Dentler Rowland, whom everyone described as eccentric, was an elderly deaf gunsmith who lived alone in a ramshackle shack at the edge of town. He did excavations and, between 1924 and 1930, had the good fortune to report finding several sets of stone and pottery figurines in nearby mounds. The *Arkansas Democrat* in 1924 reported:

> the most impressive features of the Rowland collection is a life size head carved in novaculite, a stone so hard that it cuts glass. The

> forehead is wide and low, and surmounted by a turban-like headdress strongly suggestive of the head coverings of ancient Egyptians . . . The cheekbones are prominent and the nose broad and flat with the tip well upturned. The most outstanding feature of the figure is the fact that it is embellished with gold, silver and copper.

Later Rowland found a pottery vessel in the shape of a pig (*Arkansas Gazette,* April 22, 1928). No other digger of the era had the luck of Mr. Rowland. Remarkably, both the History Commission and the Natural History Museum in Little Rock accepted his finds as authentic and purchased specimens, as did Dr. W. Foster, professor of science at the University of Tulsa. Foster contacted the Smithsonian for comments but was told that the U.S. National Museum had no similar objects and its experts would at present make no attempt to classify them. How diplomatic!

Hero Collectors and Antiquities Dealers

Until very recently, Arkansas newspapers portrayed local collectors, no matter how they obtained their artifacts, as honorable people doing interesting, worthwhile things. Antiquities dealers, particularly in the Great Depression, also were positively portrayed.

The seven commentaries about collectors and collections in the sample all were published after 1925, when major Arkansas newspapers began publishing photographs. They feature frames of points, groups of pots, and positive images of the local diggers. The newspapers reflect the popular local opinion that the collectors were experts on Indian lore. A few of the wise insights by W. H. Kirkpatrick, a 77 year old collector from the northern Arkansas town of Alpena, are typical (*Arkansas Gazette,* November 23, 1930):

> The small heads, Mr. Kirkpatrick explains, were used for killing birds and very small animals. The largest ones were used in hunting larger game, including bear and deer . . . The flint weapons or tools always were fashioned by the Indians at a brook or beside a brook where cold water was available. The bits of flint were heated to a high degree of temperature and then placed on a large heated rock. A thong of deer hide, the pitch of an elderberry branch or some other substance which would absorb water, having been dipped in the cold spring or brook, then was touched to the hot flint with such skill that bits of the stone flaked off, leaving the weapon or implement in the desired shape.

With such local authority figures passing on erroneous popular myths for generations in Arkansas, even in the state's most progressive newspaper, it is little wonder that scientific archaeological interpretation has at times had tough competition.

However, even the misleading Mr. Kirkpatrick may have passed on valuable ethnographic hearsay about the Arkansas Cherokees of the 1820s near Alpena.

> Much of Mr. Kirkpatrick's information about the Indian sojourn was gleaned from the tales told by Roland Boyd, whose parents were among the first white settlers in this section. Mr. Boyd died some 30 years ago but many of the tales he told of his boyhood associations with the Indians still are fresh in the memory of Mr. Kirkpatrick.
>
> Mr. Boyd liked to tell, Mr. Kirkpatrick recalls, of attending one of the Cherokees' annual green corn dances, an event celebrating the appearances of the first blades of corn in the spring. These dances, Mr. Boyd said, lasted all night around huge bonfires, and some times throughout most of the next day (*Arkansas Gazette,* November 23, 1930).

This valuable account strongly supports the idea that aspects of the traditional seasonal ritual cycle were still characteristic of at least some of the Arkansas Cherokee at the time. Archaeologists can now expect to find early-nineteenth-century Cherokee ceremonial grounds in the state.

Another positive collector profile in the *Arkansas Gazette* (May 22, 1926), that of J. W. Bailey of Atkins, provides some useful material. For instance, he indicates that the first significant finds of Protohistoric-period burials in the central Arkansas River valley took place in 1898, when a major flood caved in the bank of the river. The article also explains that Mr. Bailey sold a major central Arkansas River valley pottery collection to W. P. Agee. In later years, the Agee collection went to the Arkansas History Commission. In 1966, the Commission transferred its archaeological collection, including the materials from Agee (and J. W. Bailey), to the museum of the University of Arkansas. As anthropology curator of the museum, I was happy to find this explanation of why there are so many central Arkansas River valley pieces in the former History Commission collection.

During the first half of the twentieth century, the Arkansas River valley was the home of some of the largest mail-order antiquities dealers in the country (Hoffman 1985). Two, G. E. Pilquist and H. Daniel, were major middlemen during the 1930s and marketed much of the Spiro loot. They both received highly complimentary newspaper profiles. In fact, during the height of the Great Depression, Pilquist was characterized as almost a savior by the *Arkansas Democrat* (April 6, 1933):

> Many formerly prosperous farmers who once tilled the fertile soil of the Arkansas River valley with little interest in the valuable collections that lay buried beneath their cotton rows have turned archeologists since the coming of the Depression and its five cent cotton and are helping to keep the proverbial wolf from their door by selling Indian relics.

> Pilquist, who has bought more of the Carden Bottoms relics than any other individual, is most busy on "Red Cross days:" when unfortunate farmers of Yell County go to Dardanelle to secure relief. On these days many of the farmers sell him whatever relics they have been able to find.

Conclusions

I hope that I have presented enough specific examples to make the case for the significance of newspaper articles as valuable archaeological resources. I certainly enjoyed the reading. Parenthetically, after going through the many 1870–1930 articles, it occurred to me that Arkansas archaeology in those days was entirely a male domain. Not until 1960 did Hester Davis break the archaeological gender barrier in the state, at least on other than a spousal basis. Black men were mentioned twice, once in the 1870s, replete with stereotypic dialect and fear of the dead, and the other in a respectful way as the discoverer of the 30-foot Hindoo goddess carved out of petrified wood.

Newspaper articles about archaeology need to be systematically collected, scanned, indexed, and placed in a data file to be consistently useful. Even in a small state like Arkansas this will be a challenging job, one that will require some outside funding. Once it is completed, however, there will be available an important new data source that can be routinely consulted as background information before and during modern research.

References Cited

Abernathy, Leslie C.

1978a *An Archaeological Survey of Portions of Jacksonport State Park to be Affected by Revetment.* Report. Arkansas Archeological Survey, Fayetteville. Submitted to the Little Rock District, Army Corps of Engineers, Little Rock.

1978b The Eye Accustomed to the Survey of These Relics: Historical Archeology and the Arkansas Past. Paper presented to annual meeting of the Arkansas Historical Association, Pine Bluff.

1982 Help! 3.5 Billion Possible Two Meter Square Excavation Units in Arkansas, or, a Consideration of State-wide Research Design in Historical Archeology. *The Conference on Historic Sites Archeology Papers 1979,* 14:71–86.

Abernathy, Leslie C., and Robert D. Jones

1979 *Henderson Farm Reconnaissance*. In *An Archaeological Survey of the Proposed Buffalo River Trail, Hemmed-in Hollow, Ponca Area, Newton County, Arkansas and a Reconnaissance of the Henderson Farm Historic Site*. Report. Arkansas Archeological Survey, Fayetteville. Submitted to the National Park Service, Southwest Regional Office.

Abraham, Jennifer

1998 Rural Domesticity in the Piney Woods of South Mississippi, ca. Late 1850–1940. Paper presented at the annual meeting of the Society for Historical Archaeology, Atlanta.

Adams, William Hampton

1979 *Interim Report: Test Excavations at Waverly Ferry, Clay County, Mississippi.* Report. Soil Systems, Inc., Bloomington, Indiana. Submitted to the U.S. Army Corps of Engineers, Mobile District.

1980 (ed.) *Waverly Plantation: Ethnoarcheology of a Tenant Farming Community.* Report. Resource Analysts, Inc. Submitted to U.S. Heritage Conservation and Recreation Service, Atlanta.

Adams, William H., and Steven D. Smith

1985 Historical Perspectives on Black Tenant Farmer Material Culture: The Henry C. Long General Store Ledger at Waverly Plantation, Mississippi. In *The Archeology of Slavery and Plantation Life,* edited by T. A. Singleton, 309–34. Academic Press, San Diego.

Adams, William H., Steven D. Smith, David F. Barton, Timothy Riordan, and Steven Poyer

1981 *Bay Springs Mill: Historical Archeology of a Rural Mississippi Cotton Milling Community.* Report. Submitted to the U.S. National Park Service, Albuquerque.

Aldenderfer, Mark S.

1982 Methods of Cluster Validation in Archaeology. *World Archaeology* 14:61–72.

Aldenderfer, Mark S., and Roger K. Blashfield
1984 *Cluster Analysis.* Sage, Beverly Hills.

Allen, Dan S., and Glyn D. DuVall
1995 *A Phase I Historic Archaeological Survey and Limited Testing of Ames Plantation, Fayette and Hardeman Counties, Tennessee.* Report. DuVall and Associates, Nashville. Submitted to the Hobart Ames Foundation, University of Tennessee and the Tennessee Historical Commission, Nashville.

Allen, D. W., and B. J. McLane (comp.)
1991a *Arkansas Land Patents: Pulaski County (Granted through 30 June 1908).* Compiled from Completion of the GLO Records Automation Project of the Bureau of Land Management, February 8, 1991. Arkansas Research, Conway.
1991b *Arkansas Land Patents: Lonoke and Prairie Counties (Granted through 30 June 1908).* Compiled from Completion of the GLO Records Automation Project of the Bureau of Land Management, February 8, 1991. Arkansas Research, Conway.

Allsopp, F. W.
1922 *History of the Arkansas Press for a Hundred Years and More.* Parke-Harper, Little Rock.

Anderberg, Michael A.
1973 *Cluster Analysis for Applications.* Academic Press, New York.

Anderson, David G.
1975 Excavation Strategies at the Zebree Site: 1975 Field Season. In *A Preliminary Report of the Zebree Project New Approaches in Contract Archeology in Arkansas,* edited by Dan F. Morse and Phyllis A. Morse, 30–43. Research Report No. 8. Arkansas Archeological Survey, Fayetteville.
1979 *Excavations at Four Fall Line Sites: The Southeastern Columbia Beltway Project.* Report No. R-2008. Commonwealth Associates.
1988 *Cultural Resources Investigations in the L'Anguille River Basin Lee, St. Francis, Cross, and Poinsett Counties, Arkansas Final Data Appendix and Catalog.* Report, Contract DACW66-87-C-0046. Submitted to U.S. Army Corps of Engineers, Memphis District.
1989 *Cultural Resource Investigations in the L'Anguille River Basin, Lee, St. Francis, Cross, and Poinsett Counties, Arkansas.* Report. Garrow and Associates, Atlanta. Submitted to U.S. Army Corps of Engineers, Memphis District.
1994 *The Savannah River Chiefdoms, Political Change in the Late Prehistoric Southeast.* University of Alabama Press, Tuscaloosa.
1996 Approaches to Modeling Regional Settlement in the Archaic Period Southeast. In *The Archaeology of the Mid-Holocene Southeast,* edited by Kenneth E. Sassaman and David G. Anderson, 157–76. University Presses of Florida, Gainesville.

Anderson, David G., Hazel R. Delcourt, Paul A. Delcourt, John E. Foss, and Phyllis A. Morse
1989 *Cultural Resource Investigations in the L'Anguille River Basin Lee, St. Francis, Cross, and Poinsett Counties, Arkansas.* Report, Contract DACW66-87-C-0046. Garrow and Associates, Atlanta. Submitted to U.S. Army Corps of Engineers, Memphis District.

Anderson, David G., and Glen T. Hanson
1988 Early Archaic Settlement in the Southeastern United States: A Case Study from the Savannah River Basin. *American Antiquity* 53:262–86.
Anderson, David G., and Virginia Horak
1995 *Archaeological Site File Management: A Southeastern Perspective.* Readings in Archeological Resource Protection Series No. 3. Interagency Archeological Services Division, National Park Service, Atlanta.
Anderson, David G., J. W. Joseph, Mary Beth Reed, and Steven D. Smith
1997 *Fort Polk Historic Preservation Plan Prehistory and History in Western Louisiana: A Technical Synthesis of Cultural Resource Investigations at Fort Polk.* National Park Service, Southeast Archeological Center, Tallahassee, Fla.
Anderson, David G., and Joseph Schuldenrein
1985 *Prehistoric Human Ecology along the Upper Savannah River: Excavations at the Rucker's Bottom, Abbeville, and Bullard Site Groups.* Russell Papers 1985. Interagency Archeological Services Division, National Park Service, Atlanta.
Anonymous
1883 Ancient Mounds in Arkansas. *Frank Leslie's Illustrated Newspaper,* New York. May 26:222–24.
Arkansas Alumnus
1930 Indian Remains in Arkansas Should Be Preserved in State Museum. *Arkansas Alumnus* 7(5):5–6. University of Arkansas, Fayetteville.
Arkansas Democrat, Little Rock, Arkansas
June 26, 1902
July 6, 1924:6
January 4, 1925:6
May 25, 1927
March 3, 1929
November 10, 1929:xxx 1, 5
October 12, 1930
November 16, 1930
November 6, 1932
April 6, 1933
Arkansas Gazette, Little Rock, Arkansas
August 4, 1975
September 17, 1876:2
November 1, 1879:8 (City Board of Health, A Sky-High Lift of the Quarantine)
August 20–24, 1880
January 27, 1883:4 (Antiquities Found By an Agent of the Smithsonian Institute, Near This City)
March 28, 1888:5 (The New Town of Toltec on St. Louis, Arkansas and Texas Road)
February 8, 1891:5
June 19, 1892:3 (Lands of Toltec, The Overflow Shows Why They Were Selected By the Mound Builders)
January 26, 1909
March 2, 1921

August 9, 1925
May 22, 1926:4–5
April 22, 1928
November 23, 1930
February 28, 1934
December 26, 1943

Arkansas True Democrat, Little Rock, Arkansas
May 25, 1859

Arnold, M. S.
1983 The Relocation of Arkansas Post to Ecores Rouges 1779. *Arkansas Historical Quarterly* 42:317–31.
1985 *Unequal Laws Unto a Savage Race: European Legal Traditions in Arkansas, 1686–1836.* University of Arkansas Press, Fayetteville.
1991 *Colonial Arkansas, 1686–1804.* University of Arkansas Press, Fayetteville.

Arnold, M. S., and D. J. Core (comp. and ed.)
1986 *Arkansas Colonials: A Collection of French and Spanish Records Listing Early Europeans in the Arkansas, 1686–1804.* Grand Prairie Historical Society, Arkansas County, Gillett.

Atkinson, James R.
1975 *Archaeological Site Survey in the Tallahala Reservoir Area, Jasper County, Mississippi: 1975.* Report. Department of Anthropology, Mississippi State University. Submitted to the U.S. National Park Service, Southeast Regional Office, Atlanta.
1979 A Historic Contact Indian Settlement in Oktibbeha County, Mississippi. *Journal of Alabama Archaeology* 25(1):61–82.
1985a The Akia and Ogoula Tchetoka Chickasaw Village Locations in 1736 during the French-Chickasaw War. *Mississippi Archaeology* 20(1):53–72.
1985b A Surface Collection from the Chickasaw Agency Site, 22-CS-421, on the Natchez Trace in Chickasaw County, Mississippi. *Mississippi Archaeology* 20(2):46–63.
1986a The Location of the Nineteenth Century Choctaw Village of Wholkey in Chickasaw County, Mississippi. *Mississippi Archaeology* 21(1):70–72.
1986b The Origins of the Chickasaw Indians as Evidenced by Cultural Remains in the Upper Tombigbee River Valley in Northeast Mississippi. Unpublished manuscript.
1987a The de Soto Route through North Mississippi in 1540–1541. *Mississippi Archaeology* 22(1):61–73.
1987b Historic Chickasaw Cultural Material: A More Comprehensive Identification. *Mississippi Archaeology* 22(2):32–62.
n.d. Excavations at the Chickasaw Agency Site, 22-CS-421, on the Natchez Trace. Final Report. In preparation, 1997, to submit to the National Park Service.

Atkinson, James R., and Jack D. Elliott Jr.
1978 *A Cultural Resources Survey of Selected Construction Areas in the Tennessee-Tombigbee Waterway: Alabama and Mississippi.* Report. Department of Anthropology, Mississippi State University. Submitted to U.S. Army Corps of Engineers, Mobile District.

Atwill, Lionel
1992 Bow Camp. *Field and Stream* 97(2):37–39, 95.

Autin, W. J., S. F. Burns, B. J. Miller, R. T. Saucier, and John I. Snead
1991 Quaternary Geology of the Lower Mississippi Valley. In *The Geology of North America.* Vol. K-2, *Quaternary Nonglacial Geology: Conterminous U.S.,* 547–81. Geological Society of America, Boulder.

Avery, George
1996 The Los Adaes Station Archaeology Program: '95 Stump Excavations. *Newsletter of the Louisiana Archaeological Society* 23(2):8–20.

Baird, W. D.
1980 *The Quapaw Indians: A History of the Downstream People.* University of Oklahoma Press, Norman.

Baker, R. P.
1988 *From Memdag to Norsk: A Historical Directory of Arkansas Post Offices, 1832–1971.* Arkansas Genealogical Society, Hot Springs.

Baker, T.
1992 Bow Design and Performance. In *The Traditional Bowyer's Bible.* Vol. 1. Edited by J. Hamm, 43–116. Lyons and Burford, New York.
1994 Bows of the World. In *The Traditional Bowyer's Bible.* Vol. 3. Edited by J. Hamm, 43–114. Lyons and Burford, New York.

Ball, Donald B.
1976 *A Bibliography of Tennessee Anthropology, Including Cherokee, Chickasaw, and Melungeon Studies.* Miscellaneous Paper No. 1. Tennessee Anthropological Association, Knoxville.

Barnes, James E., and Jerome C. Rose
1990 Dental Morphological Variants and Kinship among Prehistoric Caddo. Paper presented at the 55th Annual Meeting of the Society for American Archeology, Las Vegas.

Bartlein, P. J., T. Webb III, and E. Fleuri
1984 Holocene Climatic Change in the Northern Midwest: Pollen-derived Estimates. *Quaternary Research* 22:361–74.

Bastian, Tyler
1966 Initial Report on the Longest Site. *Great Plains Newsletter* 3(1):1–3.

Baxter Bulletin, Mountain Home, Arkansas
April 3, 1903
October 8, 1909:6
February 24, 1911:1
April 21, 1911:1
April 18, 1913
April 24, 1914:1
June 5, 1914:1
December 10, 1914:1
December 11, 1914
February 11, 1916:5
March 31, 1916:3
May 9, 1916:2
June 2, 1916:1
April 20, 1917:2

May 15 1918:1
February 6, 1920:1
March 20, 1921
December 29, 1922:1
April 11, 1924:1
October 10, 1925
January 28, 1927:1
May 13, 1927:1
November 11, 1932

Baxter, M. J.
1993 *Exploratory Multivariate Analysis in Archaeology.* Edinburgh University Press, Edinburgh.

Bell, Robert E.
1984a The Plains Villagers: The Washita River. In *Prehistory of Oklahoma,* edited by Robert E. Bell, 307–24. Academic Press, New York.
1984b Protohistoric Wichita. In *Prehistory of Oklahoma,* edited by Robert E. Bell, 363–78. Academic Press, New York.

Bennett, W. J., Jr., J. Blakely, R. Brinkman, R. Bennett, J. Northrip, W. Isenberger, and M. Bennett
1993 *Archeological Investigations at Seventeen Euro-American Farmsteads, Fort Chaffee, Arkansas.* Final Report 188. Archaeological Assessments, Inc., Nashville. Submitted to the U.S. Army Corps of Engineers, Little Rock District, Little Rock.

Bennett, W. J., Jr., A. F. Gettys, Judith Stewart-Abernathy, and Roger Saucier
1982 *A Cultural Resources Survey in the Larkin Creek Watershed, Lee and St. Francis Counties, Arkansas.* Final Report 21. Archaeological Assessments, Inc. Submitted to the Memphis District, U.S. Army Corps of Engineers.

Bense, Judith A.
1994 *Archaeology of the Southeastern United States: Paleoindian to World War I.* Academic Press, San Diego.

Blaine, Jay C.
1992 A Summary and Discussion of Additional Findings of the Gilbert Site, an Eighteenth-Century Norteno Occupation in Rains County, Texas. *Bulletin of the Texas Archeological Society* 63:175–96.

Blaine, Jay C., and R. K. Harris
1967 Guns. In The Gilbert Site: A Norteno Focus Site in Northeastern Texas, edited by Edward B. Jelks, 33–86. *Bulletin of the Texas Archeological Society* 37.

Blakely, J., W. J. Bennett Jr., and W. Isenberger
1990 *Euro-American Occupation of Eastern Center Valley, Arkansas: 1875–1941.* Final Report, Archaeological Assessments, Nashville. Submitted to the U.S. Army Corps of Engineers, Little Rock District, Little Rock.

Blitz, John H.
1985 *An Archaeological Study of the Mississippi Choctaw Indians.* Archaeological Report 16. Mississippi Department of Archives and History, Jackson.

Bolton, Herbert E.
1915 *Texas in the Middle Eighteenth Century: Studies in Spanish Colonial History and Administration.* University of California Press, Berkeley.
1970 (ed. and annot.) *Athanase De Mezieres and the Louisiana-Texas Frontier, 1768–1780.* Vol. 1. Kraus Reprint, New York.

Bonow, Hazen
1976 First Historical Dig: "Mooney's Landing." *Arkansas Archaeological Society Field Notes* 142:3.

Booneville Enterprise, Booneville, Arkansas
November 12, 1875:1

Bowman, Isaiah
1911 *Forest Physiography: Physiography of the United States and Principles of Soils in Relation to Forestry.* John Wiley and Sons, London.

Brain, Jeffrey P.
1973 *Trudeau, An 18th Century Tunica Village.* Bulletin No. 3. Lower Mississippi Valley Survey, Peabody Museum, Harvard University, Cambridge.
1979 *Tunica Treasure.* Vol. 71, Papers of the Peabody Museum of Archaeology and Ethnology. Harvard University, Cambridge.
1988 *Tunica Archaeology.* Vol. 78, Papers of the Peabody Museum of Archaeology and Ethnology. Harvard University, Cambridge.

Braun, E. L.
1974 [1950] *Deciduous Forests of Eastern North America.* Hafner Press, New York.

Bringier, L.
1821 Notices of the Geology, Mineralogy, Topography, Productions, and Aboriginal Inhabitants of the Regions Around the Mississippi and its Confluent Waters—in a letter from L. Bringier, Esq. of Louisiana, to Rev. Elias Cornelius—Communicated for This Journal. *American Journal of Science and Arts* 3(1):15–46.

Britt, Tad
1998 Preliminary Results of Survey and Testing of Four Civil War Era Steamboats, Yazoo River, Leflore County, Mississippi. Paper presented at the South Central Historical Archeology Conference, Jackson, Miss.

Brooks, Robert L.
1989 Village Farming Societies. In *From Clovis to Comanchero: Archeological Overview of the Southern Great Plains,* by Joe S. Hays, Douglas W. Owsley, Richard L. Jantz, Murray K. Marks, and Mary H. Manhein, 137–56. Research Series No. 35. Arkansas Archeological Survey, Fayetteville.
1994 Warfare on the Southern Plains. In *Skeletal Biology in the Great Plains: Migration, Warfare, Health, and Subsistence,* edited by Douglas W. Owsley and Richard L. Jantz, 307–23. Smithsonian Institution Press, Washington, D.C.

Brose, David S.
1991 *Yesterday's River: The Archaeology of 10,000 Years along the Tennessee-Tombigbee Waterway.* Cleveland Museum of Natural History, Cleveland.

Brown, Ian W.
1975a Excavations at Fort St. Pierre. *Conference on Historic Sites Archaeology Papers* 9:60–85.
1975b *Archaeological Investigations at the Historic Portland and St. Pierre Sites in the Lower Yazoo Basin, Mississippi.* Master's thesis, Brown University, Providence, R.I.
1976a Fort St. Pierre, a Mini-Pompeii. Paper presented at the annual meeting of the Society for Historical Archaeology, Philadelphia, Pa.
1976b The Portland Site (22M12), an Early 18th Century Historic Indian Site in Warren County, Mississippi. *Mississippi Archaeology* 11(1):2–11.
1978 Artifact Patterning and Activity Areas: The Evidence from Fort St. Pierre, Mississippi. *Conference on Historic Site Archaeology Papers* 12:309–321.
1979a Historic Artifacts and Sociocultural Change: Some Warnings from the Lower Mississippi Valley. *Conference on Historic Sites Archaeology Papers* 13:109–21.
1979b *Early 18th Century French-Indian Culture Contact in the Yazoo Bluffs Region of the Lower Mississippi Valley*. Ph.D. diss., Brown University, Providence, R.I.
1985 *Natchez Indian Archaeology: Culture Change and Stability in the Lower Mississippi Valley.* Archaeological Report No. 15. Mississippi Department of Archives and History, Jackson.

Brown, James A.
1971 *Pottery Vessels.* Spiro Studies, Vol. 3. Stovall Museum of Science and History, University of Oklahoma Research Institute, Norman.
1975 Spiro Art and Its Mortuary Contexts. In *Death and the Afterlife in Pre-Columbian America*, edited by Elizabeth P. Benson, 1–32. Dumbarton Oaks Research Library and Collections, Washington, D.C.
1983 Spiroan Exchange Connections Revealed by Sources of Imported Raw Materials. In *Southeastern Natives and Their Pasts: A Collection of Papers Honoring Dr. Robert E. Bell,* edited by Don G. Wyckoff and Jack L. Hoffman, 129–62. Studies in Oklahoma's Past No. 11. Oklahoma Archeological Survey.
1984 Arkansas Valley Caddoan: The Spiro Phase. In *Prehistory of Oklahoma,* edited by Robert E. Bell, 241–63. Academic Press, New York.
1996 *The Spiro Ceremonial Center: The Archaeology of Arkansas Valley Caddoan Culture in Eastern Oklahoma.* Vols. 1 and 2. Memoirs of the Museum of Anthropology No. 29. University of Michigan, Ann Arbor.

Brues, Alice M.
1957 Skeletal Material from the Nagle Site. *Bulletin of the Oklahoma Anthropological Society* 5:101–6.
1958 Skeletal Material from the Horton Site. *Bulletin of the Oklahoma Anthropological Society* 6:27–32.
1959 Skeletal Material from the Morris Site (Ck-39). *Bulletin of the Oklahoma Anthropological Society* 7:63–70.
1962 Skeletal Material from the McLemore Site. *Bulletin of the Oklahoma Anthropological Society* 10:68–78.

Bruseth, James E., Diane E. Wilson, and Timothy K. Perttula
1995 The Sanders Site: A Spiroan Entrepôt in Texas? *Plains Anthropologist* 40(153):223–36.

Buchner, C. Andrew
1992 *Archaeological Investigations at the Lewis Site (3LE266): A Twentieth-Century Black Owned Farmstead on the St. Francis Floodway, Lee County, Arkansas.* Report. Garrow and Associates. Submitted to Department of the U.S. Army Corps of Engineers, Memphis District.

Buchner, C. Andrew, and Mitchell Childress
1991 *Archaeological Investigations at 3SF332: An Early Mississippian and Tenant Period Site on Cutoff Bayou, St. Francis County, Arkansas.* Report. Garrow and Associates, Inc. Submitted to the U.S. Army Corps of Engineers, Memphis District.

Buchner, C. Andrew, and Guy G. Weaver
1990 *A Report of Archaeological Testing at Site 3CT263 within the Proposed Edmonson Wastewater Pond, Crittenden County, Arkansas.* Report. Garrow and Associates, Inc. Submitted to the U.S. Army Corps of Engineers, Memphis District.

Bureau of Land Management
1993 Automated Records Project: Pre-1908 Homestead and Cash Entry Patents (CD-ROM). General Land Office, Bureau of Land Management, U.S. Department of the Interior, Springfield, Va.

Burnett, Barbara A.
1988 The Biological Synthesis. In *Human Adaptation in the Ozark and Ouachita Mountains,* by George Sabo III, Ann M. Early, Jerome C. Rose, Barbara A. Burnett, Louis Vogel Jr., and James P. Harcourt, 193–220. Research Series No. 31. Arkansas Archeological Survey, Fayetteville.

1990a Bioarcheology of the Goldsmith Oliver 2 Site and the Protohistoric Period in Arkansas. In *Goldsmith Oliver 2 (3PU306): A Protohistoric Archeological Site near Little Rock, Arkansas,* by Marvin D. Jeter et al., 146–216. Report. Arkansas Archeological Survey, Fayetteville. Submitted to Federal Aviation Administration, Fort Worth.

1990b The Bioarcheological Synthesis of the Gulf Coastal Plain Study Area. In *The Archeology and Bioarcheology of the Gulf Coastal Plain,* by D. A. Story, J. A. Guy, B. A. Burnett, M. D. Freeman, J. C. Rose, D. G. Steele, B. W. Olive, and K. J. Reinhard, 385–508. Research Series No. 38. Arkansas Archeological Survey, Fayetteville.

Burns, R. M., and B. H. Honkala (eds.)
1990 *Silvics of North America.* Vols. 1 and 2. U.S. Department of Agriculture Forest Service Handbook 654. U.S. Government Printing Office, Washington, D.C.

Burton, James D.
1973 *Osage-orange . . . an American Wood.* U.S. Department of Agriculture Forest Service Bulletin FS-248.

Bushnell, David J.
1927 *Drawings by A. DeBatz in Louisiana, 1732–1735.* Smithsonian Miscellaneous Collections 80 (5). Washington, D.C.

Cable, John S.

1996 Haw River Revisited: Implications for Modeling Late Glacial and Early Holocene Hunter-Gatherer Settlement Systems in the Southeast. In *The Paleoindian and Early Archaic Southeast,* edited by David G. Anderson and Kenneth E. Sassaman, 107–48. University of Alabama Press, Tuscaloosa.

Cande, Kathleen H.

1991 *Archeological Test Excavations at Three Historic Sites (3DR226, 3DR227, 3DR229) Within the Proposed Lake Monticello, Drew County, Arkansas.* Report. Arkansas Archeological Survey, Fayetteville. Submitted to the Mehlburger Firm, Little Rock.

1992 The Ozarks as Destination: Data Recovery Excavations at the Lambert Farmstead, Mountainburg, Arkansas. Paper presented at the annual meeting of the Southeastern Archeology Conference, Little Rock.

1995a *The Ozarks as Destination: Phase III Archeological Investigations at the Lambert Farmstead (3CW674) and Phase II Testing at the Dement Farmstead and Cemetery (3CE685), Crawford County.* Report. Arkansas Archeological Survey, Fayetteville. Submitted to Arkansas Highway and Transportation Department, Little Rock.

1995b Phase II and III Archeological Investigations on Historic Rural Domestic Sites In and Near National Forest Lands in Arkansas. In *An Overview of Late Historic Domestic Sites in Ouachita and Ozark-St. Francis National Forests,* by H. A. Davis, 18–38. Report. Arkansas Archeological Survey, Fayetteville. Submitted to Ozark-St. Francis National Forest, Russellville.

Cande, Robert F.

1978 *An Archaeological Investigation of the Proposed Sewerage Improvements, Brookland Arkansas.* Ms. on file, Arkansas Archeological Survey, Fayetteville.

1979 *Phase II Archaeological Investigations at the Proposed Location of the Industrial Park Expansion, Corning, Arkansas.* Manuscript on file, Arkansas Archaeological Survey, Fayetteville.

Cande, Robert F., Robert H. Lafferty III, Michael C. Sierzchula, M. Tracy Oates, and James Barnes

1990 *A Cultural Resources Survey of Steele, New Franklin, and Main Ditches and National Register of Historic Places Significance Testing of Sites 23PM574, 575, 577, and 23PM578, Pemiscot County, Missouri.* Mid-Continental Research Associates Report 89-8. Submitted to the Memphis District Corps of Engineers, Contract No. 66-89-D-0053.

Carstens, Kenneth C.

1984 In Search of Fort Jefferson: Past, Present, and Future Studies. *Proceedings of the Symposium on Ohio Valley Urban and Historic Archaeology* 2:45–56.

1997 Current Research at the Gower House (15LV178), Livingston County, Kentucky. *Ohio Valley Historical Archaeology* 12:39–57.

n.d.a *Personnel of George Rogers Clark's Fort Jefferson and Civilian Community of Clarksville, 1780–1781 (Based on the Lost Vouchers of George Rogers Clark).* Heritage Press, Bowie, Md. In press.

n.d.b Fort Smith, 1861–1865, A Federal Civil War Gun Emplacement in Western Kentucky. In *Current Research in Kentucky,* edited by Charles E. Hockensmith et al. Kentucky Heritage Council, Frankfort. In press.

Castille, George J.

1979 *A Test of Two Methods of Archeological Analysis: The Welcome Plantation Artifact Pattern.* Master's thesis, Louisiana State University, Baton Rouge.

Castille, George J., Douglas D. Bryant, Johan M. Exnicios, William D. Reeves, and Susan D. De France

1986 *Urban Archaeology in Old New Orleans: Historical and Archaeological Investigations within the Greater New Orleans Bridge No. Right-Of-Way.* Coastal Environments, Inc., Baton Rouge.

Castille, George J., David B. Kelley, Sally K. E. Reeves, and Charles E. Pearson

1982 *Archaeological Excavations at Esplanade Avenue and North Rampart Street, New Orleans, Louisiana.* Report. Coastal Environments, Inc. Submitted to the U.S. National Park Service, Southwest Regional Office, Santa Fe, N.M.

Castille, George J., and Kathleen G. McCloskey

1981 *A Cultural Resources Reconnaissance of Tezcuco, Monroe, and Brislie Plantations, Ascension Parish, Louisiana.* Report. Coastal Environments, Inc., Baton Rouge. Submitted to Ebasco Services.

Castille, George J., and Richard A. Weinstein

1986 A Cultural Resources Evaluation of Plantation Landing. Ms. on file, Louisiana Division of Archeology, Baton Rouge.

Catlin, George

1973 *Notes on the Manners, Customs, and Conditions of the North American Indians. Written during Eight Years Travel (1832–1839) amongst the Wildest Tribes of Indians in North America.* Vol. 1. With an introduction by Marjorie Halpin. Dover, New York.

Chase, David W.

1966 Fort Toulouse, First Investigations, 1966. *Conference on Historic Site Archaeology Papers* 2:33.

Chastain, J. L.

1827 Plat of Township 1 South of the Base line, Range 10 West of the 5th Principal Meridian, according to the field notes, 4th May 1827, in the Surveyor's Office, St. Louis. State Land Office, Little Rock.

Chatwin, Bruce

1987 *The Songlines.* Elisabeth Sifton Books, Viking Press, New York.

Cherry, Michelle

1998 An Historical and Archaeological Investigation of Old Augusta (Perry County, Mississippi). Paper presented at the annual meeting of the Society for Historical Archaeology, Atlanta.

Childress, Mitchell R.

1990 *Analysis and Interpretation of Artifact Collections from Four Archaeological Sites within the Country Club Gardens Permit Area, West Memphis, Crittenden County, Arkansas.* Report. Garrow and Associates, Inc. Submitted to the U.S. Army Corps of Engineers, Memphis District.

Childress, Mitchell R., John L. Hopkins, and Guy G. Weaver
1995 *Cultural Resources Investigations at King-Riverside Park, Shelby County, Tennessee.* Garrow and Associates, Inc., Atlanta. Submitted to Kersey/Wike Associates, Inc., and the Memphis Park Commission, Memphis.

Cimprich, John, and Robert C. Mainfort Jr.
1989 The Fort Pillow Massacre: A Statistical Note. *Journal of American History* 76(3):830–37.

Clayton, Lawrence A., Vernon James Knight Jr., and Edward C. Moore (eds.)
1993 *The de Soto Chronicles: The Expedition of Hernando de Soto to North America in 1539–1543.* Vol. 1. University of Alabama Press, Tuscaloosa.

Cleland, Charles E.
1983a *A Computer Compatible System for the Categorization, Enumeration, and Retrieval of Nineteenth and Early Twentieth Century Archaeological Material Culture. Part II: Manual for Identification and Classification.* Report. Michigan State University Museum. Submitted to the U.S. Army Corps of Engineers, Mobile District, and the U.S. National Park Service.
1983b Merchants, Tradesmen, and Tenants: The Economics of Diffusion of Material Culture on a Late Nineteenth Century Site. *Geoscience and Man* 23:35–44.

Cobb, Tom, Henry Miller, Barbara Musholt, and Donna Pyles
1971 A Plantation Survey in the Vicinity of Arkansas Post. Ms. on file. Arkansas Archeological Survey, Fayetteville.

Coleman, Roger
1987 *The Arkansas Post Story: Arkansas Post National Memorial.* Professional Papers No. 12. National Park Service, Southwest Cultural Resources Center, Santa Fe.
1990 *Archaeological Investigation for Construction of a Pedestrian Trail and Identification of Laundress Row, Fort Smith National Historic Site, Arkansas.* Southwest Cultural Resources Center Professional Paper No. 30. U.S. National Park Service, Santa Fe.
1996 Birds of Passage: Subsistence Farming in the Ouachita Mountains: Archaeological Investigation of the David Moore Farmstead, Polk County, Arkansas. Paper presented to the annual meeting of the Society for Historical Archaeology, Cincinnati, Ohio.

Collins, Brian R., Jane K. Kowalewski, and Guy G. Weaver
1997 *Phase I Cultural Resource Assessment of the First Place Parking Garage, Memphis, Shelby County, Tennessee.* Report. Brockington and Associates, Memphis. Submitted to Landmark America, LLC, Memphis.

Collins, Henry B., Jr.
1927 Potsherds from Choctaw Village Sites in Mississippi. *Journal of the Washington Academy of Sciences* 17:10.

Connaway, John M.
n.d. The Fishweirs of Mississippi. Report in preparation. Historic Preservation Division, Mississippi Department of Archives and History, Clarksdale.

Connaway, John M., Jay K. Johnson, and Patricia Galloway (eds.)

n.d. The Oliver Site (22-Co-503), Coahoma County, Mississippi. Collected papers. In preparation.

Cotter Record, Cotter, Arkansas

August 14, 1913:1

Council, R. Bruce

1985 *Historical Documentation and Site Reconnaissance of the Memphis Navy Yard Archaeological Site, Memphis, Shelby County, Tennessee*. Report. Submitted to the Tennessee Department of Transportation, Nashville.

Creel, Darrell

1991 Bison Hides in Late Prehistoric Exchange in the Southern Plains. *American Antiquity* 56(1):40–49.

Crosby, Alfred W., Jr.

1972 *The Columbian Exchange: Biological and Cultural Consequences of 1492.* Greenwood Press, Westport, Conn.

Curtiss, E.

1879a Letter to [F. W. Putnam]. Peabody Museum Archives Accession 80-20. Harvard University, Cambridge.

1879b Notes. Peabody Museum Archives Accession 80-20. Harvard University, Cambridge.

Davis, Hester A.

1966 An Introduction to Parkin Prehistory. *Arkansas Archaeologist* 7(1–2):1–40.

1967 History's Mysteries in Arkansas. *Arkansas Historical Quarterly* 26(1):3–10.

1987 The Cherokee in Arkansas: An Invisible Resource. In *Visions and Revisions: Ethnohistoric Perspectives on Southern Cultures,* edited by G. Sabo III and W. M. Schneider, 48–58. University of Georgia Press, Athens.

1988 Double the Work, Double the Treasure: Federal Archeology in Arkansas, 1966–1986. *Advances in Southeastern Archeology 1966–1986, Contributions of the Federal Archaeological Program.* Southeastern Archaeological Conference Special Publication No. 6, 4–6.

1991 (ed.) *Arkansas Before the Americans.* Research Series No. 40. Arkansas Archeological Survey, Fayetteville.

Delcourt, H. R., and P. A. Delcourt

1989a Palynological and Plant-Macrofossil Analysis: Hood Lake, Poinsett County, Arkansas. In *Cultural Resource Investigations in the L'Anguille River Basin Lee, St. Francis, Cross, and Poinsett Counties, Arkansas,* 16–31. Report, Contract DACW66-87-C-0046. Garrow and Associates, Inc., Atlanta. Submitted to Memphis District, Corps of Engineers.

1989b Final Report of Palynological and Plant-Macrofossil Analysis, Hood Lake, Poinsett County, Arkansas: Palynological and Plant Macrofossil Data. In *Cultural Resource Investigations in the L'Anguille River Basin Lee, St. Francis, Cross, and Poinsett Counties, Arkansas,* A-210 to A-246. Report, Contract DACW66-87-C-0046. Garrow and Associates, Inc., Atlanta. Submitted to Memphis District, Corps of Engineers.

1991a Late-Quaternary Vegetation History of the Interior Highland Region of Missouri, Arkansas, and Oklahoma. In *Restoration of Old Growth Forests in the Interior Highlands of Arkansas and Oklahoma,* edited by D. Henderson and L. D. Hedrick, 15–30. Ouachita National Forest and Winrock International, Morrilton, Ark.

1991b *Quaternary Ecology: A Paleo Ecological Perspective.* Chapman and Hall, London.

1994 Postglacial Rise and Decline of *Ostrya Virginiana* (Mill.) K. Koch and *Carpinus Caroliniana* Walt. in Eastern North America: Predictable Responses of Forest Species to Cyclic Changes in Seasonality of Climates. *Journal of Biogeography* 21:137–50.

Delcourt, P. A., and H. R. Delcourt

1987 *Long-term Forest Dynamics of the Temperate Zone.* Ecological Studies 63. Springer-Verlag, New York.

1989 Final Report of Palynological and Plant-Macrofossil Analysis, Hood Lake, Poinsett County, Arkansas. In *Cultural Resource Investigations in the L'Anguille River Basin, Lee, St. Francis, Cross, and Poinsett Counties, Arkansas,* by D. G. Anderson, H. R. Delcourt, P. A. Delcourt, J. E. Foss, and P. A. Morse, 16–31. Report, Contract No. DACW66-87-C-0046. Garrow and Associates, Inc., Atlanta. Submitted to the U.S. Army Corps of Engineers, Memphis District.

1996 Quaternary Paleoecology of the Lower Mississippi Valley. *Engineering Geology* 4:219–42.

Delcourt, P. A., H. R. Delcourt, R. C. Brister, and L. E. Lackey

1980 Quaternary Vegetation History of the Mississippi Embayment. *Quaternary Research* 13:111–32.

Delcourt, P. A., H. R. Delcourt, and J. L. Davidson

1983 Mapping and Calibration of Moderm Pollen-Vegetation Relationships in the Southeastern United States. *Review of Palaeobotany and Palynology* 39:1–45.

Delcourt, P. A., H. R. Delcourt, D. F. Morse, and P. A. Morse

1993 History, Evolution, and Organization of Vegetation and Human Culture. In *Biodiversity of the Southeastern United States Lowland Terrestrial Communities,* edited by W. H. Martin, S. G. Boyce, and A. C. Echternacht, 47–79. John Wiley and Sons, New York.

Delcourt, H. R., P. A. Delcourt, and P. D. Royall

1997 Late-Quaternary Vegetational History of the Western Lowlands. In *The Sloan Site: A Paleoindian Dalton Cemetery in Arkansas,* edited by D. F. Morse, 103–22. Smithsonian Institution Press, Washington, D.C.

Delcourt, P. A., H. R. Delcourt, and T. Webb III

1984 Atlas of Mapped Distributions of Dominance and Modern Pollen Percentages for Important Tree Taxa of Eastern North America. *American Association of Stratigraphic Palynologists Contribution Series* 14:1–131.

Dellinger, Samuel C.

1940a Letter to James Ford, February 20.

1940b Letter to Philip Phillips, March 8.

DePratter, Chester B.

1991 W.P.A. Archaeological Excavations in Chatham County, Georgia:

1937–1942. *Laboratory of Archaeology Series Report Number 29.* University of Georgia, Athens.

Derrick, Sharon McCormick, and Diane E. Wilson

1997 Cranial Modeling as an Ethnic Marker among the Prehistoric Caddo. *Bulletin of the Texas Archeological Society* 68:139–46.

Derry, Linda

1992 Fathers and Daughters: Land Ownership, Kinship Structure, and Social Space in Old Cahawba. In *The Art and Mystery of Historical Archaeology: Essays in Honor of James Deetz,* edited by Anne Elizabeth Yentsch and Mary C. Beaudry, 215–27. CRC Press, Boca Raton, Fla.

1997 Emancipation Archaeology: Does it Play in Selma? *Historical Archaeology* 31(3):18–26.

1998 Creating an Archaeological Park at Old Cahawba, AL: Making Archaeology Relevant. Paper presented at the South Central Historical Archeology Conference, Jackson, Miss.

Dickinson, Samuel D.

1936 Ceramic Relationships of the Pre-Caddo Pottery from the Crenshaw Site. *Bulletin of the Texas Archeological and Paleontological Society* 8:56–59.

1941 Certain Vessels from the Clements Place, an Historic Caddo Site. *Bulletin of the Texas Archeological and Paleontological Society* 13:117–34.

1989 Colonial Arkansas Place Names. *Arkansas Historical Quarterly* 48(2):137–68.

Dickinson, Samuel D., and Samuel C. Dellinger

1940 A Survey of the Historic Earthenware of the Lower Arkansas Valley. *Bulletin of the Texas Archeological and Paleontological Society* 12:76–89.

Dickinson, Samuel D., and Harry J. Lemley

1939 Evidences of the Marksville and Coles Creek Complexes at the Kirkham Place, Clark County, Arkansas. *Bulletin of the Texas Archeological and Paleontological Society* 11:139–89.

Din, G. C., and A. P. Nasatir

1983 *The Imperial Osages: Spanish-Indian Diplomacy in the Mississippi Valley.* University of Oklahoma Press, Norman.

Divine, Douglas Wayne

1972 *Guide to Arkansas Geology.* Ph.D. diss., Northeast Louisiana University, Monroe.

Dollar, Clyde D.

1966a The First Fort Smith Report. Ms. on file. Arkansas Archeological Survey, Fayetteville.

1966b *Preliminary Site Report: Spadra Bluff Indian Trading Factory, Arkansas.* Report submitted to the U.S. National Park Service, Richmond, Va.

1977 *An Archaeological Assessment of Historic Davidsonville.* Research Report No. 17. Arkansas Archeological Survey, Fayetteville.

1983 *Archaeological Investigation and Historical Documentation in the Vicinity of the Old Commissary Building, Fort Smith National Historic Site, Fort Smith, Arkansas.* Historic Preservation Associates, Fayetteville.

Donahue, Randolph E.

1983 *A Computer Compatible System for the Categorization, Enumeration, and Retrieval of Nineteenth and Early Twentieth Century Archaeological*

Material Cultural. Part III: Archaeological Information System: Software & Manual for Use. Report. Michigan State University Museum. Submitted to the U.S. Army Corps of Engineers, Mobile District and the U.S. National Park Service.

Dow, Laura Ann Brantly
1987 *The Genetic Affinities and Adaptive Success of Three Groups of Late Prehistoric Amerindians from Texas.* Master's thesis, University of Texas, Austin.

Dubes, Richard C.
1993 Cluster Analysis and Related Issues. In *Handbook of Pattern Recognition and Computer Vision,* edited by C. H. Chen, L. F. Pau, and P. S. P. Wang, 3–32. World Scientific, River Edge, New Jersey.

Dubes, Richard C., and Anil K. Jain
1976 Clustering Techniques: The User's Dilemma. *Pattern Recognition* 8(4):247–60.

Duffield, Lathel F., and Edward B. Jelks
1961 *The Pearson Site: A Historic Indian Site at Iron Bridge Reservoir, Rains County, Texas.* Anthropology Series No. 4. Department of Anthropology, University of Texas, Austin.

Dunnahoo, Patrick
1993 *Of Clear, Cool Water and Gentle Hills: The Story of the Four Forks of Arkansas' Saline River.* Published by author, Benton, Ark.

Dye, David H.
1993 Reconstruction of the de Soto Expedition Route in Arkansas: The Mississippi Alluvial Plain. In *The Expedition of Hernando de Soto West of the Mississippi, 1541–1553,* edited by Gloria A. Young and Michael P. Hoffman, 36–57. University of Arkansas Press, Fayetteville.

Early, Ann M.
1982a "Ouachita Mountains Region" and "Middle Saline Region" Sections of Southwest Arkansas, by F. F. Schambach, A. M. Early, E. T. Hemmings, D. B. Kelley, and M. Swanda. In *A State Plan for the Conservation of Archeological Resources in Arkansas,* edited by H. A. Davis. Research Series No. 21. Arkansas Archeological Survey, Fayetteville.
1982b Caddoan Settlement Systems in the Ouachita River Basin. In *Arkansas Archeology in Review,* edited by Neal L. Trubowitz and Marvin D. Jeter, 192–232. Research Series No. 15. Arkansas Archeological Survey, Fayetteville.
1986 Dr. Thomas L. Hodges and His Contributions to Arkansas Archeology. *Arkansas Archeologist* 23, 24:1–11.
1988 *Standridge: Caddoan Settlement in a Mountain Environment.* Research Series No. 29. Arkansas Archeological Survey, Fayetteville.
1993a (ed.) *Caddoan Saltmakers in the Ouachita Valley: The Hardman Site.* Research Series No. 43. Arkansas Archeological Survey, Fayetteville.
1993b Finding the Middle Passage: The Spanish Journey from the Swamplands to Caddo Country. In *The Expedition of Hernando de Soto West of the Mississippi, 1541–1543,* edited by Gloria A. Young and Michael P. Hoffman, 68–70. University of Arkansas Press, Fayetteville.

1993c Ceramics. In *Caddoan Saltmakers in the Ouachita Valley,* edited by A. M. Early, 63–144. Research Series No. 43. Arkansas Archeological Survey, Fayetteville.

Elliott, Daniel T.

1995 *Clark Hill River Basin Survey.* Savannah River Archaeological Research Papers 7. Savannah River Archaeological Research Program, South Carolina Institute of Archaeology and Anthropology, University of South Carolina, Columbia.

Elliott, Jack E., Jr.

1987 *Report on a Reconnaissance Survey of the Beauvoir Grounds, Biloxi, Mississippi.* Report. Mississippi Department of Archives and History, Jackson.

1989 *Rosalie, the Fort of Natchez: Its National Significance and Integrity.* Report. Historic Preservation Division, Mississippi Department of Archives and History. Submitted to Secretary of the Interior.

1994 Extinct Townsites and Cultural Resource Considerations. Symposium organized and chaired by Jack D. Elliot Jr., at meeting of the State Historic Preservation Officers, Southeastern Region, Columbus, Miss.

1998a *The Fort of Natchez and the Colonial Origins of Mississippi.* Eastern National, n.p. (revised version of 1990 article originally published in *Journal of Mississippi History*).

1998b Concerning Cutoff Dates for State Archaeological Inventories. *Mississippi Archaeological Association Newsletter* 33 (September):2–6.

Ernest, David M.

1994 *The Oakleaf Hotel: A Study of Urban Residence Dynamics in Late 19th and Early 20th Century Little Rock, Arkansas.* Master's thesis, University of Arkansas, Fayetteville.

Etchieson, Meeks, and Roger E. Coleman

1996 Texas Fever and Free Range Herding in Arkansas: Material Culture of the Federal Tick Eradication Program. Paper presented at the annual meeting of the Society for Historical Archaeology, Cincinnati, Ohio.

Ewen, Charles R.

1992 *Archaeological Investigations at the Norwood Property (3HE236-JR1), Old Washington Historic State Park.* Report, AAS Project 755. Arkansas Archeological Survey, Fayetteville. Submitted to Arkansas Department of Parks and Tourism, Little Rock.

Feathers, James K.

1989 Effects of Temper on Strength of Ceramics: A Response to Bronitsky and Hamer. *American Antiquity* 54(3):579–88.

Fehon, Jacqueline R., and Alfred D. Viscito

1974 *Archaeological and Historical Inventory and Preliminary Field Reconnaissance of Village Creek, Jackson and Lawrence Counties, Arkansas.* Research Report 2. Arkansas Archeological Survey, Fayetteville.

Fenneman, Nevin M.

1938 *Physiography of Eastern United States.* McGraw-Hill, New York.

Ferguson, Leland

1992 *Uncommon Ground: Archaeology and Early African America, 1675–1800.* Smithsonian Institution Press, Washington, D.C.

First State Abstract and Insurance Corporation
1975 Abstract of Title, Supplemental No. 9918. Lands in Section 10, Township 1 South Range 10 West, Lonoke County, Arkansas. Certified from Original Entry to December 1, 1952. Prepared for Arkansas Department of Parks and Tourism, Little Rock.

Fisher-Carroll, Rita L.
1997 *Sociopolitical Organization at Upper Nodena (3MS4) from a Mortuary Perspective.* Master's thesis, University of Arkansas, Fayetteville.

Flores, Dan L. (ed.)
1984 *Jefferson and Southwestern Exploration: The Freeman and Custis Accounts of the Red River Expedition of 1806.* University of Oklahoma Press, Norman.
1985 *Journal of an Indian Trader: Anthony Glass and the Texas Trading Frontier, 1790–1810.* Texas A&M University Press.

Ford, James A.
1936 *Analysis of Indian Village Site Collections from Louisiana and Mississippi.* Anthropological Study No. 2. Department of Conservation, Louisiana Geological Survey, New Orleans.
1961 *Menard Site: The Quapaw Village of Osotouy on the Arkansas River.* Anthropological Papers No. 48 (2). American Museum of Natural History, New York.

Ford, James A., and Robert N. Neitzel
1958 *Excavations at the Menard Site, Arkansas County, Arkansas 1958.* Report. American Museum of Natural History. Submitted to the U.S. National Park Service, Southwest Archaeological Center, Macon, Ga.

Ford, R. I.
1972 Barter, Gift, or Violence: An Analysis of Tewa Intertribal Exchange. In *Social Exchange and Interaction,* edited by E. M. Wilmsen, 21–45. Anthropological Papers No. 46. Museum of Anthropology, University of Michigan, Ann Arbor.

Fort Smith Elevator, Fort Smith, Arkansas
July 4, 1884:1

Fort Smith Times-Record, Fort Smith, Arkansas
October 9, 1937

Foss, John E.
1989 Soils and Landscapes along the L'Anguille River in Arkansas. In *Cultural Resource Investigations in the L'Anguille River Basin Lee, St. Francis, Cross, and Poinsett Counties, Arkansas,* A-247–A-261. Report, Contract DACW66-87-C-0046. Garrow and Associates, Inc., Atlanta. Submitted to Memphis District, Corps of Engineers.

Fowler, M. L.
1989 *The Cahokia Atlas: A Historical Atlas of Cahokia Archaeology.* Studies in Illinois Archaeology No. 6. Illinois Historic Preservation Agency, Springfield.

Fox, Gregory L.
1992 *A Critical Evaluation of the Interpretive Framework of the Mississippi Period in Southeast Missouri.* Ph.D. diss., University of Missouri, Columbia.

Fritz, Gayle J.

1989 Evidence of Plant Use from Copple Mound at the Spiro Site. In *Contributions to Spiro Archeology; Mound Excavations and Regional Perspectives,* edited by J. Daniel Rogers, Don G. Wyckoff, and Dennis Peterson, 65–67. Studies in Oklahoma's Past No.16. Oklahoma Archaeological Survey, Norman.

1990 Multiple Pathways to Farming in Precontact Eastern North America. *Journal of World Prehistory* 4(4):387–431.

Galloway, Patricia

1982 (ed.) *LaSalle and His Legacy: Frenchmen and Indians in the Lower Mississippi Valley.* University Press of Mississippi, Jackson.

1995 *Choctaw Genesis.* University of Nebraska Press, Lincoln.

Garrow, Patrick, John L. Hopkins, and Linda Kennedy

1998 *Working on the Railroad: The Archeology and History of the MATA North End Terminal Site, Memphis, Tennessee.* Report. TRC Garrow Associates, Atlanta. Submitted to Memphis Area Transit Authority, Memphis.

Gerstacker, Frederick

1968 *Wild Sports in the Far West: The Narrative of a German Wanderer Beyond the Mississippi, 1837–43.* Duke University Press, Durham, N.C.

Gillam, J. Christopher

1995 *Paleoindian Settlement in the Mississippi Valley of Arkansas.* Master's thesis, University of Arkansas, Fayetteville.

1996a A View of Paleoindian Settlement from Crowley's Ridge. *Plains Anthropologist* 41:273–86.

1996b Early and Middle Paleoindian Sites in the Northeastern Arkansas Region. In *The Paleoindian and Early Archaic Southeast,* edited by D. G. Anderson and K. E. Sassaman, 404–12. University of Alabama, Tuscaloosa.

Glascock, Michael D.

1992 Characterization of Archaeological Ceramics at MURR by Neutron Activation Analysis and Multivariate Statistics. In *Chemical Characterization of Ceramic Pastes in Archaeology,* edited by H. Neff, 11–26. Prehistory Press, Madison.

Goodspeed Publishing Co.

1889 *Biographical and Historical Memoirs of Pulaski, Jefferson, Lonoke, Faulkner, Grant, Saline, Perry, Garland, and Hot Spring Counties, Arkansas.* Goodspeed, Chicago. [No date] facsimile ed. Southern Historical Press, Easley, S.C.

Goodwin, R. Christopher, Peter Gendel, and Jill-Karen Yakubik

1983 *Historic Archeology at the Old Courthouse Site, Convent, St. James Parish, Louisiana.* Report. Goodwin and Associates, New Orleans. Ms. on file, Louisiana Division of Archeology, Baton Rouge.

Goodwin, R. Christopher, Jill-Karen Yakubik, and Peter Gendel

1983 *Historic Archeology at Star and Bourbon Plantations.* Report. Goodwin and Associates, New Orleans. Submitted to U.S. Army Corps of Engineers, New Orleans District.

Goodwin, R. Christopher, Jill-Karen Yakubik, and Cyd Goodwin

1983 *The Historic Archaeology of Elmwood Plantation.* Report. Goodwin and

Associates, New Orleans. Submitted to Division of Archaeology, Department of Culture, Recreation, and Tourism, Baton Rouge.

Goodwin, R. Christopher, Jill-Karen Yakubik, Peter A. Gendel, Kenneth Jones, Debra Stayner, Cyd H. Goodwin, Gallow W. Selby, and Janice Cooper

1985 *Preserving the Past for the Future: A Comprehensive Archaeology and Historic Sites Inventory of Jefferson Parish, Louisiana.* Report. Goodwin and Associates, New Orleans. Ms. on file, Louisiana Division of Archeology, Baton Rouge.

Goodyear, Albert C.

1974 *The Brand Site: A Techno-functional Study of a Dalton Site in Northeast Arkansas.* Research Series 7. Arkansas Archeological Survey, Fayetteville.

1979 *A Hypothesis for the Use of Cryptocrystalline Raw Materials Among Paleo-Indian Groups of North America.* Research Manuscript Series 156. South Carolina Institute of Archaeology and Anthropology.

1982 The Chronological Position of the Dalton Horizon in the Southeastern United States. *American Antiquity* 47:382–95.

Graham, Russell W., C. Vance Haynes, Donald L. Johnson, and Marvin Kay

1981 Kimmswick: Clovis Adaptations to Midwestern Environments. *Science* 213:1115–17.

Graham, Russell W., and Marvin Kay

1988 Taphonomic Comparisons of Cultural and Noncultural Faunal Deposits at the Kimmswick and Barnhart Sites, Jefferson County, Missouri. In *Late Pleistocene and Early Holocene Paleoecology and Archeology of the Eastern Great Lakes Region,* edited by Richard S. Laub, Norton G. Miller, and David W. Steadman, 227–40. Bulletin of the Buffalo Society of Natural Sciences, vol. 33. Buffalo, N.Y.

Gramling, Robert

1980 *Underwater Investigation of a Small Gasoline-Powered Stern-Wheeler, Aliceville Lake, Lowndes County, Mississippi.* Report. Delta Research. Submitted to Heritage Conservation and Research Services, Interagency Archaeological Services, Atlanta.

Greengo, Robert E.

1957 *Appraisal of the Archaeological Resources of the Dardanelle Reservoir, Arkansas.* Report. Smithsonian Institution River Basin Surveys, Lincoln, Nebr.

Gregg, Susan A., Keith W. Kintigh, and Robert Whallon

1991 Linking Ethnoarchaeological Interpretation and Archaeological Data: The Sensitivity of Spatial Analytical Methods to Postdepositional Disturbance. In *The Interpretation of Archaeological Spatial Patterning,* edited by E. M. Kroll and T. D. Price, 149–96. Plenum, New York.

Gregory, Hiram F., Jr.

1973 *Eighteenth-Century Caddoan Archaeology: A Study of Models and Interpretation.* Ph.D. diss., Southern Methodist University. University Microfilms, Ann Arbor.

Gregory, Hiram F., Jay C. Blaine, and Sheila Morrison

1982 Presidio de Nuestra Senora Del Pilar de los Adaes: Excavations 1981–1982. Ms. on file, Louisiana Division of Archeology, Baton Rouge.

Gregory, Hiram F., David T. Eschenfelder, Connie B. Eschenfelder, James McCorkle, George A. Strokes, Nancy Bernstein, and Jay C. Blaine.
1984 *A Civil War Military Site Survey: Natchitoches Parish and Environs.* Report. Northwestern State University, Williamson Museum, Natchitoches, LA. Submitted to the Louisiana Division of Archeology, Baton Rouge.

Gregory, Hiram F., Aubra Lee, Jay C. Blaine, David Eschenfelder, and Douglas Raymond
1984 *Excavations 1982: Presidio de Nuestra Senora de Pilar de los Adaes.* Report. Northwestern State University, Natchitoches, La. Submitted to the Office of State Parks, Louisiana Department of Culture, Recreation and Tourism, Baton Rouge.

Gregory, Hiram F., and James McCorkle
1981 *Los Adaes: Historical and Archaeological Background.* Report. Northwestern State University, Natchitoches, La. Submitted to the Office of State Parks, Louisiana Department of Culture, Recreation and Tourism, Baton Rouge.

Gregory, Hiram F., and Clarence H. Webb
1965 European Trade Beads from Six Sites in Natchitoches Parish, Louisiana. *Florida Anthropologist* 18 (3, Pt. 2):15–44.

Griffin, James B.
1952 Prehistoric Cultures of the Central Mississippi Valley. In *Archaeology of the Eastern United States,* edited by J. B. Griffin, 226–38. University of Chicago Press, Chicago.
1961 Relationships between the Caddoan Area and the Mississippi Valley. *Bulletin of the Texas Archeological Society* 31:27–43.
1973 Review of *Archaeological Survey in the Lower Yazoo Basin, Mississippi, 1945–1955,* by P. Phillips. *American Antiquity* 38(3):374–80.
1978 Foreword. In *Mississippian Settlement Patterns,* edited by B. D. Smith, xv–xxii. Academic Press, New York.

Guccione, M. J., R. H. Lafferty III, and L. S. Cummings
1988 Environmental Constraints of Human Settlement in an Evolving Holocene Alluvial System, the Lower Mississippi Valley. *Geoarchaeology* 3:65–84.

Guccione, M. J., W. Prior, and E. M. Rutledge
1990 The Tertiary and Early Quaternary Geology of Crowley's Ridge, Northeast Arkansas and Southeast Missouri. In *Field Guide to the Mississippi Alluvial Valley, Northeast Arkansas and Southeast Missouri,* edited by M. J. Guccione and E. M. Rutledge, 23–44. South-Central Cell, Friends of the Pleistocene, Fayetteville, Ark.

Guccione, M. J., and R. B. Van Arsdale
1995 *Origin and Age of the St. Francis Sunklands Using Drainage Patterns and Sedimentology.* Report submitted to the U.S. Geological Survey.

Guendling, Randall L.
1989a *An Archival Research Study and Archeological Reconnaissance Level Survey of the Cabot Land Application Area, Lonoke County, Arkansas.* Report, AAS Project 712. Arkansas Archeological Survey, Fayetteville. Submitted to Garver and Garver, Inc., Little Rock.
1989b *An Archival and Field Research Study of Cultural Resources within the*

National Cemetery Expansion Area, Pulaski County, Arkansas. Report, AAS Project 714. Arkansas Archeological Survey, Fayetteville. Submitted to Veterans Administration Medical Center, North Little Rock.

1990 *Intensive Survey and Test Excavation of the Cabot Land Application Area, Lonoke County, Arkansas.* Report, AAS Project 726. Arkansas Archeological Survey, Fayetteville. Submitted to Garver and Garver, Inc., Little Rock.

1993a *Archeological Assessment of the Sanders Block, Old Washington State Park, Hempstead County, Arkansas.* Report. Arkansas Archeological Survey, Fayetteville. Submitted to Arkansas Department of Parks and Tourism, Little Rock.

1993b *An Assessment of Archeological Resources in the Area of Bankruptcy Court Additions, Little Rock, Arkansas.* Report, AAS Project 868. Arkansas Archeological Survey, Fayetteville. Submitted to Witsell, Evans, and Rasco, P.A., Little Rock.

Guendling, Randall L., and Mary L. Kwas

1997 *The Historical Archeology of Arkansas's Old State House.* Report. Arkansas Archeological Survey, Fayetteville. Submitted to Department of Arkansas Heritage and Arkansas Commemorative Commission, Little Rock.

Gulf South Research Institute

1977 *Performance of a Cultural Resources Survey, Tennessee-Tombigbee Waterway, Tombigbee River Channel, Alabama and Mississippi.* Report. Gulf South Research Institute. Submitted to the U.S. Army Corps of Engineers, Vicksburg District.

Gums, Bonnie S.

1997 A Comparison of French Colonization in the Illinois Country and the Gulf Coastal Region. Paper presented at the annual meeting of the Society for Historical Archaeology, Corpus Christi, Tex.

Gums, Bonnie S., and Gregory A. Waselkov

1998 Alabama Clay: Nineteenth Century Potteries around Mobile Bay. Paper presented at the annual meeting of the Society for Historical Archaeology, Atlanta.

Haag, William G.

1953 Choctaw Archaeology. *Southeastern Archeological Conference Newsletter* 3(3):25–28.

Haas, Mary R.

1950 *Tunica Texts.* University of California Press, Berkeley and Los Angeles.

Haggett, Peter

1966 *Locational Analysis in Human Geography.* Edward Arnold, London.

Hahn, Thurston H. G., III, Sammy Crawford, and Charles E. Pearson

1994 *Historical and Archaeological Investigations of Doro Plantation, Bolivar County, Mississippi. Beulah Levee Project: Archaeology and History.* Vol. 2. Report. Coastal Environments. Submitted to the U.S. Army Corps of Engineers, Vicksburg District.

Hahn, Thurston H. G. III, Allen R. Saltus Jr., and Stephen R. James Jr.

1994 *Delta Landing: Historical and Archaeological Investigations of Three Sunken Watercraft at Delta, Madison Parish, Louisiana.* Report. Coastal

Environments, Inc., Baton Rouge. Submitted to U.S. Army Corps of Engineers, Vicksburg District, Vicksburg, Miss.

Hally, D. J., and M. Williams
1994 Macon Plateau Site Community Pattern. In *Ocmulgee Archaeology 1936–1986,* edited by D. J. Hally, 84–95. University of Georgia Press, Athens.

Hambacher, Michael J.
1983 *22LO741: A Nineteenth Century Multipurpose Light Industrial Site in Lowndes County, Mississippi.* Report. Michigan State University Museum. Submitted to National Park Service, Mid-Atlantic Regional Office, Philadelphia, Pa.

Hamm, Jim
1989 *Bows and Arrows of the Native Americans: A Complete Step-by-Step Guide to Wooden Bows, Sinew-backed Bows, Composite Bows, Strings, Arrows and Quivers.* Lyons and Burford in cooperation with Bois d'Arc Press, New York.
1992 Bowhunting: Traditional Choices. *Field and Stream* 97(6):24–25.
1994 Plains Indian Bows. In *The Traditional Bowyer's Bible.* Vol. 3. Edited by J. Hamm, 115–42. Lyons and Burford, New York.

Harcourt, James P.
1993 *Slackwater Harbor (Helena).* Report, AAS Project 785. Arkansas Archeological Survey, Fayetteville. Submitted to Phillips County Port Authority, Helena, Ark.

Harcourt, James P., and Jack H. Stewart
1993 *The NOARK Project: The Archaeology of the NOARK Pipeline in the Arkansas River Valley, Northeast Arkansas and Portions of the Ozarks.* Final Report. Arkansas Archeological Survey, Fayetteville.

Hardcastle, R.
1992 Osage Flat Bow. In *The Traditional Bowyer's Bible.* Vol. 1. Edited by J. Hamm, 131–48. Lyons and Burford, New York.

Harper, Loyd, Ruby Harper, R. K. Harris, Inus M. Harris, Edward B. Jelks, and J. Ned Woodall
1967 Ornaments. In *The Gilbert Site: A Norteno Focus Site in Northeast Texas,* edited by Edward B. Jelks, 87–104. *Bulletin of the Texas Archeological Society* 37.

Harrington, Mark R.
1920 *Certain Caddo Sites in Arkansas.* Indian Notes and Monographs, Miscellaneous Series No. 10. Museum of the American Indian, New York.
1960 *The Ozark Bluff Dwellers.* Museum of the American Indian, Heye Foundation, Indian Notes and Monographs No. 12. Museum of the American Indian, New York.

Harris, R. King, Inus Marie Harris, J. C. Blain, and J. Blain
1965 A Preliminary Archaeological and Documentary Study of the Womack Site, Lamar County, Texas. *Bulletin of the Texas Archeological Society* 36:287–364.

Hartigan, John A.
1975 *Clustering Algorithms.* John Wiley and Sons, New York.
1985 Statistical Theory in Clustering. *Journal of Classification* 2:63–76.

Hartley, John D., and A. F. Miller
1977 *Archaeological Investigations at the Bryson-Paddock Site: An Early Contact Period Site on the Southern Plains.* Archeological Site Report No. 32. Oklahoma River Basin Survey, University of Oklahoma Office of Research Administration, Norman.

Haynes, C. Vance, Jr.
1992 Contributions of Radiocarbon Dating to the Geochronology of the Peopling of the New World. In *Radiocarbon after Four Decades,* edited by R. E. Taylor, A. Long, and R. S. Kra, 355–74. Springer-Verlag, New York.

Heldman, Donald P.
1973 *Archaeological Investigations of Fort Toulouse: 1972–73.* Report to the Alabama Historical Commission, Montgomery, and the National Park Service, Washington, D.C.

Hemmings, E. Thomas
1982 *Human Adaptation in the Grand Marais Lowland.* Research Series No. 17. Arkansas Archeological Survey, Fayetteville.

Hempstead, F.
1978 [1890] *A Pictorial History of Arkansas from Earliest Times to the Year 1890.* N. D. Thompson, St. Louis. Facsimile ed. Southern Historical Press, Easley, S.C.

Henige, David
1993 Proxy Data, Historical Method, and the de Soto Expedition. In *The Expedition of Hernando de Soto West of the Mississippi, 1541–1543,* edited by G. A. Young and M. P. Hoffman, 155–72. University of Arkansas Press, Fayetteville.

Hilliard, J. E., and G. Sabo III
1984 Intrasite Analysis and Comparison of the Uses of Various Types of Small Subsurface Tests at the James Leeper Site, Fayetteville, Arkansas. Paper presented at Annual Meeting of the Society for Historical Archeology, Williamsburg, Va.

Hodges, T. L., and Mrs. T. L. Hodges
1942 Possibilities for the Archeologist and Historian in Eastern Arkansas. *Arkansas Historical Quarterly* 2(2):141–63.

Hoffman, Michael P.
1981 Arkansas for Arkansans: S. C. Delinger and His Contributions to the Study of Southeastern Prehistory. Paper presented at 46th Annual Meeting of the Society for American Archaeology, San Diego.
1985 Arkansas Antiquities Dealers in the 1920–1950 Era. Paper presented at the annual meeting of the Southern Anthropological Society, Fayetteville, Ark.
1986 The Protohistoric Period in the Lower and Central Arkansas River Valley in Arkansas. In *The Protohistoric Period in the Mid-South: 1500–1700,* edited by D. H. Dye and R. C. Brister, 24–37. Archaeological Reports No. 18. Mississippi Department of Archives and History, Jackson.
1992 Protohistoric Tunican Indians in Arkansas. *Arkansas Historical Quarterly* 51(1):30–53.
1993 Identification of Ethnic Groups Contacted by the de Soto Expedition

in Arkansas. In *The Expedition of Hernando de Soto West of the Mississippi, 1541–1543,* edited by Gloria A. Young and Michael P. Hoffman. University of Arkansas Press, Fayetteville.

Hogue, S. Holmes, Susanne Bufkin, and Heather Rushing
1996 European Contact, Burial Behavior, Health, and Diet: A Case Study from Starkville, Miss. *Mississippi Archaeology* 31(2): 1–22.

Holder, Preston
1957 *Archaeological Field Research on the Problem of the Locations of Arkansas Post, Arkansas, 1686–1804.* National Park Service, Southeast Archaeological Center, Macon, Ga.

Holland, Claudia C.
1986 *Investigating Twentieth-Century Plantation Tenancy through Ethnoarchaeology: An Example from Central Louisiana.* Master's thesis, Louisiana State University, Baton Rouge.

Holland-Braund, Kathryn E.
1996 *Deerskins and Duffels: The Creek Indian Trade with Anglo-America, 1685–1815.* Bison Books, University of Nebraska Press, Lincoln.

Hon, David N. S.
1988 *Scientific Assessment of the Preservation Treatments Conducted on the U.S.S.* Cairo *and Development of Preservation Alternatives.* Final Report (revised). Clemson University, Clemson, S.C. Submitted to National Park Service, Southeast Region, Atlanta.

House, John H.
1975a A Functional Typology for Cache Project Surface Collections. In *The Cache River Archeological Project: An Experiment in Contract Archeology,* assembled by Michael B. Schiffer and John H. House, 55–73. Research Series 8. Arkansas Archeological Survey, Fayetteville.

1975b Prehistoric Lithic Resource Utilization in the Cache Basin: Crowley's Ridge Chert and Quartzite and Pitkin Chert. In *The Cache River Archeological Project: An Experiment in Contract Archeology,* assembled by Michael B. Schiffer and John H. House, 281–91. Research Series 8. Arkansas Archeological Survey, Fayetteville.

1977a Survey Data and Regional Models in Historical Archeology. In *Research Strategies in Historical Archeology,* edited by Stanley South, 241–60. Academic Press, New York.

1977b Regional Data in Historic Archeology: Examples from Environmental Impact Surveys. *Conference on Historic Sites Archeology Papers,* 10:140–51.

1984 Tom Watts Collection Contributed to the Survey and the Jefferson County Courthouse Historical Museum. *Arkansas Archeological Society Field Notes* 196:3–4.

1987 Kent Phase Investigations in Eastern Arkansas, 1978–1984. *Mississippi Archeology* 22:46–60.

1991a Resurveying the Bartholomew Bypass Route near Pine Bluff. *Arkansas Archeological Society Field Notes* 243:3.

1991b *Monitoring Mississippian Dynamics: Time, Settlement and Ceramic Variation in the Kent Phase, Eastern Arkansas.* Ph.D. diss., Southern Illinois University, Carbondale.

1993 Dating the Kent Phase. *Southeastern Archeology* 12:21–32.

1997 Excavations at the Menard-Hodges Site, 1997. Paper presented at the annual meeting of the Arkansas Archeological Society, Little Rock.

1998 Excavations at the Menard-Hodges Site, 1998. Paper presented at the annual meeting of the Arkansas Archeological Society, Little Rock.

House, John H., and Michael B. Schiffer

1975 Archeological Survey in the Cache River Basin. In *The Cache River Archeological Project: An Experiment in Contract Archeology*, assembled by Michael B. Schiffer and John H. House, 37–53. Research Series 8. Arkansas Archeological Survey, Fayetteville.

House, J. H., T. C. Klinger, and M. B. Schiffer

1975 A Test of the Dalton Settlement Pattern Hypothesis Using Cache Project Survey Data. In *The Cache River Archeological Project: An Experiment in Contract Archeology,* edited by M. Schiffer and J. House, 93–101. Research Series No. 8. Arkansas Archeological Survey, Fayetteville.

Hubbert, Charles W.

1977 *A Cultural Resource Survey of the Bay Springs Segment of the Tennessee-Tombigbee Waterway.* Report of Investigations 3. Office of Archaeological Research, University of Alabama, Tuscaloosa.

Hudson, Charles M.

1976 *The Southeastern Indians.* University of Tennessee Press, Knoxville.

1985 De Soto in Arkansas: A Brief Synopsis. *Field Notes of the Arkansas Archeological Society* 205:3–12.

1993 Reconstructing the de Soto Expedition Route West of the Mississippi River: Summary and Contents. In *The Hernando de Soto Expedition West of the Mississippi, 1541–1543,* edited by Gloria A. Young and Michael P. Hoffman, 143–54, University of Arkansas Press, Fayetteville.

Hudson, Jack C., and Kay Goelzer Hudson

1974 An Analysis of a Cache of Gunflints from a Site in New Orleans: Gallier House (16OR46). *Conference on Historic Sites Archaeology Papers,* 7:2–11.

Hudson, Charles M., Marvin T. Smith, and Chester B. DePratter

1990 The Hernando de Soto Expedition: From Mabila to the Mississippi River. In *Towns and Temples along the Mississippi,* edited by D. H. Dye and C. A. Cox, 181–207. University of Alabama Press, Tuscaloosa.

Huttig News, Huttig, Arkansas

January 30, 1909:1

February 6, 1909:1

Jackson, Donald Dean (ed.)

1962 *Letters of the Louis and Clark Expedition: With Related Documents 1783–1854.* 2 vols. University of Illinois Press, Urbana.

Jackson, H. Edwin

1992 *The Ables Creek Site: A Protohistoric Cemetery in Southeast Arkansas.* Research Series No. 42. Arkansas Archeological Survey, Fayetteville.

Jackson, H. Edwin, and Marvin D. Jeter

1991 Late Archaic Settlement and Poverty Point Connections in the Lowlands of Southeast Arkansas: An Initial Assessment. *Mississippi Archaeology* 26(2):33–55.

Jain, A. K., and R. C. Dubes
1988 *Algorithms for Clustering Data.* Prentice Hall, Englewood Cliffs, N.J.

Janzen, Daniel H., and Paul S. Martin
1982 Neotropical Anachronisms: The Fruits the Gomphotheres Ate. *Science* 215(1):19–27.

Jelks, Edward B.
1967 The Gilbert Site: A Norteno Focus Site in Northeast Texas. *Bulletin of the Texas Archeological Society* 37:1–247.

Jenkins, Ned J., and Richard A. Krause
1986 *The Tombigbee Watershed in Southeastern Prehistory.* University of Alabama Press, Tuscaloosa.

Jennings, Jesse D.
1952 Prehistory of the Lower Mississippi Valley. In *Archaeology of Eastern United States,* edited by J. B. Griffin, 256–71. University of Chicago Press, Chicago.

Jeter, Marvin D.
1982 The Archeology of Southeast Arkansas: An Overview for the 1980s. In *Arkansas Archeology in Review,* edited by N. L. Trubowitz and M. D. Jeter, 76–131. Research Series No. 15. Arkansas Archeological Survey, Fayetteville.

1986 Tunicans West of the Mississippi: A Summary of Early Historic and Archaeological Evidence. In *The Protohistoric Period in the Mid-South: 1500–1700,* edited by D. H. Dye and R. C. Brister, 38–63. Archaeological Reports No. 18. Mississippi Department of Archives and History.

1988 (ed.) *The Burris Site and Beyond: Archeological Survey and Testing along a Pipeline Corridor and Excavation at a Mississippian Village, Northeast Arkansas.* Research Report No. 27. Arkansas Archeological Survey, Fayetteville.

1990a Review of *Tunica Archaeology,* by Jeffrey P. Brain. *Southeastern Archaeology* 9(2):147–49.

1990b (ed.) *Edward Palmer's Arkansaw Mounds.* University of Arkansas Press, Fayetteville.

1996 Review: *Archaeology of the Southeastern United States: Paleoindian to World War I,* by Judith A. Bense. *Mississippi Archaeology* 31(2):73–81.

n.d.a The Eagle Lake Mounds Site (3BR4), Southern Bradley County, Arkansas. Report in preparation for publication by the Arkansas Archeological Survey, Fayetteville.

n.d.b Archeological Salvage Investigations at the Saline-fifteen Site (3BR119). Report in preparation, Arkansas Archeological Survey, Fayetteville, for submission to Arkansas Highway and Transportation Department.

Jeter, Marvin D., Kathleen H. Cande, and John J. Mintz
1990 *Goldsmith Oliver 2 (3PU306): A Protohistoric Archeological Site near Little Rock, Arkansas.* Report. Arkansas Archeological Survey, Fayetteville. Submitted to Federal Aviation Administration, Fort Worth.

Jeter, Marvin D., and H. Edwin Jackson
1994 Poverty Point Extraction and Exchange: The Arkansas Lithic

Connections. In *Exchange in the Lower Mississippi Valley and Contiguous Areas at 1100 B.C.*, edited by J. L. Gibson, 133–206. *Louisiana Archaeology* 17.

Jeter, Marvin D., Hector Neff, Michael D. Glascock, and James W. Cogswell
n.d. Chemical Comparisons of Southeast Arkansas Ceramics and Clays: Refining the Mississippi Valley and Southeastern Databases. Manuscript in preparation.

Jeter, Marvin D., Jerome C. Rose, G. Ishmael Williams Jr., and Anna M. Harmon
1989 *Archeology and Bioarcheology of the Lower Mississippi Valley and Trans-Mississippi South in Arkansas and Louisiana.* Research Series No. 37. Arkansas Archeological Survey, Fayetteville.

Jeter, Marvin D., and G. Ishmael Williams Jr.
1989 Lithic Horizons and Early Cultures. In *Archeology and Bioarcheology of the Lower Mississippi Valley and Trans-Mississippi South in Arkansas and Louisiana,* edited by Marvin D. Jeter, J. C. Rose, G. I. Williams Jr., and A. M. Harmon, 71–110. Research Series No. 37. Arkansas Archeological Survey, Fayetteville.

John, Elizabeth A. H.
1975 *Storms Brewed in Other Men's Worlds: The Confrontation of Indians, Spanish and French in the Southwest 1540–1795.* Texas A&M University Press, College Station.
1992 A Case Study in the Interdependence of Archeology and History: The Spanish Fort Sites on the Red River. *Bulletin of the Texas Archeological Society* 63:197–209.

John Milner Associates
1978 *A Final Report on Archeological Investigations, Historical Research, and Architectural Analysis for Windsor Ruins Historic Site, Claiborne County, Mississippi.* Report. John Milner Associates. Submitted to Mississippi Department of Archives and History, Jackson.

Johnson, Jay K., Patricia Galloway, and Walter Belokon
1989 Historic Chickasaw Settlement Patterns in Lee County, Mississippi: A First Approximation. *Mississippi Archaeology* 24(2):45–52.

Johnson, Jay K., Geoffrey R. Lehmann, James R. Atkinson, Susan L. Scott, and Andrea Shea
1991 *Protohistoric Chickasaw Settlement Patterns and the de Soto Route in Northeast Mississippi.* Final report, National Endowment for the Humanities Grant No. RO-21879-89 and National Geographic Grant No. 4006–89.

Jolley, Robert L.
1984 *An Archaeological Assessment of the Proposed Peabody Place Mall and Office Complex, Memphis, Tennessee.* Report. Cultural Resource Consultants, Nashville. Submitted to Belz Enterprises, Memphis.

Jones, George T., Donald K. Grayson, and Charlotte Beck
1983 Artifact Class Richness and Sample Size in Archaeological Surface Assemblages. In *Lulu Linear Punctated: Essays in Honor of George Irving Quimby,* edited by R. C. Dunnell and D. K. Grayson, 55–73. Anthropological Papers No. 72. University of Michigan, Museum of Anthropology, Ann Arbor.

Joseph, J. W.
1986 *Archaeological Testing at the Site of the Peabody Place Mall and Office Complex, Memphis, Tennessee, Phase I Investigations.* Report. Garrow and Associates, Atlanta. Submitted to Belz Enterprises, Memphis.

Joutel, Henri
1714 *A Journal of the Last Voyage Perform'd by Monsr. De La Sale, to the Gulph of Mexico, to Find out the Mouth of the Mississippi River.* English translation of the 1713 French original, published by A. Bell, London. Reprinted in 1966 by Readex Microprint Corporation.

Jurney, David H.
1975 The Tilles House: A Preliminary Report of a Weekend Test Excavation. Ms. on file, Arkansas Archeological Survey, Fayetteville.

Jurney, David H., and William Young
1995 Southwestern Pottery and Turquoise in Northeastern Texas. *Caddoan Archeology Newsletter* 6(2):15–28.

Kaye, Samuel H.
1988 An 1822–1836 Trash Pit in Columbus, Mississippi. Ms. report on file, Mississippi Department of Archives and History, Jackson.

Keel, Bennie C., John E. Cornelison Jr., and David M. Brewer
1996 *Regionwide Archeological Survey Plan, Southeast Field Area, National Park Service.* Southeast Archeological Center, National Park Service, Tallahassee, Fla.

Keene, David
1991 Fort De Chartres: Archaeology in the Illinois Country. In *French Colonial Archaeology: The Illinois Country and the Western Great Lakes,* edited by John A. Walthall, 29–41. University of Illinois Press, Chicago.

Kelley, David B.
1981 *A Cultural Resources Survey of Levee Enlargement and Berm Areas, Lakeport to Harwood, Chicot County, Arkansas.* Report. Coastal Environments, Inc., Baton Rouge. Submitted to U.S. Army Corps of Engineers, Vicksburg District.
1997 (ed.) *Two Caddoan Farmsteads in the Red River Valley: The Archeology of the McLelland and Joe Clark Sites.* Research Series No. 51. Arkansas Archeological Survey, Fayetteville.

Kelley, David B., Donald G. Hunter, Paul S. Gardner, Daniel C. Weinand, Angela Tine, and Larry L. Tiesen
1996 The McLelland and Joe Clark Sites: Protohistoric-Historic Caddo Farmsteads in the Red River Valley of Northwest Louisiana. *Southeastern Archeology* 15(1):81–102.

Kern, John R.
1979 *Study of Archaeological, Architectural and Historic Resources within the Memphis Metropolitan Area: TN, AR, MS: Horn Lake Creek Area.* Gilbert-Commonwealth, Inc. Submitted to Corps of Engineers Memphis District, Memphis.
1980 *Study of Archaeological, Architectural and Historic Resources within the Memphis Metropolitan Area TN, AR, MS: Wolf-Loosahatchie River.* Gilbert-Commonwealth, Inc. Submitted to Corps of Engineers Memphis District, Memphis.

1981a *Study of Archaeological, Architectural and Historic Resources within the Memphis Metropolitan Area: TN, AR, MS: Memphis Metro Area.* Gilbert-Commonwealth. Submitted to Corps of Engineers Memphis District, Memphis.

1981b *Study of Archaeological, Architectural and Historical Resources within the Memphis Metropolitan Area TN, AR, and MS: Nonconnah Creek.* Gilbert-Commonwealth, Inc. Submitted to Corps of Engineers Memphis District, Memphis.

Kern, John R., Steven F. Miller, Ira Berlin, and Joseph P. Reidy

1981 *Phase II Historical Investigations at Sharpley's Bottom Historic Sites, Tombigbee River Multiresource District, Alabama and Mississippi.* Interim Report. Commonwealth Associates, Inc., Jackson, Miss. Submitted to National Park Service, Southwest Region, Santa Fe.

Kidd, Stephen

1998 The Identification of Structures at Old Augusta (Perry County, Mississippi). Paper presented at the annual meeting of the Society for Historical Archaeology, Atlanta.

Kidder, Tristram R.

1986 *Final Report on Archaeological Test Excavations in the Central Boeuf Basin, Louisiana, 1985.* Lower Mississippi Survey Bulletin No. 10. Peabody Museum, Harvard University, Cambridge.

1988 The Koroa Indians of the Lower Mississippi Valley. *Mississippi Archaeology* 23(2):1–42.

1991 Review of *Coles Creek and Mississippi Period Foragers in the Felsenthal Region of the Lower Mississippi Valley,* edited by Frank F. Schambach. *Mississippi Archaeology* 26(2):78–85.

1992 Excavations at the Jordan site (16MO1), Morehouse Parish, Louisiana. *Southeastern Archaeology* 11(2):109–31.

1993 The Glendora Phase: Protohistoric-Early Historic Culture Dynamics on the Lower Ouachita River. In *Archaeology of Eastern North America: Papers in Honor of Stephen Williams,* edited by James B. Stoltman. Archaeological Report No. 25. Mississippi Department of Archives and History, Jackson.

King, Frances B.

1990 The Archeobotany of the Bangs Slough Site: Presettlement Environment and Evidence of Aboriginal Plant Use. In *Coles Creek and Mississippi Period Foragers in the Felsenthal Region of the Lower Mississippi Valley,* edited by Frank F. Schambach, 85–94. Research Series No. 39. Arkansas Archeological Survey, Fayetteville.

King, J. E., and W. H. Allen Jr.

1977 A Holocene Vegetation Record from the Mississippi River Valley, Southeastern Missouri. *Quaternary Research* 8:307–23.

Kintigh, Keith W., and Albert J. Ammerman

1982 Heuristic Approaches to Spatial Analysis in Archaeology. *American Antiquity* 47(1):31–63.

Kline, Gerald W.

1991 Abstract of *Archaeological Testing and Data Recovery at the Morning Sun Farmstead Site (40SY508), Shelby County, Tennessee. Tennessee Anthropological Association Newsletter* 16(5):2–8.

Klinger, Timothy C.
1976 *An Assessment of Impacts on the Cultural Resources of the Davidsonville State Park Resulting from Proposed Park Improvements.* Report. Arkansas Archeological Survey, Fayetteville. Submitted to the Arkansas Department of Parks and Tourism, Little Rock.
1977 Parkin Archeology: A Report on the 1966 Field School Test Excavations at the Parkin Site. *Arkansas Archeologist* 16–18:45–80.
1986 *Village Creek: An Explicitly Regional Approach to the Study of Cultural Resources.* Research Report 26. Arkansas Archeological Survey, Fayetteville. (Originally prepared 1976.)

Klinger, Timothy C., Roy Cochran Jr., and Clyde D. Dollar
1983 *Berry Cemetery and George Berry Washington: Archaeological Mitigation and Historical Documentation of 3CT47 along the Big Creek Enlargement and Diversion, Item 1, Crittenden County, Arkansas.* Report. Historic Preservation Associates, Inc., Fayetteville. Submitted to U.S. Army Corps of Engineers, Vicksburg Division.

Klinger, Timothy C., Steven M. Imhoff, and Roy J. Cochran Jr.
1983 *Brougham Lake.* Final Report 83-7, Contract DACW66-80-C-0082. Historic Preservation Associates. Submitted to the U.S. Army Corps of Engineers, Memphis District.

Klinger, Timothy C., and Richard P. Kandare
1988 *Hunter-Dawson: Archeological Investigations at the Hunter-Dawson State Historic Site, 23NM542, in New Madrid, New Madrid County, Missouri.* Historic Preservation Associates Reports 88–3, Fayetteville, Ark.

Klinger, Timothy C., and Mark A. Mathis (comp.)
1978 *St. Francis II: An Archeological Assessment of Three COE-Sponsored Channelization Projects in the St. Francis Basin, Arkansas.* Research Report No. 14. Arkansas Archeological Survey, Fayetteville.

Knapp, Mrs. Gilbert
1876a Letter to W. H. Barry, 8 April, National Anthropological Archives Accession 5153. Smithsonian Institution, Washington, D.C.
1876b Letter to J. Henry, 11 April. National Anthropological Archives Accession 5153. Smithsonian Institution, Washington, D.C.
1878 Earth-works on the Arkansas River, Sixteen Miles below Little Rock. *Annual Report of the Board of Regents of the Smithsonian Institution* 1877:251. Washington, D.C.

Kniffen, Fred B., Hiram F. Gregory, and George A. Stokes
1987 *The Historic Indian Tribes of Louisiana from 1541 to the Present.* Louisiana State University Press, Baton Rouge.

Knight, V. J., Jr. (ed.)
1996 *The Moundville Expeditions of Clarence Bloomfield Moore.* University of Alabama Press, Tuscaloosa.

Kowalewski, Stephen A., and James W. Hatch
1991 The Sixteenth-Century Expansion of Settlement in the Upper Oconee Watershed, Georgia. *Southeastern Archaeology* 10:1–17.

Krieger, Alex D.
1946 *Culture Complexes and Chronology in Northern Texas, with Extensions of Puebloan Datings to the Mississippi Valley.* Publication 4640. University of Texas, Austin.

Kutzbach, J. E., and T. Webb III
1993 Conceptual Basis for Understanding Late-Quaternary Climates. In *Climates Since the Last Glacial Maximum,* edited by H. E. Wright Jr., J. E. Kutzbach, T. Webb III, W. F. Ruddiman, F. A. Street-Perrott, and P. J. Bartlein, 5–11. University of Minnesota Press, Minneapolis.

Kwas, Mary L., and Randall L. Guendling
1999 William E. Woodruff and the Cherry-Cumberland Street Print Shop. Sponsored Research Program, Arkansas Archeological Survey, report submitted to Arkansas Territorial Restoration, Little Rock.

Lafferty, Robert H., III
1994 Prehistoric Exchange in the Lower Mississippi Valley. In *Prehistoric Exchange Systems in North America,* edited by Timothy G. Baugh and Jonathan E. Ericson, 177–213. Plenum Press, New York.

Lafferty, Robert H., III, Robert F. Cande, Michael C. Sierzchula, James T. Toney, and Margaret J. Guccione
1993 *Archeological Testing of 20 Archeological Sites, Eaker Air Force Base, Mississippi County, Arkansas.* Report. Mid-Continental Research Associates, Lowell, Ark. Submitted to Earth Technology Corporation and U.S. Air Force Civil Engineers.

Lafferty, Robert H., III, Margaret J. Guccione, Linda J. Scott, D. Kate Aasen, Beverly J. Watkins, Michael C. Sierzchula, and Paul F. Baumann
1987 *A Cultural Resources Survey, Testing and Geomorphic Examination of Ditches 10, 12, and 29, Mississippi County, Arkansas.* Report 86-5, Contract No. DACW66-86-C-0034. Mid-Continental Research Associates, Inc. Submitted to the U.S. Army Corps of Engineers, Memphis District.

Lafferty, Robert H., III, and Kathleen M. Hess (eds.)
1995 *Archeological Investigations in the New Madrid Floodway.* Report 95-7. Mid-Continental Research Associates, Lowell, Ark. Submitted to U.S. Army Corps of Engineers, Memphis District.

Lafferty, Robert H., III, Lawrence G. Santeford, Phyllis A. Morse, and L. M. Chapman
1984 *A Cultural Resources Survey and Evaluation in the Tyronza River Watershed Phase I Area, Mississippi County, Arkansas.* Mid-Continental Research Investigations No. 84-2. Submitted to USDA, Soil Conservation Service, Little Rock.

Lafferty, Robert H., III, Lawrence G. Santeford, Carol S. Spears, Neal H. Lopinot, Sharon A. Lopinot, Michael C. Sierzchula, and Kathleen M. Hess
1985 *Cultural Resources Data Recovery in Basins 14, 15, 20, and 21 of the Fourche Creek Watershed, Randolph County, Arkansas.* Report No. 85-5. Mid-Continental Research Associates, Lowell, Ark. Submitted to USDA, Soil Conservation Service, Little Rock.

Lafferty, Robert H., III, Carol S. Spears, Phyllis A. Morse, and Hope N. Gillespie
1985 *A Cultural Resources Survey, Testing and Predictive Model in the Tyronza River Watershed Phase II Mississippi and Poinsett Counties, Arkansas.* Associates Report 85-1, Contract No. 53-7103-4-36817. Mid-Continental Research Associates, Inc. Submitted to USDA, Soil Conservation Service, Little Rock.

Lafferty, Robert H., III, and Barbara J. Watkins
1987 Previous Research and Cultural History. In *A Cultural Resources Survey: Testing and Geomorphic Examination of Ditches 10, 12, and 29, Mississippi County, Arkansas*, by Robert H. Lafferty III and others, 41–66. Report No 86-5. Mid-Continental Research Associates. Submitted to U.S. Army Corps of Engineers, Memphis.

Laubin, Reginald, and Gladys Laubin
1980 *American Indian Archery.* University of Oklahoma Press, Norman and London.

Ledbetter, R. Jerald, W. Dean Wood, Karen G. Wood, Robbie F. Ethridge, and Chad O. Braley
1987 *Cultural Resource Survey of Allatoona Lake Area, Georgia.* Report, Contract DACW01-85-C-0183. Southeastern Archaeological Services, Inc., Athens. Submitted to U.S. Army Corps of Engineers, Mobile District.

Lemley, Harry J.
1936 Discoveries Indicating a Pre-Caddo Culture on Red River in Arkansas. *Bulletin of the Texas Archeological and Paleontological Society* 8:25–55.
1942 Prehistoric Novaculite Quarries of Arkansas. *Bulletin of the Texas Archeological and Paleontological Society* 14:32–37.

Lemley, Harry J., and S. C. Dickinson
1937 Archaeological Investigations on Bayou Macon in Arkansas. *Bulletin of the Texas Archeological and Paleontological Society* 9:11–47.

Lewis, Thomas M. N., Madeline Kneberg Lewis, and Lynne P. Sullivan
1995 *The Prehistory of the Chickamauga Basin.* Vol. 1. Compiled and edited by Lynne P. Sullivan. University of Tennessee Press, Knoxville.

Lopinot, Neal H.
n.d. Plant Remains from Site 3BR119. In *Archeological Salvage Investigations at the Saline-Fifteen Site (3BR119)*, by M. D. Jeter. Report in preparation, Arkansas Archeological Survey, Fayetteville, for submission to Arkansas Highway and Transportation Department.

Lottinville, Savoie (ed.)
1980 *A Journal of Travels into the Arkansas Territory During the Year 1819*, by Thomas Nuttall. University of Oklahoma Press, Norman.

Luckett, William Wallace
1937 Report on the Lower Water Battery Magazine. Included in 1966 "Background Information: The Fort Donelson River Batteries." On file, Fort Donelson National Battlefield, Dover, Tenn.

Lumb, Lisa C., and Charles H. McNutt
1988 *Chucalissa: Excavations in Units 2 and 6, 1959–67.* Occasional Papers No. 15. Anthropological Research Center, Memphis State University, Memphis.

Lynott, Mark J.
1980 Prehistoric Bison Populations of North-Central Texas. *Bulletin of the Texas Archeological Society* 50:89–101.

Lyon, Edwin A.
1996 *A New Deal for Southeastern Archaeology.* University of Alabama Press, Tuscaloosa.

Mainfort, Robert C., Jr.
1979 *Indian Social Dynamics in the Period of European Contact: Fletcher Site Cemetery, Bay County, Michigan.* Anthropological Series 1 (4). Publications of the Museum, Michigan State University, East Lansing.
1980 *Archaeological Investigations at Fort Pillow State Historic Area 1976–1978.* Research Series No. 4. Tennessee Department of Conservation, Division of Archaeology, Nashville.
1991 An Overview of Late Mississippian Sites in West Tennessee. Paper presented to the Southeastern Archaeological Conference, Jackson, Miss.
1996 Late Period Chronology in the Central Mississippi Valley: A Western Tennessee Perspective. *Southeastern Archaeology* 15(2): 172–81.

Manger, Walter L.
1986 Regional Geological Setting and the Availability of Various Raw Materials. In *Village Creek: An Explicitly Regional Approach to the Study of Cultural Resources,* edited by T. C. Klinger, 204–13. Research Report 26. Arkansas Archeological Survey, Fayetteville.

Marked Tree Gazette, Marked Tree, Arkansas
March 25, 1910:1

Marshall Republican, Marshall, Arkansas
April 27, 1934:4

Martin, Patrick E.
1978 *An Inquiry into the Locations and Characteristics of Jacob Bright's Trading House and William Montgomery's Tavern.* Research Series No. 11. Arkansas Archeological Survey, Fayetteville.

Martin, William A., and Robert D. Jones
1978 *The Conway Water Supply: An Intensive Archeological and Historical Survey of a Proposed Reservoir Area in Conway County, Arkansas.* Report. Arkansas Archeological Survey, Fayetteville. Submitted to the U.S. Army Corps of Engineers, Little Rock District.

Mason, Otis Tufton
1972 *North American Indian Bows, Arrows and Quivers.* Carl J. Pugliese, Yonkers, N.Y.

Mathis, Mark A.
1986 Prehistoric Chert Utilization: An Analysis Using the 1976 Village Creek Collections. In *Village Creek: An Explicitly Regional Approach to the Study of Cultural Resources*, assembled by Timothy C. Klinger, 272–308. Research Report 26. Arkansas Archeological Survey, Fayetteville.

Mattison, Ray H.
1957 *Report on the Historical Investigations of Arkansas Post, Arkansas.* U.S. National Park Service, Region Two, Omaha.

McBride, Kim A.
1984 Differentials in Wealth in Nineteenth Century Rural Mississippi: The Effects of Race, Social Class, Household Structure, and Economic Change. Paper presented at the annual meeting of the Society for Historical Archaeology, Williamsburg, Va.

McBride, W. Stephen
1984 From Town to Country: Changing Refuse Disposal Patterns at

Barton Townsite, 1848–1935. Paper presented at the annual meeting of the Society for Historical Archaeology, Williamsburg, Va.
1987 A Village Blacksmith in the Antebellum South: Archaeological Investigations at the Griswold Shop, Barton, Mississippi. *Southeastern Archaeology* 6(2):79–92.
1994 Colbert and Barton, Extinct Townsites on the Upper Tombigbee. Paper presented at the meeting of State Historic Preservation Officers, Southeastern Region, Columbus, Miss.

McClurkan, Burney B.
1968 *Archaeological Investigations at Fort Curtis, Helena Arkansas.* Report. Arkansas Archeological Survey, Fayetteville. Submitted to the Phillips County Historical Society, Helena, Ark.
1971 The Search for Fort Desha. *Arkansas Archeological Society Field Notes* 77:5–6.
1972 Fort Desha, the Location of Arkansas Post ca. 1735–1750. *Conference on Historic Sites Archaeology Papers* 6:32–39.

McCrocklin, Claude
1985 The Red River Coushatta Indian Villages of Northwest Louisiana, 1790–1835. *Louisiana Archeology* 12:129–78.
1992a Three Historic Sites on Red River: Tara (3MI292) and 3MI297. *Arkansas Archeologist* 31:31–41.
1992b Three Historic Sites on Red River: A Possible Historic Delaware Indian Site. *Arkansas Archeologist* 31:42–52.

McGimsey, Charles R., III
1997 Federal Archeology. Paper presented at the Mid-South Archaeological Conference, Jonesboro, Ark.

McNutt, Charles H.
1996 The Central Mississippi Valley: A Summary. In *Prehistory of the Central Mississippi Valley*, 187–257. University of Alabama Press, Tuscaloosa.

Medford, Larry D.
1972 Agricultural Destruction of Archeological Sites in Northeast Arkansas. In *Site Destruction Due to Agricultural Practices*, by J. L. Ford, M. A. Rolingson, and L. D. Medford, 41–82. Research Series 3. Arkansas Archeological Survey, Fayetteville.

Meyers, Robert A.
1997 Cherokee Pioneers in Arkansas: The St. Francis Years, 1785–1813. *Arkansas Historical Quarterly* 56 (2):127–57.

Milligan, Glenn W.
1980 An Examination of the Effect of Six Types of Error Perturbation on Fifteen Clustering Algorithms. *Psychometrika* 45(3):325–42.
1996 Clustering Validation: Results and Implications for Applied Analyses. In *Clustering and Classification*, edited by P. Arabie, L. J. Hubert, and G. De Soete, 341–76. World Scientific, River Edge, N.J.

Milligan, Glenn W., and Martha C. Cooper
1985 An Examination of Procedures for Determining the Number of Clusters in a Data Set. *Psychometrika* 50(2):159–79.

Milner, George R., David G. Anderson, and Marvin T. Smith
n.d. The Distribution of Eastern Woodland Peoples at the Prehistoric and

Historic Interface. In *Societies in Eclipse,* edited by D. S. Brose, C. W. Cowan, and R. C. Mainfort. Smithsonian Institution Press, Washington, D.C. In press.

Minnerly, W. Lee

1982 *Oral Historical, Documentary, and Archaeological Investigations of Colbert, Barton, and Vinton, Mississippi: An Interim Report On Phase I of the Tombigbee Historic Townsites Project -Volume I: Text.* Report. Michigan State University Museum. Submitted to the U.S. National Park Service, Mid-Atlantic Regional Office, Philadelphia, Pa.

1983a *A Computer Compatible System for the Categorization, Enumeration, and Retrieval of Nineteenth and Early Twentieth Century Archaeological Material Culture -Part I: Codebook.* Report. Michigan State University Museum. Submitted to the U.S. Army Corps of Engineers, Mobile District, and the U.S. National Park Service, Mid-Atlantic Regional Office, Philadelphia, Pa.

1983b *Oral Historical, Documentary, and Archeological Investigations of Barton and Vinton, Mississippi: An Interim Report on Phase II of the Tombigbee Historic Townsites Project.* Report. Michigan State University Museum. Submitted to the U.S. National Park Service, Mid-Atlantic Regional Office, Philadelphia, Pa.

Mooney, Timothy

1994 *Many Choctaw Standing: An Archaeological Study of Culture Change in the Early Historic Period.* Master's thesis, University of North Carolina, Chapel Hill.

Moore, Clarence B.

1908 Certain Mounds of Arkansas and of Mississippi. *Journal of the Academy of Natural Sciences of Philadelphia* 13:480–600.

1911 Some Aboriginal Sites on Mississippi River. *Journal of the Academy of Natural Sciences of Philadelphia* 14:366–480.

1913 Some Aboriginal Sites in Louisiana and in Arkansas. *Journal of the Academy of Natural Sciences of Philadelphia* 16(1):5–93.

Moore, Jackson W., Jr.

1962 Status of the Fort Smith Excavations. *Arkansas Archeologist* 3(10):10.

1963a The Archeology of Fort Smith I. *Arkansas Archeologist* 4(10):14.

1963b The Archeology of Fort Smith I. Ms. on file, U.S. National Park Service, Southeast Archaeological Center, Macon, Ga.

1963c *The Archeology of Fort Smith I: Fort Smith National Historic Site.* U.S. National Park Service, Southeast Region, Atlanta.

Moorehead, Warren K.

1931 *Archaeology of the Arkansas River Valley.* Yale University Press, New Haven.

Morse, Dan F.

1969 Introducing Northeast Arkansas Prehistory. *Arkansas Archeologist* 10:13–30.

1970 Preliminary Notes on a Recent Mastodon and Tapir Find in Northeast Arkansas. *Arkansas Archeologist* 11(3):9–20.

1971a The Hawkins Cache: A Significant Dalton Find in Northeast Arkansas. *Arkansas Archeologist* 12(1):9–20.

1971b An Historic Indian Grave near Blytheville, Arkansas. *Arkansas Archeologist* 12(3):56–60.

1973 Dalton Culture in Northeast Arkansas. *Florida Anthropologist* 25:28–38.

1975a Paleo-Indian in the Land of Opportunity: Preliminary Report on the Excavations at the Sloan Site (3GE94). In *The Cache River Archeological Project: An Experiment in Contract Archeology*, compiled by Michael B. Schiffer and John H. House, 135–43. Research Series 8. Arkansas Archeological Survey, Fayetteville.

1975b Reply to Schiffer. In *The Cache River Archeological Project: An Experiment in Contract Archeology*, compiled by Michael B. Schiffer and John House, 113–19. Research Series 8. Arkansas Archeological Survey, Fayetteville.

1977a Dalton Settlement Systems: Reply to Schiffer (2). *Plains Anthropologist* 22:149–58.

1977b The Penetration of Northeast Arkansas by Mississippian Culture. In *For the Director: Research Essays in Honor of James B. Griffin,* edited by Charles E. Cleland, 186–211. Anthropological Papers 61. Museum of Anthropology, University of Michigan.

1989 (ed.) *Nodena*. Research Series No. 30. Arkansas Archeological Survey, Fayetteville.

1990 The Nodena Phase. In *Towns and Temples along the Mississippi,* edited by D. H. Dye and C. A. Cox, 69–97. University of Alabama Press, Tuscaloosa.

1997a *Sloan: A Paleoindian Dalton Cemetery in Arkansas.* Smithsonian Institution Press, Washington, D.C.

1997b The Dalton Culture. In *The Paleoindians of the North American Midcontinent,* edited by A. Montet-White, 60–67. Musee Departmental de Prehistoire, Solutre.

Morse, Dan F., David G. Anderson, and Albert C. Goodyear III

1996 The Pleistocene-Holocene Transition in the Eastern United States. In *Humans at the End of the Ice Age: The Archeology of the Pleistocene-Holocene Transition,* edited by Lawrence Guy Strauss, Berit Valentin Eriksen, Jon M. Erlandson, and David R. Yesner, 319–38. Plenum Press, New York.

Morse, Dan F., and Phyllis A. Morse

1964 The Brake Site: A Possible Early 19th Century Log Cabin in Stewart County, Tennessee. *Florida Anthropologist* 17(3):165–76.

1977 *Excavation, Data Interpretation, and Report on the Zebree Homestead Site, Mississippi County, Arkansas.* Arkansas Archeological Survey, Fayetteville. Submitted to the U.S. Army Corps of Engineers, Memphis District.

1980 Zebree Archeological Project: Excavation, Data Interpretation, and Report on the Zebree Homestead Site, Mississippi County, Arkansas. Ms. on file, U.S. Corps of Engineers, Memphis.

1983 *Archaeology of the Central Mississippi Valley.* Academic Press, New York.

1990 The Spanish Exploration of Arkansas. In *Columbian Consequences.* Vol. 2, *Archaeological and Historical Perspectives on the Spanish Borderlands East,* edited by D. H. Thomas, 197–210. Smithsonian Institution Press, Washington, D.C.

1996 Changes in Interpretation in the Archaeology of the Central Mississippi Valley Since 1983. *North American Archaeologist* 17:1–35.

Morse, Phyllis A.

1977a *Later Historic Settlement along Big Lake in Excavation, Data Interpretation, and Report on the Zebree Homestead Site, Mississippi County, Arkansas.* Report. Arkansas Archeological Survey, Fayetteville. Submitted to the U.S. Army Corps of Engineers, Memphis District.

1977b The Forgotten Pioneers. In *Excavation, Data Interpretation, and Report on the Zebree Homestead Site, Mississippi County, Arkansas.* Report. Arkansas Archeological Survey, Fayetteville. Submitted to the U.S. Army Corps of Engineers, Memphis District.

1981 *Parkin: The 1978–1979 Archeological Investigations of a Cross County, Arkansas Site.* Research Series 13. Arkansas Archeological Survey, Fayetteville.

1986 *Archeological Survey of Old Greensboro, Craighead County, Arkansas.* Report. Arkansas Archeological Survey, Fayetteville. Submitted to the Farrville Water Expansion System, Perryville.

1990 The Parkin Site and the Parkin Phase. In *Towns and Temples along the Mississippi,* edited by D. H. Dye and C. A. Cox, 118–34. University of Alabama Press, Tuscaloosa.

Neitzel, Robert S.

1965 *Archeology of the Fatherland Site: The Grand Village of the Natchez.* American Museum of Natural History Anthropological Papers 51 (1). New York.

1983 *The Grand Village of the Natchez Revisited: Excavations at the Fatherland Site, Adams County, Mississippi, 1972.* Archaeological Report No. 12. Mississippi Department of Archives and History, Jackson, Miss.

Neuman, Robert W.

1958 Archaeological Investigations at the George Washington Carver National Monument, Missouri. Ms. on file, Missouri Department of Natural Resources, Jefferson City.

Neumann, Georg K.

1942 Types of Artificial Cranial Deformation in the Eastern United States. *American Antiquity* 7(3):306–10.

Newcomb, W. W., Jr.

1961 *The Indians of Texas.* University of Texas Press, Austin.

Norris, F. Terry

1991 St. Genevieve, A French Colonial Village in the Illinois Country. In *French Colonial Archaeology: The Illinois Country and the Western Great Lakes,* edited by John A. Walthall, 133–48. University of Illinois Press, Chicago.

Nuttall, Thomas

1980 *A Journal of Travels into the Arkansas Territory during the Year 1819.* Edited by Savoie Lottinville. University of Oklahoma Press, Norman.

O'Brien, Michael J.

1994 *Cat Monsters and Head Pots.* University of Missouri Press, Columbia.

1995 Archaeological Research in the Central Mississippi Valley: Culture History Gone Awry. *Review of Archaeology* 16(1):23–36.

O'Brien, Michael J., Thomas D. Holland, R. J. Hoard, and Gregory L. Fox
1994 Evolutionary Implications of Design and Performance Characteristics of Prehistoric Pottery. *Journal of Archaeological Method and Theory* 1:259–304.

Orser, Charles E., Jr.
1990 Historical Archaeology on Southern Plantations and Farms: Introduction. *Historical Archaeology* 24(4):1–6.

Orser, Charles E., Jr., and Claudia C. Holland
1986 Public Archeology at a Late-Nineteenth to Late-Twentieth Century Urban House Site, Shreveport Louisiana. Ms. on file, Louisiana Division of Archeology, Baton Rouge.

Osceola Times, Osceola, Arkansas
August 9, 1873
April 14, 1888:1
July 19, 1902:6

O'Shea, John M.
1984 *Mortuary Analysis.* Academic Press, New York.

Owens, Harry P.
1979 *An Assessment of Historic Period Cultural Resources along the Yazoo River between River Miles 75.6 and 273.0, Including Tchula Lake and Honey Island, Mississippi.* Report. University of Mississippi. Submitted to the U.S. Army Corps of Engineers, Vicksburg District, Vicksburg, Miss.

Owsley, Douglas W.
1989 The History of Bioarcheological Research in the Southern Great Plains. In *From Clovis to Comanchero: Archeological Overview of the Southern Great Plains,* by Joe S. Hays, Douglas W. Owsley, Richard L. Jantz, Murray K. Marks, and Mary H. Manhein, 123–36. Research Series No. 35. Arkansas Archeological Survey, Fayetteville.

Owsley, Douglas, and Richard L. Jantz
1989 A Systematic Approach to the Skeletal Biology of the Southern Plains. In *From Clovis to Comanchero: Archeological Overview of the Southern Great Plains,* by Joe S. Hays, Douglas W. Owsley, Richard L. Jantz, Murray K. Marks, and Mary H. Manhein, 137–56. Research Series No. 35. Arkansas Archeological Survey, Fayetteville.

Palmer, E.
1917 [Posthumous] Arkansas Mounds. *Publications of the Arkansas Historical Association* 4:390–448.

Peacock, Evan
1992 Rationale for the Preservation of Representative Historic Sites in the National Forests of Mississippi. Ms. on file, Tombigbee Ranger District, Ackerman, Miss.
1994 Representation and Significance on Late Nineteenth Century House Sites on Tombigbee and Holly Springs National Forests. Paper presented at the Southeast Region State Historic Preservation Officers' Conference, Columbus, Miss.

Pearson, Charles E.
1981 *El Nuevo Constante: Investigations of An Eighteenth Century Spanish Shipwreck off the Louisiana Coast.* Anthropological Study No. 4.

Louisiana Archaeological Survey and Antiquities Commission, Baton Rouge.

Pearson, Charles E., and Allen R. Saltus Jr.

1993 *Underwater Archaeology on the Ouachita River, Arkansas: The Search for the Chieftain, Haydee, and Homer.* Report. Coastal Environments, Inc. Submitted to the U.S. Army Corps of Engineers, Vicksburg District, Vicksburg, Miss.

Peattie, Donald Culross

1953 *A Natural History of Western Trees.* Houghton Mifflin, Boston.

Penman, John T.

1983 Archaeology and Choctaw Removal. In *Southeastern Natives and Their Pasts,* edited by D. G. Wyckoff and J. C. Hofman. Studies in Oklahoma's Past No. 11. Oklahoma Archaeological Survey, Norman.

Perino, Gregory

1965 The Paleo-Indian Era: Distribution of Finds, Arkansas. *Bulletin of the Southeastern Archaeological Conference* 2:18–20.

1967 *The Cherry Valley Mounds and Banks Mound 3.* Memoir 1. Central States Archaeological Society.

1980 Possible Early Trade of European Goods Indian to Indian. *Central States Archaeological Journal* (January):7–8.

Perttula, Timothy K.

1992 *The Caddo Nation: Archaeological and Ethnohistoric Perspectives.* University of Texas Press, Austin.

Pfeiffer, Michael A.

1993 "Which Front Door Do I Use?" and Other Ozark Exotica. Paper presented at the annual meeting of the Society for Historical Archaeology, Kansas City, Mo.

Phillips, Philip

1970 *Archaeological Survey in the Lower Yazoo Basin, Mississippi, 1949–1955.* Vol. 60, pts. 1 and 2. Papers of the Peabody Museum of Archaeology and Ethnology. Harvard University, Cambridge.

Phillips, Philip, and James A. Brown

1978 *Pre-Columbian Shell Engravings from the Craig Mound at Spiro, Oklahoma,* Part 1. Peabody Museum of Archaeology and Ethnology. Harvard University, Cambridge.

Phillips, Philip, James A. Ford, and James B. Griffin

1951 *Archaeological Survey in the Lower Mississippi Alluvial Valley, 1940–1947.* Papers of the Peabody Museum of Archaeology and Ethnology, vol. 25. Harvard University, Cambridge.

Pietak, Lynn

1998 Preliminary Results of Data Recovery Excavations at the Old Colclough Homestead Site, Oktibbeha County, Mississippi. Paper presented at the South Central Historical Archeology Conference, Jackson, Miss.

Pine Bluff Commercial, Pine Bluff, Arkansas

February 26, 1885:3

Ponder, Robert

1998 Preliminary Investigations into African-American Slave Lifeways in the Piney Woods (Forrest County, Mississippi). Paper presented at the annual meeting of the Society for Historical Archaeology, Atlanta.

Pope, Saxton T.

1962 *Bows and Arrows.* University of California Press, Berkeley.

Pope, W. F.

1895 *Early Days in Arkansas, Being for the Most Part the Personal Recollections of an Old Settler.* Frederick W. Allsopp, Little Rock.

Poplin, Eric C., and Marian D. Roberts

1992 *Fort Jackson Military Reservation Historic Preservation Plan–Cultural Overview.* Prepared for Fort Jackson–Directorate of Public Works and the U.S. Army Corps of Engineers-Savannah District. Columbia, S.C. and Savannah, Ga.

Porter, D. A., and M. J. Guccione

1994 Deglacial Flood Origin of the Charleston Alluvial Fan, Lower Mississippi Alluvial Valley. *Quaternary Research* 41:278–84.

Post Office Department

1980 *Reports of Site Locations, 1827–1950.* Microfilm Publication M1126, Roll 36, Lonoke County. National Archives and Records Service. Washington, D.C.

Powell, J. W.

1894 Report of the Director. *Annual Report of the Bureau of Ethnology, 1890–1891.* Vol. 12. Washington, D.C.

Price, Cynthia R.

1977 *An Archaeological and Historical Literature Review of the Cape Girardeau-Jackson Metropolitan Area, Cape Girardeau County, Missouri.* Report. Southeastern Missouri Archeological Research Facility, University of Missouri. Submitted to the U.S. Army Corps of Engineers, St. Louis District, St. Louis.

1979 *Nineteenth Century Ceramics . . . in the Eastern Ozark Border Region.* Monograph No.1. Southwest Missouri State University Center for Archaeological Research, Springfield.

1980 *Old Eminence: Report of Initial Investigation in the Ozark National Scenic Riverways at the First County Seat of Shannon County.* Report. Center for Archaeological Research, Southwest Missouri State University. Submitted to the U.S. National Park Service, Lincoln, Nebr.

1981a *Report of Initial Investigations at the Isaac Kelley Site, 23CT-111, in the Ozark National Scenic Riverways, Carter County, Missouri: 1980–81.* Submitted to the U.S. National Park Service, Midwest Archaeological Center, Lincoln, Nebr.

1981b Analysis of the Historic Period Materials and Assessment of Site Function. In *Changing Settlement Systems in the Fourche Creek Watershed in the Ozark Border Region of Southeast Missouri and Northeast Arkansas,* edited by J. E. Price and C. R. Price, 625–76. Report submitted to Interagency Archaeological Services, Denver.

1984a Old Eminence. *Missouri Archaeological Society Quarterly* 1(2):8–18.

1984b Excavations at the Historic Period Sites. In *Archaeological Investigations in the Ozark National Scenic Riverways, 1982–1983,* by J. E. Price, C. R. Price, R. Saucier, P. Delcourt, H. Delcourt, and

N. Smith, 14–165. Report. Submitted to the U.S. National Park Service, Midwest Archaeological Center, Lincoln, Nebr.

1985 Excavations at the Historic Period Sites. In *Archaeological Investigations in the Ozark National Scenic Riverways, 1983–1984*, by J. E. Price et al., 13–142. Report. Submitted to the U.S. National Park Service, Midwest Archaeological Center, Lincoln, Nebr.

1987a Patterns of Cultural Behavior and Intra-site Distributions of Faunal Remains at the Widow Harris Site. *Historical Archaeology* 19(2):40–56.

1987b Frontier Settlement in the Current River Valley: Variation in Organizational Patterning. In *Visions and Revisions, Ethnohistoric Perspectives on Southern Cultures,* edited by G. Sabo III and W. M. Schneider, 114–31. University of Georgia Press, Athens.

1993 *Determination of Eligibility and Effect, Herrygers Site, 23WE693, Wayne County, Missouri.* Report. Submitted to the Mark Twain National Forest, Doniphan, Mo.

Price, Cynthia R., and James E. Price

1981 Investigations of Settlement and Subsistence Systems in the Ozark Border Region of Southeast Missouri during the First Half of the 19th Century: The Widow Harris Cabin Project. *Ethnohistory* 28(3):237–58.

Price, James E.

1975 *An Assessment of the Cultural Resources of the Little Black Watershed. University of Missouri, Columbia.* Report. Submitted to the USDA, Soil Conservation Service, St. Louis, Mo.

1976a Snider Cabin Site in Western Carter County: A Historical Review. Ms. on file, Missouri Department of Natural Resources, Jefferson City.

1976b *An Assessment of the Cultural Resources of the Fourche Creek Watershed.* Report. University of Missouri, Columbia. Submitted to the USDA, Soil Conservation Service, St. Louis, Mo.

1978a The Settlement Pattern of the Powers Phase. In *Mississippian Settlement Patterns,* edited by B. D. Smith, 201–31. Academic Press, New York.

1978b The Widow Harris Cabin Site. *Arkansas Amateur* 27(9):5–7.

Price, J. E., and J. J. Krakker

1975 *Dalton Occupation of the Ozark Border.* Museum Brief 20. University of Missouri, Columbia.

Price, James E., and Cynthia R. Price

1975 *An Assessment of the Cultural Resources of the Little Black Watershed.* Prepared for the Soil Conservation Service. University of Missouri, Columbia.

1978a Pioneer Settlement and Subsistence on the Ozark Border: Preliminary Report on the Widow Harris Cabin Site Project. *Conference on Historic Site Archaeology Papers* 12:145–69.

1978b *An Investigation of Settlement Patterns and Subsistence on the Ozark Escarpment in Southeast Missouri During the First Half of the Nineteenth Century.* Final Report. Submitted to the National Endowment for the Humanities, Washington, D.C.

1979 *Greenville on the St. Francis. Report on a Brief Literature Search and Archaeological Testing Program at the Town of Old Greenville, Wayne County Missouri.* Report. Submitted to the U.S. Department of Interior, National Park Service in compliance with Antiquities Permit Number 78-MO-028.

1981 *Changing Settlement Systems in the Fourche Creek Watershed in the Ozark Border Region of Southwest Missouri and Northeast Arkansas.* Report 251. Center for Archaeological Research, Southwest Missouri State University.

Prouty, Fred M., and Gary L. Barker

1996 *A Survey of Civil War Period Military Sites in West Tennessee.* Report of Investigations No. 11. Tennessee Department of Environment and Conservation, Division of Archaeology, Nashville.

Purdy, Barbara A.

1982 *The Malone Lake Canoe: An Historic Craft from the Tombigbee River, Mississippi.* Report of Investigations No. 1. Office of Cultural/ Archaeological Research, University of West Florida, Pensacola.

Putnam, F. W.

1880 Report of the Curator [for 1879]. *Thirteenth Annual Report of the Peabody Museum: Reports of the Peabody Museum, Harvard University* 2(4):715–51. Cambridge.

Quimby, George I., Jr.

1942a The Natchezan Culture Type. *American Antiquity* 7(3):255–75.

1942b Indian Trade Objects in Michigan and Louisiana. *Papers of the Michigan Academy of Science Arts and Letters* 27(4):43–551.

1957 The Bayou Goula Site, Iberville Parish, Louisiana. *Fieldiana: Anthropology* 47(2).

Quinn, David B.

1979 The Expedition of Hernando de Soto and His Successor, Luis de Moscoso, 1538–1543. In *New American World: A Documentary History of North America to 1612.* Vol. 2. Edited, with a commentary, by David B. Quinn, 90–198. Arno Press, New York.

Rankin, Robert L.

1993 Language Affiliations of Some de Soto Place Names in Arkansas. In *The Expedition of Hernando de Soto West of the Mississippi, 1541–1543,* edited by Gloria A. Young and Michael P. Hoffman, 210–21. University of Arkansas Press, Fayetteville.

Ray, Jack H.

1995 Lithic Analysis. In *Woodland and Mississippian Occupations at the Hayti Bypass Site, Pemiscot County, Missouri,* edited by M. D. Conner, 172–75. Special Publication No. 1. Center for Archaeological Research, Southwest Missouri State University, Springfield.

Read, Dwight W.

1989a Statistical Methods and Reasoning in Archaeological Research: A Review of Praxis and Promise. *Journal of Quantitative Anthropology* 1:5–78.

1989b Intuitive Typology and Automatic Classification: Divergence or Full Circle? *Journal of Anthropological Archaeology* 8:158–88.

Reams, Robert, and Jerome Cramer
1998 A Passport-in-Time Excavation of a Piney Woods Logging and Turpentine Camp. Paper presented at the annual meeting of the Society for Historical Archaeology, Atlanta.

Reaves, Robert G., and Burney B. McClurkan
1970 The Dansbury Creek Site (3CV24). *Arkansas Archeological Society Field Notes* 70:3–4.

Redfield, Alden
1970 Dalton Forms from the Lower Mississippi Alluvial Valley. *Bulletin of the Southeastern Archaeological Conference* 13:99–107.
1971 *Dalton Project Notes.* Vol. 1. University of Missouri, Museum of Anthropology, Columbia.

Redfield, Alden, and John H. Moselage
1970 The Lace Place, A Dalton Project Site in the Western Lowland in Eastern Arkansas. *Arkansas Archeologist* 11:21–44.

Redman, Charles L., and Patty Jo Watson
1970 Systematic Intensive Surface Collection. *American Antiquity* 35(3):279–91.

Reynolds, J. H.
1906 Aboriginal and Indian Remains. *Publications of the Arkansas Historical Association* 1:274–77.

Rigaud, Jean-Philippe, and Jan F. Simek
1991 Interpreting Spatial Patterns at the Grotte XV: A Multiple Method Approach. In *The Interpretation of Archaeological Spatial Patterning,* edited by E. M. Kroll and T. D. Price, 199–220. Plenum, New York.

Riordan, Timothy B.
1980 *Archaeological Investigations at Waverly Ferry, Clay County, Mississippi: Mitigation Interim Report.* Report. Soils Systems, Inc., Bloomington, Ind. Submitted to the U.S. Army Corps of Engineers Mobile District, Mobile.

Robbins, Wilfred William, John Peabody Harrington, and Barbara Freire-Marreco
1916 *Ethnobotany of the Tewa.* Bulletin 55. Smithsonian Institution Bureau of American Ethnology, Washington.

Rogers, J. Daniel
1996 Markers of Social Integration: The Development of Centralized Authority in the Spiro Region. In *Political Structure and Change in the Prehistoric Southeastern United States,* edited by John F. Scarry, 53–68. University Press of Florida, Gainesville.

Rohrbaugh, Charles L.
1982a *Spiro and Fort Coffee Phases: Changing Cultural Complexes of the Caddoan Area.* Ph.D. diss., Graduate School of the University of Wisconsin-Madison. University Microfilms International, Ann Arbor.
1982b An Hypothesis for the Origin of the Kichai. In *Pathways to Plains Prehistory: Anthropological Perspectives of Plains Natives and Their Pasts,* edited by Don G. Wyckoff and Jack L. Hoffman, 51–63. Memoir 3. Oklahoma Anthropological Society.
1984 Arkansas Valley Caddoan: Fort Coffee and Neosho Foci. In *Prehistory of Oklahoma,* edited by Robert E. Bell, 265–83. Academic Press, Orlando.

Rolingson, Martha Ann

1976 The Bartholomew Phase: A Plaquemine Adaptation in the Mississippi Valley. In *Cultural Change and Continuity: Essays in Honor of James Bennett Griffin,* edited by C. E. Cleland, 99–119. Academic Press, New York.

1982a (ed.) *Emerging Patterns of Plum Bayou Culture.* Research Series No. 18. Arkansas Archeological Survey, Fayetteville.

1982b Contributions to the Toltec (Knapp) Site Research by the Smithsonian Institution. In *Emerging Patterns of Plum Bayou Culture: Preliminary Investigations of the Toltec Mounds Research Project,* edited by M. A. Rolingson, 71–86. Research Series No. 18. Arkansas Archeological Survey, Fayetteville.

1990 The Toltec Mounds Site: A Ceremonial Center in the Arkansas River Lowland. In *The Mississippian Emergence,* edited by B. D. Smith, 27–49. Smithsonian Institution Press, Washington, D.C.

1992 Excavations of Mound S at the Toltec Mounds Site: Preliminary Report. *Arkansas Archeologist* 31:1–30.

1993 Robert Chowning Makes Major Donation to the Survey. *Arkansas Archeological Society Field Notes* 250:3.

1998 *Toltec Mounds and Plum Bayou Culture: Mound D Excavations.* Research Series No. 54. Arkansas Archeological Survey, Fayetteville.

Rolingson, Martha Ann, and J. Michael Howard

1997 Igneous Lithics of Central Arkansas: Identification, Sources, and Artifact Distribution. *Southeastern Archaeology* 16(1):33–50.

Rolingson, Martha Ann, and Frank F. Schambach

1981 *The Shallow Lake Site (3UN9/52) and Its Place in Regional Prehistory.* Research Series No. 12. Arkansas Archeological Survey, Fayetteville.

Rose, Jerome C. (ed.)

1985 *Gone to a Better Land: A Biohistory of a Rural Black Cemetery in the Post-Reconstruction South.* Research Series No. 25. Arkansas Archeological Survey, Fayetteville.

Royall, P. D., P. A. Delcourt, and H. R. Delcourt

1991 Late Quaternary Paleoecology and Paleoenvironments of the Central Mississippi Alluvial Valley. *Geological Society of America Bulletin* 103:157–70.

Sabo, George, III, and Jerry Hilliard

1980 *Additional Test Excavations at the Clayton House, Belle Grove Historical District, Fort Smith, Arkansas.* Report. Arkansas Archeological Survey, Fayetteville. Submitted to the Fort Smith Heritage Foundation and the City of Fort Smith.

Sabo, George, III, David B. Waddell, and John H. House

1982 *A Cultural Resource Overview of the Ozark-St. Francis National Forests.* Report. Arkansas Archeological Survey, Fayetteville. Submitted to the USDA Forest Service, Ozark and St. Francis National Forests, Russellville, Ark.

Saltus, Alan

1986 *Submerged Cultural Resources Investigation of the Maurepas Basin with Intensive Surveys at Warsaw Landing, Blood River and Springfield Area, Natalbany, Louisiana.* Report submitted to the U.S. Department of

Interior and to the Division of Archeology, Department of Culture, Recreation, and Tourism, Baton Rouge.

1988 *Submerged Cultural Resources Investigation of Various Waterways of Lake Pontchartrain's North Shore.* Report submitted to the U.S. Department of Interior and to the Division of Archeology, Louisiana Department of Culture, Recreation, and Tourism, Baton Rouge.

Santeford, Lawrence G.

1980a Limited Perspectives on Log House Society in the Cypress Creek Basin, Conway County, Arkansas. In *The Conway Water Supply: An Intensive Archaeological and Historical Survey of a Proposed Reservoir Area in Conway County, Arkansas,* edited by L. G. Santeford and W. A. Martin, 137–90. Research Report 20. Arkansas Archeological Survey, Fayetteville.

1980b Log House Society: Archeology and Transitions in Nineteenth and Twentieth Century Conway County, Arkansas. Paper presented at the annual meeting of the Society for Historical Archeology, Albuquerque, N.M.

1982 *Results of a Data Recovery Program at a Late-Nineteenth to Twentieth Century Log House: Site 3RA83 in Basin Structure 19, the Fourche Creek Watershed, Randolph County, Arkansas.* Report. Arkansas Archeological Survey, Fayetteville. Submitted to the USDA Soil Conservation Service, Little Rock.

Santeford, Lawrence G., William A. Martin, and E. Thomas Hemmings

1985 *Excavations at Four Sites in the Cypress Creek Basin, Conway County, Arkansas.* Research Report No. 24. Arkansas Archeological Survey, Fayetteville.

Santeford, Lawrence G., and Carol S. Spears

1994 *3JE357: A 19th Century Site in Jefferson County, Arkansas.* SPEARS Project Report 83. Spears Professional Environmental and Archeological Research Service, West Fork, Arkansas. Submitted to the Arkansas Highway and Transportation Department, Little Rock.

Santeford, Lawrence G., Carol S. Spears, Annie L. Moerbe, Kirsten L. Hoffman, and James E. Duncan

1993 *Empty Rooms and Broken Dishes: Results of Testing Ten Historic Sites in the Sullivan Creek Project Area, Independence and Sharp Counties, Arkansas.* SPEARS Project Report 65. Submitted to the Arkansas Game and Fish Commission, Little Rock.

Sassaman, Kenneth E., and David G. Anderson

1995 *Middle and Late Archaic Archaeological Records of South Carolina, A Synthesis for Research and Resource Management.* Research Papers 6. Savannah River Archaeological Research Program, South Carolina Institute of Archaeology and Anthropology, University of South Carolina, Columbia.

Saucier, R. T.

1970 Origin of the St. Francis Sunk Lands, Arkansas and Missouri. *Geological Society of America Bulletin* 81:2847–54.

1974 *Quaternary Geology of the Lower Mississippi Valley.* Research Series No. 6. Arkansas Archeological Survey, Fayetteville.

1982 Geomorphology, Geological History, and Paleogeography. In *A Cultural Resources Survey in the Larkin Creek Watershed, Lee and St. Francis Counties, Arkansas*, by W. J. Bennett Jr., A. F. Gettys, Judith Stewart-Abernathy, and Roger Saucier, 16–32. Final Report 21. Archaeological Assessments, Inc. Submitted to the Memphis District, U.S. Army Corps of Engineers.

1987 The Physical Setting of the Ouachita, Saline, and Little Missouri Rivers, Southern Arkansas. *Arkansas Archeologist* 25–26:63–74.

1994 *Geomorphology and Quaternary Geologic History of the Lower Mississippi Valley.* U.S. Army Corps of Engineers, Waterways Experiment Station, Vicksburg, Mississippi.

1997 Late Quaternary Geologic History of the Western Lowlands. In *Sloan: A Paleoindian Dalton Cemetery in Arkansas,* edited by D. F. Morse, 96–102. Smithsonian Institution Press, Washington, D.C.

Saucier, Roger T., and Lawson M. Smith

1986 *Geomorphic Mapping and Landscape Classification of the Ouachita and Saline River Valleys, Arkansas.* Report No. 51. Archeological Assessments, Inc., Nashville, Ark.

Saunders, Joe W., Thurman Allen, and Roger T. Saucier

1994 Four Archaic? Mound Complexes in Northeast Louisiana. *Southeastern Archaeology* 13(2):134–53.

Saunders, Joe W., Reca Jones, Kathryn Moorehead, and Brian Davis

1998 "Watson Brake Objects," an Unusual Archaic Artifact Type from Northeast Louisiana and Southwest Mississippi. *Southeastern Archaeology* 17(1):72–79.

Schambach, Frank F.

1970 *Pre-Caddoan Cultures in the Trans-Mississippi South: A Beginning Sequence.* Ph.D. diss., Harvard University, Cambridge.

1971 The Trans-Mississippi South: The Case for a New Natural Area West of the Lower Mississippi Valley and East of the Plains. Paper presented at the 13th Caddo Conference, Austin, Tex.

1979 Summary of Local and Regional Archeology. In *Hampton: An Archeological and Historical Overview of a Proposed Strip Mine Tract in South Central Arkansas*, assembled by T. C. Klinger, 21–30. Research Reports No. 19. Arkansas Archeological Survey, Fayetteville.

1981 A Description and Analysis of the Ceramics. In *The Shallow Lake Site (3UN9/52) and Its Place in Regional Prehistory*, by M. A Rolingson and F. F. Schambach, 101–76. Research Series No. 12. Arkansas Archeological Survey, Fayetteville.

1982a An Outline of Fourche Maline Culture in Southwest Arkansas. In *Arkansas Archeology in Review,* edited by N. L. Trubowitz and M. D. Jeter, 132–97. Research Series No. 15. Arkansas Archeological Survey, Fayetteville.

1982b "Felsenthal Region" Sections of Southwest Arkansas, by F. F. Schambach, A. M. Early, E. T. Hemmings, D. B. Kelley, and M. Swanda. In *A State Plan for the Conservation of Archeological Resources in Arkansas,* edited by H. A. Davis. Research Series No. 21. Arkansas Archeological Survey, Fayetteville.

1990 (ed.) *Coles Creek and Mississippi Period Foragers in the Felsenthal Region of the Lower Mississippi Valley.* Research Series No. 39. Arkansas Archeological Survey, Fayetteville.

1993a The End of the Trail: Reconstruction of the Route of Hernando de Soto's Army through Southwest Arkansas and East Texas. In *The Route of Hernando de Soto West of the Mississippi, 1541–1543,* edited by G. A. Young and M. P. Hoffman, 78–105. University of Arkansas Press, Fayetteville.

1993b Some New Interpretations of Spiroan Culture History. In *Archaeology of Eastern North America: Papers in Honor of Stephen Williams,* edited by James B. Stoltman, 187–230. Archaeological Report No. 25. Mississippi Department of Archives and History, Jackson.

1993c Spiroan Entrepôts at and beyond the Western Border of the Trans-Mississippi South. *Caddoan Archeology Newsletter* 4(2):11–26.

1994 A Probable Spiroan Entrepôt in the Red River Valley in Northeast Texas. Poster presentation, 59th Annual Meeting of the Society for American Archeology, Anaheim, California.

1995 A Probable Spiroan Entrepôt in the Red River Valley in Northeast Texas. *Caddoan Archeology Newsletter* 6(1):10–25.

1996 The Womack, Gilbert, and Pearson Sites: Early Eighteenth Century Tunican Entrepôts in Northeast Texas? *Caddoan Archeology* 7(3):9–31.

1997 Continuing the Discussion of the Spiroans and Their Entrepôts: A Reply to Brooks's Critique of My New Paradigm for the Archeology of the Arkansas Valley. *Caddoan Archeology* 7(4):17–46.

1998 *Pre-Caddoan Cultures in the Trans-Mississippi South: A Beginning Sequence.* Research Series No. 53. Arkansas Archeological Survey, Fayetteville.

Schambach, Frank F., and Ann M. Early

1982 Southwest Arkansas. In *A State Plan for the Conservation of Archeological Resources in Arkansas,* edited by Hester A. Davis, SW1-110. Research Series No. 21. Arkansas Archeological Survey, Fayetteville.

Schambach, Frank F., and John E. Miller

1984 A Description and Analysis of the Ceramics. In *Cedar Grove: An Interdisciplinary Investigation of a Late Caddo Farmstead in the Red River Valley,* edited by Neal L. Trubowitz, 109–70. Research Series No. 23. Arkansas Archeological Survey, Fayetteville.

Schambach, Frank F., and Martha Ann Rolingson

1981 Conclusions. *In The Shallow Lake Site (3UN9/52) and Its Place in Regional Prehistory,* by M. A. Rolingson and F. F. Schambach, 177–203. Research Series No. 12. Arkansas Archeological Survey, Fayetteville.

Schiffer, Michael B.

1975a An Alternative to Morse's Dalton Settlement Pattern Hypothesis. *Plains Anthropologist* 20:253–66.

1975b Some Further Comments on the Dalton Settlement Pattern Hypothesis. In *The Cache River Archeological Project: An Experiment in*

Contract Archeology, assembled by Michael B. Schiffer and John House, 103–12. Research Series 8. Arkansas Archeological Survey, Fayetteville.

Schiffer, Michael B., and John H. House (comp.)
1975 *The Cache River Archeological Project: An Experiment in Contract Archeology.* Research Series No. 8. Arkansas Archeological Survey, Fayetteville.

Scholtz, James A.
1968 Archeological Sites and Land-Leveling in Eastern Arkansas. *Arkansas Archeologist* 9(1–2):1–9.

Scott, L. J., and D. K. Aasen
1987 Interpretation of Holocene Vegetation in Northeastern Arkansas. In *A Cultural Resources Survey, Testing, and Geomorphic Examination of Ditches 10, 12, and 29, Mississippi County, Arkansas,* edited by R. H. Lafferty III, M. J. Guccione, L. J. Scott, D. K. Aasen, B. J. Watkins, M. C. Sierzchula, and P. F. Bauman, 133–50. Report No. 86-5. Mid-Continental Research Associates, Lowell, Ark. Submitted to the U.S. Army Corps of Engineers, Memphis District.

Shaeffer, James B.
1957 The Nagle Site, Ok-4. *Bulletin of the Oklahoma Anthropological Society* 5:93–99.

Shea, John Gilmary
1861 *Early Voyages Up and Down the Mississippi.* Joel Munsell, Albany, N.Y.

Shenkel, J. Richard
1971 Archaeological Investigations of Madame John's Legacy, 1971. Ms. on file, Department of Anthropology and Geography, University of New Orleans, New Orleans.

Shenkel, J. Richard, and Jack Hudson
1972 Historic Archaeology in New Orleans. *Conference on Historic Site Archaeology Papers* 6:40–44.

Shenkel, J. Richard, Robert Sauder, and Edward R. Chatelain
1979 *Archaeology of the Jazz Complex and Beauregard (Congo) Square, Louis Armstrong Park, New Orleans, Louisiana.* Research Report 2. University of New Orleans Archaeological and Cultural Research Program, New Orleans.

Sierzchula, M. C., R. H. Lafferty III, H. Wagner, J. T. Toney, L. G. Santeford, M. T. Oates, and W. J. Bennett Jr.
1995 *Archeological Testing of 13 Historic Sites, Fort Chaffee Military Garrision, Sebastian County, Arkansas.* Final Report 94-2. Mid-Continental Research Associates, Springdale, Ark. Submitted to the U.S. Army Corps of Engineers, Little Rock District.

Sims, Doug, and John Connaway
1998 A Preliminary Review of Mississippi's Fishweirs. Paper presented at the South Central Historical Archeology Conference, Jackson, Miss.

Singleton, Teresa A.
1985 (ed.) *The Archaeology of Slavery and Plantation Life.* Academic Press, New York.
1989 The Potential for Afro-American Archaeology in Mississippi: A Brief Overview of Afro-American Settlement. Paper presented at Digging

the Afro-American Past: Historical Archaeology and the Black Experience Conference, Oxford, Miss.

1990 The Archaeology of the Plantation South: A Review of Approaches and Goals. *Historical Archaeology* 24(4):70–77.

1991 The Potential for African American Archaeology in Mississippi. *Mississippi Archaeology* 26(1):19–32.

Smith, Bruce D.

1975 *Middle Mississippian Exploitation of Animal Populations.* Anthropological Papers of the Museum of Anthropology, University of Michigan 57, Ann Arbor.

1984a Mississippian Expansion: Tracing the Historical Development of an Explanatory Model. *Southeastern Archaeology* 3(1):13–32.

1984b A Review of the Investigations at Cedar Grove. In *Cedar Grove: An Interdisciplinary Investigation of a Late Caddo Farmstead in the Red River Valley,* edited by Neal L. Trubowitz, 274–77. Research Series No. 23. Arkansas Archeological Survey, Fayetteville.

1985 Introduction to the 1985 Edition. In *Report on the Mound Explorations of the Bureau of Ethnology,* by Cyrus Thomas, 5–19. Smithsonian Institution Press, Washington, D.C.

Smith, E. N., Jr.

1984 Late-Quaternary Vegetational History at Cupola Pond, Ozark National Scenic Riverways, Southeastern Missouri. Master's thesis, University of Tennessee, Knoxville.

Smith, F. L., and R. T. Saucier

1971 *Geological Investigation of the Western Lowlands Area, Lower Mississippi Valley.* Technical Report S-71-5. U.S. Army Corps of Engineers Waterways Experiment Station, Vicksburg, Miss.

Smith, Gerald P.

1977 Fort Pillow State Park, Memphis State University Archaeological Field School Excavations, July 13–August 13, 1976. Report on file, Department of Anthropology, Memphis State University.

1985 *Fort Germantown Historic Park: Historic Background, Archaeological Investigations and Recommendations.* Report submitted to the City of Germantown, Tenn.

1987 *Fort Germantown: 1986 Excavations.* Report submitted to the City of Germantown, Tenn.

1990 The Walls Phase and Its Neighbors. In *Towns and Temples along the Mississippi,* edited by D. H. Dye and C. A. Cox, 135–69. University of Alabama Press, Tuscaloosa.

1991 *Archaeological Testing at the Porter-Leath Children's Center, Memphis, Tennessee.* Report. Cultural Resource Services, Memphis. Submitted to the City of Memphis, Division of Housing and Community Development.

1992 *Porter-Leath Children's Center: Sarah's Place Construction Monitoring.* Report. Cultural Resource Services, Memphis. Submitted to the City of Memphis, Division of Housing and Community Development.

Smith, Jeffrey L., and Janice V. Perino

1981 Osage Orange *(Maclura pomifera)*: History and Economic Uses. *Economic Botany* 35(1):24–41.

Smith, Ralph A.
1958 Account of the Journey of Benard de la Harpe: Discovery Made by Him of Several Nations Situated in the West. *Southwestern Historical Quarterly* 62(1–4).

Smith, Samuel D.
1972a Prospectus for Historic Site Archeology in Northeast Arkansas. *Craighead County Historical Quarterly* 11(2):7–17.
1972b Arkansas Kiln Sites. *Arkansas Archeological Society Field Notes* 95:7–10.
1974a *Preliminary Report of an Historical and Archeological Assessment of the First Hermitage. Tennessee Division of Archaeology.* Report submitted to the Ladies Hermitage Association and the Tennessee American Revolution Bicentennial Commission, Nashville.
1974b *A Survey and Assessment of the Archaeological Resources of Cadron Settlement.* Research Report No. 1. Arkansas Archeological Survey, Fayetteville.
1976 (ed.) *An Archaeological and Historical Assessment of the First Hermitage.* Research Series No. 2. Tennessee Department of Conservation, Division of Archaeology, Nashville.
1978 Davidsonville Bricks. *Arkansas Archeologist* 19:31–35.
1980 *Preliminary Report Concerning Fort San Fernando de las Barrancas Archaeological Project, Memphis, Tennessee.* Tennessee Department of Conservation, Division of Archaeology. Report submitted to the Tennessee Historical Commission and the Shelby County Historical Commission, Memphis.
1982 *Archaeological Excavations in Search of the Site of Fort San Fernando de las Barrancas.* Tennessee Department of Conservation, Division of Archaeology. Report submitted to the Tennessee Historical Commission and the Shelby County Historical Commission, Memphis.
1990 Site Survey as a Method for Determining Historic Site Significance. *Historical Archaeology* 24(2):34–41.
1996a Historical Overview. In *A Bibliographic History of Historical Archaeology in Tennessee*, by Samuel D. Smith, 1–24. Miscellaneous Publication No. 4. Tennessee Department of Environment and Conservation, Division of Archaeology, Nashville.
1996b A Summary of Fifty Years of Historical Archaeology in Tennessee. Paper presented at the annual meeting of the Society for Historical Archaeology, Cincinnati, Ohio.

Smith, Samuel D., and William V. Davidson
1975 County Seat Towns as Archaeological Sites: Some Arkansas Examples. *The Conference on Historic Site Archaeology Papers* 8:33–51.

Smith, Samuel D., Fred M. Prouty, and Benjamin C. Nance
1991 *A Preliminary Survey of Historic Period Gunmaking in Tennessee.* Report of Investigations No. 8. Tennessee Department of Environment and Conservation, Division of Archaeology, Nashville.

Smith, Samuel D., and Stephen T. Rogers
1979 *A Survey of Historic Pottery Making in Tennessee.* Research Series No. 3. Tennessee Department of Conservation, Division of Archaeology, Nashville.

Smith, Steven D., David F. Barton, and Timothy B. Riordan

1982 *Ethnoarchaeology of the Bay Springs Farmsteads: A Study of Rural American Settlement.* Report. Submitted to the U.S. National Park Service, Washington, D.C.

Smith, Steven D., Philip G. Rivet, Kathleen M. Byrd, and Nancy W. Hawkins

1983 *Louisiana's Comprehensive Archaeological Plan.* Division of Archaeology, Office of Cultural Development. Baton Rouge.

Southwest Times Record, Fort Smith, Arkansas

April 5, 1925:8

November 29, 1925:12

Spears, Carol, S., Nancy Myer, and Hester A. Davis

1975 *Watershed Summary of Archeological and Historical Resources in the White River Basins, Arkansas and Missouri.* Research Report 5. Arkansas Archeological Survey, Fayetteville.

Squier, E. G., and E. H. Davis

1848 *Ancient Monuments of the Mississippi Valley.* Vol. 1, Smithsonian Contributions to Knowledge. Washington, D.C.

Starr, Mary Evelyn

1996 *Phase I Archaeological Survey and Deep Testing at Presidents Island and the Frank C. Pidgeon Industrial Park, Shelby County, Tennessee.* Report. Garrow and Associates, Memphis. Submitted to the Memphis and Shelby County Port Commission, Memphis.

Stein, Julie K., Kenneth C. Carstens, and Kit W. Wesler

1983 Geoarchaeology and Historic Archaeology: An Example from Fort Jefferson, Kentucky. *Southeastern Archaeology* 2(2):132–44.

Stewart, T. D.

1941 The Circular Type of Cranial Deformation in the United States. *American Journal of Physical Anthropology* 28:343–51.

Stewart-Abernathy, Judith C.

1982 *Background and Literature Study for the L'Anguille River Project Area.* Final Report 21. Archaeological Assessments, Inc. Submitted to the Memphis District, U.S. Army Corps of Engineers.

1989 *Arkansas Territorial Restoration Walkway Improvement Project (3PU30), Pulaski County, Arkansas.* Report, AAS Project 706. Arkansas Archeological Survey, Fayetteville. Submitted to Arkansas Territorial Restoration, Little Rock.

Stewart-Abernathy, Leslie C.

1980a *Test Excavations at the Clayton House, Belle Grove Historic District, Fort Smith, Arkansas.* Report submitted to the Fort Smith Heritage Foundation and the City of Fort Smith, Ark.

1980b *A Report of the Archaeological Monitoring of the Sewer Line Excavation for Arkansas Post National Memorial, Arkansas.* Report submitted to the U.S. National Park Service, Southwest Region, Santa Fe, N.M.

1980c *The Seat of Justice, 1815–1830: An Archeological Reconnaissance of Davidsonville, 1979.* Research Report No. 21. Arkansas Archeological Survey, Fayetteville.

1980d *Preliminary Archeological Study of Camp Robinson, Arkansas.* Report submitted to the Camp Robinson Study Committee, Joint Committee of the Arkansas State Legislature.

1980e Historical Archeology and Folklore. Paper presented at the combined annual meetings of the Arkansas Folklore Association and the Ozark Folklore Society, Mountain View.

1980f The Other Four and a Half Centuries: Historical Archeology in Arkansas. Paper presented at the annual meeting of the Society for American Archaeology, Philadelphia, Pa.

1980g The Eye Accustomed to the Survey of These Relics: Historical Archeology and the Arkansas Past. Paper presented at the annual meeting of the Society for Historical Archaeology, Albuquerque, N.M.

1981 *Test Excavations in the Area of the Detached Kitchen, Bozeman House (3CL228), Clark County, Arkansas.* Report. Arkansas Archeological Survey, Fayetteville. Submitted to the Arkansas State Historic Preservation Office.

1982a 1982 Society Historical Excavations: Block-Catts Kitchen Ell (3HE236-19). *Arkansas Archeological Society Field Notes* 185:7.

1982b *Final Evaluation Report, the Sawdust Hill Community: Graphic Documentation of the Historic Occupation of the Parkin Site (3CS29).* Report. Arkansas Archeological Survey, Fayetteville. Submitted to the Arkansas Endowment for the Humanities, Little Rock.

1982c The Black Community at Sawdust Hill: Further History of the Parkin Site, 3CS29, Cross County, Arkansas. Paper presented at the annual meeting of the Southeastern Archaeological Conference, Memphis.

1982d There Are No Vacant Lots: Historical Archeology and Historic Preservation. Paper presented at the annual meeting of the Historic Preservation Alliance of Arkansas, Batesville.

1982e The Other Four and a Half Centuries: Historical Archeology and the Arkansas Archaeological Survey. In *Arkansas Archeology in Review,* edited by N. L. Trubowitz and M. D. Jeter, 301–9. Research Series No. 15. Arkansas Archeological Survey, Fayetteville.

1983a Urban Farmsteads in Old Washington: The Dynamics of Spatial and Chronological Patterning in Two House Lots from the Mid-1800s to the Present. Paper presented at the annual meeting of the Society for Historical Archaeology, Denver.

1983b Old Davidsonville on the Arkansas Frontier: Reconnaissance at a Townsite for the Parks and the Past, for the Public and the Present. In *Forgotten Places and Things,* edited by Albert E. Ward, 141–47. Center for Anthropological Studies, Albuquerque, N.M.

1984a Ashley Mansion Site, Little Rock. *Newsletter of the Society for Historical Archaeology* 17(3):31–32.

1984b Historical Archeology in Your Backyard. Paper presented at the annual meeting of the Historic Preservation Alliance of Arkansas, El Dorado, Ark.

1985a The Moser Farmstead: Ethnoarcheology in Pre–World War Ozarkia. *Pioneer America Society Transactions* 8:27–36.

1985b Of Chickens, Sir Walter Scott, and the Columbian Exposition of 1893: A View of the World Economy from an Ozark Farmstead before the Great War. Paper presented at the annual meeting of the Society for Historical Archaeology, Boston.

1985c Tenant Farm Activity Period: Some Suggested Research Questions. Unpublished handout prepared for a conference on historical archeology issues in cultural resource management, Little Rock. Copy on file Arkansas Technical University Field Station, Arkansas Archeological Survey, Russellville.

1986a Urban Farmsteads: Household Responsibilities in the City. *Historical Archaeology* 20(2):5–15.

1986b *The Block House Piers: A Contribution to the Archaeological Underpinning of Historic Preservation in Washington, Arkansas.* Report submitted to the Arkansas Department of Parks and Tourism, Little Rock.

1986c *The Moser Farmstead, Independent but not Isolated: The Archeology of a Late Nineteenth Century Ozark Farmstead.* Research Series No. 26. Arkansas Archeological Survey, Fayetteville.

1986d Household Consumption in an Ozark Mountain Farmstead before the Great War: An Archaeological Perspective on Consumption and Cognition in an Agricultural Hinterland. Paper presented at the annual meeting of the Association for Consumer Research, Toronto.

1987a From Memories and from the Ground: Historical Archeology at the Moser Farmstead in the Arkansas Ozarks. In *Visions and Revisions, Ethnohistoric Perspectives on Southern Cultures* , edited by G. Sabo III and W. M. Schneider, 98–113. University of Georgia Press, Athens.

1987b *Interim Report, Mitigation of 3JE140, Jefferson County, Arkansas.* Report. Arkansas Archeological Survey, Fayetteville. Submitted to the Little Rock District, U.S. Army Corps of Engineers.

1987c Excavations at the Boyd Point Site (3JE140), Jefferson County, Arkansas. Paper presented at the annual meeting of the Arkansas Archeological Society, Lake DeGray State Park.

1988a Queensware from a Southern Store: Perspectives on the Antebellum Ceramics Trade from a Merchant Family's Trash in Washington, Arkansas. Poster paper session, annual meeting of the Society for Historical Archaeology, Reno, Nev.

1988b The West Memphis Boatwrecks. *Society for Historical Archaeology Newsletter* 12(4):16–17.

1990 Introduction and Overview (for a Symposium Titled "Ghost Boats on the Mississippi: Opportunity, Obligation, and Watercraft at West Memphis, Arkansas, in the Drought Summer of 1988"). Paper presented at the annual meeting of the Society for Historical Archaeology, Tucson.

1991 African-American Archaeology in Arkansas: An Update. *African-American Archaeology Newsletter* 5:2–4.

1992a Separate Kitchens and Intimate Archeology: Constructing Urban Slavery on the Antebellum Cotton Frontier in Washington, Arkansas. Paper presented at the annual meeting of the Society for American Archeology, Pittsburgh, Pa.

1992b Industrial Goods in the Service of Tradition: Consumption and Cognition on an Ozark Farmstead before the Great War. In *The Art and Mystery of Historical Archaeology: Essays in Honor of James Deetz,* edited by Anne Elizabeth Yentsch and Mary C. Beaudry, 101–26. CRC Press, Boca Raton, Fla.

1992c Cutting Christians into Shoestrings in the Twinkling of a Bedpost: Urban Archeology on the Cotton Frontier. Paper presented at the annual meeting of the Society for Historical Archeology, Kingston, Jamaica.

1992d The Taylor Log House: 1991 Fieldwork and Results, and 1992 Plans. *Arkansas Archeological Society Field Notes* 245:8–10.

1994a Courthouse Turned Corn Crib: Visibility, Myth, and Extinct Towns of Arkansas. Paper presented at a meeting of the State Historic Preservation Officers, Southeastern Region, Columbus, Miss.

1994b From Suburban Farmstead to Urban Park: Archaeological Considerations at the Pike-Fletcher-Terry House/Decorative Arts Museum, Little Rock. Invited presentation at the Decorative Arts Museum, Little Rock.

1994c The Taylor Log House, Documentation for Criterion D, Archaeological Significance, National Register Nomination Form for the Taylor House, 3DR26. Submitted to the Arkansas State Historic Preservation Office, Little Rock.

1994d Historical Archeology in Arkansas. *Preservation Digest* (April 1994): 5. Published by the Arkansas Historic Preservation Alliance, Little Rock.

1994e The Early Historic Settlement Landscape of Phillips County. Presentation at Phillips County Community College, Helena, Ark.

1995 Separate Kitchens and Intimate Archeology: Constructing Urban Slavery on the Antebellum Cotton Frontier in Washington, Arkansas. Paper presented at the annual meeting of the Society for Historical Archeology, Washington, D.C.

1996a Ghost Boats on the Mississippi, Opportunity, Obligation, and Watercraft at West Memphis, Arkansas in the Drought Summer of 1988. Paper presented at the Mississippi River Conference, Memphis.

1996b Some Archaeological Considerations on the Arkansas Cherokee. Paper presented at the National Trail of Tears Association Symposium, Little Rock.

1997a Just Putting It Back the Way It Was: Constructions of an Antebellum Townscape in Washington, Arkansas. Paper presented at the annual meeting of the Society for Historical Archeology, Corpus Christi, Tex.

1997b Some Archeological Considerations on the Arkansas Cherokee. In *Proceedings, Trail of Tears Association Symposium*, Department of Arkansas Heritage, Little Rock, 55–71. (Revised version published with same title in *Arkansas Archeologist* 37(1996):39–54.

1998a Still Looking for Arkansas Post: Lake Dumond, 1998. Paper presented at the annual meeting of the Arkansas Archeological Society, Camden, Ark.

1998b A Reply to: "Concerning Cutoff Dates for State Archaeological Inventories" by Jack Elliott, Historic Preservation Division, Mississippi Department of Archives and History. *Mississippi Archaeological Association Newsletter* 33:6–11.

n.d. (ed.) Ghostboats on the Mississippi: Discovering Our Working Past. With contributions by Hester A. Davis, Mary Ann Goodman, Charles L. Pearson, and Allen R. Saltus Jr. Final report submitted 1998 for publication by the Arkansas Archeological Survey, Fayetteville.

Stewart-Abernathy, Leslie C., and Mary Farmer
1988 Queensware from a Southern Store: Perspectives on the Antebellum Ceramics Trade from a Merchant Family's Trash in Washington, Arkansas. Poster paper session, annual meeting of the Society for Historical Archaeology, Reno, Nev.
1997 Lake Dumond: The Search for Arkansas Post, 1997. Paper presented at the annual meeting of the Arkansas Archeological Society, Little Rock.

Stewart-Abernathy, Leslie C., and Barbara L. Ruff
1986 A Good Man in Israel: Zooarcheology and Assimilation in Antebellum Washington, Arkansas. Paper presented at the annual meeting of the Society for Historical Archaeology, Sacramento, Calif.
1989 A Good Man in Israel: Zooarcheology and Assimilation in Antebellum Washington, Arkansas. *Historical Archaeology* 23(2):96–112.

Stewart-Abernathy, Leslie C., and Beverly S. Watkins
1982 Historical Archeology. In *A State Plan for the Conservation of Archaeological Resources in Arkansas,* edited by H. A. Davis, HA1–HA53. Research Series No. 21. Arkansas Archeological Survey, Fayetteville.

Story, Dee Ann, Byron Barber, Estalee Barber, Evelyn Cobb, Herschel Cobb, Robert Coleman, Kathleen Gilmore, R. K. Harris, and Norma Hoffrichter
1967 Indian Artifacts: Pottery Vessels. In *The Gilbert Site: A Norteno Focus Site in Northeast Texas,* edited by Edward B. Jelks, 87–104. *Bulletin of the Texas Archeological Society* 37.

Story, Dee Ann, Janice A. Guy, Barbara A. Burnett, Martha Doty Freeman, Jerome C. Rose, D. Gentry Steele, Ben W. Olive, and Karl J. Reinhard
1990 *The Archeology and Bioarcheology of the Gulf Coastal Plain.* Research Series No. 38, vols. 1 and 2. Arkansas Archeological Survey, Fayetteville.

Suhm, Dee Ann, and Edward B. Jelks (eds.)
1962 *Handbook of Texas Archeology: Type Descriptions.* Texas Archeological Society, Special Publication No. 1 and Texas Memorial Museum, Bulletin No. 4, Austin.

Suhm, Dee Ann, Alex D. Krieger, and Edward B. Jelks
1954 *An Introductory Handbook of Texas Archaeology.* Bulletin of the Texas Archeological and Paleontological Society No. 25, Austin.

Surrey, N. M. Miller
1968 *The Commerce of Louisiana during the French Regime, 1699–1763.* Reprint of the edition of 1916, AMS Press, New York.

Swanda, Michael L.
1980 Sites Lost and Found: Mapping the Archives in Dallas County, or, Of Course the Site Is There! Paper presented at the annual meeting of the Society for Historical Archaeology, Albuquerque.

Swanton, John R.
1911 *Indian Tribes of the Lower Mississippi Valley and Adjacent Coast of the Gulf of Mexico.* Bulletin 43. Smithsonian Institution, Bureau of American Ethnology, Washington, D.C.

1919 *A Structural and Lexical Comparison of the Tunica, Chitimacha, and Atakapa Languages.* Bulletin 68. Smithsonian Institution, Bureau of American Ethnology, Washington, D.C.

1939 *Final Report of the United States de Soto Expedition Commission.* U.S. House of Rep. Doc. 71, 76th Cong., 1st Sess., Washington, D.C. (reprinted 1985, Smithsonian Institution Press, Washington, D.C.).

1942 *Source Material on the History and Ethnology of the Caddo Indians.* Bulletin 132. Smithsonian Institution, Bureau of American Ethnology, Washington, D.C.

1946 *The Indians of the Southeastern United States.* Bulletin 137. Smithsonian Institution, Bureau of American Ethnology, Washington, D.C.

Teller, J. T.

1990 Volume and Routing of Late-Glacial Runoff from the Southern Laurentide Ice Sheet. *Quaternary Research* 34:12–23.

Teltser, Patrice A.

1988 *The Mississippian Archaeological Record on the Malden Plain, Southeast Missouri: Local Variability in Evolutionary Perspective.* Ph.D. diss., University of Washington, Seattle.

Terrell, Bruce G.

1990 *Louisiana Submerged Cultural Resource Plan.* Division of Archeology, Louisiana Department of Culture, Recreation, and Tourism, Baton Rouge.

Thomas, Cyrus

1894 Report of the Mound Explorations of the Bureau of Ethnology. *Annual Report of the Bureau of Ethnology* 12:17–342. Washington, D.C.

1985 *Report on the Mound Explorations of the Bureau of Ethnology.* Smithsonian Institution Press, Washington, D.C. Reprinted. Originally published 1894, in the 12th Annual Report of the Bureau of American Ethnology, 1890–1891. U.S. Government Printing Office, Washington, D.C.

Thomas, Prentice, Jr., and L. Janice Campbell

1993 *Elgin Air Force Base Historic Preservation Plan: Technical Synthesis of Cultural Resources Investigations at Elgin, Santa Rosa, Okaloosa and Walton Counties, Florida.* Report of Investigations No. 192. New World Research, Inc., Fort Walton Beach, Fla.

Thorne, Robert M.

1988 Archaeological Data Recovery in Transition: Observations from Mississippi. In *Advances in Southeastern Archeology 1966–1986, Contributions of the Federal Archaeological Program.* Southeastern Archaeological Conference Special Publication No. 6, 30–33.

Thurman, Melburn D.

1984 *Building a House in 18th Century Ste. Genevieve.* Pendragon's Press, Ste. Genevieve, Mo.

Tordoff, Judith D., and John R. Kern

1981 *Phase II Archaeological Investigations at Sharpley's Bottom Historic Sites, Tombigbee River Multiresource District, Alabama and Mississippi.* Interim Report. Commonwealth Associates, Inc., Jackson, Miss. Submitted to the U.S. National Park Service, Atlanta.

Tregle, Joseph G., Jr. (ed.)
1975 *The History of Louisiana: Translated from the French of M. Le Page du Pratz.* A facsimile reproduction of the 1774 edition with foreword, editor's note, introduction, and index added. Louisiana State University Press, Baton Rouge.

Trubowitz, Neal L.
1984 European Contact and the Cedar Grove Site. In *Cedar Grove: An Interdisciplinary Investigation of a Late Caddo Farmstead in the Red River Valley,* edited by Neal L. Trubowitz, 30–43. Research Series No. 23. Arkansas Archeological Survey, Fayetteville.

U.S. Army Corps of Engineers
1985 *L'Anguille River, Arkansas Reevaluation Report Volume 1. Main Report and Environmental Impact Statement.* Final Report. Submitted to the Memphis District, U.S. Army Corps of Engineers.

Usner, Daniel H., Jr.
1988 Economic Relations in the Southeast until 1783. In *Handbook of North American Indians.* Vol. 4, *History of Indian-White Relationships,* edited by Wilcomb E. Washburn, 391–95, Smithsonian Institution, Washington, D.C.
1992 *Indians, Settlers, and Slaves in a Frontier Exchange Economy: The Lower Mississippi Valley before 1783.* University of North Carolina Press, Chapel Hill.

Varner, John Grier, and Jeanette Johnson Varner
1951 *The Florida of the Inca.* University of Texas Press, Austin.

Vehik, S. H.
1994 Cultural Continuity and Discontinuity in the Southern Prairies and Cross Timbers. In *Plains Indians, A.D. 500–1500: The Archaeological Past of Historic Groups,* edited by K. H. Schlesier, 239–63. University of Oklahoma Press, Norman.

Voget, Fred W.
1974 *Osage Indians I: Osage Research Report.* Garland, New York.

Voss, Jerome A., and John H. Blitz
1983 An Archaeological Survey in the Choctaw Homeland. *Mississippi Archaeology* 18(2):49–56.
1988 Archaeological Investigations in the Choctaw Homeland. *American Antiquity* 53(1):125–45.

Walker, John W.
1971 *Excavation of the Arkansas Post Branch of the Bank of the State of Arkansas, Arkansas Post National Memorial, Arkansas.* Report. Submitted to U.S. National Park Service, Southeast Archaeological Center, Macon, Ga.

Walthall, John A.
1991a (ed.) *French Colonial Archaeology: The Illinois Country and the Western Great Lakes.* University of Illinois Press, Chicago.
1991b French Colonial Fort Massac: Architecture and Ceramic Patterning. In *French Colonial Archaeology: The Illinois Country and the Western Great Lakes,* edited by John A. Walthall, 42–64. University of Illinois Press, Chicago.
1991c An Analysis of Late Eighteenth Century Ceramics from Arkansas Post at Ecores Rouges. *Southeasten Archaeology* 10(2):98–113.

Ward, Rufus

1984 Nineteenth Century Choctaw Indian Reservation Sites in Lowndes County, Mississippi. *Mississippi Archaeology* 19(2):39–45.

Waring, George H.

1983 *Horse Behavior: The Behavioral Traits and Adaptations of Domestic and Wild Horses, Including Ponies.* Noyes, Park Ridge, N.J.

Waselkov, Gregory A.

1989 Indian Maps of the Colonial Southeast. In *Powhatan's Mantle: Indians in the Colonial Southeast,* edited by Peter H. Wood, Gregory A. Waselkov, and M. Thomas Hatley, 292–343. University of Nebraska Press, Lincoln.

1997 French Colonial Archaeology at Old Mobile: An Introduction. Paper presented at the annual meeting of the Society for Historical Archaeology, Corpus Christi, Tex.

Washington Telegraph, Washington, Arkansas

December 22, 1916:1

Watkins, Beverly

1980a Find Me a Steamboat Wreck! A Historian in Contract Archeology. Paper presented at the annual meeting of the Society for Historical Archeology, Albuquerque.

1980b The Bird and Welch Potteries: Small Industry in Nineteenth Century Arkansas. Paper presented at the annual meeting of the Society for Historical Archeology, Albuquerque.

1982 History of the Felsenthal Region. In *Human Adaptation in the Grand Marais Lowland,* by E. T. Hemmings, 79–97. Research Series No. 17. Arkansas Archeological Survey, Fayetteville.

1984 History of the Upper Felsenthal Region. In *Archaeology and Paleogeography of the Upper Felsenthal Region: Cultural Resources Investigations in the Calion Navigation Pool, South-Central Arkansas,* edited by R. A. Weinstein and D. B. Kelley, 51–60. Report. Coastal Environments, Baton Rouge. Submitted to the U.S. Army Corps of Engineers, Vicksburg District.

Wauchope, Robert L.

1966 *Archaeological Survey of Northern Georgia.* Memoir 21. Society for American Archaeology.

Weaver, Guy

1988 *Archeological Testing at the Site of the Peabody Place Mall and Office Complex, Memphis, Tennessee: Phase II Construction.* Report. Garrow and Associates, Inc., Memphis. Submitted to the Division of Housing and Community Development, City of Memphis.

1990a *A Report of Archeological Investigations at the Woodruff-Fontaine House Cistern, Memphis, Shelby County, Tennessee.* Report. Garrow and Associates, Inc., Memphis. Submitted to the Memphis Chapter Association for the Preservation of Tennessee Antiquities.

1990b Urban Archaeology on Beale Street, Memphis, Tennessee. Paper presented at the Fifth Annual Illinois Historical Archaeological Conference, Makanda, Ill.

1991 *Analysis and Interpretation of Artifact Collections from Site 3CT271, Randolf Estate Development, Crittenden County Arkansas.* Report. Garrow and Associates, Inc., Memphis. Submitted to the U.S. Army Corps of Engineers, Memphis District, Memphis.

1992 That Crooked Little Street: Archeology on Beale Street, Memphis Tennessee. Paper presented at the annual meeting of the Society for Historical Archaeology, Kingston, Jamaica.

1994a *A Report of an Intensive Archaeological Survey and Cemetery Delineation along Goodman Road (State Route 302), DeSoto County, Mississippi.* Report. Garrow and Associates, Inc., Atlanta. Submitted to D. R. Bridgforth and R. R. Bridgeforth Estates, Southhaven, Miss.

1994b *Preliminary Report: Phase I and Phase II Cultural Resource Investigations at the Wagner Street Development Area, AutoZone Corporate Headquarters Site, 40SY528, Area 2, Memphis, Shelby County, Tennessee.* Report. Garrow and Associates, Inc., Memphis. Submitted to the Division of Engineering, City of Memphis.

1996a *Preliminary Report and Management Summary: Phase II Archaeological Testing of the MATA North End Terminal Site (40SY590), Memphis, Shelby County, Tennessee.* Report. Garrow and Associates, Inc., Memphis. Submitted to the Memphis Area Transit Authority, Memphis.

1996b The Memphis Cobblestone Landing. Paper presented at the annual meeting of the Mid-South Archaeological Conference, Memphis.

1997a *Archeological Investigations at the Massey-Robins Cemetery, Shelby County, Tennessee.* Report. Brockington and Associates, Memphis. Submitted to Dexter Development Partners, Inc., Memphis.

1997b *Phase I and II Cultural Resource Investigations at Archaeological Sites 40SY610, 40SY611, and 40SY612, Gibson Guitar Corporation Manufacturing and Visitors Center, Memphis, Tennessee.* Report. Brockington and Associates, Memphis. Submitted to Williamson, Haizlip, and Pounders, Inc., Memphis.

1997c The Cobblestone Landing at Memphis. Paper presented at the annual meeting of the Society for Historical Archaeology, Corpus Christi, Tex.

1998 Tin-Can Politics: The Urgency of Urban Archaeology. Paper presented at the annual meeting of the Society for Historical Archaeology, Atlanta.

Weaver, Guy G., Brian R. Collins, and Jane Kowalewski

1998 *Archaeological Investigations at the Burkle House, Memphis, Tennessee.* Report. Weaver and Associates, Inc., Memphis. Submitted to Slavehaven, Inc., Memphis.

Weaver, Guy G., Brian R. Collins, and Gerald P. Smith

1997 *Supplemental Phase II Archaeological Data Recovery of Feature 85, MATA North End Terminal (40SY590), Memphis, Shelby County, Tennessee.* Report. Department of Anthropology, University of Memphis, Memphis. Submitted to Memphis Area Transit Authority, Memphis.

Weaver, Guy G., and John L. Hopkins

1993 *A Cultural Resources Survey of the Proposed Helena, Arkansas, and Vicinity Project, Reaches IA, 2A, and IB, Phillips County, Arkansas.* Report. Garrow and Associates, Inc., Atlanta. Submitted to U.S. Army Corps of Engineers, Memphis District.

1998 *Archaeological Testing and Assessment at the Hildebrand/McTighe House (40SY615), Memphis, Shelby County, Tennessee: Preliminary Report.*

Report. Weaver and Associates, Memphis. Submitted to the Memphis-Shelby County Airport Authority, Memphis.

Weaver, Guy G., John L. Hopkins, and Emmanuel Breitburg
1991 *Archeological Data Recovery at the Rum Boogie Site (40SY494), Peabody Place Mall and Office Complex, Memphis, Tennessee.* Report. Garrow and Associates, Inc., Memphis. Submitted to the Division of Housing and Community Development, City of Memphis.

Weaver, Guy G., John L. Hopkins, Mary Kwas, and Jonathan Bloom
1990 *Archaeological Testing and Data Recovery at the Morning Sun Farmstead Site (40SY508), Shelby County, Tennessee.* Report. Garrow and Associates, Inc., Atlanta. Submitted to Tennessee Department of Transportation, Nashville.

Weaver, Guy G., John L. Hopkins, Marsha Oates, and Gary Patterson
1994 *The Tom Lee Monument Relocation Project at Beale Street Landing (40SY352).* Report. Garrow and Associates, Inc., Atlanta. Submitted to City of Memphis.

Weaver, Guy G., John L. Hopkins, Gary Patterson, and Marsha R. Oates
1996 *The Memphis Landing Cultural Resources Assessment and Preservation Plan, City of Memphis, Shelby County, Tennessee, Parts 1 and 2.* Report. Garrow and Associates, Inc., Memphis. Submitted to the Division of Engineering, City of Memphis.

Weaver, Guy G., John L. Hopkins, Louella Whitson Weaver, Jane Kowalewski, and Mitch Childress
1995 *Cultural Resource Investigations at the AutoZone Corporate Headquarters Site (40SY528), Memphis, Shelby County, Tennessee.* Report. Garrow and Associates, Memphis. Submitted to AutoZone and City of Memphis, Division of Housing and Community Development.

Weaver, Guy G., and Jane Kowaleski
1998 The Saffron Plague: Archaeology of the Yellow Fever Epidemics in Memphis, Tennessee. Paper presented at the South Central Historical Archeology Conference, Jackson, Miss.

Weaver, Louella W., Charlotte Watrin, Marjorie Holmes, and Ronald Brister
1997 *Archeological Investigations at the Magevney House, Memphis, Tennessee: 1981–1984.* Occasional Paper No. 17. Anthropological Research Center, University of Memphis.

Webb, Clarence H.
1962 Early 19th Century Trade Material from the Colfax Ferry Site, Natchitoches Parish, Louisiana. *Southeastern Archaeological Conference Newsletter* 9(1):30–33.
1982 *The Poverty Point Culture.* 2d ed., rev. *Geoscience and Man* 17. School of Geoscience, Louisiana State University, Baton Rouge.
1984 Early Caddo Cultures (Caddo I and II). Pictures of Record Slide Set, Pictures of Record, Inc., Weston, Conn.

Webb, Clarence H., and Ralph R. McKinney
1975 Mounds Plantation (16CD12), Caddo Parish, Louisiana. *Louisiana Archaeology* 2:39–127.

Wedel, Mildred Mott
1971 J. B. Benard, Sieur De La Harpe: Visitor to the Wichitas in 1719. *Great Plains Journal* 10(1):37–70.

1974 The Benard De La Harpe Historiography on French Colonial Louisiana. *Louisiana Studies* 13(1):9–67. Louisiana Studies Institute, Northwestern State College.

1978 *La Harpe's 1719 Post on Red River and Nearby Caddo Settlements.* Bulletin 30. Texas Memorial Museum, University of Texas, Austin.

1981 *The Deer Creek Site, Oklahoma: A Wichita Village Sometimes Called Ferdinandina, An Ethnohistorian's View.* Oklahoma Historical Society Series in Anthropology No. 5.

Weinstein, Richard A., and David B. Kelley

1984 Archaeology and Paleogeography of the Upper Felsenthal Region: Cultural Resources Investigations in the Calion Navigation Pool, South-Central Arkansas. Report. Coastal Environments, Inc., Baton Rouge. Submitted to Vicksburg District, U.S. Army Corps of Engineers.

Weniger, Del

1996 Catalpa *(Catalpa bignonioides, Bignoiaceae)* and Bois D'Arc *(Maclura pomifera, Moraceae)* in Early Texas Records. *SIDA* 17(1):231–42.

Wesler, Kit W.

1983 Socioeconomic Distinctions in Nineteenth-Century Sites: Two Experiments and a Caution. *Proceedings of the Symposium on Ohio Valley Urban and Historic Archaeology* 1:138–46.

1984a A Spatial Perspective on Artifact Group Patterning within the Houselot. *Proceedings of the Symposium on Ohio Valley Urban and Historic Archaeology* 2:37–44.

1984b Posthole Testing and Pattern Recognition at the Whitehaven Mansion, 15McN65. *Tennessee Anthropologist* 9(1):32–47.

1987 Posthole Testing and Pattern Recognition Revisited: The Moore House, Ballard County, Kentucky. *Proceedings, Symposium on Ohio Valley Urban and Historic Archaeology* 5:30–41.

1993a The Historical Archaeology of Wickliffe Mounds: An Archaeology of Archaeology and Tourism. Paper presented at the Southeastern Archaeological Conference, Raleigh, N.C.

1993b Preliminary Testing at the Lloyd Tilghman House, Paducah, Kentucky. *Ohio Valley Historical Archaeology* 10:1–5.

1997 Preliminary Comments on Test Excavations at the Curtis-Sullivan House, Ballard County, and the Richard Morrill House, Graves County, Kentucky. Paper presented at the Symposium on Ohio Valley Urban and Historic Archaeology, Paducah, Ky.

1998 Test Excavations at the DeLassus-Kern House, Ste. Genevieve, Missouri. Paper presented at the Symposium on Ohio Valley Urban and Historic Archaeology, Louisville, Ky.

Westbury, William A.

1971 *1969 Excavations at Spadra Bluff, 3JO33.* Report. Arkansas Archeological Survey, Fayetteville. Submitted to the U.S. National Park Service, Southeast Region, Atlanta.

1975 *Investigations at Arkansas Post, National Memorial, Arkansas.* Report. Archeology Research Program, Southern Methodist University, Dallas. Submitted to the U.S. National Park Service, Southwest Division, Santa Fe, N.M.

1976 *Archaeological Assessment of Arkansas Post.* Report No. 96. Archeology Research Program, Southern Methodist University, Dallas.

Whelan, James Patrick, Jr., and Charles E. Pearson.

1988 *Archeology of an Early Twentieth Century Black Community: The Good Land Cypress Sawmill Company, Terrebonne Parish, Louisiana.* Report. Coastal Environments, Inc., Baton Rouge. Submitted to the Office of Highways, Louisiana Department of Transportation and Development, Baton Rouge.

White, Anta M.

1963 Analytic Description of the Chipped-stone Industry from Snyders Site, Calhoun County, Illinois. In *Miscellaneous Studies in Typology and Classification,* 1–70, by Anta M. White, Lewis R. Binford, and Mark L. Papworth. Anthropological Papers No. 19. Museum of Anthropology, University of Michigan, Ann Arbor.

White, Patsy

1970 Investigation of the Cemetery at the Gee's Landing Site. *Arkansas Archeologist* 11:1–20.

1987 The Gordon Site: A Middle Coles Creek to Late Mississippi Period Occupation in Ashley County, Southeast Arkansas. *Arkansas Archeologist* 25–26:1–51.

Wilkinson, Leland

1989 *SYSTAT: The System for Statistics.* Systat, Evanston, Ill.

Willey, G. R., and J. A. Sabloff

1974 *A History of American Archaeology.* W. H. Freeman, San Francisco.

Williams, J. Mark

1995 Chiefly Compounds. In *Mississippian Communities and Households,* edited by J. Daniel Rogers and Bruce D. Smith, 124–34. University of Alabama Press, Tuscaloosa.

Williams, Stephen

1954 *An Archaeological Study of the Mississippian Culture in Southeast Missouri.* Ph.D. diss., Yale University, New Haven.

1962 Historic Archeology in the Lower Mississippi Valley. *Southeastern Archaeological Conference Newsletter* 9(1):53–63.

1965 Lower Mississippi Valley. *Bulletin of the Southeastern Archaeological Conference* 2:9–10.

1991 *Fantastic Archaeology: The Wild Side of North American Prehistory.* University of Pennsylvania Press, Philadelphia.

Williams, Stephen, and Jeffrey P. Brain

1983 *Excavations at the Lake George Site, Yazoo County, Mississippi, 1958–1960.* Peabody Museum of Archaeology and Ethnology, Harvard University, Cambridge.

Williams, W. D.

1989 Louis Bringier and His Description of Arkansas in 1812. *Arkansas Historical Quarterly* 48:108–36.

Wilson, Diane E.

1993 Incidence of Degenerative Joint Disease among the Sanders Site (41LR2) Population. Paper presented at the 35th Caddo Conference, Norman, Okla.

Wilson, Diane E., and Sharon McCormick Derrick
1996 Cranial Modeling as an Ethnic Marker among the Caddo. Paper presented at the 61st Annual Meeting of the Society for American Archaeology, New Orleans.

Wilson, Kristin
1998 *Disinterment/Reinterment of the Turner Cemetery, Marshal County, Mississippi.* Report. TRC Garrow, Atlanta. Submitted to Lewis and Lewis, LLC, Olive Branch, Miss.

Winberry, John, J.
1979 The Osage Orange: A Botanical Artifact. *Pioneer America* 11(3):134–41.

Witte, Adolph Henry
1938 Spanish Fort, An Historic Wichita Site. *Bulletin of the Texas Archeological and Paleontological Society* 10:234–44.

Yakubik, Jill-Karen
1988 *Ceramic Use in Late-Eighteenth Century and Early-Nineteenth Century Southeastern Louisiana.* Ph.D. diss., Tulane University, New Orleans.

Yakubik, Jill-Karen, H. A. Franks, R. C. Goodwin, and C. J. Poplin
1986 *Cultural Resources Inventory of the Bonnet Carre Spillway, St. Charles Parish, Louisiana.* R. C. Goodwin and Associates, New Orleans. Submitted to U.S. Army Corps of Engineers, New Orleans District.

Yakubik, Jill-Karen, and Rosalinda Mendez
1994 *Beyond the Great House: Archaeology at Ashland-Belle Helene Plantation.* Discovering Louisiana Archaeology 1. Louisiana Department of Culture, Recreation, and Tourism, Division of Archaeology, Baton Rouge.

Yakubik, Jill-Karen, Galloway W. Selby, Kenneth R. Jones, Debra Stayner, and Janice Cooper
1985 An Archeological and Historic Sites Inventory of Bayou Teche between Franklin and Jeunerette, Louisiana. Ms. on file, Louisiana Division of Archaeology, Baton Rouge.

Young, Amy, and Milburn Crowe
1998 Public Archaeology at Mound Bayou: Mississippi's First All-Black Town. Paper presented at the South Central Historical Archeology Conference, Jackson, Miss.

Young, Gloria A., and Michael P. Hoffman (eds.)
1993 *The Expedition of Hernando de Soto West of the Mississippi, 1541–1543.* University of Arkansas Press, Fayetteville.

Index